AF394602

EAST
END
PUBS

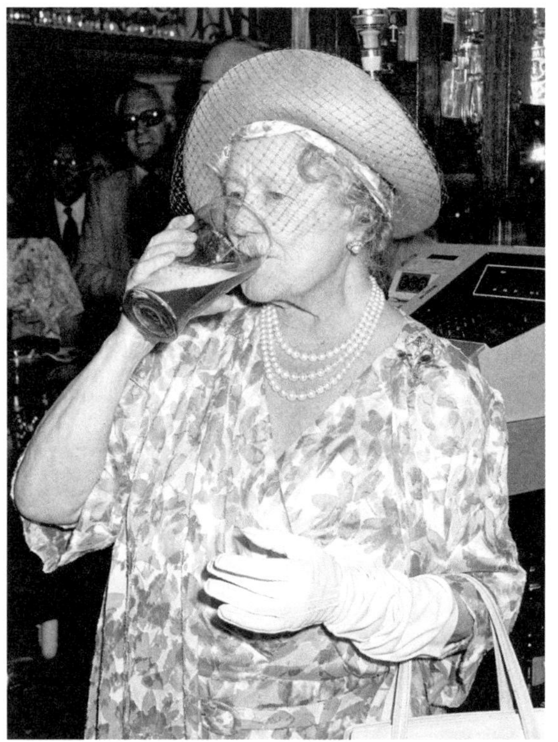

*Her Majesty Queen Elizabeth The Queen Mother imbibes
a pint of bitter at The Queen's Head in Stepney (p.116).*

ALISTAIR VON LION • TIM GEORGE

EAST END PUBS

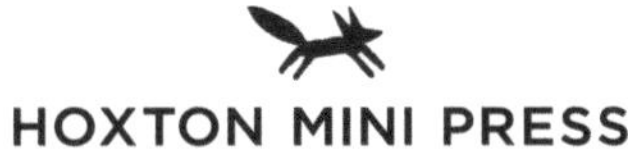

HOXTON MINI PRESS

CONTENTS

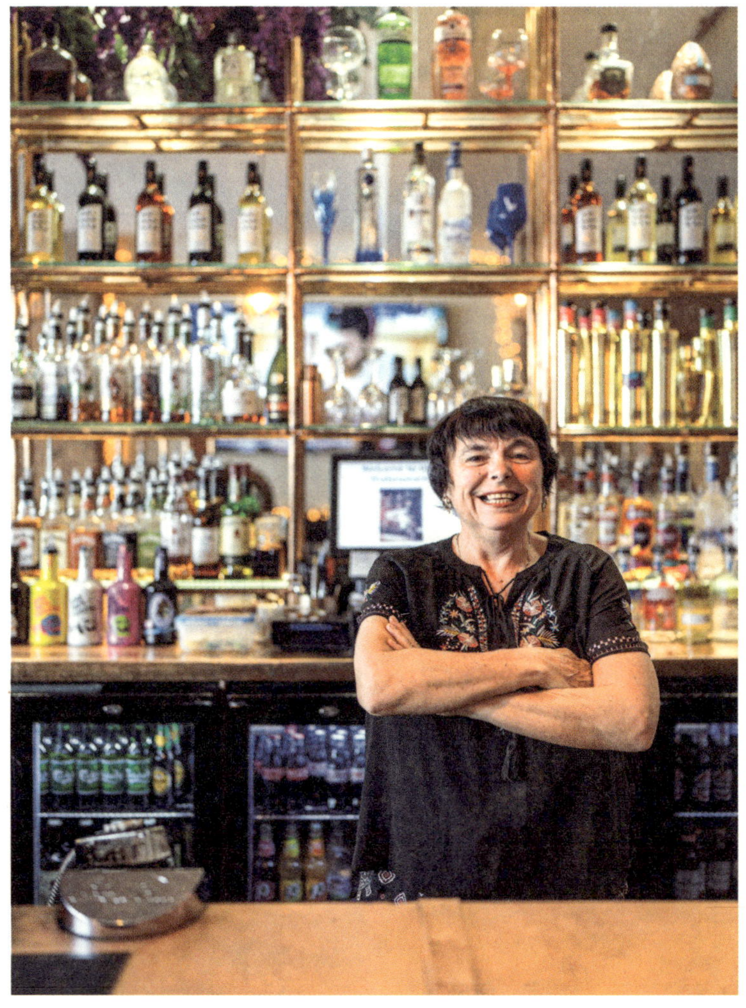

(Above) *The Shakespeare (p.240), Bethnal Green.*
(Opposite) *The Well & Bucket (p.52), Bethnal Green.*

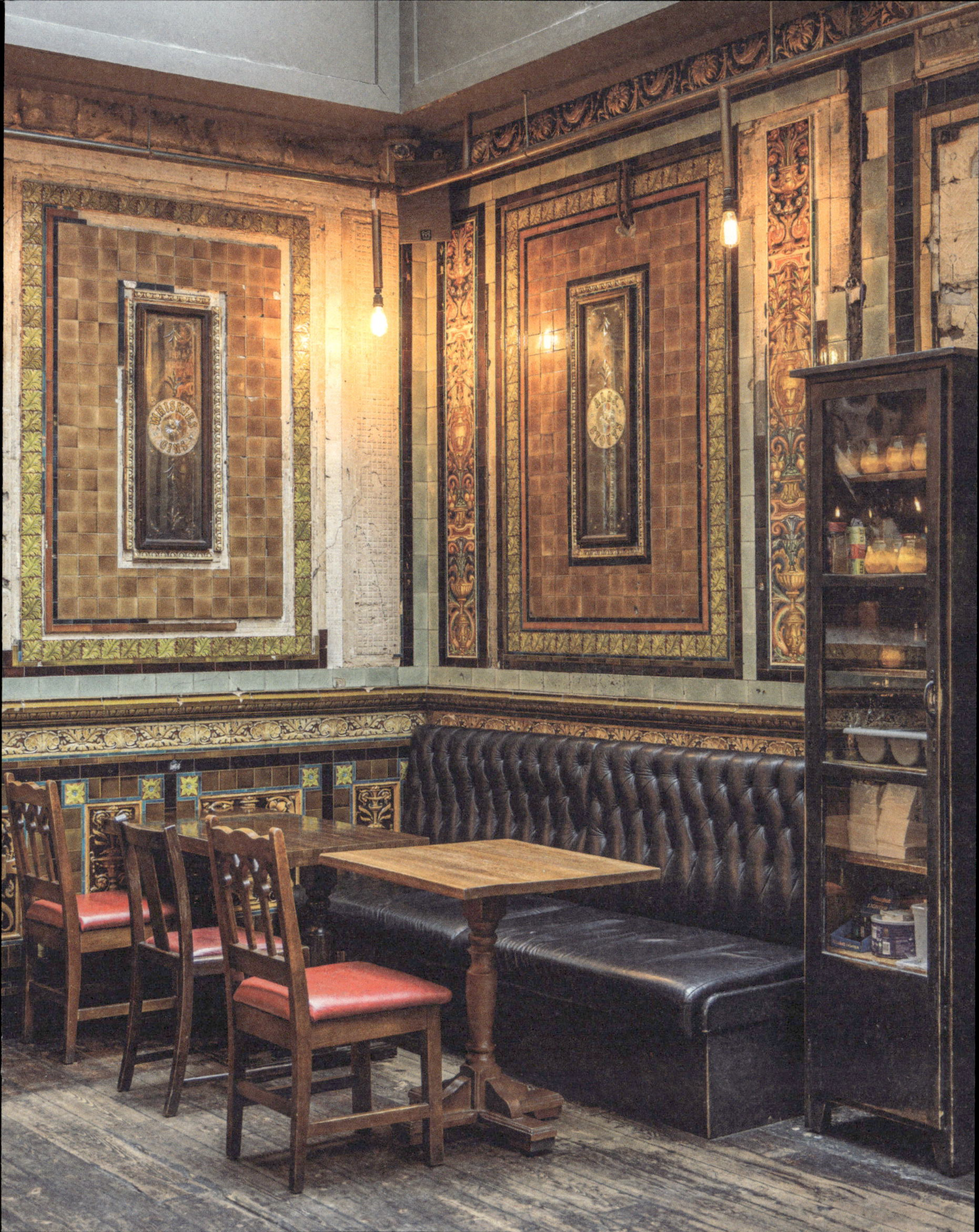

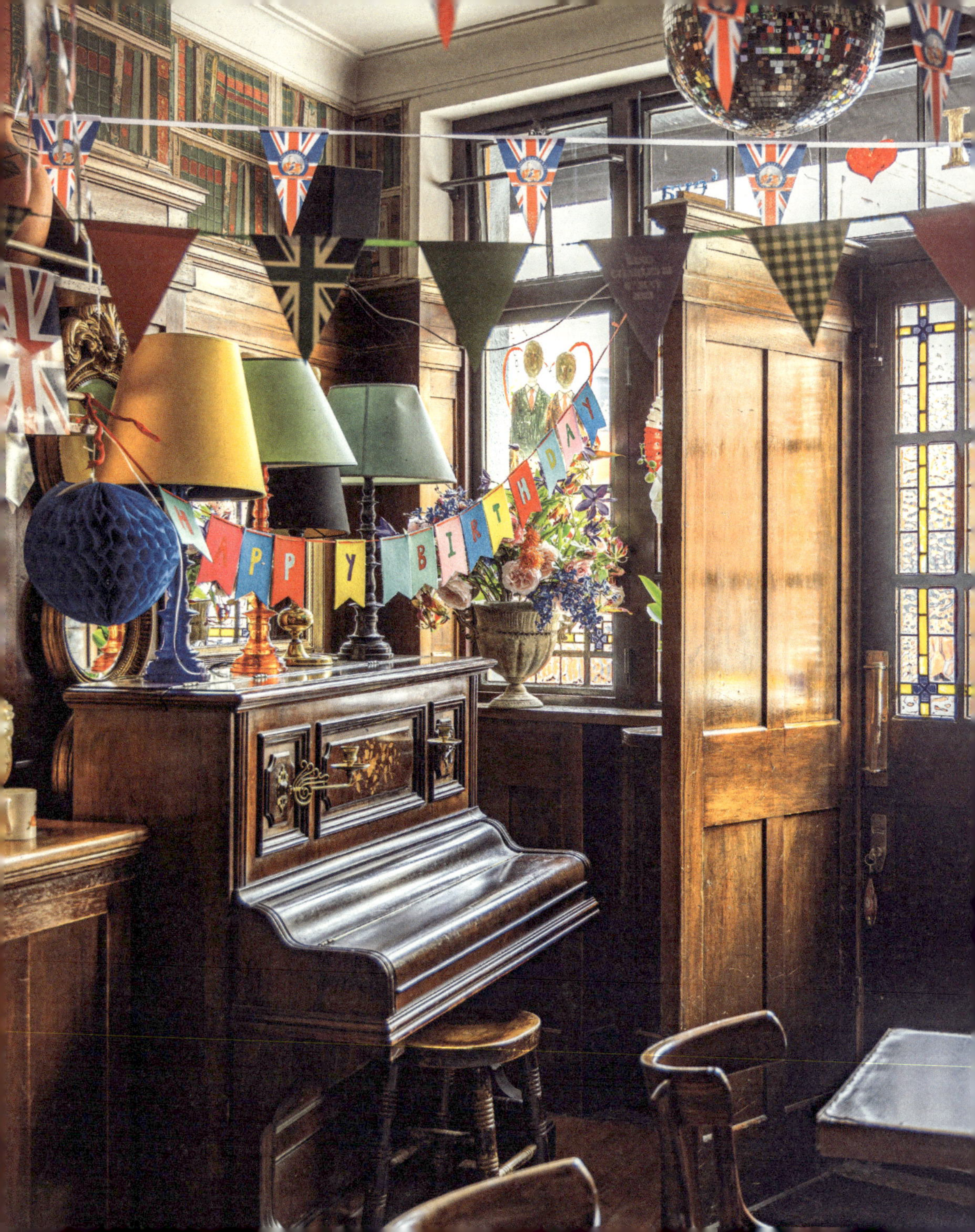

HAPPY BIRTHDAY

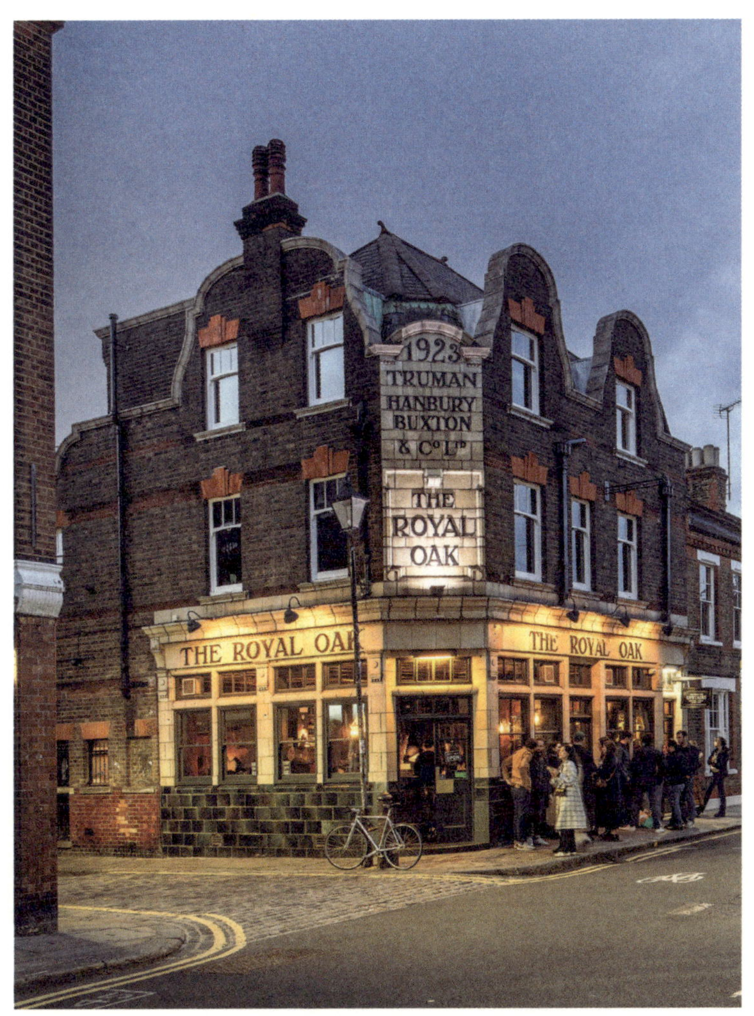

(Above) *The Royal Oak (p.28), Bethnal Green.*
(Opposite) *The Golden Heart (p.250), Spitalfields.*

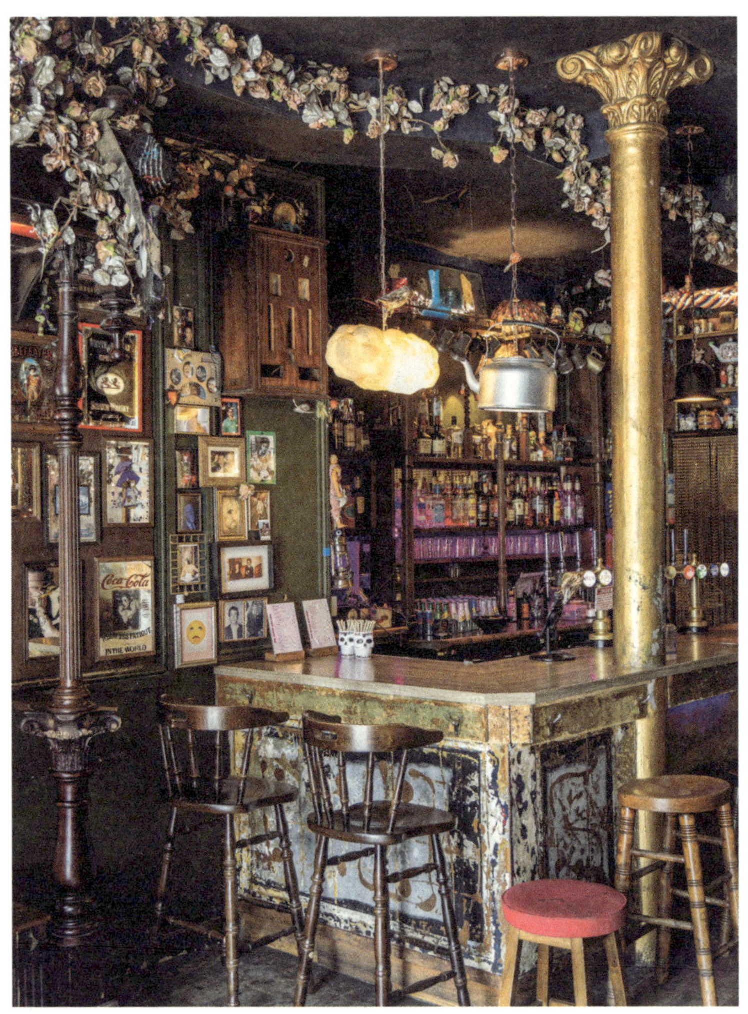

(Above) The Queen Adelaide (p.220), Bethnal Green.
(Opposite) The Victory (p.58), Bethnal Green.

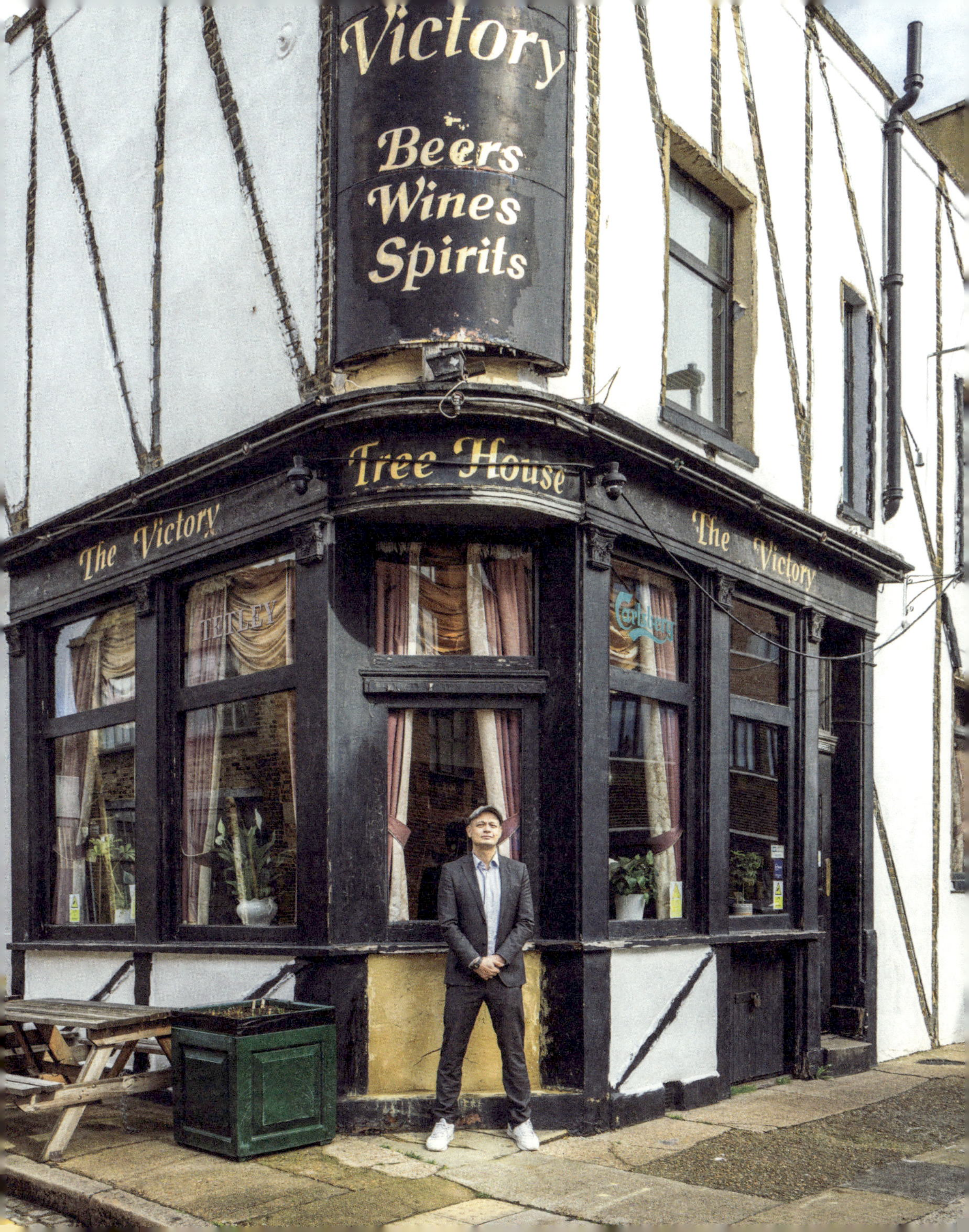
Victory
Beers
Wines
Spirits
Tree House
The Victory
The Victory
TETLEY
Carlsberg

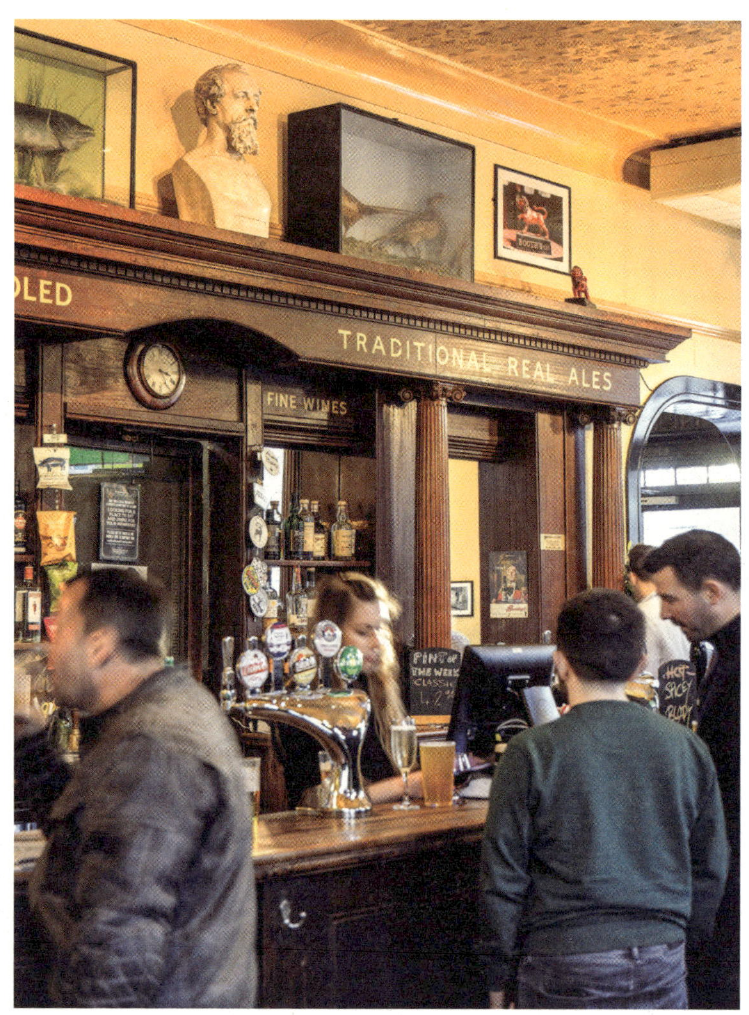

The Approach Tavern (p.48), Bethnal Green.

Introduction

The East End of London, with its tight backstreets, terraced houses, old docks and urban decay, is the site of intoxicating myths and histories that have spilled over its borders and into countless books and films – from Charles Dickens' immortalisation of the Victorian slums to the passionate tracts of social commentators such as Charles Booth. Its troubled past and ability to resiliently overcome seemingly never-ending adversity, in the shape of disease, abject poverty and bombs raining from the skies, has come to define it. But it's the evolution of the East End that makes for the most fascinating tale: from chronic destitution to an industrial powerhouse of commerce and trade, centred around the docks and brewing, through the Blitz and the postwar era where the heady optimism of the Swinging Sixties mingled with the brute force of organised crime.

Lore dictates that a Cockney, and therefore an East Ender, must be born within earshot of the bells of St Mary-le-Bow Church on Cheapside. But there are no longer any maternity hospitals from where it's possible to hear the Bow bells ring as the ever-increasing height of London's skyline has muffled their peals. So few people born in recent times can claim to be bona fide Cockneys. Such rigid definitions have never truly encapsulated the East End, which has always been home to people born all over the world – from Huguenot weavers fleeing religious persecution in France to Irish, Ashkenazi Jewish and Bangladeshi communities – all of whom brought with them culture and language that has shaped the area. In over 1,000 years of existence, the East End has only had two constants: change, and the humble public house. It is the latter's vital presence that constitutes the core of the city's soul.

Pubs have provided sanctuary, lodgings, refreshment and a place to stave off the chilblains of loneliness since time immemorial. But they are under threat. Numerous challenges have chipped away at their presence: pestilence, the Luftwaffe, beer tax, supermarket price wars, the smoking ban, the cost of living crisis and changing drinking habits. That other spectre of change – the property developer – hovers close by, ready to snap up struggling pubs and convert them into luxury housing.

Things have evolved since the days of simple ale houses, giving way to ornate gin palaces and tiled, branded pubs owned by breweries. For a time in the 19th century, almost every pub in the East End was owned by one of the 'Big Four' breweries: Truman, Hanbury & Buxton owned the Black Eagle Brewery on Brick Lane, once the largest in the world; the Albion Brewery in Whitechapel was owned by Mann, Crossman & Paulin and produced 250,000 barrels a year; Charrington ran the Anchor Brewery in Stepney, which was demolished in the 1970s to make way for a retail park; and the Barley Mow Brewery in Limehouse, owned by Taylor Walker, survived incendiary bombs during the Blitz only to close in 1960.

Many of the pubs in this book acted as taprooms to these breweries, which commanded the landscape not just as suppliers of ale, stout and porter, but also as employers. But, unlike their west London counterparts Young's and Fuller's who still operate today, not one of these East End breweries remains in business.

Pubs built by one of the dominant breweries in the late 19th century typically have a facade decorated with glazed tiles. They were a hallmark of quality used by the breweries to show that they were investing heavily in their pubs. Many opulent examples survive and the majority boast punchy colours, often consistent across the brewery's boozers (such as Charrington's signature bottle-green tiles, visible on the battle-worn frontage of The Queen Adelaide, p.220).

Today, many pubs in east London are independent houses, no longer forced to purchase their beer from the brewery that owned them. Typically, these hostelries are operated by a Guv'nor (landlord or landlady) who might have a lease or own the freehold of the building and, mirroring the glorious victualler days of yore, live upstairs.

Historically, when the East End did well, so did its pubs. The industry of thirsty labourers working the docks provided business for hundreds of taverns along the Thames, creating a 'river of beer'. But it was not to last. From the first dock closure in 1969 to the final death knell in 1981, the steady decline of this industry hit the area hard. Around 83,000 people lost their jobs in the boroughs that border the river alone. The economic struggles of the Three-Day Week in the 1970s and a lack of investment in the early 1980s compounded the issue. So too did the increased Cockney diaspora as East Enders left the city for Essex and beyond. Unsurprisingly, scores of pubs closed.

For years, these defunct pubs were left to rot like decaying teeth in a diseased mouth. They stood in opposition to the rapidly rising glass and steel towers of Canary Wharf. It wasn't until land values started to rise as a result of gentrification that many of these old pubs were converted into flats. The old faces of the manors suddenly had to coexist, not always in harmony, with more affluent newcomers disinterested in the area's working-class communities.

In the 21st century, the haves and have-nots live cheek-by-jowl in the East End. A lack of social cohesion illuminates a divided landscape where people from different generations and backgrounds often do not mix. This economic segregation lives on

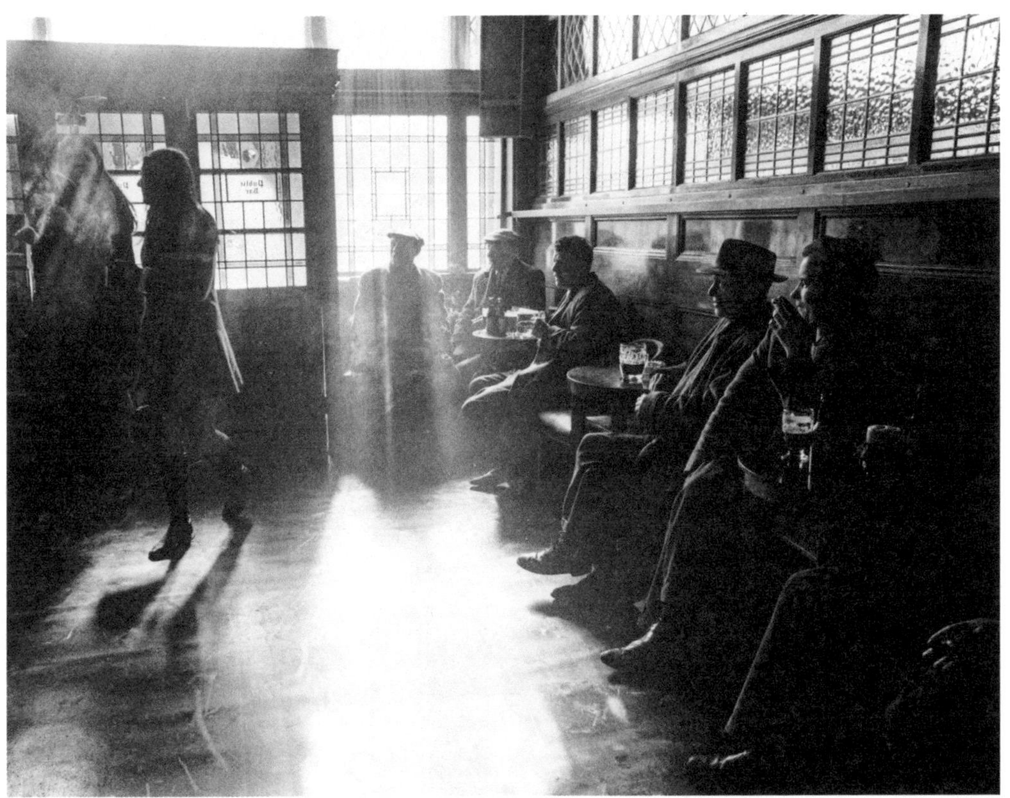

The Blind Beggar (p.32), Whitechapel. The pub gained notoriety when Ronnie Kray shot rival gangster George Cornell there in 1966.

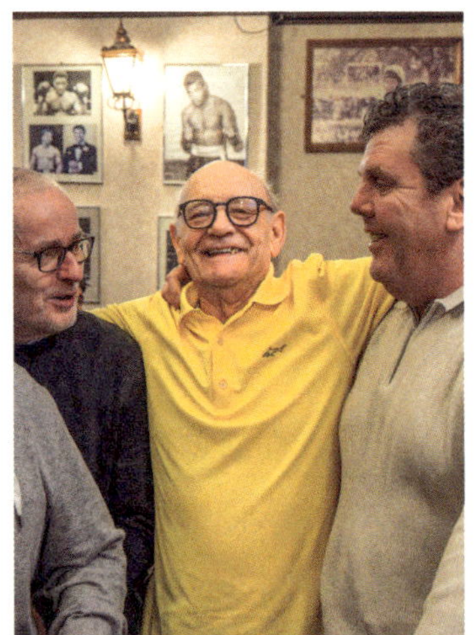
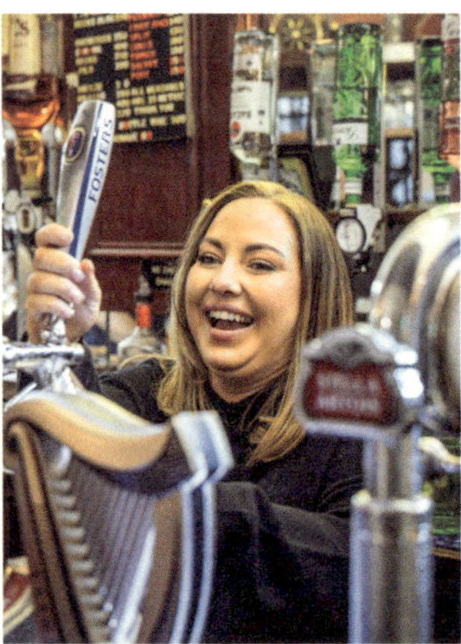
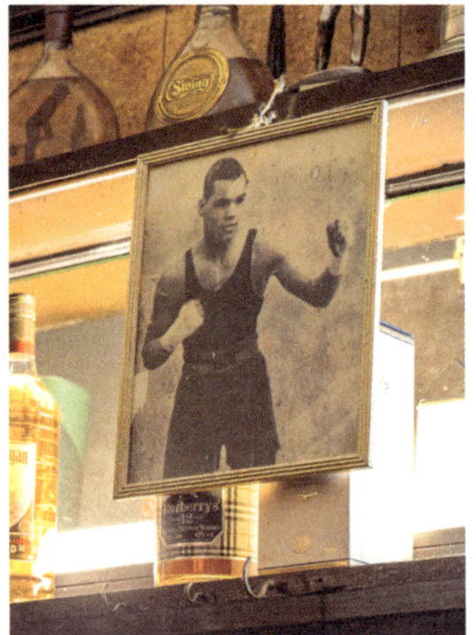
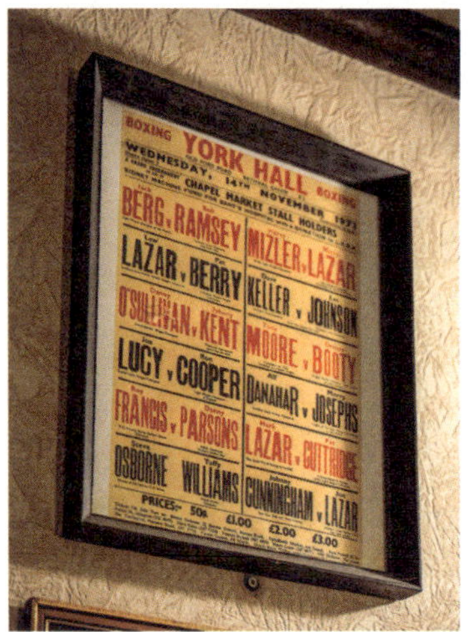

*Punters congregate at The Peacock (p.224) in Stepney
for a fond farewell to long-standing landlady Patsy Pyne.*

in the pubs too, with an increasing number of local establishments simply out of the financial reach of many East Enders.

Seasoned locals come from a time when a pub was a place for a singalong around the 'ol' Joanna' with neighbours they'd known all their lives, when it was normal for pubs to provide loan clubs, organise 'beanos' (day trips) to the coast and Christmas dinners for the elderly. The polar opposite now exists in some gentrified pubs where it is no longer even possible to sit at the bar and make friends with other solo drinkers, as the barstools have been removed to make more space for dining. Cosy snugs, dart boards and pool tables have also largely disappeared. While pubs do have to stay relevant to survive, these sudden changes – which can often feel designed to alienate lower-income customers – are lamented by those who remember how things used to be.

Many 'wet-led' venues (selling drinks only) have vanished, and pubs have had to create new revenue streams by offering sports on big screens, food and coffee. Only a handful of the old Cockney pubs remain, but the special ones that do afford visitors a slice of East End life – typified by lager and nothing more exotic than a bag of nuts, in an unmanufactured setting.

But the past was not all rose-tinted, either. Pubs were male-dominated institutions until the 1920s. Men could be profligate with their wages at the bar while, back at home, mouths went unfed as families struggled to make ends meet. Social attitudes towards unaccompanied female drinkers did not change in many pubs until after the millennium. Ironically, the lion's share of pub work was always done by women and many boozers were (and still are) run by matriarchal landladies.

This book of 65 eclectic and unique East End pubs intends to record a moment in time. Tim and I hope to share the true stories of pub life in the East End, both in the past and present. Readers can expect to learn about the buildings and the patrons and Guv'nors who have steered these good ships through choppy waters. We hope this record can help future generations understand and appreciate how the pub-going way of life has survived thanks to the efforts of treasured East End 'pub royalty' such as the unique Sandra Esquilant (p.250), raconteur Paul Drew (p.122) and third-generation Cockney landlady Emma Tarbard (p.84).

With so many pubs closed, it remains vital to recognise the community-minded pastoral work publicans have done for decades. Whether offering a kind ear in troubled times or organising a whip-round for someone in need, the role of an East End victualler is far more than just pulling pints.

These champions of the East End and the pubs they live and work in make a tremendous difference in countless people's lives. The sad sight of empty husks of pubs, which used to buzz with life, can symbolise the erosion of community life. They should serve as a reminder that if you don't love your local, one day you might lose it. In an ever-changing East End, the pub must survive to ensure such bonds never die.

Alistair Von Lion, east London, 2023

THE EAST END

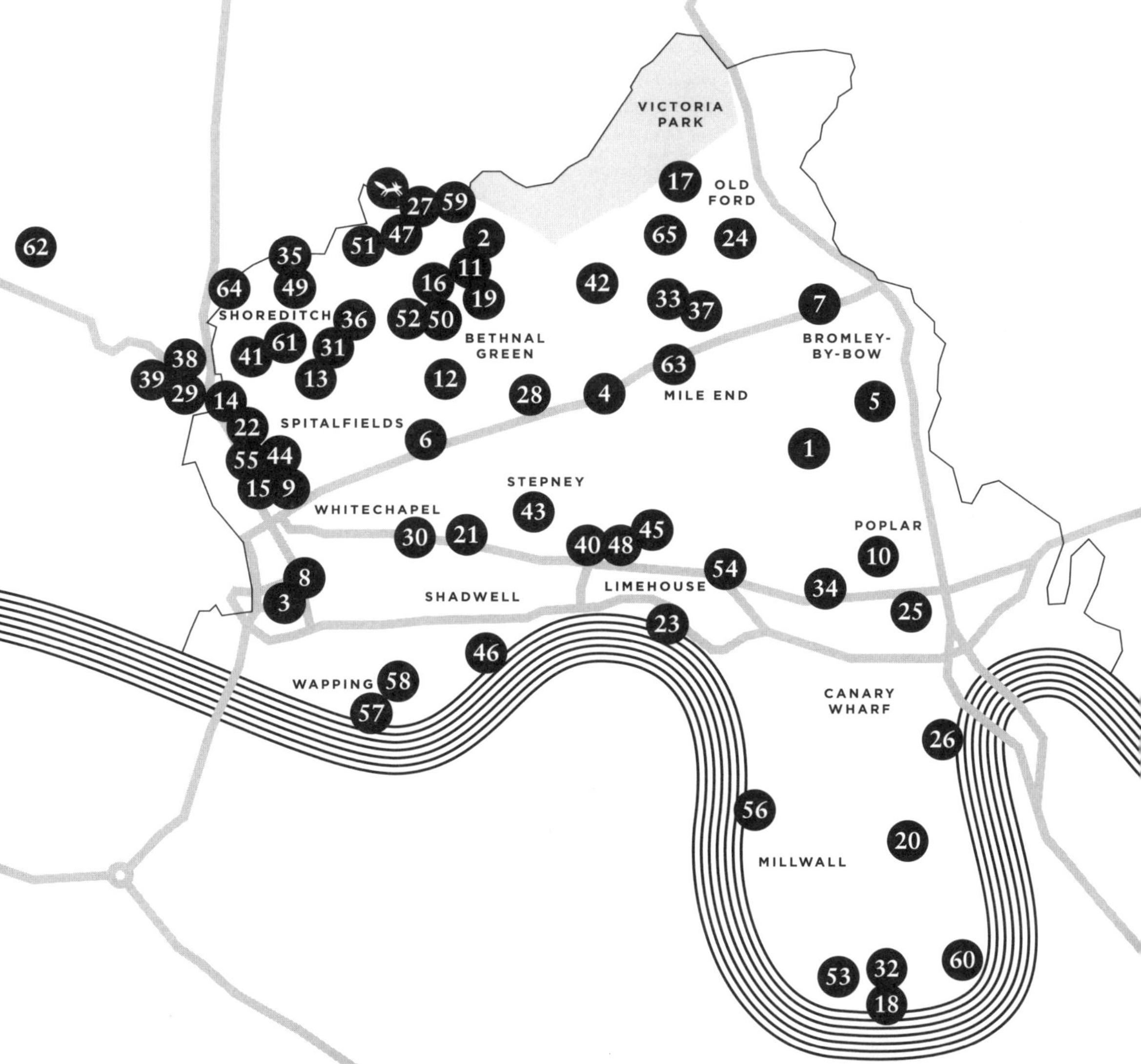

Our definition of the East End corresponds to the London Borough of Tower Hamlets, where the majority of postcodes are E1, E2, E3 & E14. This borough is bordered by the River Lea to the east, Victoria Park to the north and the River Thames to the south. According to this criteria, Hackney, Hoxton, Leyton, Walthamstow and areas further afield are not in the East End – although some parts of Hackney Wick do lie within its boundaries. A few pubs just over the border have snuck in. Why? Because they're too fantastic to leave out.

VICTORIA PARK
OLD FORD
SHOREDITCH
BETHNAL GREEN
BROMLEY-BY-BOW
MILE END
SPITALFIELDS
STEPNEY
WHITECHAPEL
POPLAR
SHADWELL
LIMEHOUSE
CANARY WHARF
WAPPING
MILLWALL

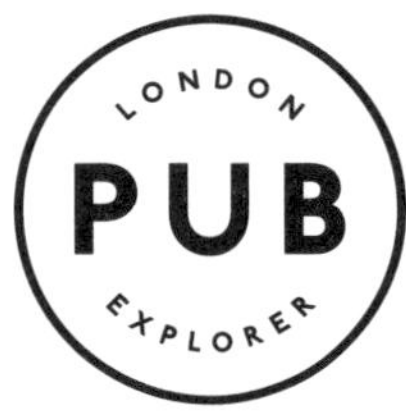

Alistair Von Lion is a London pub writer, social commentator and tour guide exploring the social history of London's pubs. He curates fascinating journeys around the mysterious backstreets of London, revealing how pubs have shaped the capital. He lives in east London, and longs for a past he never experienced.

@londonpubexplorer
londonpubexplorer.com

Tim George is a photographer documenting London's ever-changing built environment. Pubs fascinate him because they resist change and allow their patrons to travel back in time. Tim works independently on photography and graphic design from his studio in east London. He has designed several books on architecture, but this is the first book of his own photographs.

tim-george.com

Hoxton Mini Press is a small independent publisher based in east London. We make books about London – we love and breathe this city – and always with a dedication to good photography, passionate writing and lovely production. As the world goes ever more online, we believe that books should be cherished, much like the many inspiring pubs you'll find in these pages.

hoxtonminipress.com

THE PUBS

The Palm Tree

A TRUE GEM WITH A MUSICAL SOUL

Almost everything seems to be online now, and even local pubs are harnessing social media to drive footfall and increase revenue. So, it remains a treat to discover a belligerent relic that refuses to use a card reader, let alone an Instagram account. Many first-time visitors to The Palm Tree are amazed to discover how little has changed in the 46 years since Val and Alf Barrett took it over.

The Palm Tree was constructed in 1935 by Truman, Hanbury & Buxton in a neo-Georgian style as one of their interwar 'improved' pubs, intended to attract more women. It cuts an imposing figure on the Regent's Canal, standing by itself in the middle of Mile End Park, but it wasn't always so isolated – it once sat between two streets lined with the remnants of abandoned warehouses and Victorian terraced dwellings. These older buildings, many badly damaged during the Second World War, were replaced with temporary prefabricated housing, erected in haste to cope with the postwar population boom. Not that long before the Barretts took on the pub, those houses were demolished too, as was everything else on the streets aside from the Grade II-listed tavern. The Palm Tree had once stood on the corner of Palm Street and Lessada Street; but now, neither of these streets exist.

Today, the pub is managed by Val and Alf's children, Kerry and Paul, but the past

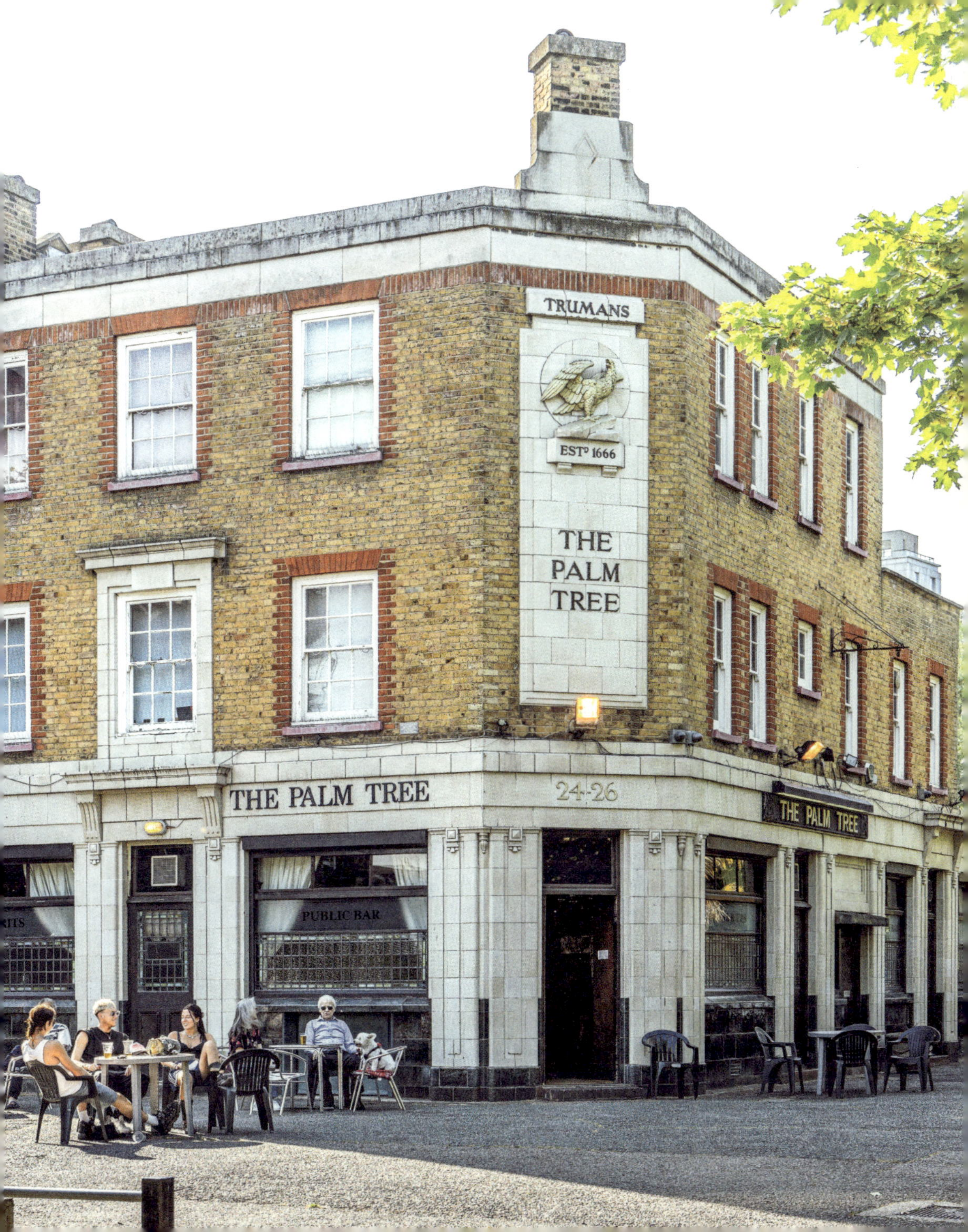
TRUMANS
ESTD 1666
THE
PALM
TREE
THE PALM TREE
24-26
PUBLIC BAR
THE PALM TREE

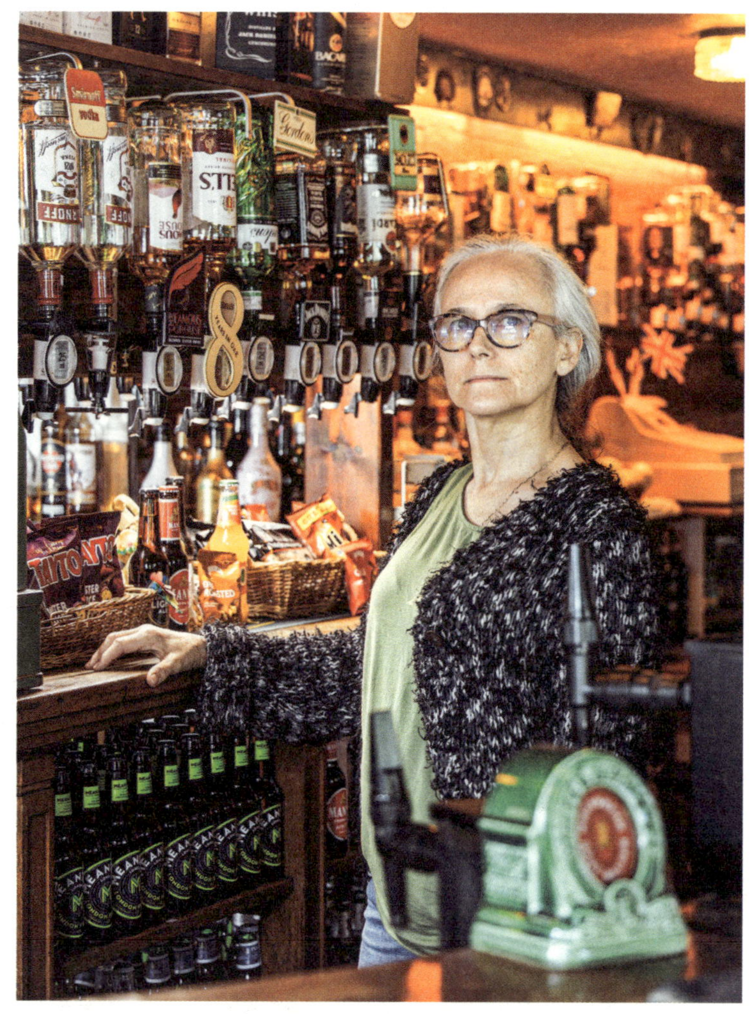

is very much still alive at The Palm Tree. Recalling a period when tradesmen and working-class locals were the only patrons, the pub retains a cash-only policy. All coins and notes are securely placed in the antique cash register, which takes pride of place in the public bar. From the opulent gold wall-paper and lavish upholstery to the low red lighting and gilded Truman's mirrors, The Palm Tree radiates an old-world elegance that was carefully curated by Val. Portraits of old boxers and crooners oversee the live music in the main bar, while those of a quieter disposition can sit in the separate saloon, decorated with sports trophies and prints of local history and lost public houses – about which Alf is most happy to school inquisitive guests.

Nowadays, the majestic old boozer really gets swinging when jazz troupes – including eminent pianist Jack Honeybourne, who is 95 years old and used to play with Dame Vera Lynn – perform every evening from Thursday to Sunday on the tiny stage. These popular events appeal as much to thirsty nostalgics as to newcomers to the manor, all of whom pack out this two-bar treasure. Its popularity was so great that, in 2018, the musicians who regularly take to the stage recorded a live session in the pub for posterity. Such talented performers as Helen Keating, actress and former landlady of the closed Foresters Arms, appeared on the limited-edition EP.

So much of what is good about the East End lives on inside this Grade II-listed icon. Any lover of real pubs would certainly cherish a visit here.

127 Grove Road, E3 5BH

Kerry Barrett, landlady of The Palm Tree,
fondly recalls moving to the pub as a child when
her parents Val and Alf took it over in 1977.

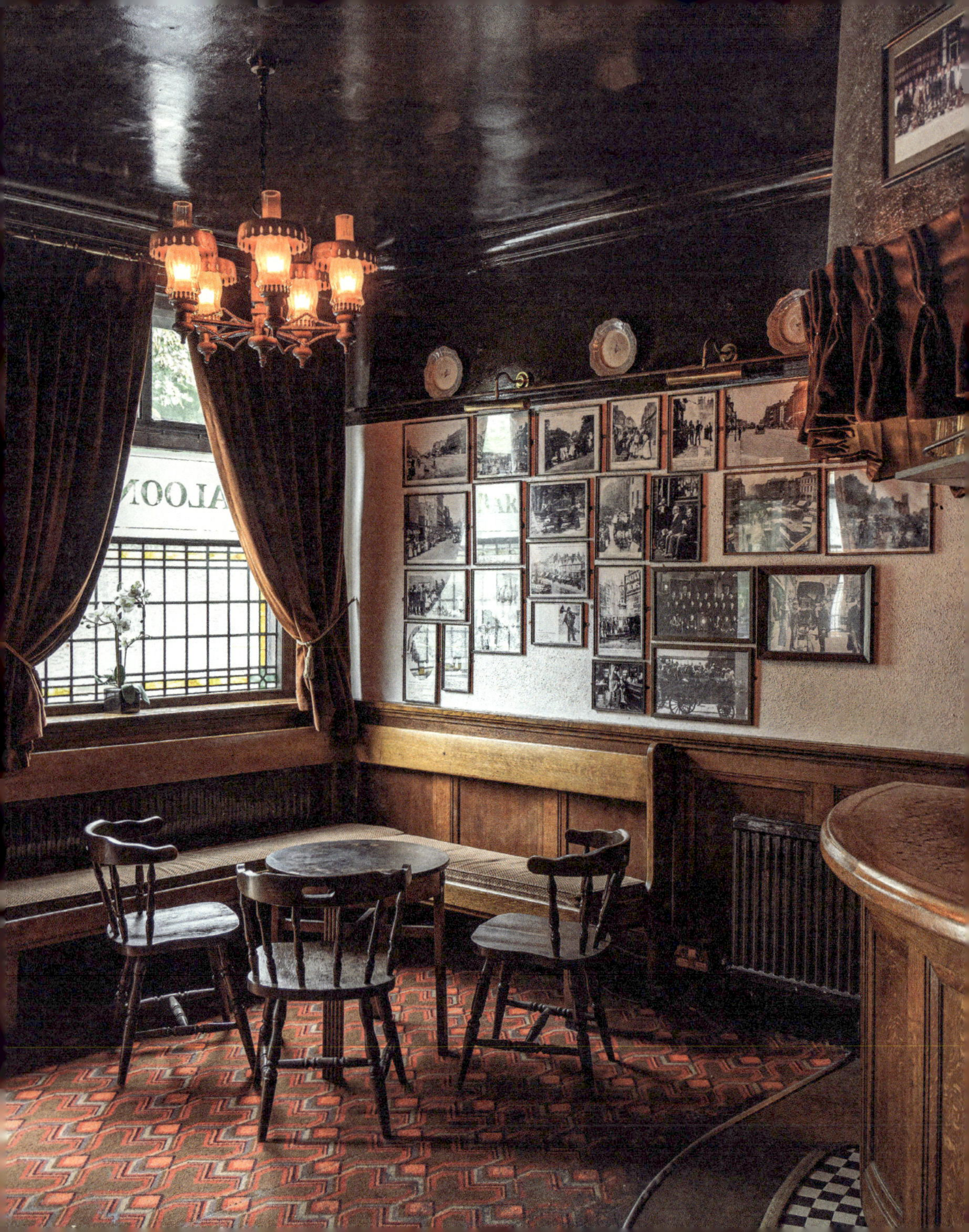

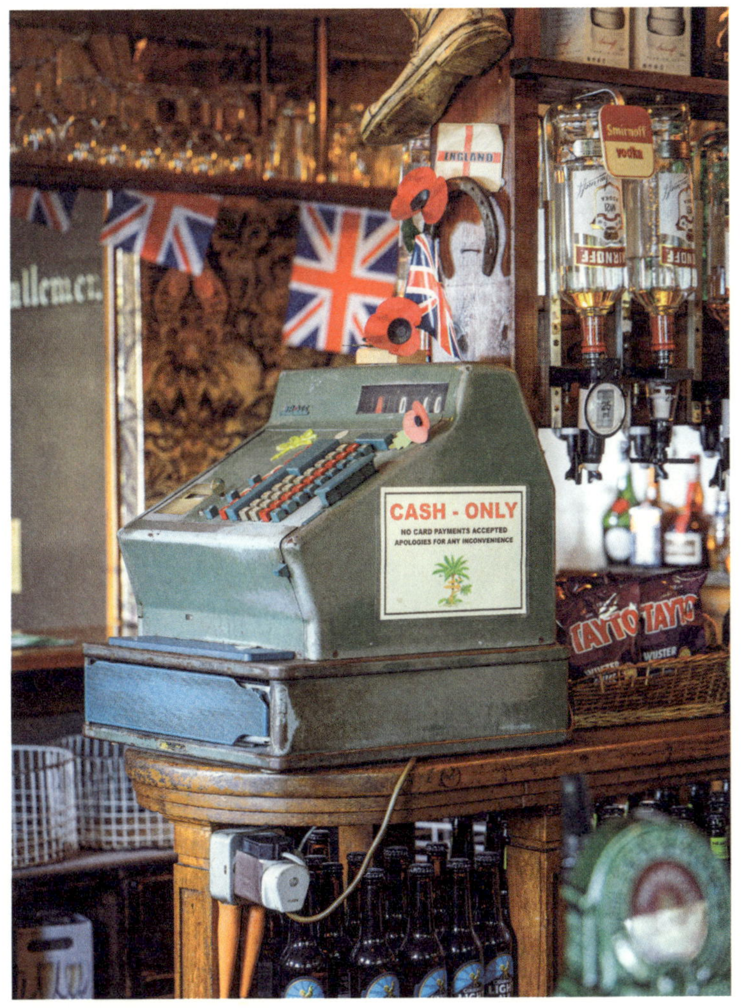

*The Palm Tree is proudly cash-only and still
uses an antique till to ring up punters' orders.*

The Royal Oak

A strong contender for the East End's most picturesque boozer, The Royal Oak was designed for brewers Truman, Hanbury & Buxton in 1923 by their in-house architect Arthur E. Sewell. Sewell designed close to 50 pubs for the firm, but this Grade II-listed gem is arguably his magnum opus.

The Royal Oak is one of the most instantly recognisable public houses in the East End. Featured in many series and films over the last 30 years, its renown is both local and international.

Famously, it serves the florists and punters of Columbia Road's weekly flower market, which was at one time located in a now-demolished covered food hall built by the Victorian social reformer and heiress Angela Burdett-Coutts. Although the arrival of lilies and chrysanthemums pre-date the pub's current iteration by more than 50 years, a pub has stood on the site since 1839 – long before Burdett-Coutts took on Bethnal Green's slums.

With its striking facade, the pub is testament to a time of great transition between the wars. In the depths of an English winter, the mood is often sombre and reflective; once summer arrives, however, the dark green tiles come alive as sunlight hits the building, completely transforming it. Pubs in Bethnal Green don't tend to be so pretty, but The Royal Oak has earned its right to be considered a thing of beauty.

Until the late 1990s, the pub opened in the small hours of Sunday morning for market traders. It was frequently packed by 7am and enjoyed a convivial atmosphere as an eclectic mix of flower sellers and sex

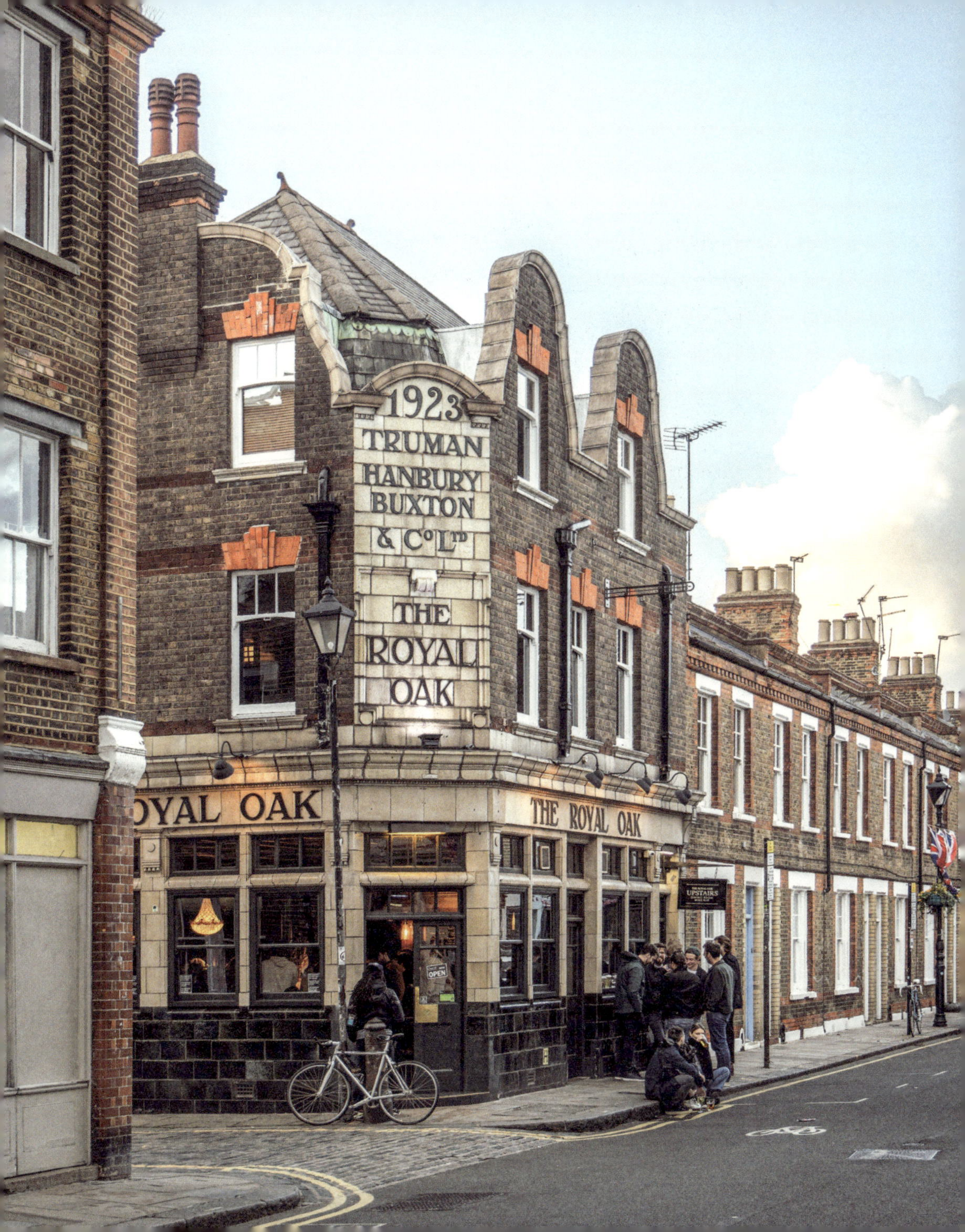

1923
TRUMAN
HANBURY
BUXTON
& C° L™
THE
ROYAL
OAK
ROYAL OAK
THE ROYAL OAK
UPSTAIRS
OPEN

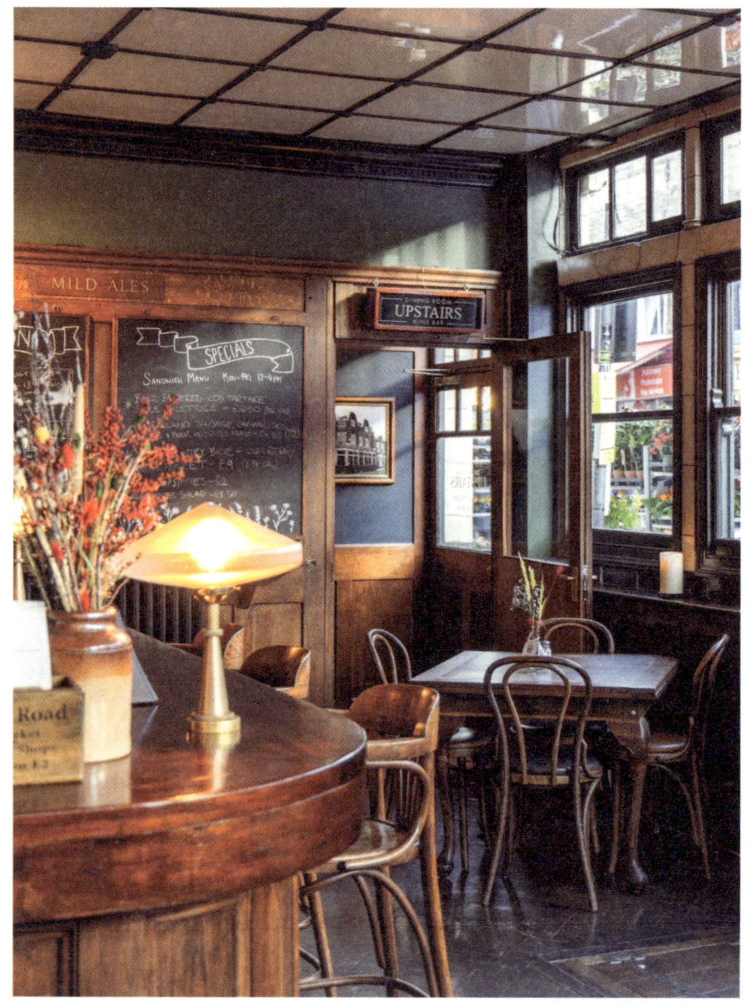

workers joined those rounding off an evening in London's nightclubs.

Like many parts of the East End, the area has undergone seismic changes. Nowadays, The Royal Oak mostly caters to young professionals popping in on their way home after work to let off some steam. They've perhaps not come from the factories and the docks as workers did in times gone by, but the hubbub is likely as loud as the din back in the 1920s.

Stools circle the island bar and although the 'saloon' and 'public' bars have merged and opened out to one room (ending the old distinction of the more private saloon and the cheaper public bar), it is still a stylish affair. Original oak panels, beautifully preserved parquet flooring and a simple glass Vitrolite ceiling project a fresh and clean minimalist aesthetic.

In times gone by, the local community was tight knit; everyone seemed to know everyone else and look out for one another. The pub was always there to welcome those living cheek-by-jowl in densely populated streets, and although the clientele may have changed significantly, The Royal Oak retains a unique energy due to its proximity to the market. Whether you are here once a year or several nights a week, it's a pub that never loses its charm or the feeling it stokes in its punters that they're a part of something.

Run independently for many years, there were concerns in 2020, when Young & Co took the pub back in-house, that the planned refurbishment might alter its DNA. Fortunately, fans of the traditional interwar interior can rest easy, as the only changes have been a lick of paint and the welcome addition of a bar footrail.

Flowers may wither and customers move on, but Truman's archetypal design and branding will always remain a constant in the ever-changing East End.

73 Columbia Road, E2 7RG

The Royal Oak retains a rare example of the Vitrolite ceilings favoured by Truman's in their interwar pubs.

The Blind Beggar

The Blind Beggar was immortalised when Ronnie Kray murdered George Cornell there in 1966, but the pub is much more than just the backdrop to the notorious violence of the Kray's Firm.

The Beggar was used as a taproom for the Albion Brewery, which stood next to the pub until its closure in 1979. Its unusual name comes from the early modern ballad *The Blind Beggar of Bethnal Green*. The beggar is often thought to be Henry de Montfort, a knight wounded and blinded during the Battle of Evesham in 1265. The story goes that de Montfort would beg at the crossroads where the current Blind Beggar (built in 1894) now stands.

While The Beggar today draws in tourists who want to see where the Krays cut their deals, locals know that they didn't actually drink in this pub. Ronnie, in particular, favoured

The Grave Maurice (which sadly closed in 2010) for its banquette-style seating, which had a clear view of the door. As well as the odd criminal, The Beggar has enjoyed regular custom from the Royal London Hospital whose staff visit to blow off steam after a tough shift. It's also common to find yourself bumping into large groups taking part in tours of the Kray's East End, who stop by to hear the story of Ronnie Kray's downfall over a pint and a burger.

That a pub with such heritage, some of it gruesome, is finding a way to keep its doors open must be celebrated. The Blind Beggar is an iconic symbol of the East End's troubled history with organised crime, which always takes root where inequality thrives.

337 Whitechapel Road, E1 1BU

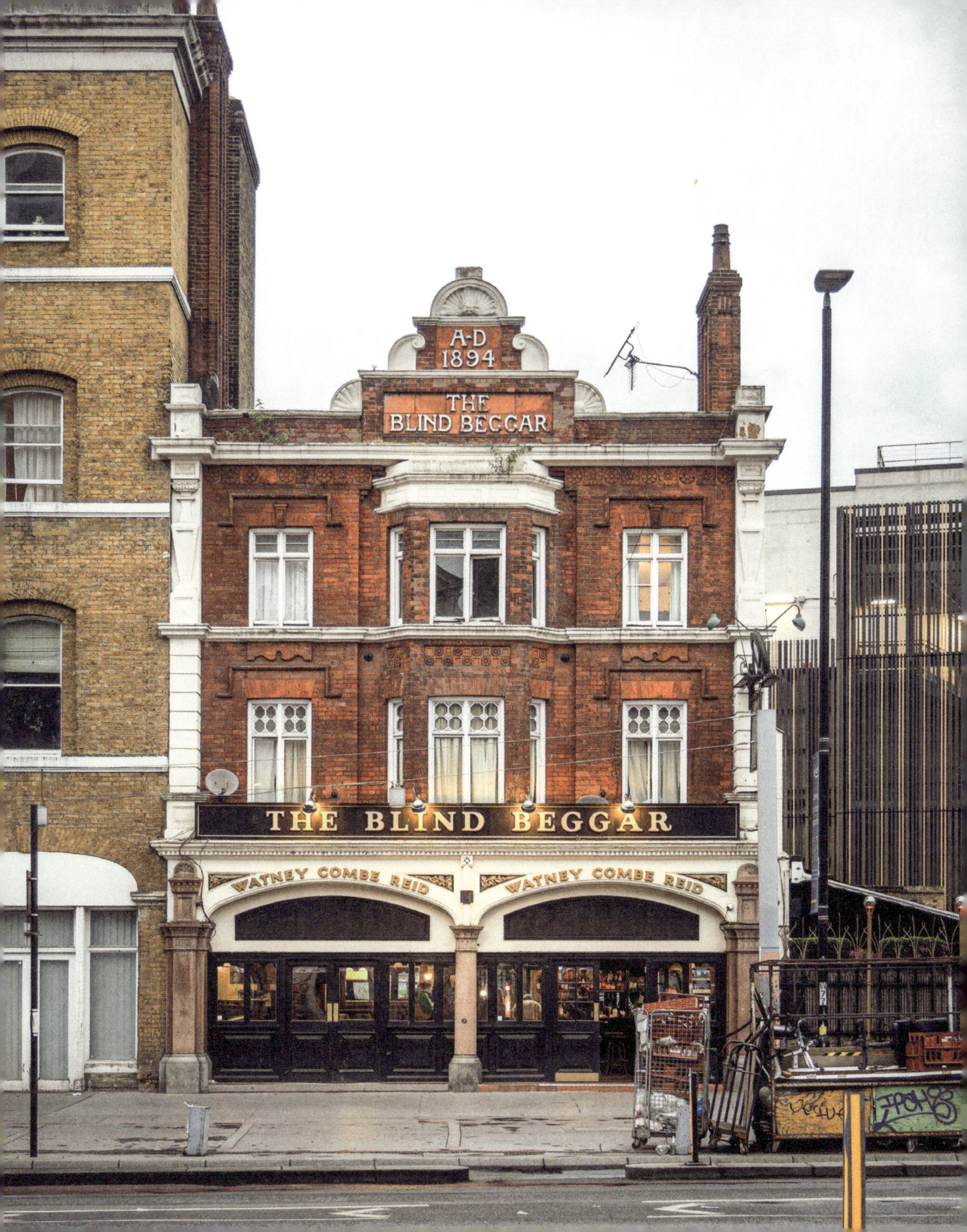
A·D
1894
THE
BLIND BEGGAR
THE BLIND BEGGAR
WATNEY COMBE REID
WATNEY COMBE REID

The Ten Bells

OLD MARKET BOOZER WITH A MODERN TWIST

The Ten Bells is often credited as being the beating heart of Spitalfields, the former home of London's fruit and vegetable market. There are certainly few public houses that can claim to have seen as much change throughout their life as this iconic Truman's hostelry.

The pub sits in the shadow of Christ Church, built by Nicholas Hawksmoor in the early 18th century to provide spiritual sustenance to London's growing population. It is one of east London's most recognisable landmarks. The pub was previously named The Eight Bells after the number of bells in the church's tower. It was renamed in the late 1780s and the moniker remains the same today (though it is worth noting that the church still has only eight bells).

From the establishment of Spitalfields Market in 1638 up until 1991, when the market closed and the vendors moved further east to Leyton, the shouts and cries of costermongers could be heard throughout the area. Spitalfields suffered economic decline once the market relocated. It was only after the regeneration of the old covered market – now selling arts and crafts, clothes and high-end street food – that the more polished Spitalfields we see today emerged from its journey through austerity and chronic want.

The three-storey pub has been a constant through all these changes and today, after a sympathetic refurbishment in 2010, makes for an alluring London pub experience.

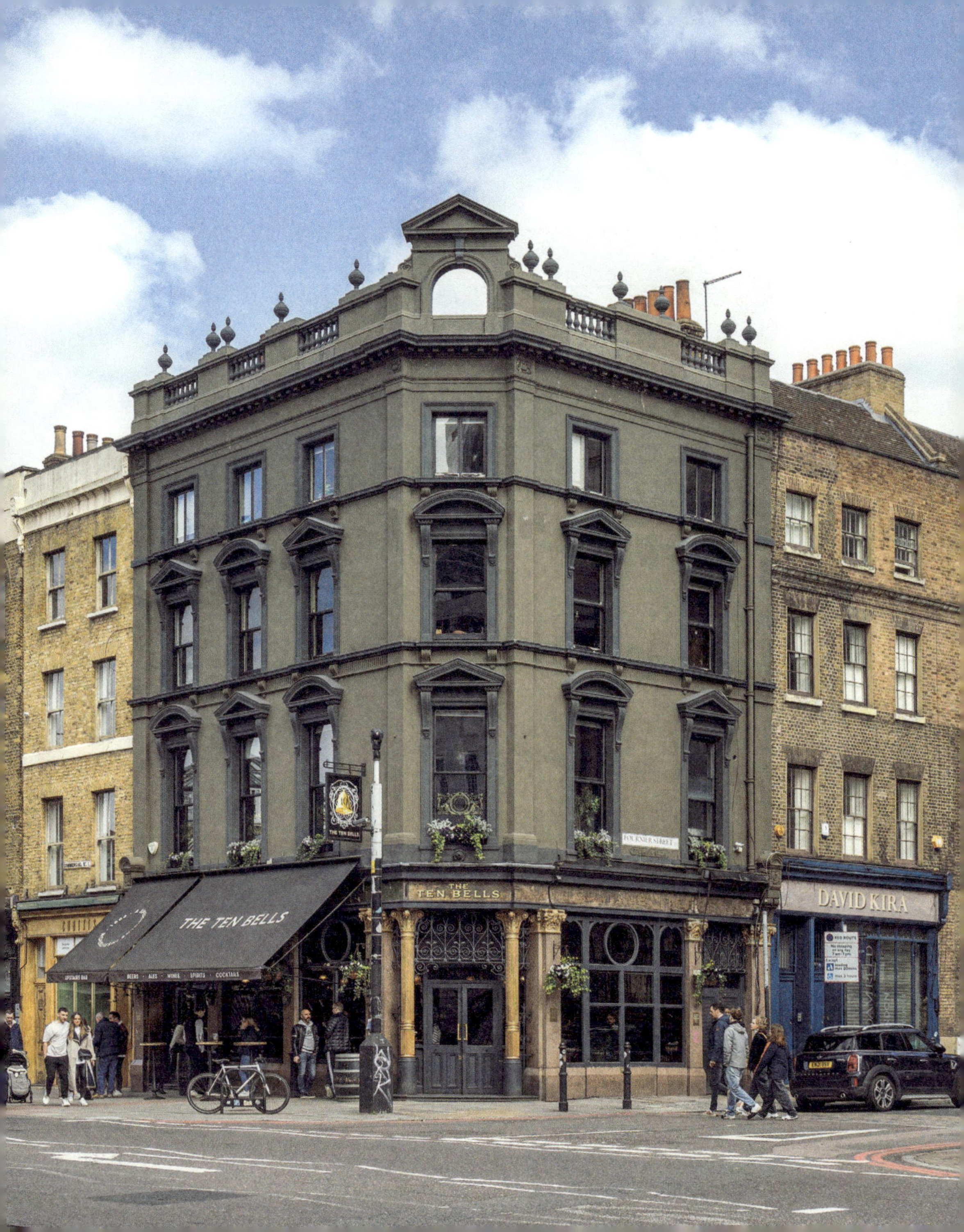
THE TEN BELLS
THE TEN BELLS
UPSTAIRS BAR
BEERS · ALES · WINES · SPIRITS · COCKTAILS
DAVID KIRA
FOURNIER STREET

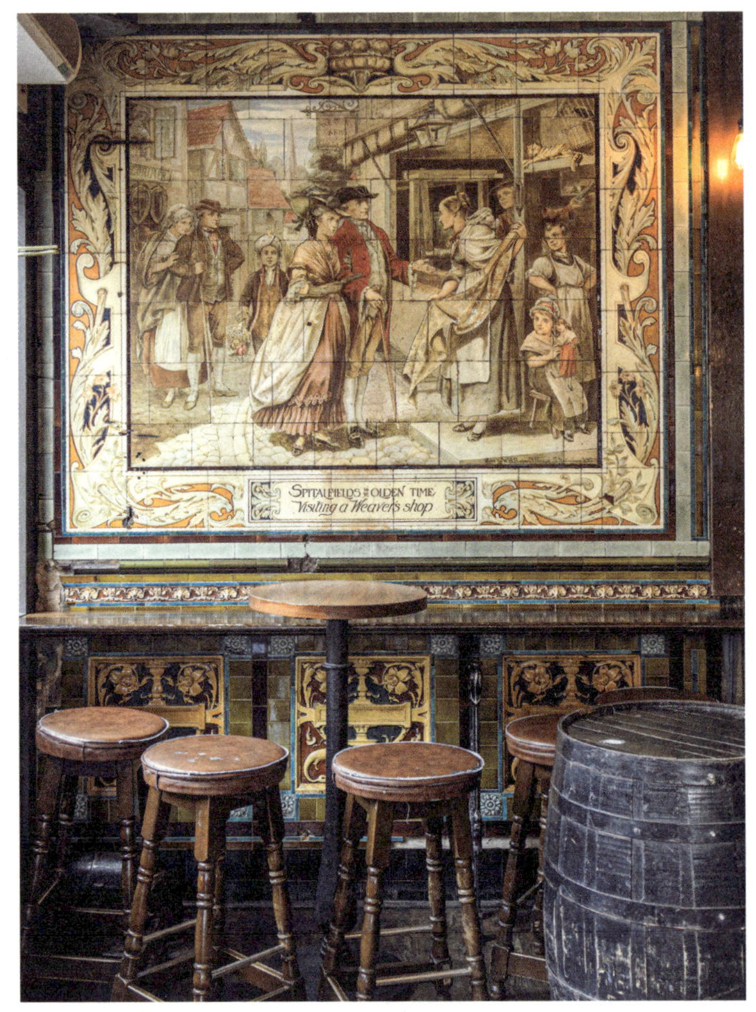
SPITALFIELDS IN THE OLDEN TIME
Visiting a Weaver's shop

This was not always the case, however. In 1976, The Ten Bells was crudely renamed The Jack the Ripper because of its link to the Victorian serial killer. Two victims, Annie Chapman and Mary Jane Kelly, were thought to have frequented the pub. The fact that walking tours would stop for a drink and have photographs taken wearing a Ripper-inspired cape and top hat added further offence. It was not until 1988 that committed campaigners Reclaim the Night successfully persuaded the pub to return to its former name. It was, however, still a spit 'n' sawdust boozer with '50p in a pint' strippers up until the late 1990s.

Today no such entertainment takes place. Instead, the hostelry is a treasure trove for lovers of fine Victorian architecture and fittings: an island bar is the cornerstone of the ground floor, offset by some rare and striking floor-to-ceiling tiling. On one wall, an intricate design paints a scene from the area's historic silk weaving industry. A newer mural on the southeastern wall by Ian Harper, *Spitalfields in Modern Times*, depicts characters from this century, including local artists Gilbert & George. It's no wonder that The Ten Bells has held Grade II-listed status since 1973.

Constantly busy with an ebb and flow reminiscent of the heyday of Old Spitalfields Market, revellers can head to the first-floor cocktail bar or climb the creaking ancient stairs to the intimate lounge, which is often used for photoshoots and private events.

The Ten Bells offers a slice of social, architectural and cultural history in an energising part of London, which continues to surprise and delight.

84 Commercial Street, E1 6QQ

Tiled murals depict scenes from the area's past and present. Here, two well-dressed Londoners visit a silk weaver, a popular trade in Spitalfields introduced by Huguenot migrants in the 17th century. Overleaf, Ian Harper's contemporary mural presents a modern Spitalfields.

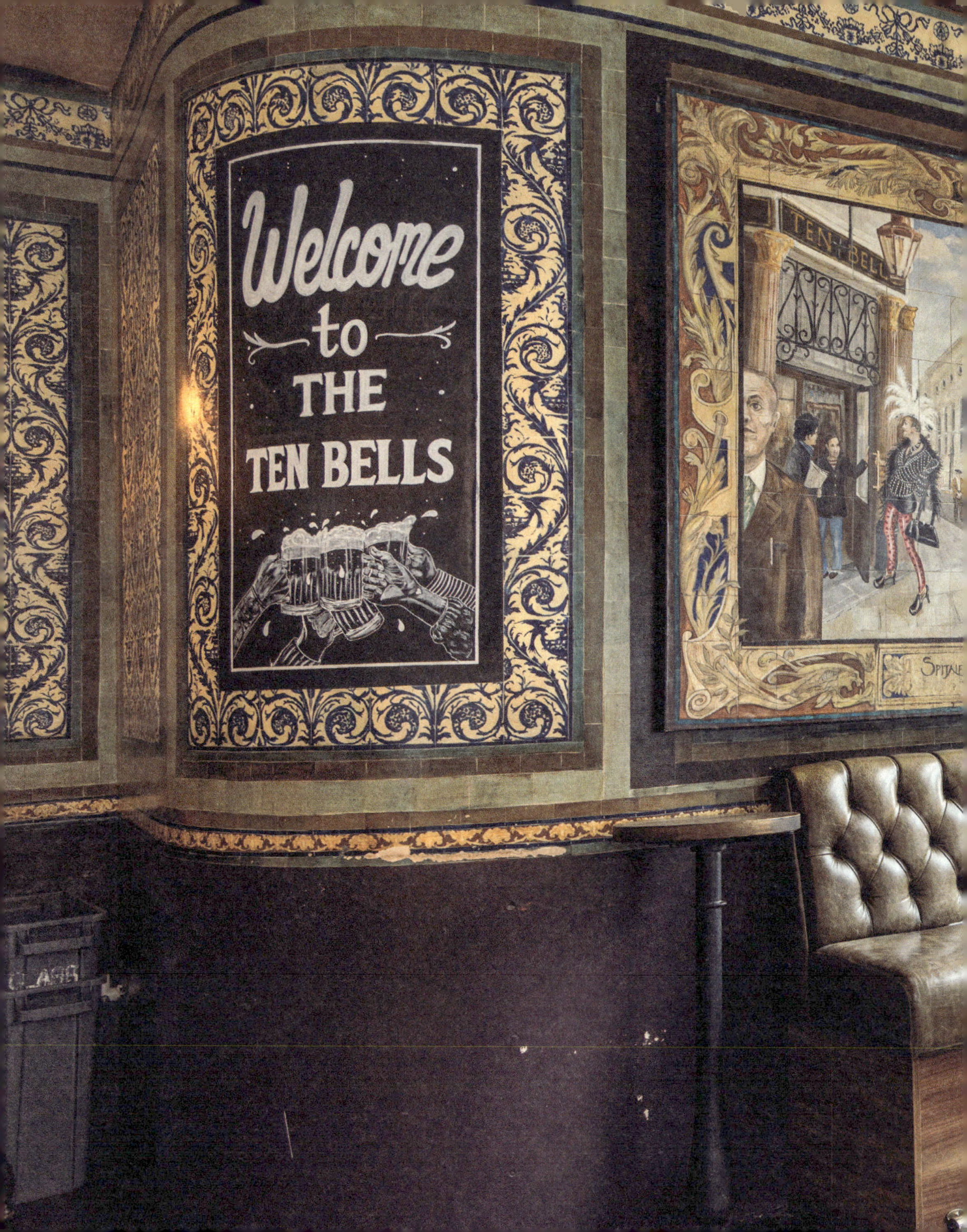

Welcome
to
THE
TEN BELLS

TEN BELLS
SPITAL

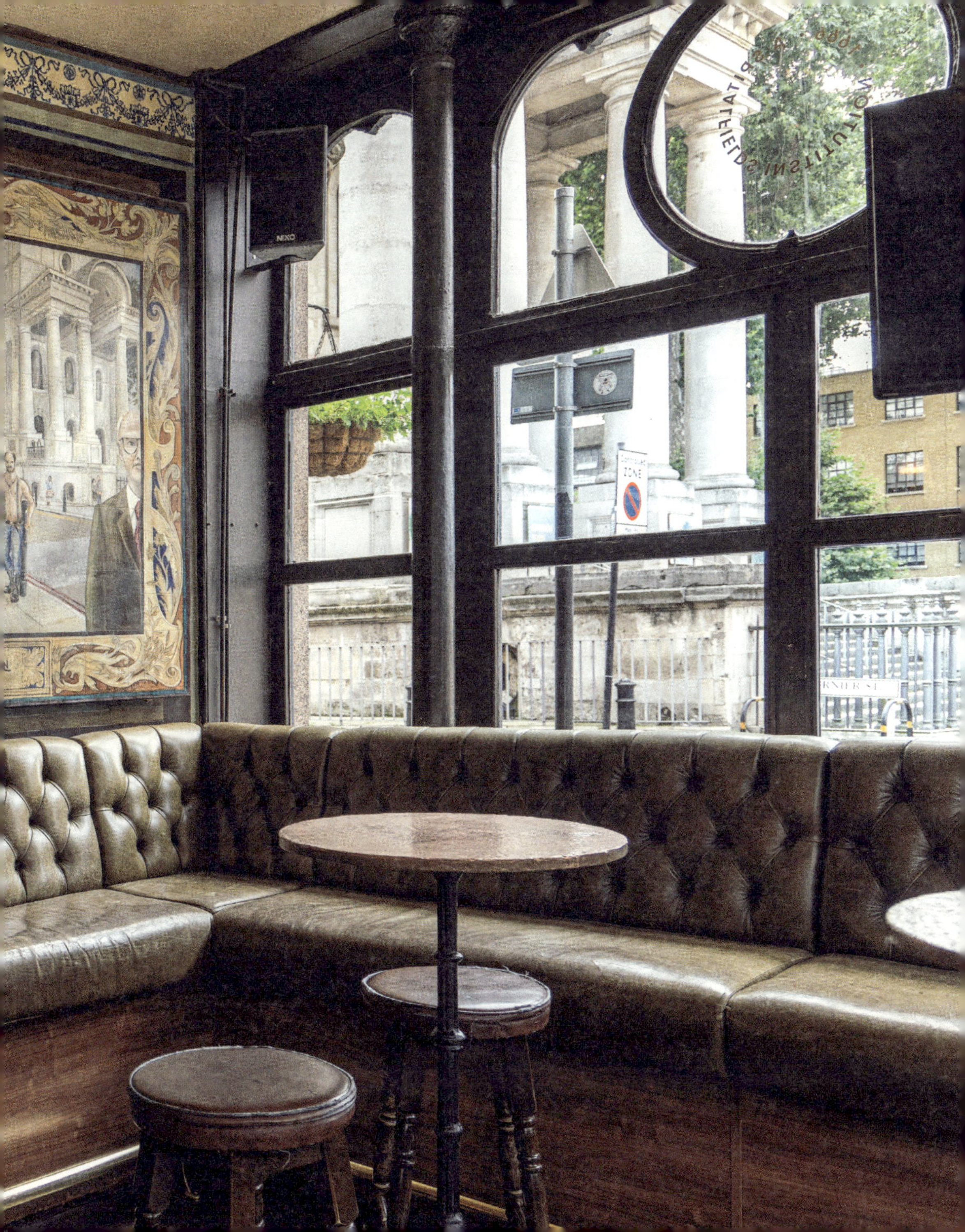
RNIER ST

The Camel

London is a city of constant change and renewal, but there are still corners of the East End that resemble the distant past – when narrow, compact streets arranged long before the arrival of the motor car housed row-upon-row of terraced dwellings, and there was a 'pub on every corner'.

While that expression is over-used by sentimental romantics, it is true that on the tree-lined backstreets of Bethnal Green, the sheer number of pubs – catering first to weavers, then factory workers and now to both the remnants of Cockney communities and professional newcomers – was at one time significant. Cast an eye over old Ordnance Survey maps of the area and you'll find them almost saturated with little PH markers, denoting a public house. They were the cornerstones of their community and had few rivals other than music halls and, much later, cinemas.

Here, on the northern side of Globe Road, set against social housing constructed by the East End Dwelling Co. in 1905, lies what was once many East Enders' favourite pub crawl: The Florist (p.84), The Greyhound and, of course, The Camel.

Two of these pubs still survive. Guv'nor Stevie Connor was already running The Greyhound (which has sadly been sold to be converted into flats) when he purchased The Camel in 1990, and it remains in the family to this day, run by his daughter Debbie. She gave up a career in finance to take up the victualler mantle and has been running a tight ship ever since. Locally

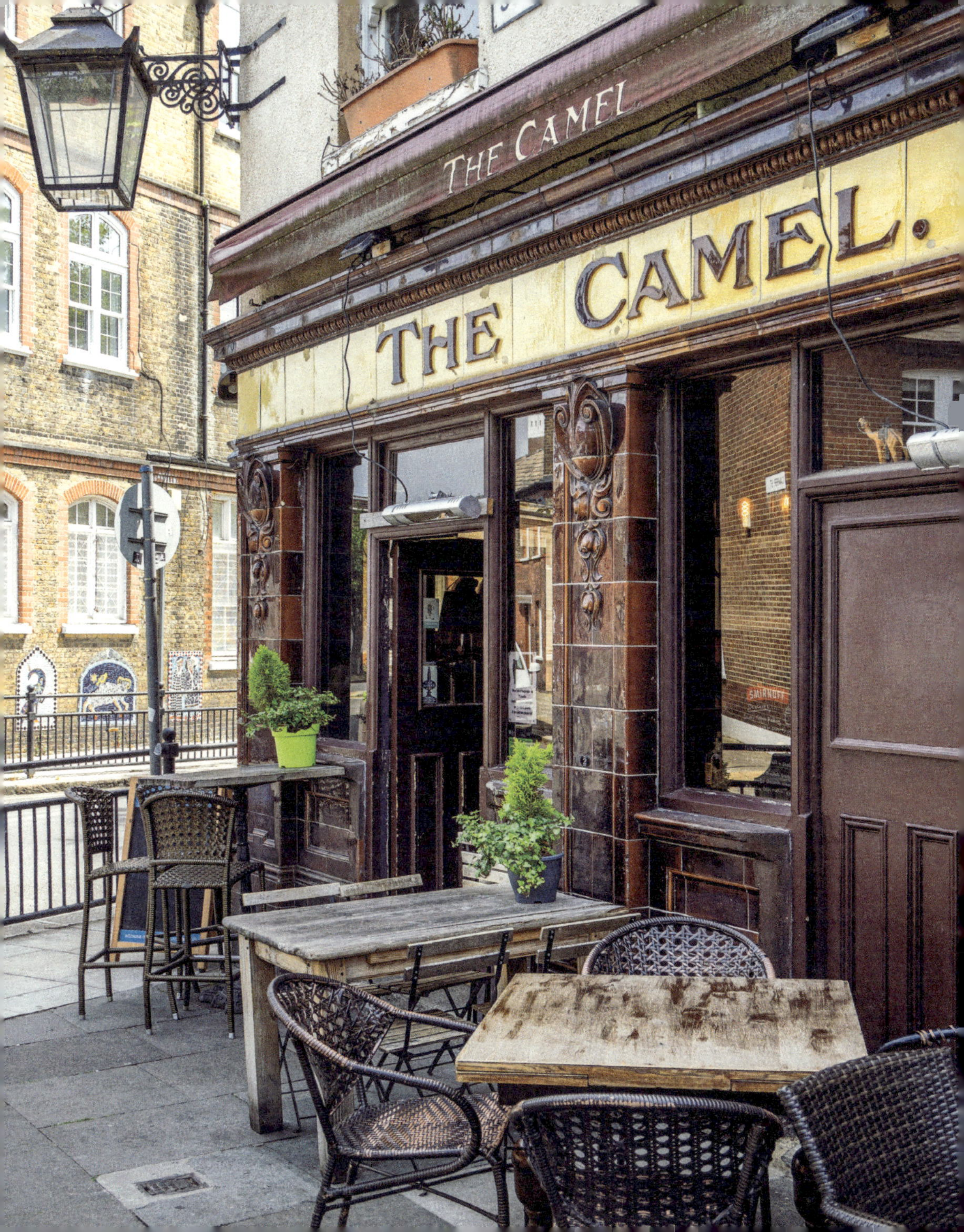

THE CAMEL
THE CAMEL.

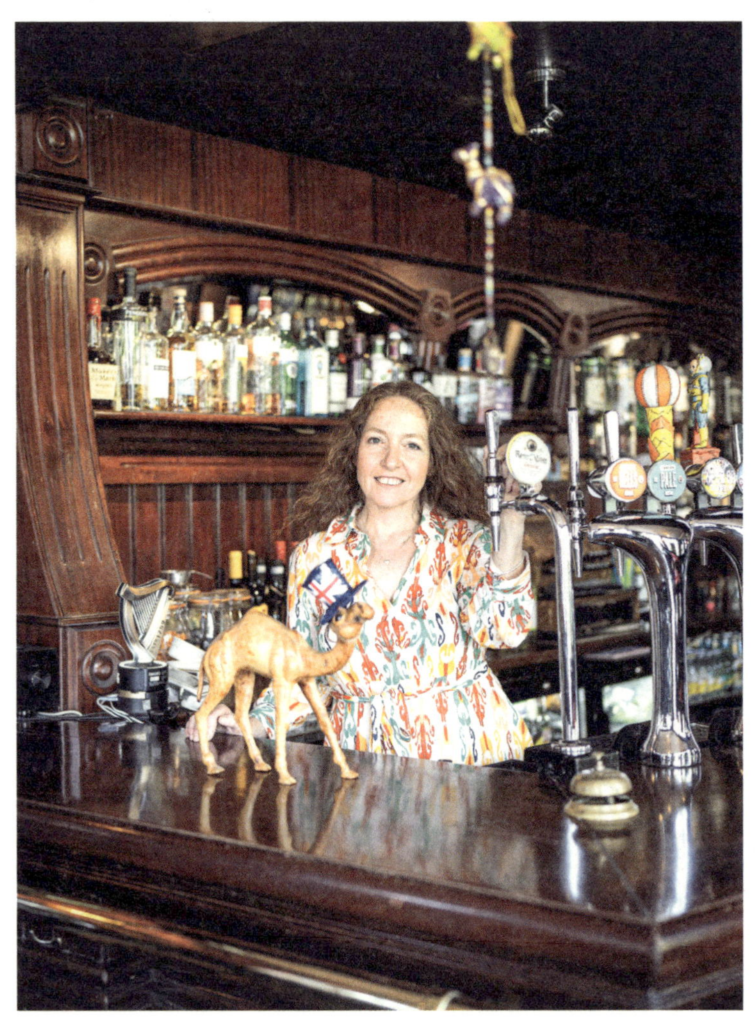

sourced libations on tap and hand pump alongside mouth-watering pies all served by Debbie's able team, The Camelettes, provide a true escape from the strains of life.

Originally named The Museum Beer Tavern, the date The Camel was renamed is uncertain but its link to the Young V&A (formerly the Museum of Childhood) goes back as far as the foundation of the museum itself in 1872. Its current name, however, is a nod to the area's rich weaving history: camel wool was used in the 19th century to produce luxury textiles and fabrics. It is a mystery how the pub's name came to be punctuated on the facade, but the Connor family respectfully added the unique full-stop to their awnings.

The current interior is furnished with opulent flock wallpaper, a gleaming lower and upper bar rail (an unusual sight now; upper bar rails allow standing drinkers to lean against them), camel paraphernalia, pictures of old punters on jaunts to the coast and a grand wooden bar, which must have many stories embedded within the polished mahogany.

The glorious brown tiles on the facade give the pub a memorable and welcoming presence against the more modern flats behind. It is how one imagines the non-evacuated East End children, who frequented the children's club at The Camel during World War II, must have seen it.

The pub takes full advantage of any warm weather with its al fresco seating. In the summer, life and laughter can be heard as you approach, and it is always heart-warming to see that the age-old tradition of meeting and making friends continues here with such gusto.

It is somewhere to go for a beer and a chat with Debbie (or any members of the team that run the bar with such ease), or for one of the exceptional pies for which they are revered locally. While the pub has an effortless feel to it, any patron will instantly understand the toil, passion and hours that go into running a first-class hostelry. May the Connor family long continue to do so with such gracious aplomb.

277 Globe Road, E2 0JE

Debbie Connor took over the pub from her father Stevie, leaving a career in the City to become a much-loved landlady.

The Carpenters Arms

TRADITIONAL PUB HERALDING THE NEW EAST END

The Carpenters Arms is famous for its association with the Kray Twins, who used it as a watering hole for their notorious criminal organisation The Firm in the 1960s. Just around the corner from Ronnie and Reggie Kray's childhood home, they purchased the pub for their mother in 1967. From then on, they used it to host parties and plot their next move. But this 19th-century boozer should be more revered for its dogged resilience, than for its connection to London's most infamous criminals.

Fast forward six decades, and The Carpenters Arms still stands while much of its old surrounds have vanished. Its near neighbour The King & Queen closed forever after it was ravaged by fire in 1996, but The Carpenters has somehow survived two closures in the last 20 years and is now thriving once more.

Its newest custodians, who also run the magnificent Highbury pub The Bank of Friendship, reopened the pub triumphantly in 2023. There are respectful nods to the legacy of brewing juggernaut Truman's throughout, the walls adorned with plenty of their branded wares and magnificent gold-leafed mirrors.

As a further mark of respect, only local brews such as Hackney's Five Points are served to a thirsty crowd, who perch on barstools and studded leather banquettes in a 1960s-inspired public bar.

The cultural shift of the pub, from serving gangsters and Brick Lane market traders to contemporary punters who favour craft beer to porter, is a sign of the times. If pubs don't evolve, they risk being forgotten. Luckily, The Carpenters Arms no doubt has a bright future ahead.

73 Cheshire Street, E2 6EG

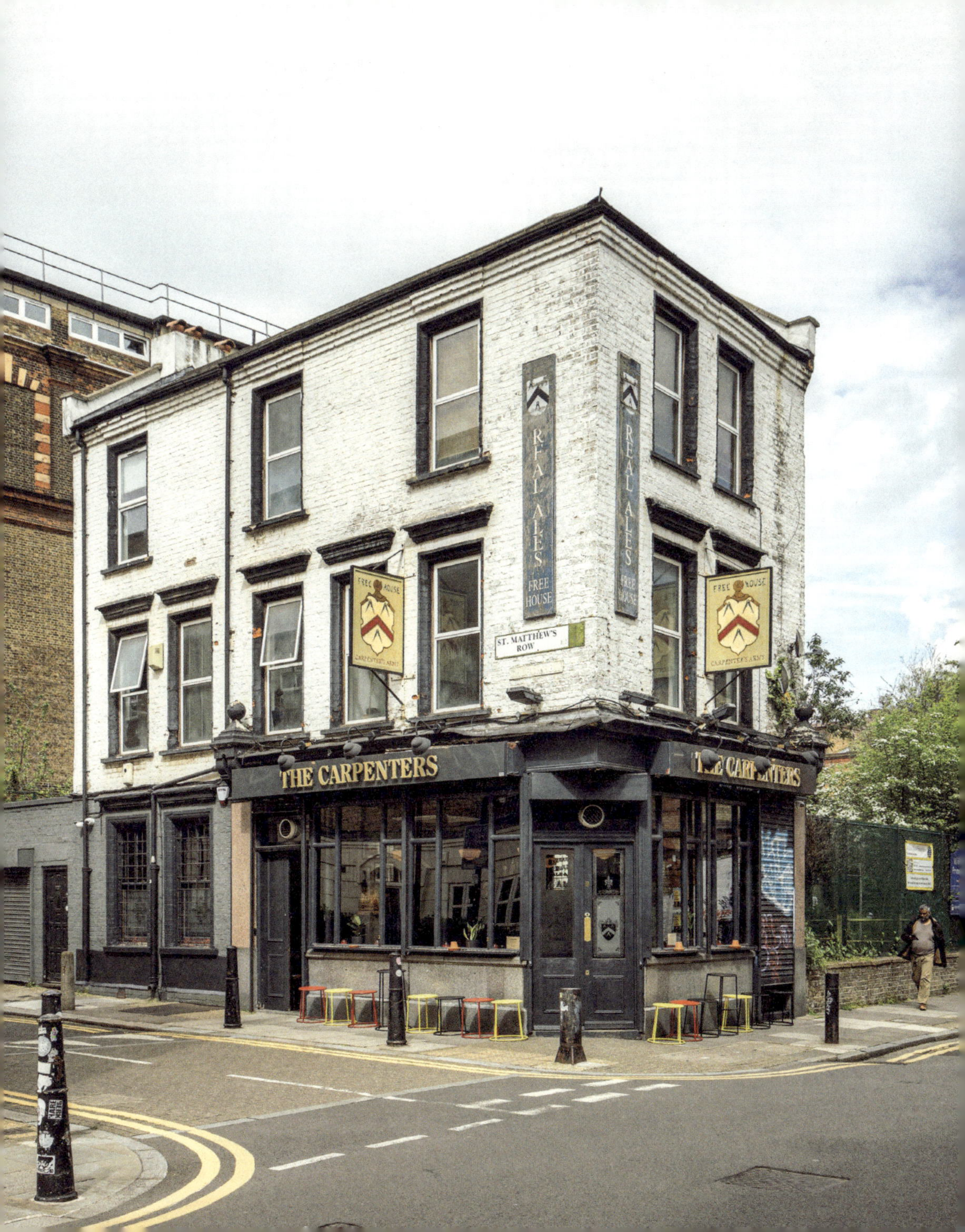

REAL ALES
FREE HOUSE
REAL ALES
FREE HOUSE
FREE HOUSE
CARPENTERS ARMS
FREE HOUSE
CARPENTERS ARMS
ST. MATTHEW'S ROW
THE CARPENTERS
THE CARPENTERS

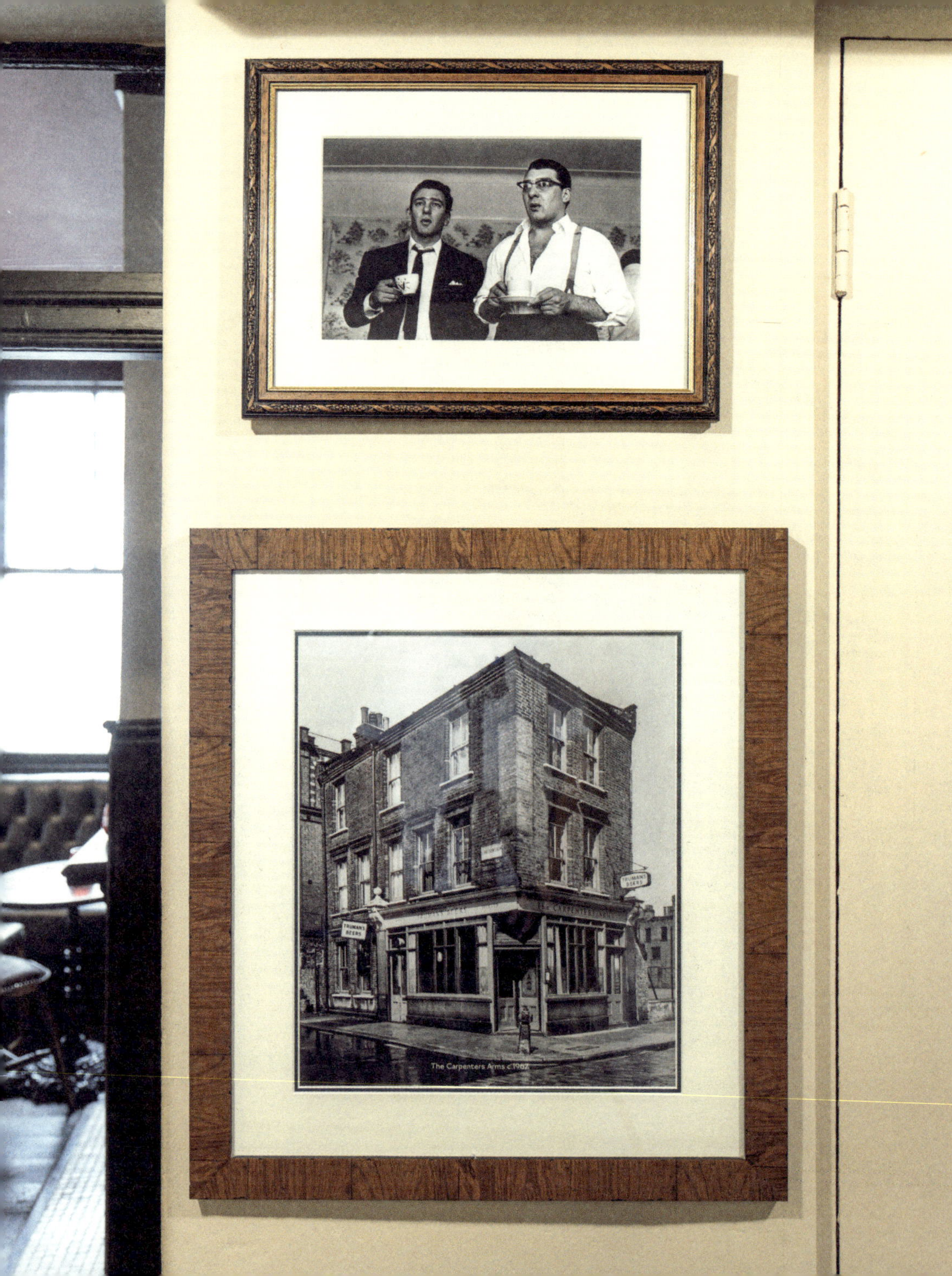
The Carpenters Arms c.1967

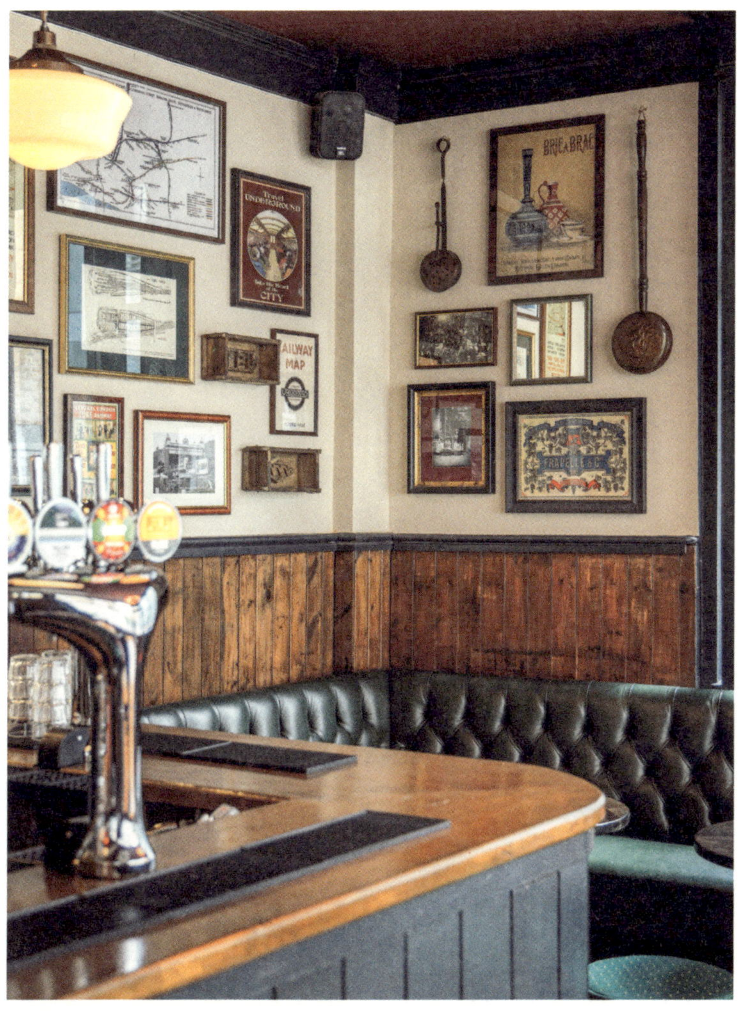

The walls of The Carpenters Arms are adorned with historic memorabilia, including a photograph of Reggie and Ronnie Kray hung above an image of the pub taken in 1967, the year they purchased it.

The Approach Tavern

RESILIENT MAINSTAY ON A LEAFY BACKSTREET

The Approach Tavern, a much-loved hostelry that first opened its doors in 1860, was named after the road taken by Queen Victoria as she journeyed through the East End on her way to open her glorious park to the public.

During the pub's long history, wars have raged and empires have fallen while economic downturns and harrowing pestilences have been endured. After resiliently surviving such a chequered history, it is no surprise that the pub yet again demonstrated its mettle when it was bombed during the Blitz.

As enemy aircraft soared over London, the King family, who ran The Approach Tavern for many years, sheltered in the pub's cellar. During one air raid, a bomb struck the front of the pub. Upon receiving the all-clear, the Kings emerged to assess the damage and discovered, to their horror, most of the top floor had been destroyed, as had the beautiful Victorian frontage.

Guv'nor Jack King surveyed the destruction while his son, Harry, aged 19, searched desperately for his beloved fish – shrapnel having smashed the tank. Despite the severe damage, the pub was painstakingly restored and eventually reopened with a new facade. Pictures of both Jack and Harry, who became Guv'nor after his father retired and later potman (an elder statesman who would collect glasses in return for a few free pints) after hanging up his own bar towel in 1996, can now be seen on the wall by the fireplace, alongside images of the bombed pub and fish tank.

Nowadays, The Approach is one of 16 pubs owned by the Hackney-based, family-owned business Remarkable Pubs. Their restorations of traditional pubs across east and north London are a pub-purist's dream, and the hallmark of a company that treasures heritage and authenticity above easy profits.

There is so much respect for the King family's legacy that little has changed in the pub over the last 80 years, aside from a

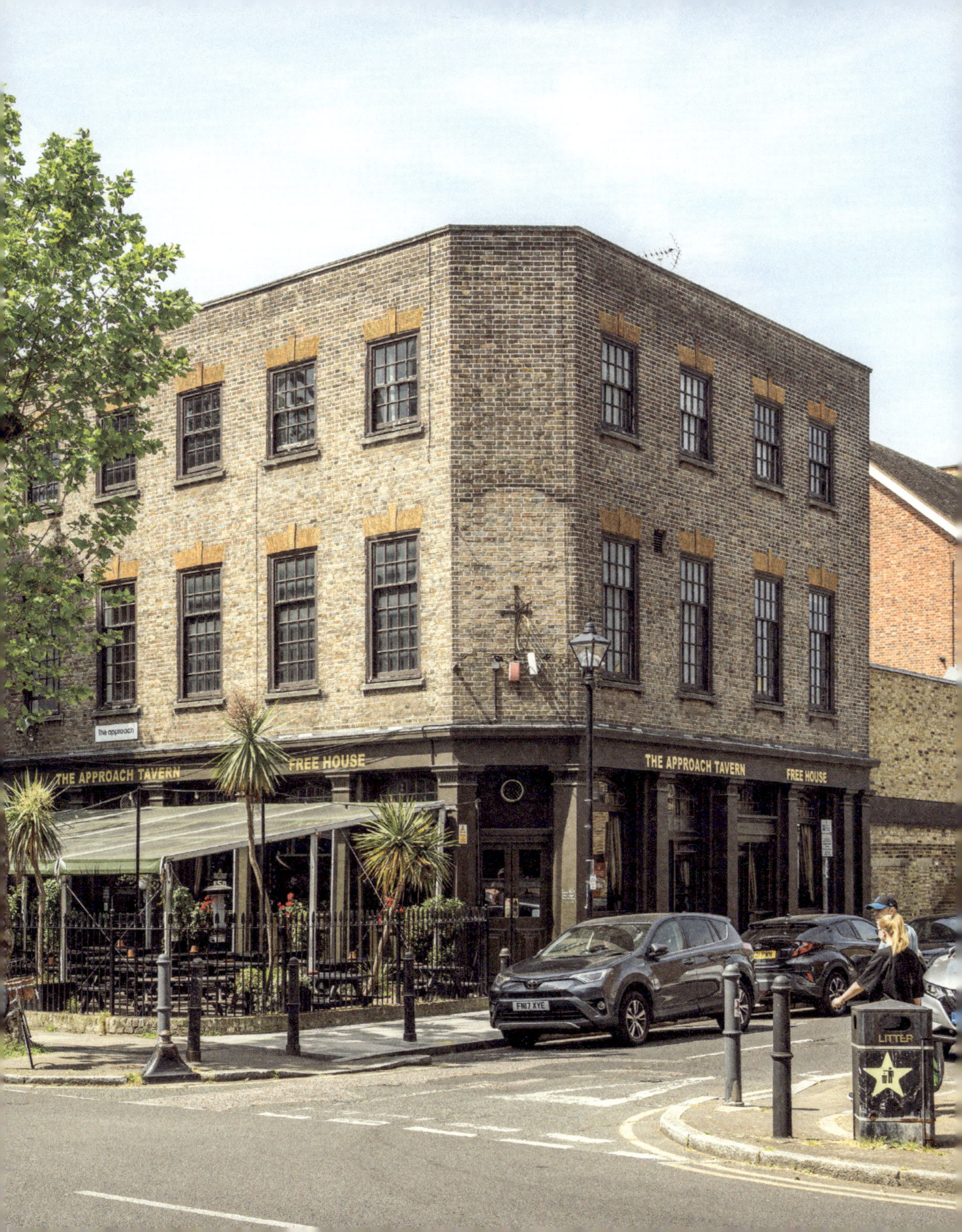
The approach
THE APPROACH TAVERN
FREE HOUSE
THE APPROACH TAVERN
FREE HOUSE
LITTER

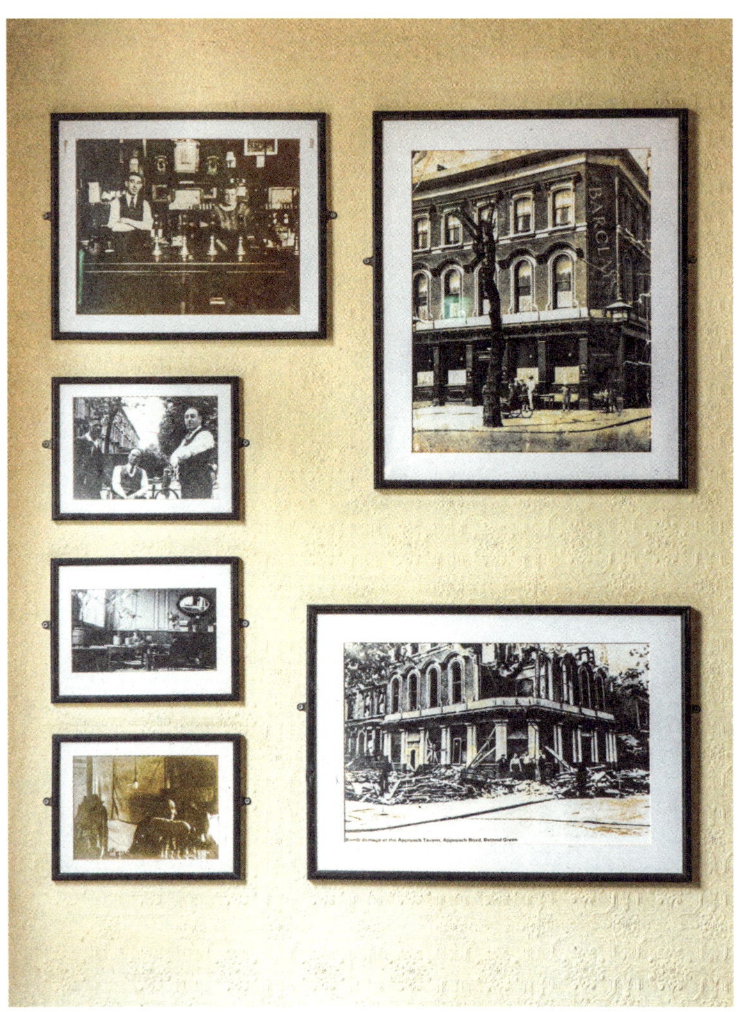

Bomb damage at the Approach Tavern, Approach Road, Bethnal Green

freshened-up bar and the removal of a wood partition to create more space. The timeless feel of a traditional East End boozer runs throughout, with dark mahogany, high ceilings and simple furnishings sitting over what would formerly have been stripped-back, spit 'n' sawdust floorboards. The Kings would no doubt approve of this fastidious continuity, which sits alongside more modern offerings in the shape of the trade-mark Remarkable jukebox.

The pub's upper floors have also seen transition over the years, shifting from the publican's family accommodation to a comedy club in the early 1990s, where performers such as Lee Hurst cut their teeth. Today, it hosts The Approach Gallery, a contemporary art gallery known for exhibiting and supporting London-based artists at the beginning of their careers.

While some believe that many similar establishments have traded in the essence of their boozer soul to chase the culinary pound, that is pleasingly not the case here. Diners and drinkers happily coexist in the vast space. You are as likely to see an old campaigner enjoying a cask-conditioned ale or a younger customer nursing a craft IPA as a group of friends sitting down to enjoy some burgers with a bottle of red. This diverse mix of customers has kept the pub busy and, in this most traditional of settings, augurs well for a bright future on the tree-lined Approach Road.

47 Approach Road, E2 9LY

Photographs of the King family, who owned and ran The Approach Tavern until 1996, adorn the walls. In one, they can be seen standing outside the wrecked pub after it was bombed during the Blitz.

The Well & Bucket

A RARE AND MARVELLOUS PUB RESURRECTED

Once in a blue moon an East End pub comes back from the dead and, when it does, it reinvigorates the whole street. Originally a Truman's pub, The Well & Bucket served beer from the Black Eagle Brewery on Brick Lane until its closure in 1989. By the time its final days had come round, it was a heavy metal venue called the Stick of Rock. After it closed, it became a Chinese restaurant, and then later a leather whole-saler called Leather Tex.

Prior to its reopening in 2013, the old treasure was in a sorry state. Battered roller shutters hid its facade and a hole-in-the-wall-cashpoint disfigured the once proud building. The local authority has historically been slow to protect pubs, but council officers did recognise the social significance of The Well & Bucket and strongly supported the attempt to bring it back to life. After it reopened, there was a domino effect and many other independent businesses opened on its stretch of terrace.

The Well & Bucket is now operated by Urban Pubs & Bars, who have beautifully restored the interiors with a design that marries the old with the new. The footrails and sanded floorboards project an air of traditional authenticity but its pièce de résistance is undeniably the original glazed tiles which were remarkably saved after years of neglect.

Like the creative streets and businesses that surround it, The Well & Bucket now hums with a constant up-beat energy. The movers and shakers of Shoreditch come here to let loose in the cavernous boozer, drawn to its cellar cocktail bar and, on sunny days, its beer garden. The fact that this pub was almost lost but now lives on is a good omen for the preservation of social history and pub heritage.

143 Bethnal Green Road, E2 7DG

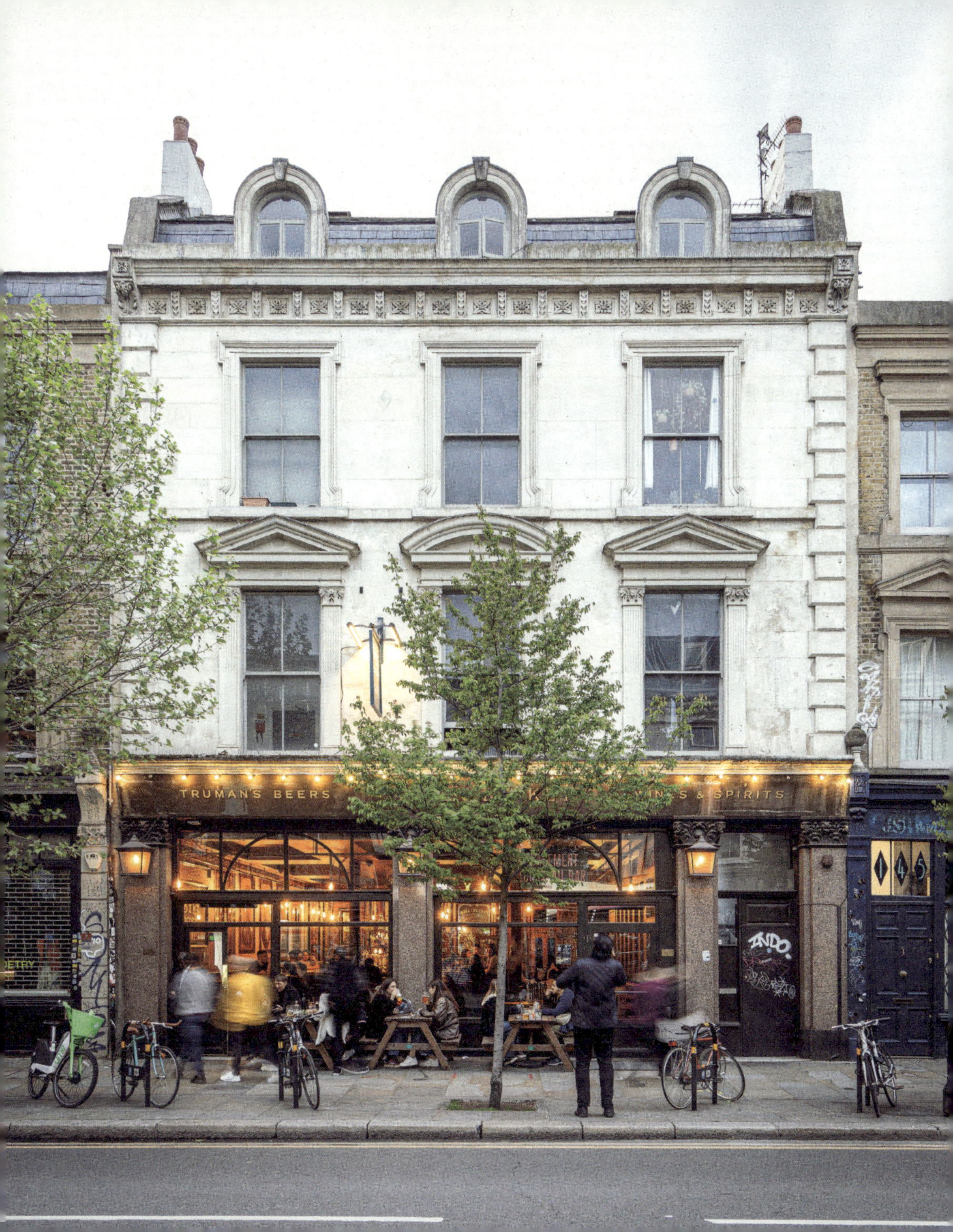

TRUMAN'S BEERS
WINES & SPIRITS
POETRY
145

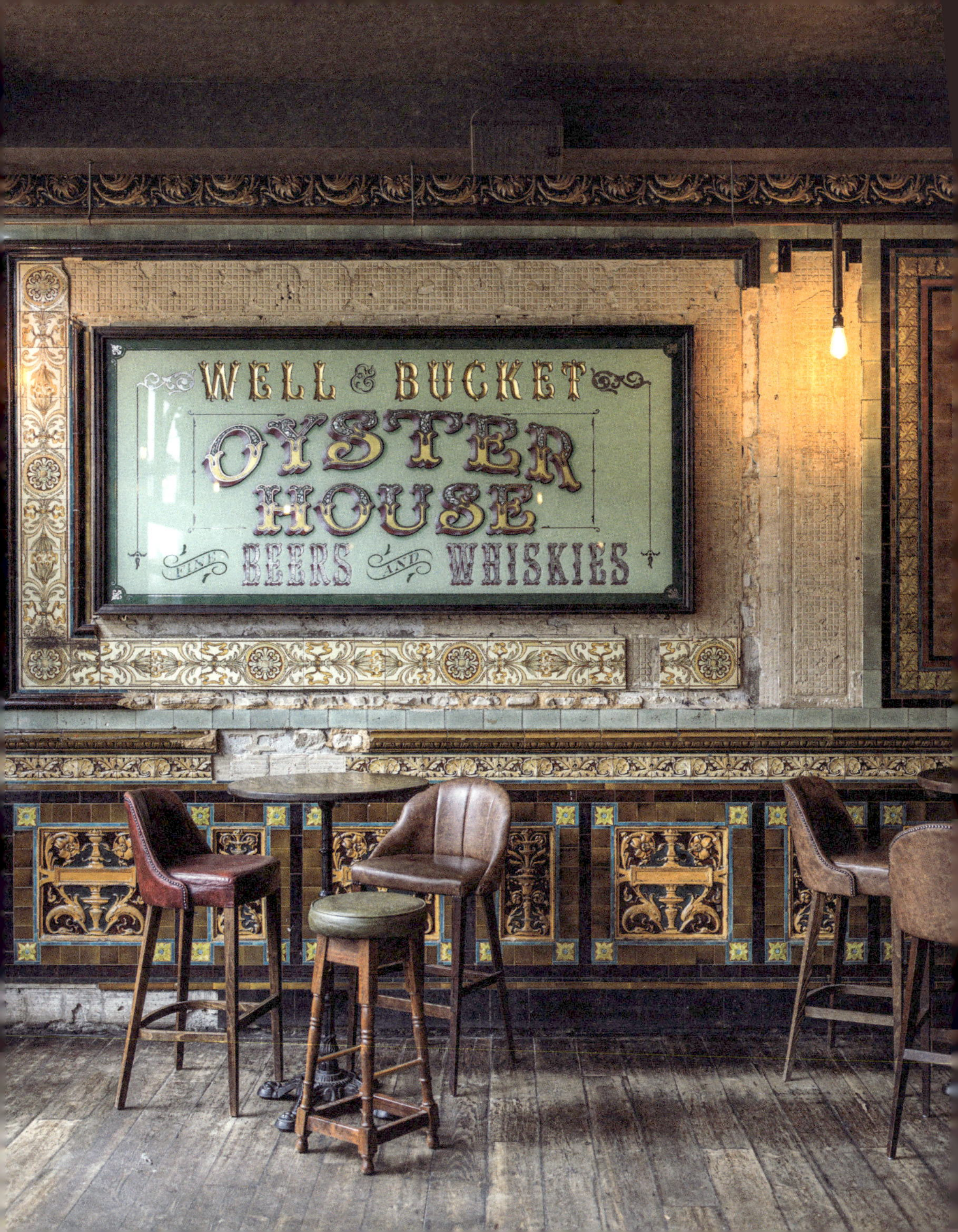

WELL & BUCKET
OYSTER
HOUSE
FINE BEERS AND WHISKIES

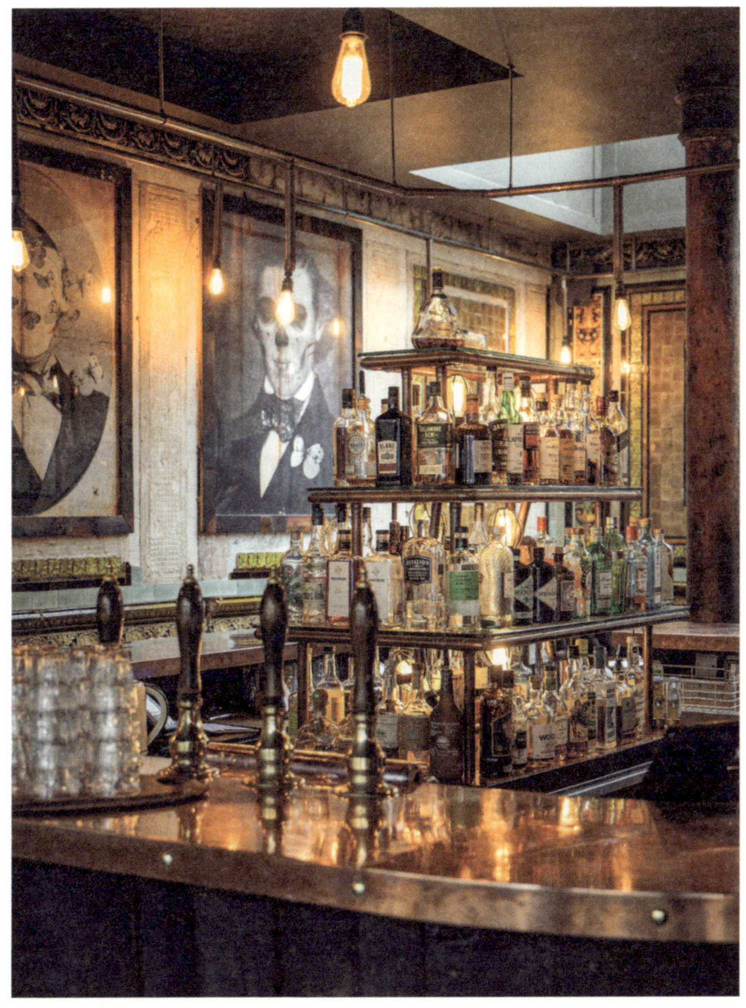

Despite suffering years of neglect, these remarkable glazed ceramic tiles survived and now give the pub a striking dash of authentic colour.

The Salmon & Ball

One of the East End's most famous boozers, the Salmon & Ball has stood on Bethnal Green Road in one guise or another since 1760. Likely named after the prevalent local trades – a weaver's ball of yarn and the fish carted by the market porters down to Old Billingsgate Market – its history is somewhat bloody.

Located next to Bethnal Green tube station, the pub bore witness to one of the largest civilian wartime tragedies in British history when, in 1943, anti-aircraft guns being tested in Victoria Park were mistaken for a German air raid. Thousands rushed for the shelter of the Underground but an old man slipped and dragged down a young mother carrying her baby, causing a panic. People were trapped but those behind continued to push to enter the station, resulting in 173 people dying of asphyxiation. The incident was hushed up to avoid damaging morale and it wasn't until 2017 that a memorial was unveiled.

The community resolutely soldiered on after this tragedy and as the East End continued to evolve, so did the famous old hostelry. Towards the end of the 20th century, it even temporarily reinvented itself as a disco pub called Tipples.

Worn carpet and a horseshoe bar create a rustic, lived-in atmosphere and it is this comforting consistency, as well as the sensibly priced drinks, that makes the Salmon & Ball a beacon for locals who flock here in their droves for the convivial conversation at the bar. Many of its customers were born in Bethnal Green and have worked and lived here their whole lives.

The Salmon & Ball is as handsome as any pub you'll have the pleasure visiting; its presence and reluctance to change makes it the most lovable of stalwarts, especially with its wallet-pleasing happy hours.

502 Bethnal Green Road, E2 0EA

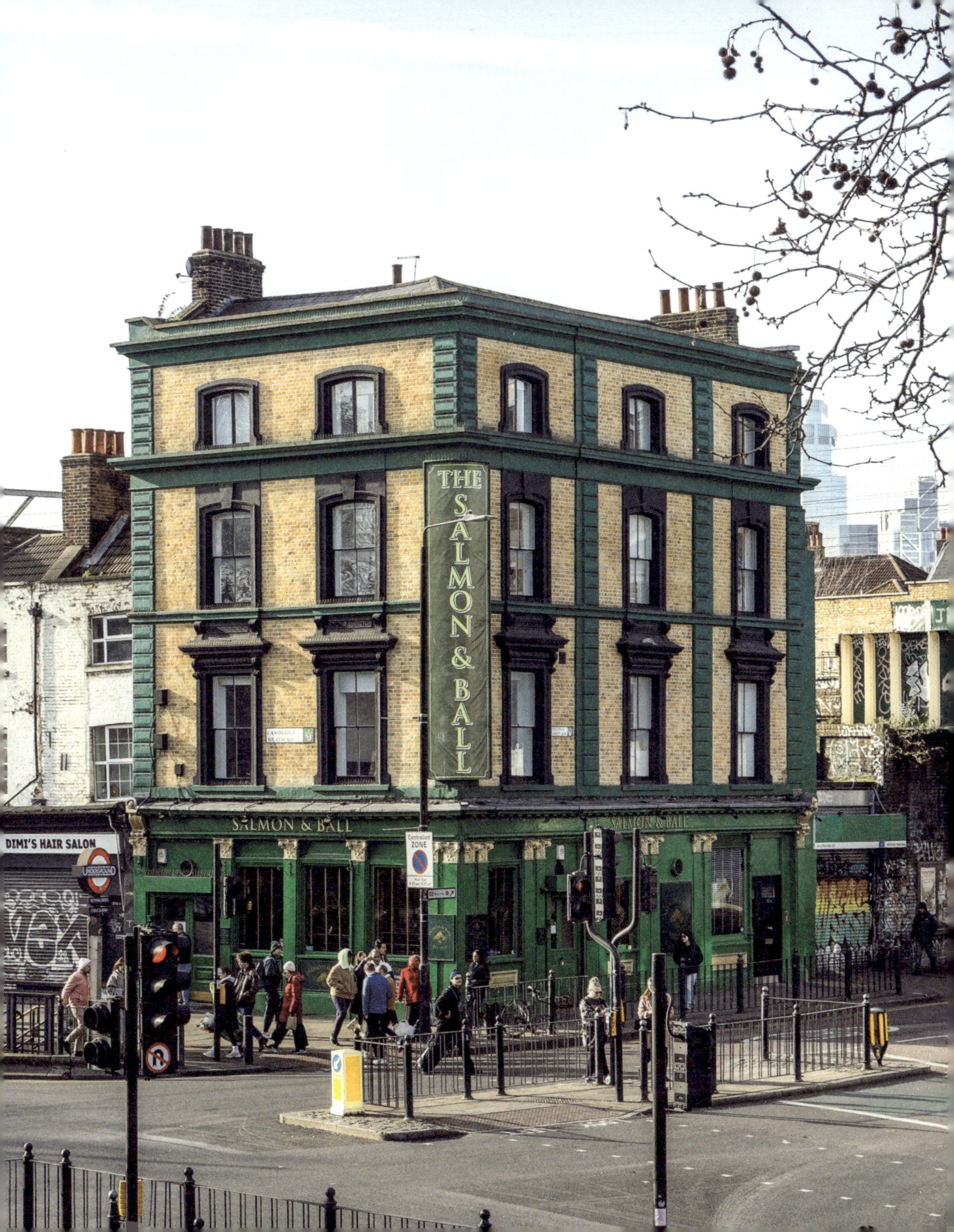
THE SALMON & BALL
SALMON & BALL
SALMON & BALL
DIMI'S HAIR SALON
UNDERGROUND
CONTROLLED ZONE

The Victory

PRIZED FAMILY-RUN PUB

Vyner Street is a carriageway that has seen many changes in the last 100 years. One long-term resident is The Victory, a cosy pub whose records date back to at least 1843 – although the Bones family, who took over the pub in 1993, believe the building dates from much earlier.

In recent decades, the East End has been the centre of London's creative boom. It is now home to a thriving art scene, and, for many years, Vyner Street came alive on the nights when its 13 art galleries stayed open late and thirsty patrons would flock to The Victory for refreshment after perusing the work of local artists. While not all the galleries survived, there are still half a dozen going strong.

This is good news for publicans Auring and Steve Bones who love welcoming art-lovers, as well as Cockney locals. The pub itself is its own work of art, with Auring and Steve's son Anthony acting as creative director, finding innovative ways to keep up with the modern world. He created a new bar, the speakeasy-style Rabbit Hole, which hosted pop-ups and events to entice new punters.

The main pub has remained true to its East End roots. Little appears to have been altered internally and it still has its trusty pool table, jukebox and fruit machine. As part of the Regent's Canal conservation area, the pub feels like a sanctuary from everyday life. Its large windows have cast an eye upon seismic change over the centuries, and they are certain to see much more during its many years ahead under the Bones' fine stewardship. Whether supping reasonably priced pints or enjoying a few frames of pool, it is the simple pleasures that make this old friend the perfect East End escape.

27 Vyner Street, E2 9DQ

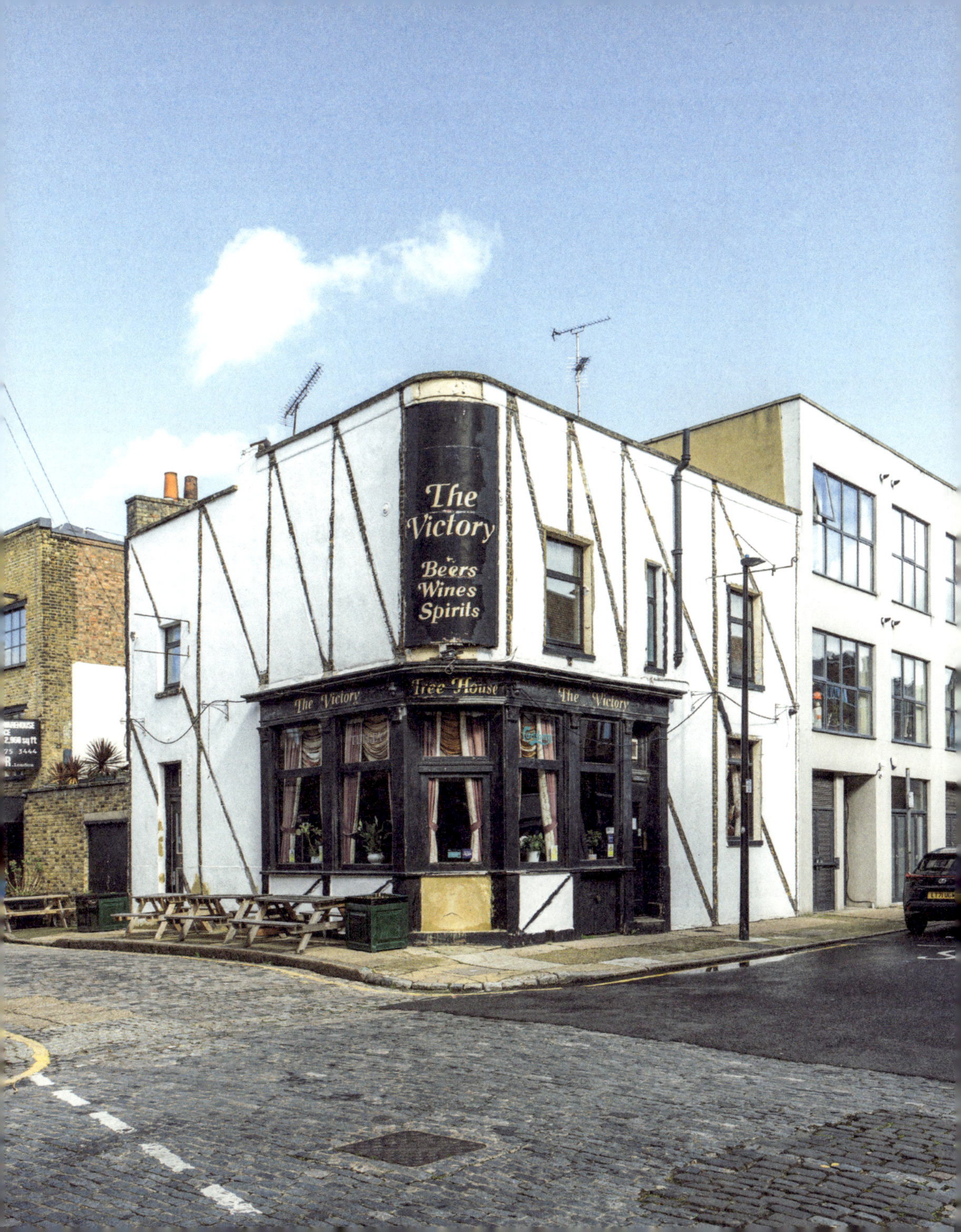
The Victory
Beers
Wines
Spirits
The Victory
Free House
The Victory

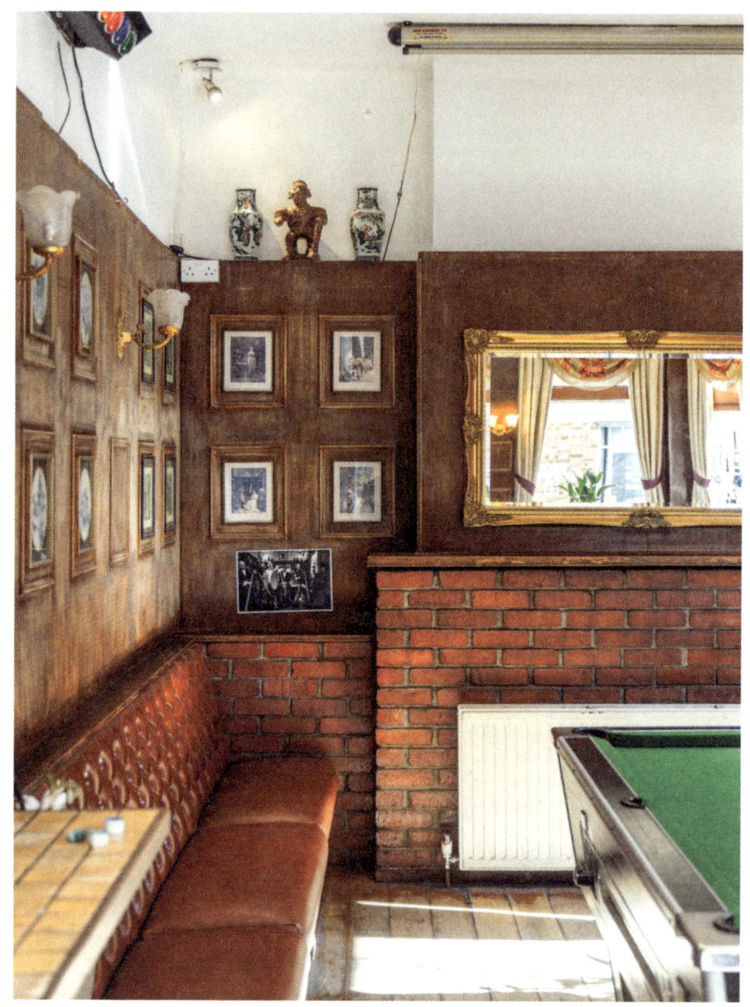

While many pubs have removed their pool tables to create more space for dining, The Victory has retained its traditional leisure pursuits and elegant interiors.

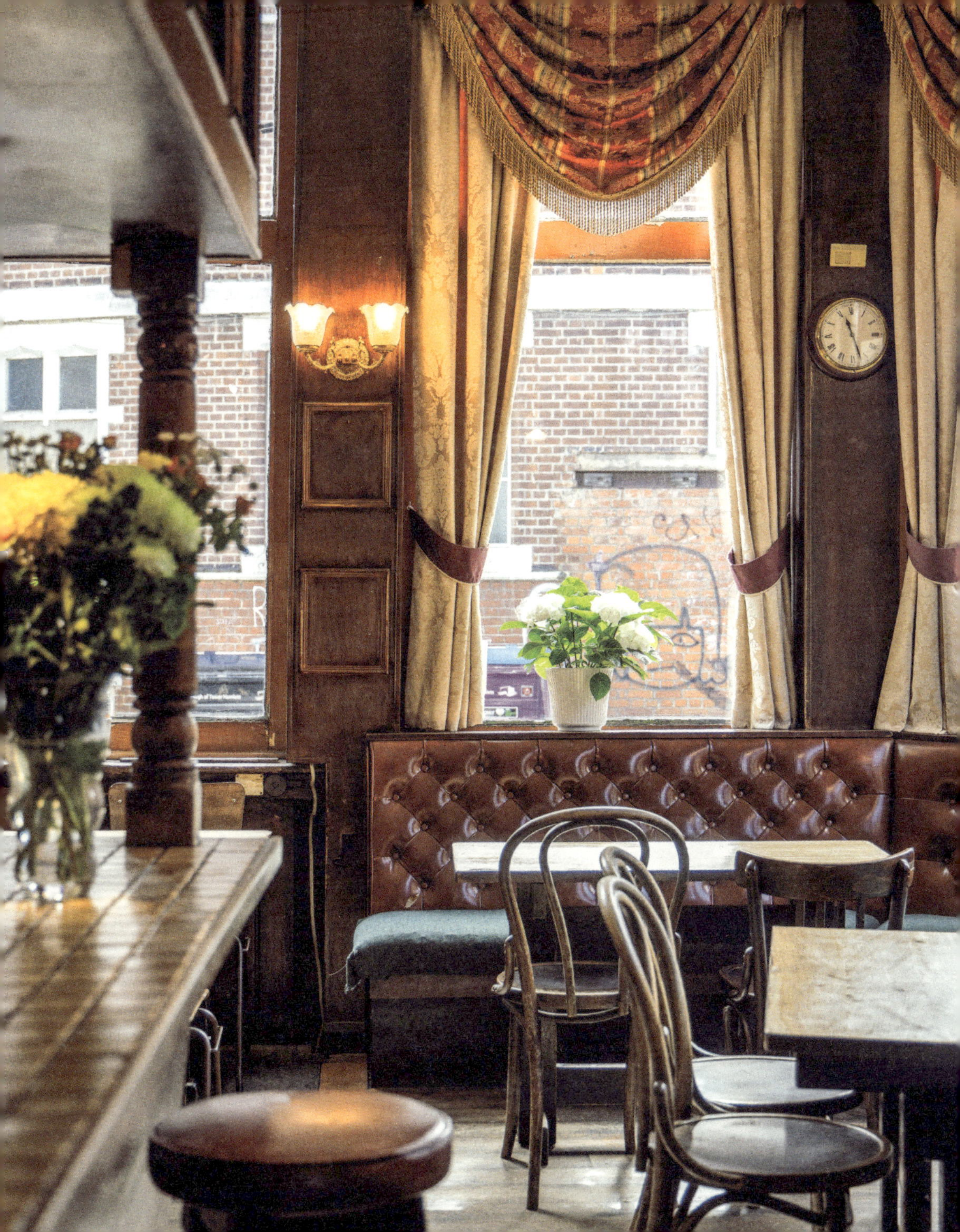

The Hare

A HEARTENINGLY AUTHENTIC LOCAL

An old pub set beside a railway arch on the ever-busy Cambridge Heath Road, The Hare is a delight for any visitor. The mellow lustre of its old Truman's tiles hint at the nostalgic East End scene that awaits visitors who enter this traditional hostelry.

It's a simple boozer with a mahogany bar, dart board, pool table, classic pub carpet and assortment of much-loved furniture naturally distressed by decades of use. The affable Guv'nor Julian Apperley has been steering the good ship since 2001. A man in tune with his regulars and the wider community, Julian moved to Clapton from Muswell Hill when he was 11 years old and has lived in the area ever since. To run a great pub well, a landlord or landlady must truly love people and the pub business itself. Julian has boundless passion for both, which is evident in the way he keeps his house, as well as the calibre of his ales and stouts.

Learning his trade at Young's of Wandsworth and later working at The Approach Tavern (p.48), Julian was raised during a time when a publican was a revered profession in the community – held in the same standing as doctors or members of the clergy. He maintains a relaxed atmosphere in his hostelry and welcomes a good blend of young people who come here to imbibe alongside more senior faces of the manor.

The Hare has an unpretentious atmosphere that allows anyone to feel at home among its neighbourly community. Its honest beauty encapsulates everything a proper local pub should be and purists on the hunt for a real boozer would do well to make a beeline here.

505 Cambridge Heath Road, E2 9BU

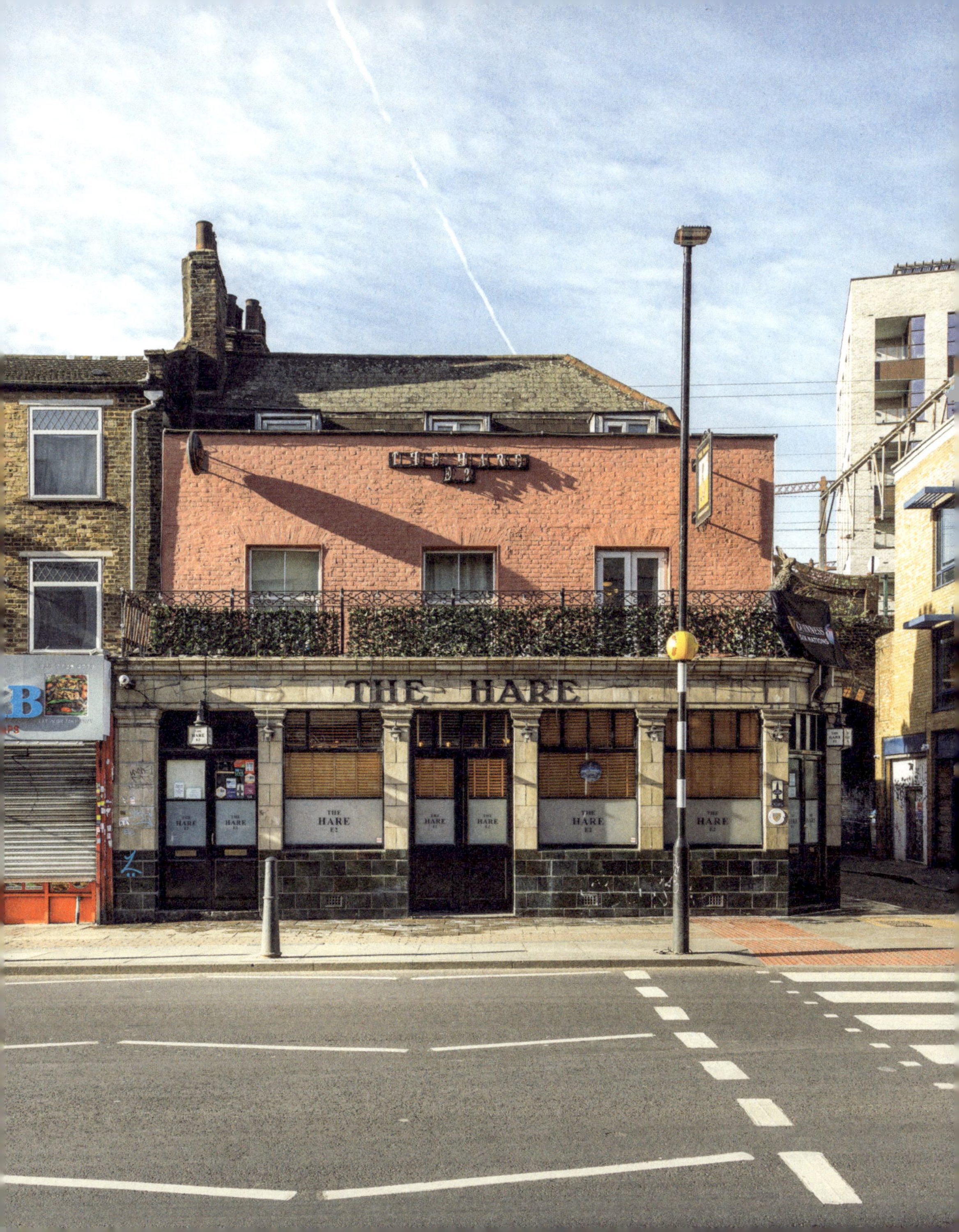
THE HARE
THE HARE E2
THE HARE E2
GUINNESS

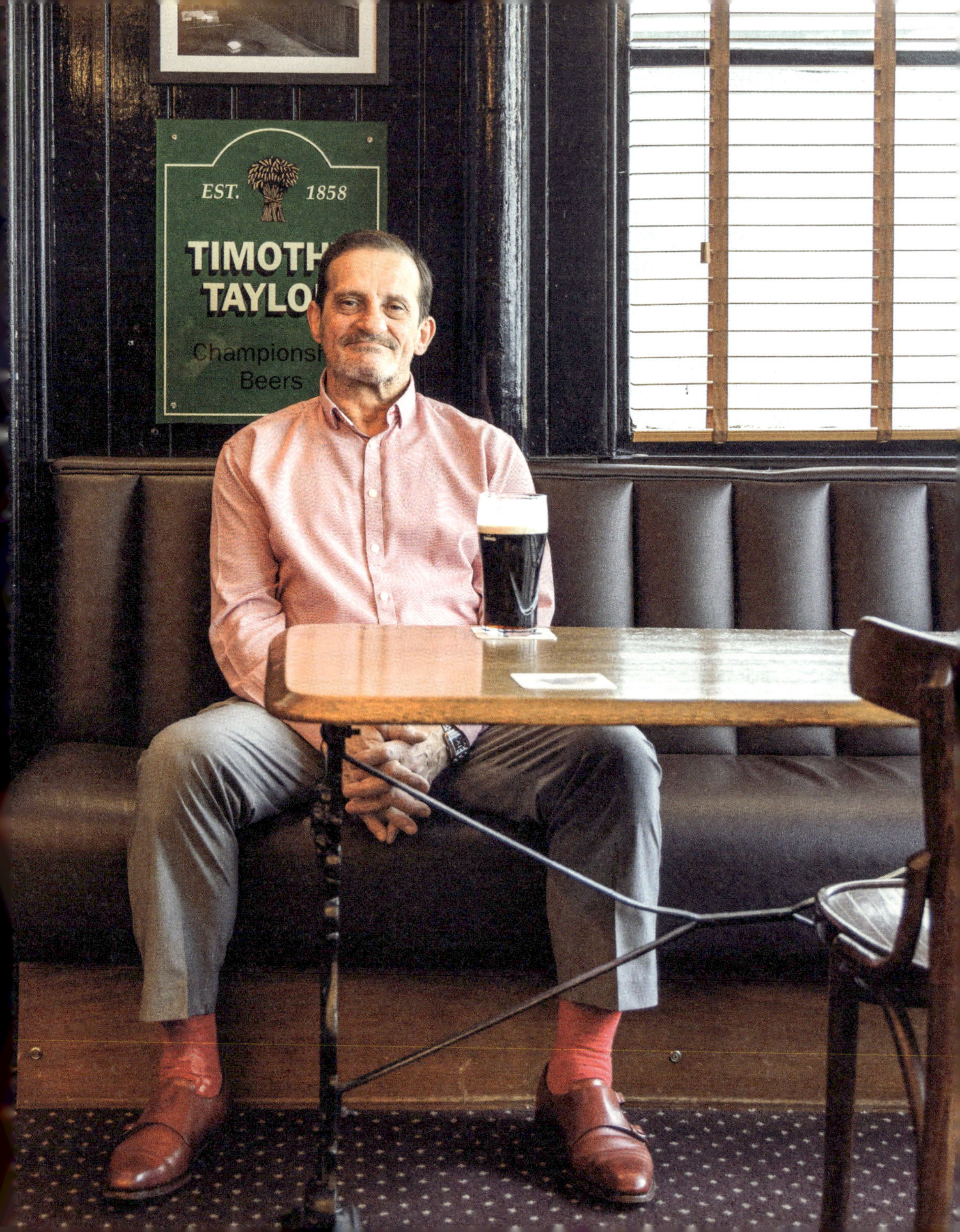

EST. 1858
TIMOTH
TAYLO
Championsh
Beers

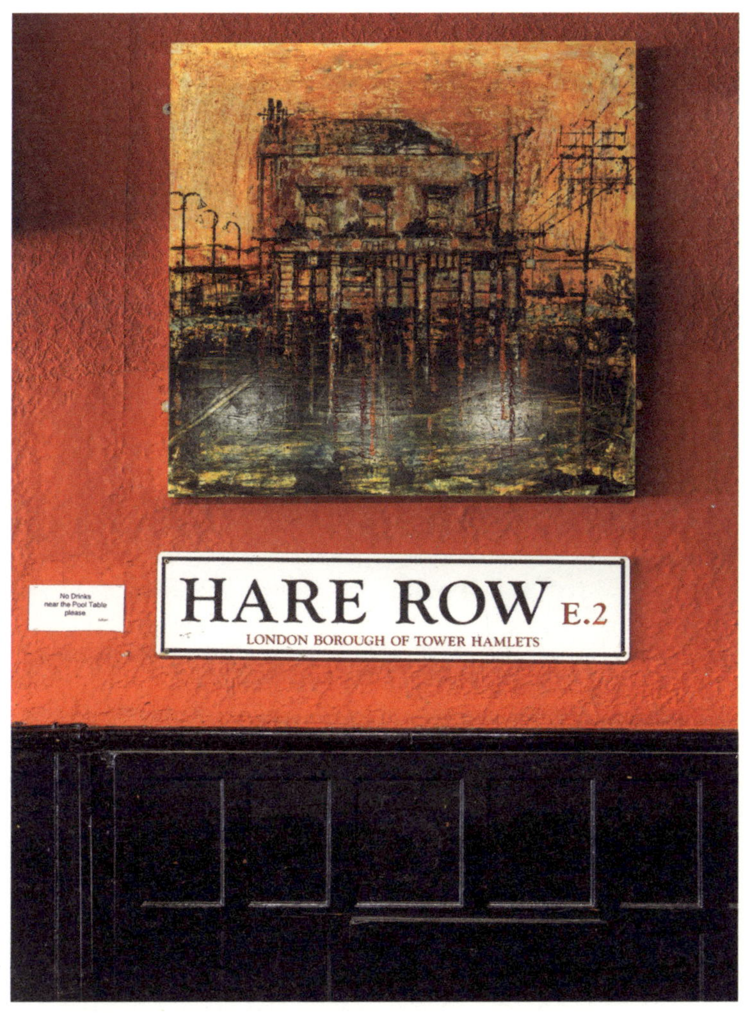

Guv'nor Julian Apperley has run The Hare since 2001. His regular newsletters keep the loyal band of punters up to date with what's going on at the pub.

The Horse & Groom

A PARTY PUB WITH LITERARY HERITAGE

On first inspection, this backstreet boozer appears to be merely a silent relic from Shoreditch's pre-gentrified past. But what an illustrious and historic past it is. The pub stands on the site of the Curtain Theatre, the Jacobean playhouse where William Shakespeare is thought to have first staged *Romeo and Juliet*. For centuries, its precise location had been lost, but it was rediscovered in 2012 and the pub's back garden has since been excavated to uncover the foundations of the old theatre.

Its battered exterior now hidden among natural wine bars and bottomless brunch spots, The Horse & Groom appears isolated and cast aside. But its rich wood interior has been well cared for, and the old panelled ceiling still looks down on an attractive bar with gleaming brass footrails and battle-worn barstools. If it were not for the large modern speakers in the corner, little would appear to have altered in the last two centuries.

During the day the pub has a lazy, easy atmosphere, slinging out cocktails as well as the traditional ales that would be slightly more familiar to Shakespeare's audiences than the espresso martinis. However, as dusk settles The Horse & Groom becomes something of a different animal. After a reboot in 2007, it became a disco pub hosting a rotating stable of live DJs until the wee hours every weekend. That these very different kinds of hospitality, the quiet afternoon refuge and the late-night rave, can coexist in the shell of an old boozer says a lot about the diversity and resilience of our East End pubs.

28 Curtain Road, EC2A 3NZ

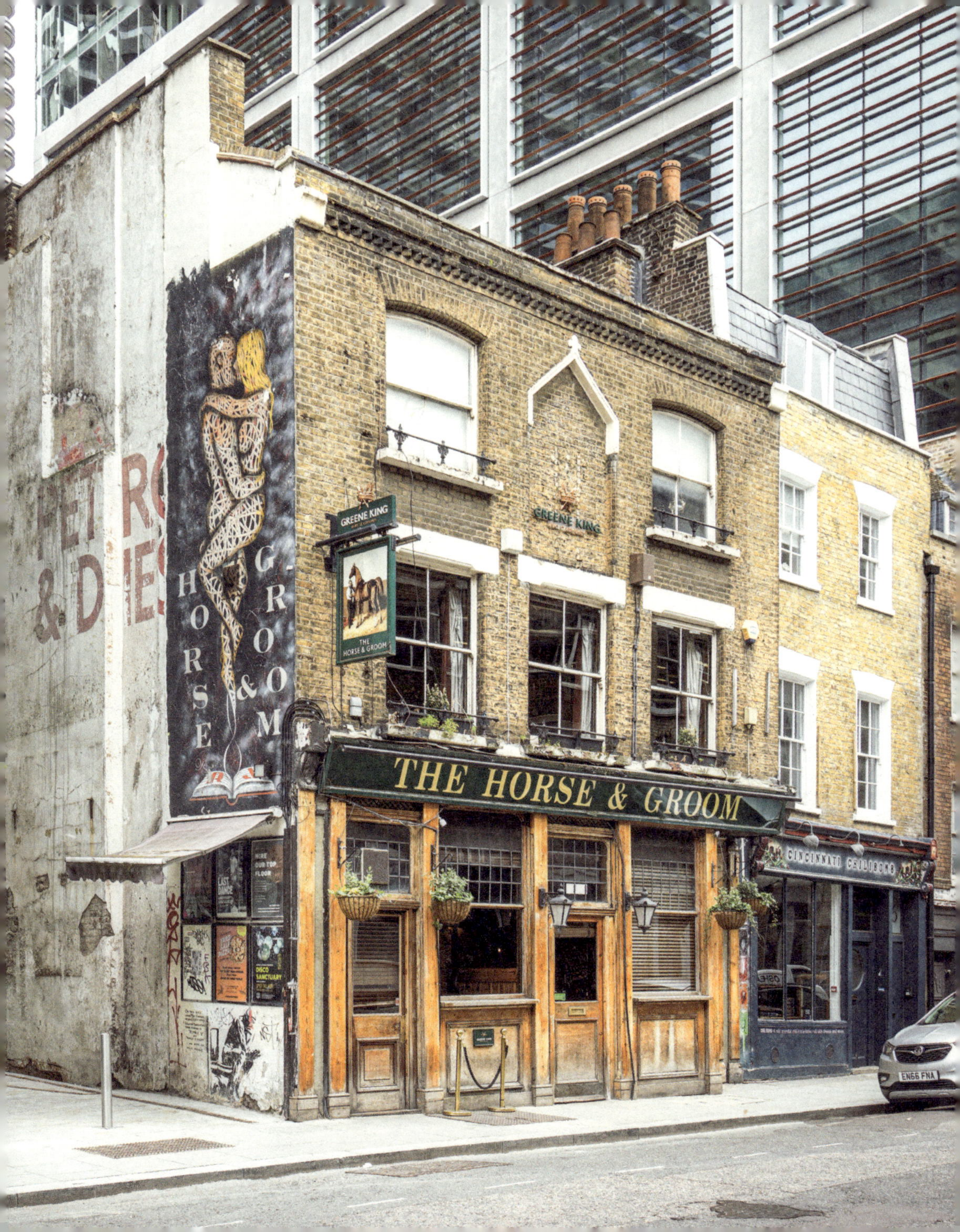
GREENE KING
GREENE KING
THE
HORSE & GROOM
HORSE
&
GROOM
THE HORSE & GROOM
CINCINNATI GRILLHOUSE

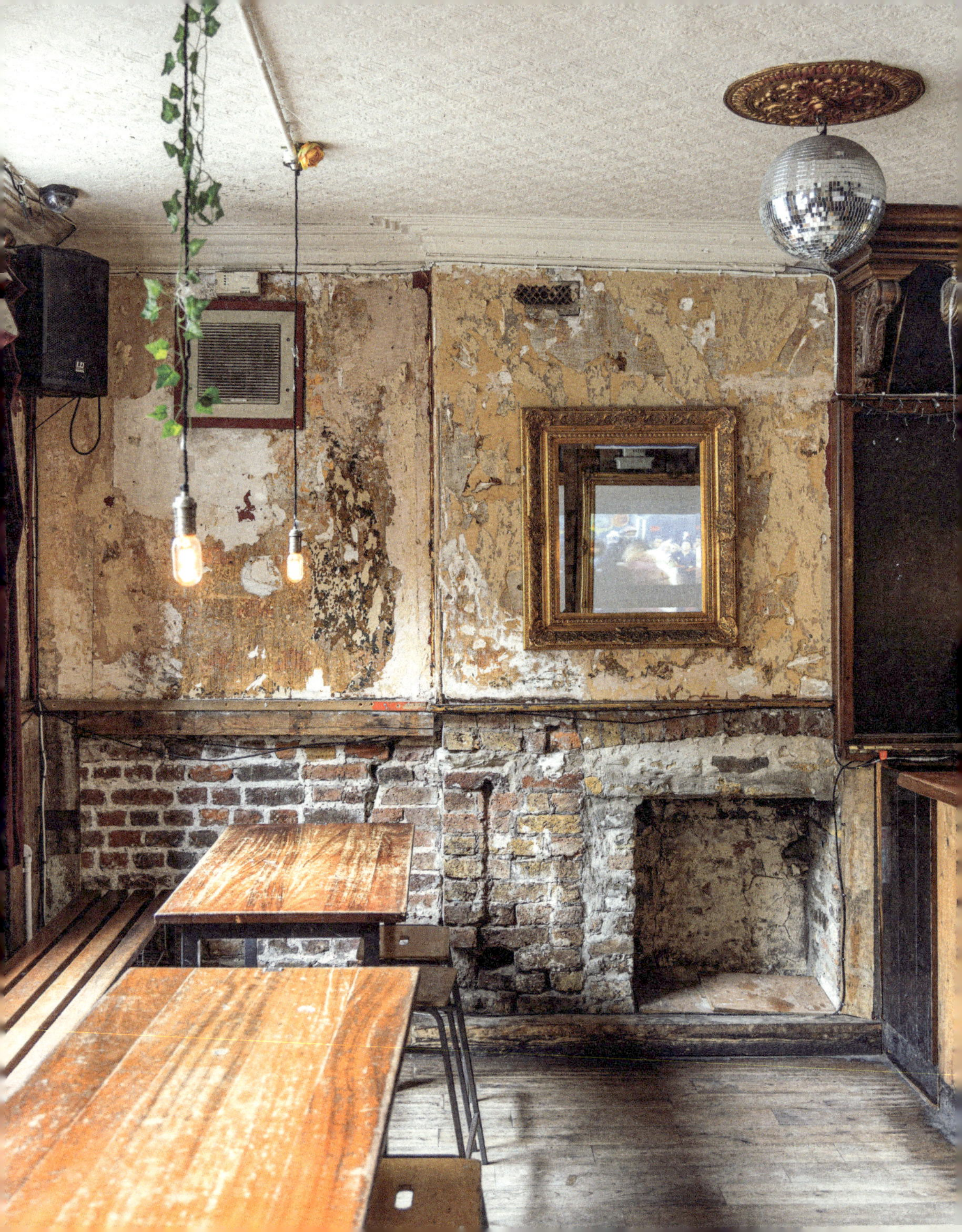

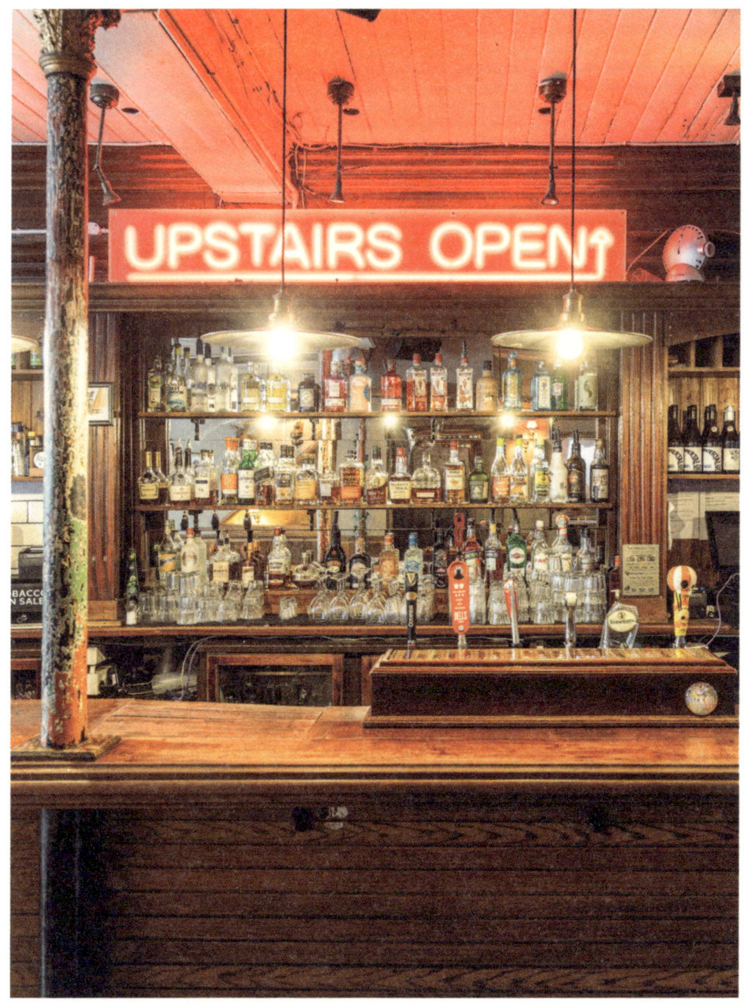

(Opposite) Visible signs of the pub's past remain, including an old, disused fireplace that would have once warmed the traders and workers of yesteryear.

The Wentworth Arms

A handsome pub once owned by Charrington, situated near the Anchor Brewery in Stepney, The Wentworth has hosted some famous East End faces over the years. None more so than the nefarious Kray Twins, who frequently drank here as it was opposite the Regal Billiard Hall, which they used as the base for The Firm from the mid-1950s.

Today, the pub is the dictionary definition of an inclusive East End local. It is one of six London pubs owned by Bedfordshire brewery Wells & Co. Anyone blessed to patronise the corner boozer will be greeted by its Guv'nors, Faolan Friel and Connor Culleton, graduates of the nearby Queen Mary University of London who worked at the pub for three years before taking on the lease in 2020.

Navigating a global pandemic only further endeared them to their loyal band of locals and saw them demonstrating maturity beyond their years – after all, they are the youngest East End publicans in the area. This experience has given Faolan and Connor a deep understanding of the importance of pubs in this tight-knit community.

The Wentworth Arms is a party pub with a constant roster of karaoke, where seasoned drinkers, punters waiting for a train and West Ham fans happily imbibe with university students. They maintain the tradition of never-ending fun, along with annual beanos to the races or the coast.

It's the ability to offer younger revellers a good time while also sating the desire of other patrons to enjoy a quiet drink in a traditional setting that makes The Wentworth Arms a true East End classic.

127 Eric Street, E3 4SR

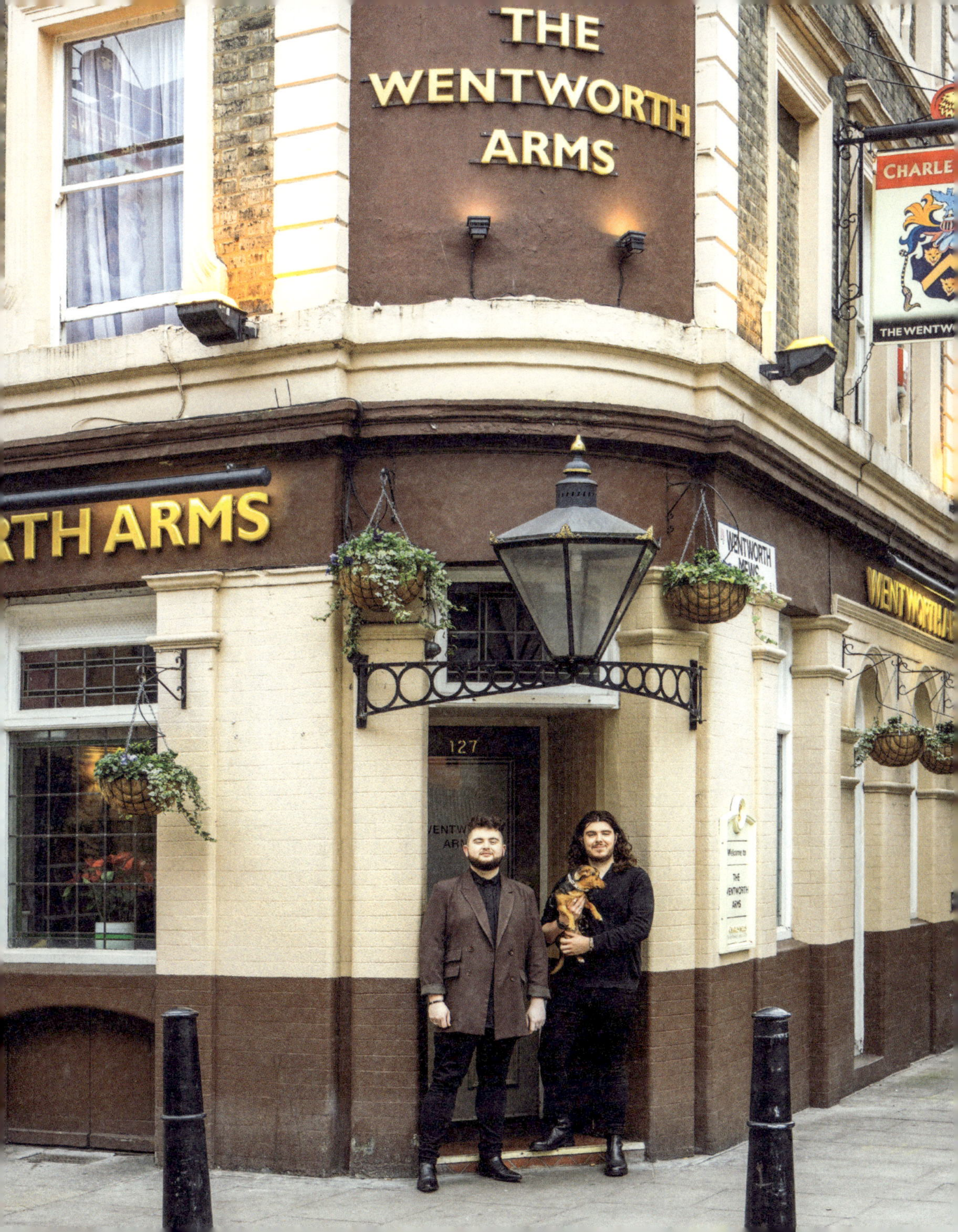

THE
WENTWORTH
ARMS
RTH ARMS
CHARLE
THE WENTW
WENTWORTH
WENTWORTH
MEWS
127
WENTW
ARM
Welcome to
THE
WENTWORTH
ARMS

The Dundee Arms

The Dundee Arms has gone through many iterations since it opened in the 19th century. Only a stone's throw from York Hall, originally opened as a public baths but, from the 1950s, becoming more famous as a boxing arena, sporting fans often end up in The Dundee for a pint. Enjoying live sport and having a few drinks is a beloved pastime in the East End, where many legendary boxers have been born and raised, from the 18th-century bare knuckle savant Daniel Mendoza to the formidable world middleweight champion Nigel Benn.

In 2015, the weathered green frontage was replaced with vibrant gold lettering, the old pub carpet was jettisoned and tired furnishings exchanged for leather banquette seating, but The Dundee Arms retains the original wood panelling from its past life. The boozer's rough and ready days – when only old geezers of the manor came for a good soak, in what was a run-down establishment that had seen little investment – are over. The Dundee Arms now welcomes a younger crowd, while retaining the essence of a quality public house. Its patrons hail from all walks of life: Cockneys returning to their old stomping ground for Fight Night at York Hall happily mix with parched visitors from the Museum of Childhood across the road. There are even dishevelled, hirsute punters nursing a pint at the bar while waiting their turn for a snip at the barbers upstairs. The ebb and flow of these various visitors, imbibing fine local offerings on tap, make for a social utopia in the East End.

339 Cambridge Heath Road, E2 9LH

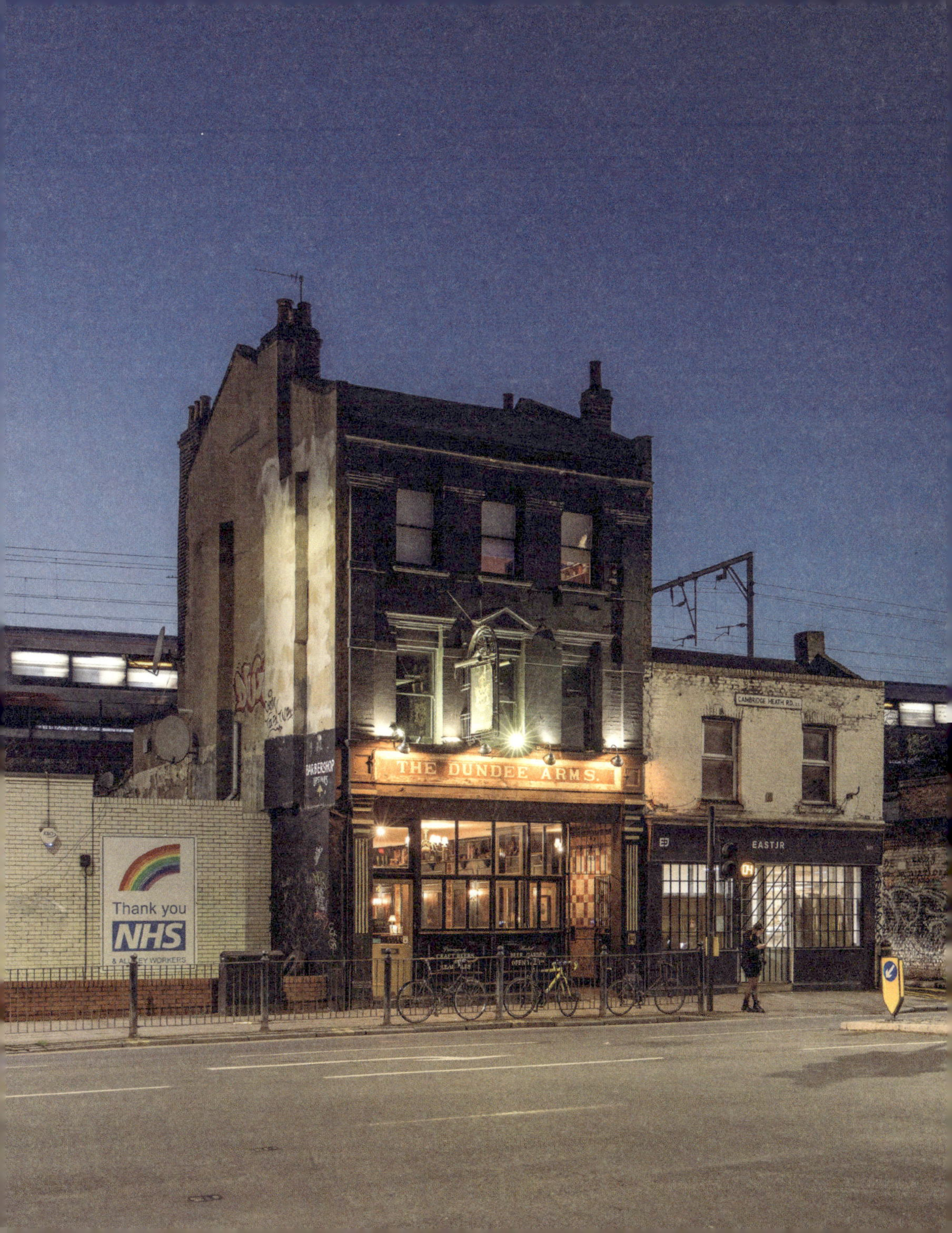
THE DUNDEE ARMS.
Thank you
NHS
& ALL KEY WORKERS
CAMBRIDGE HEATH RD.
EASTJR

The Prospect of Whitby

One of London's oldest pubs, there isn't much that hasn't already been written about The Prospect of Whitby. A riverside beacon of fine hospitality, it has existed in one guise or another along Wapping Wall since 1520.

The old adage, 'If the walls could talk, what tales would they tell?' has likely never rung truer than within this famous pub. Over the centuries, artists, buccaneers, London's criminal fraternities and film stars have all rubbed shoulders over pints and quarts with salt-of-the-earth East Enders.

Although these days only the floor can claim to be original, the pub's attractive 19th-century facade makes it a firm favourite with visitors to 21st-century Wapping keen to follow in the footsteps of famous patrons such as Samuel Pepys, Charles Dickens, J.M.W. Turner and no doubt many a smuggler.

The pub would have once been described as a well-kept secret – tucked away from prying eyes to hide nefarious deeds – but it is now a highlight on one of the most well-worn paths on the river Thames. And for good reason.

Crossing the threshold, after peering in through the galleon-like front windows, visitors are greeted by a log burner alight with flames that flicker and dance across the ancient floor. Outside, on the shoreline, an eerie gallows stands as a marker of the pub's dark past. It is a grim nod to one-time

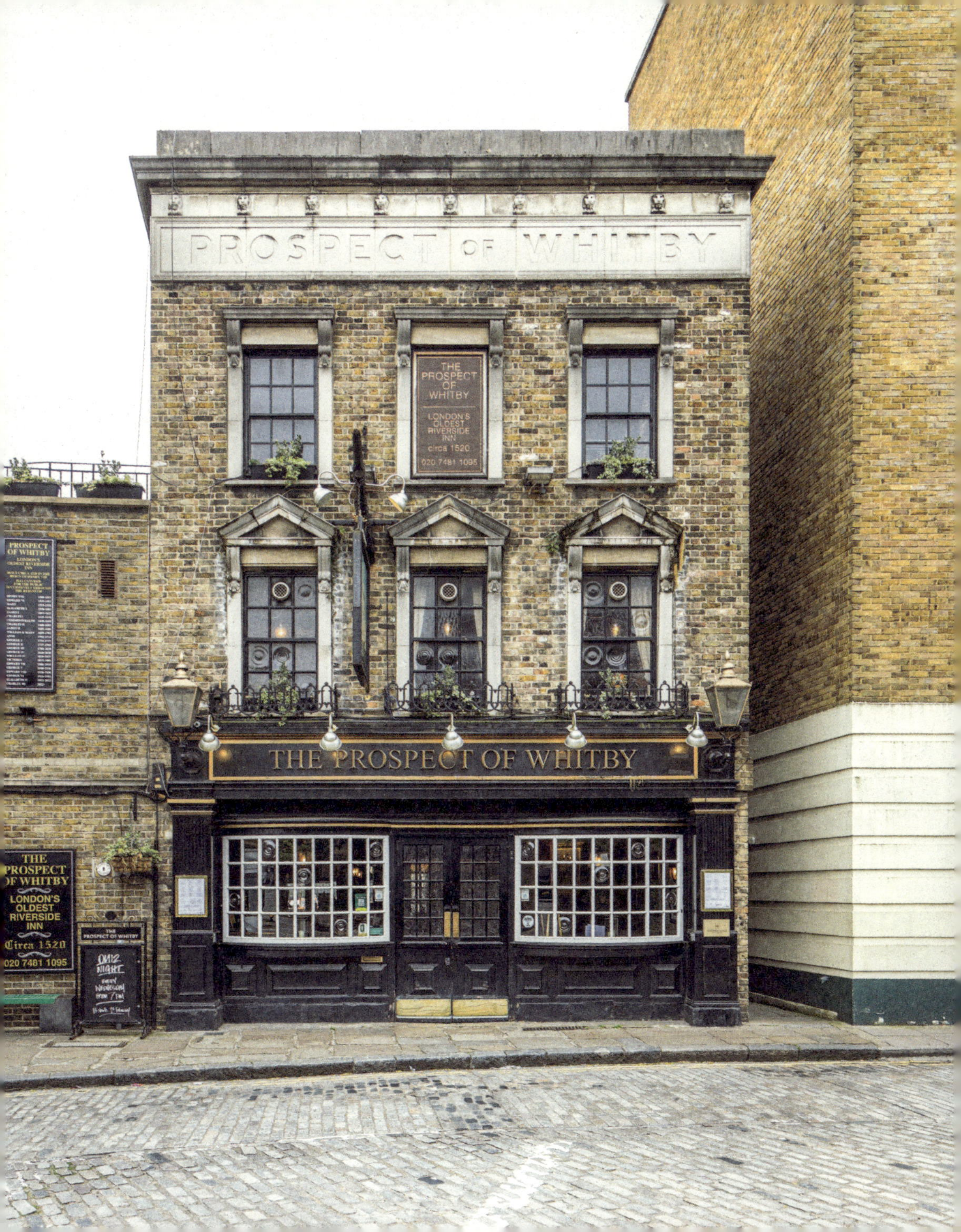

PROSPECT OF WHITBY
THE PROSPECT OF WHITBY
LONDON'S OLDEST RIVERSIDE INN
circa 1520
020 7481 1095
THE PROSPECT OF WHITBY
THE PROSPECT OF WHITBY
LONDON'S OLDEST RIVERSIDE INN
Circa 1520
020 7481 1095

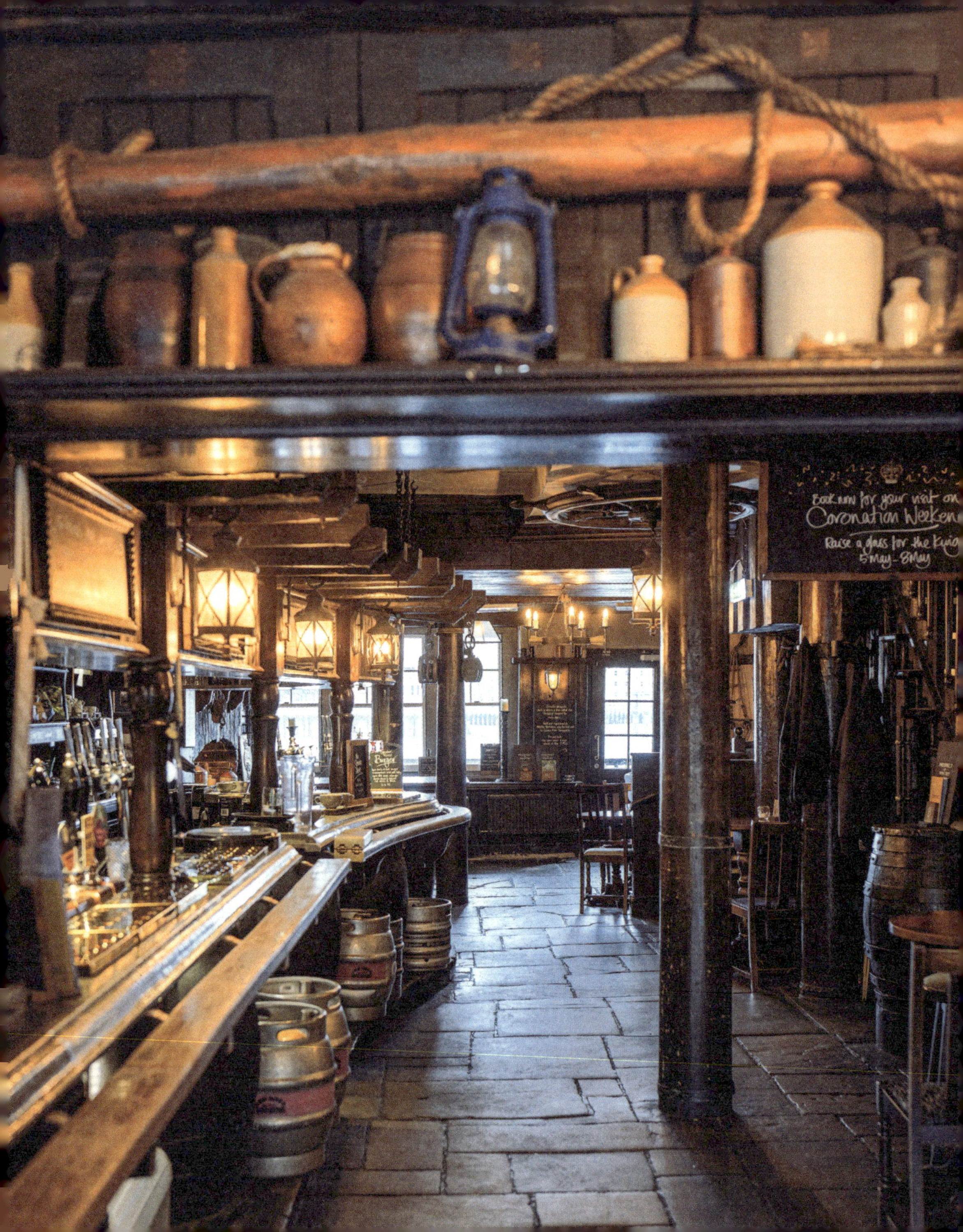
Book now for your visit on
Coronation Weeken
Raise a glass for the King
5 May - 8 May

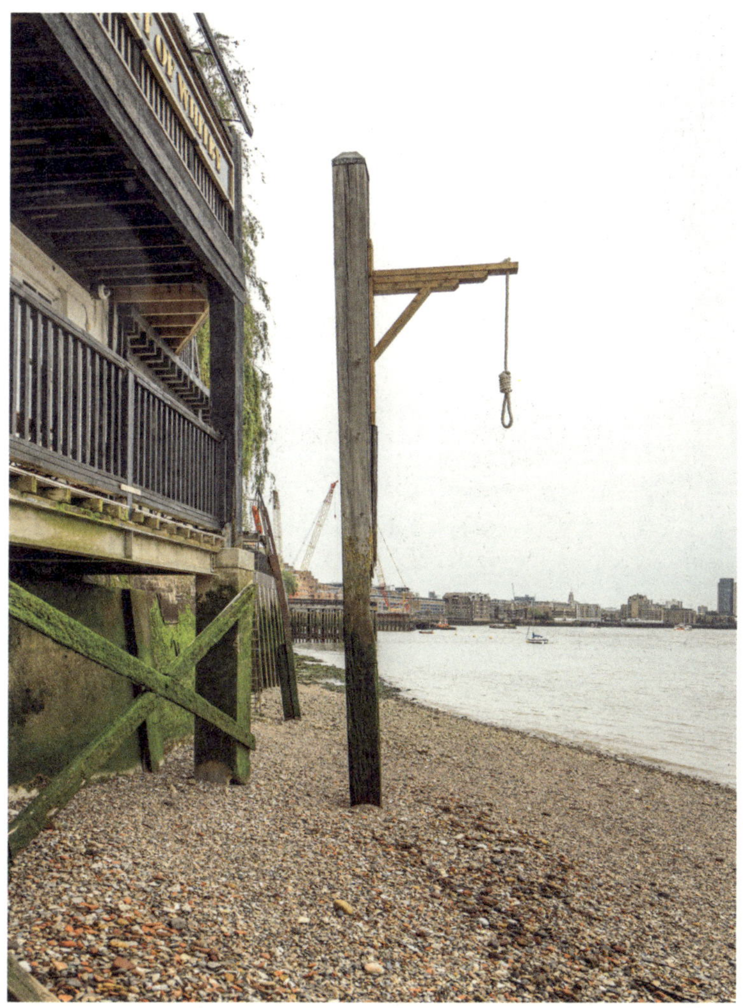

*The gallows on the shoreline outside the pub are a fitting tribute
to the rogues that met their maker at Execution Dock.*

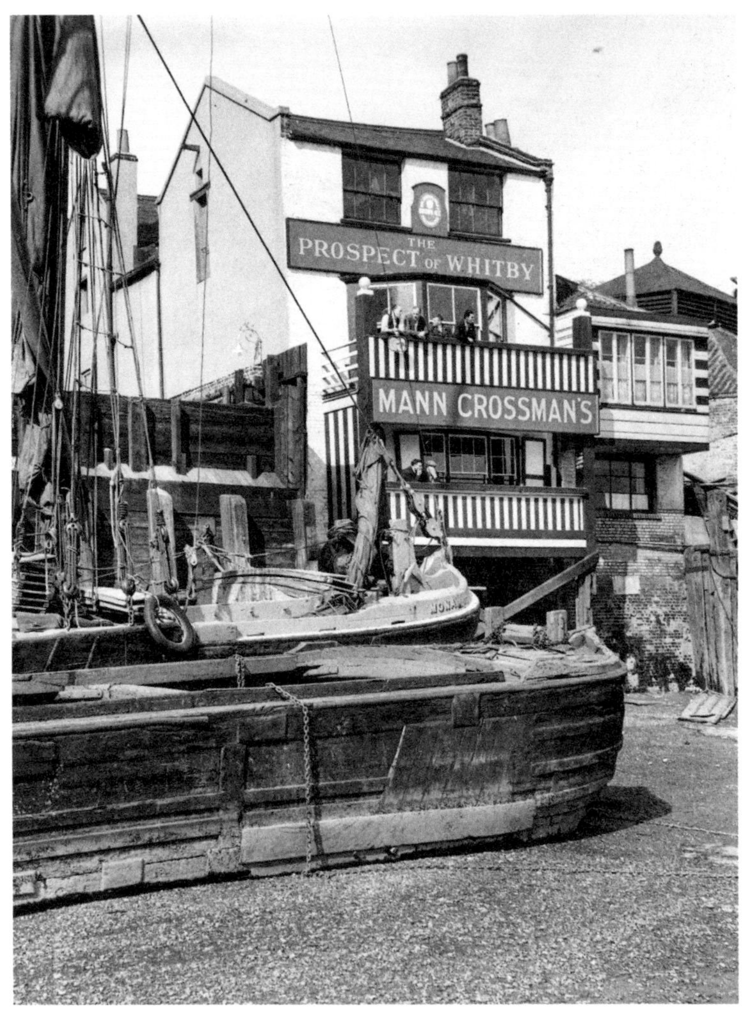
THE
PROSPECT OF WHITBY
MANN CROSSMAN'S

patron 'Hanging Judge' Jeffreys (who also drank at the Town of Ramsgate, p.132) and his victims, who met their maker at the nearby Execution Dock.

Once named The Pelican, The Prospect of Whitby reportedly took its current moniker from a cargo ship that was said to moor close to the pub. Ship barrels are set within the rare pewter-topped concave bar and dark wood runs throughout, giving it the feel of a lantern-lit captain's quarters. The mysteries of the pub's past and its iniquitous patrons reflect and creak off the ships' masts embedded within the building's structure.

Although miles away from how it would have originally looked, The Prospect is still a timeless classic and the 18th-century upstairs bar and dining area, with panelled walls and an uneven floor, is an ideal place to drink and feast.

Once the albatross has been spotted and fair weather has finally arrived, the pub comes into its own. A garden makes for a shipshape spot to take in the fine river views under a glorious weeping willow, where spray from the rip often splashes onto unsuspecting patrons.

For a crow's-nest view, a gloriously colourful deck offers a stunning panorama that ranges from Canary Wharf to the east, the City to the west and, on the other side of the river, the historically nautical Rotherhithe. It is essential to explore all the nooks and crannies on a visit to The Prospect, so as to be fully immersed in the celebrated pub culture of London and make the most of a bona fide treat for aficionados.

A pub of great riches that caters to tourists, locals and Canary Wharf drinkers alike, The Prospect of Whitby is a celebrated classic that continues to water and feed those in search of the warmest hospitality and a slice of history.

57 Wapping Wall, E1W 3SH

The Prospect of Whitby has a rich nautical history and captains of barges would have been frequent visitors.

The King's Arms

Once a pub closes, there's only a slim chance that it will ever reopen. Developers know that converting a Victorian building into six flats is more lucrative than renting it out to a pub landlord. Many developers unfortunately have little regard for the damage they inflict on the community by closing a much-needed amenity.

The King's Arms, however, was taken over in 2013 by developers who bucked that trend and instead renovated the pub. Once the doors reopened, patrons were treated to a contemporary East End local with one eye respectfully on the past. Gone are the heavy draped curtains and 1970s pub carpet; the handsome facade now feels well-matched by an airy interior.

While the painted wood panelling and minimalist aesthetic might not please die-hard purists, its stripped-back style draws on how the pub would have looked and felt as a simple backstreet inn in the early Victorian era. This thoughtful design reflects modern Bethnal Green while catering to those who long for hushed conversations over pints of porter. Anyone who treasures pub life will approve of the fact that the primary focus of The King's Arms is still selling beer, not food. Craft beers are now the pub's main wares and whether rolling IPAs or high ABV stouts, all tastes are catered for.

When a pub reopens and attracts a wider range of clientele than before, new bonds are created and relationships forged. The best pubs have always brought people together and The King's Arms does so with an effortless grace in the backstreets of Bethnal Green.

11A Buckfast Street, E2 6EY

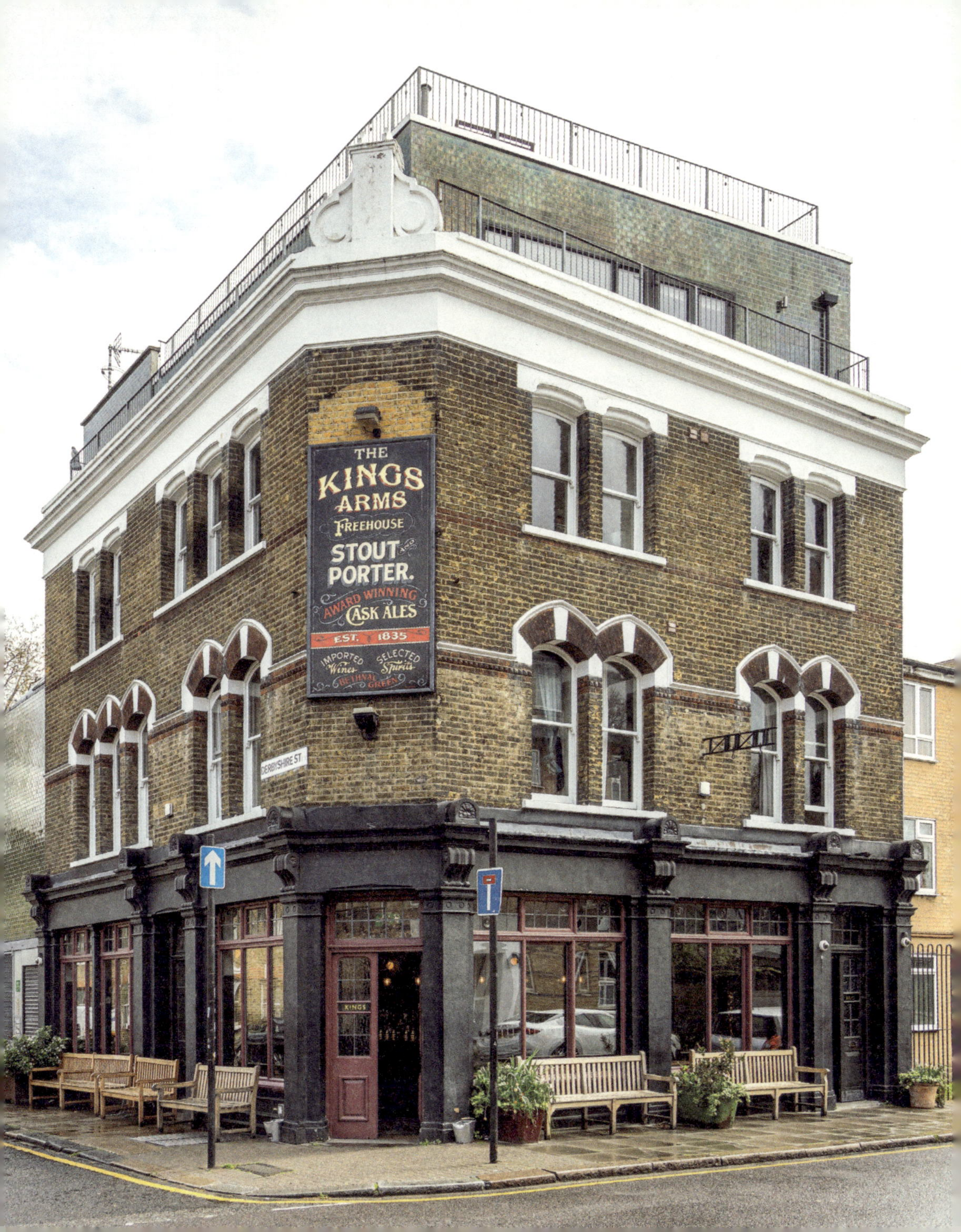
THE
KINGS
ARMS
FREEHOUSE
STOUT AND
PORTER.
AWARD WINNING
CASK ALES
EST. 1835
IMPORTED
WINES
SELECTED
Spirits
BETHNAL
GREEN
DERBYSHIRE ST
KINGS

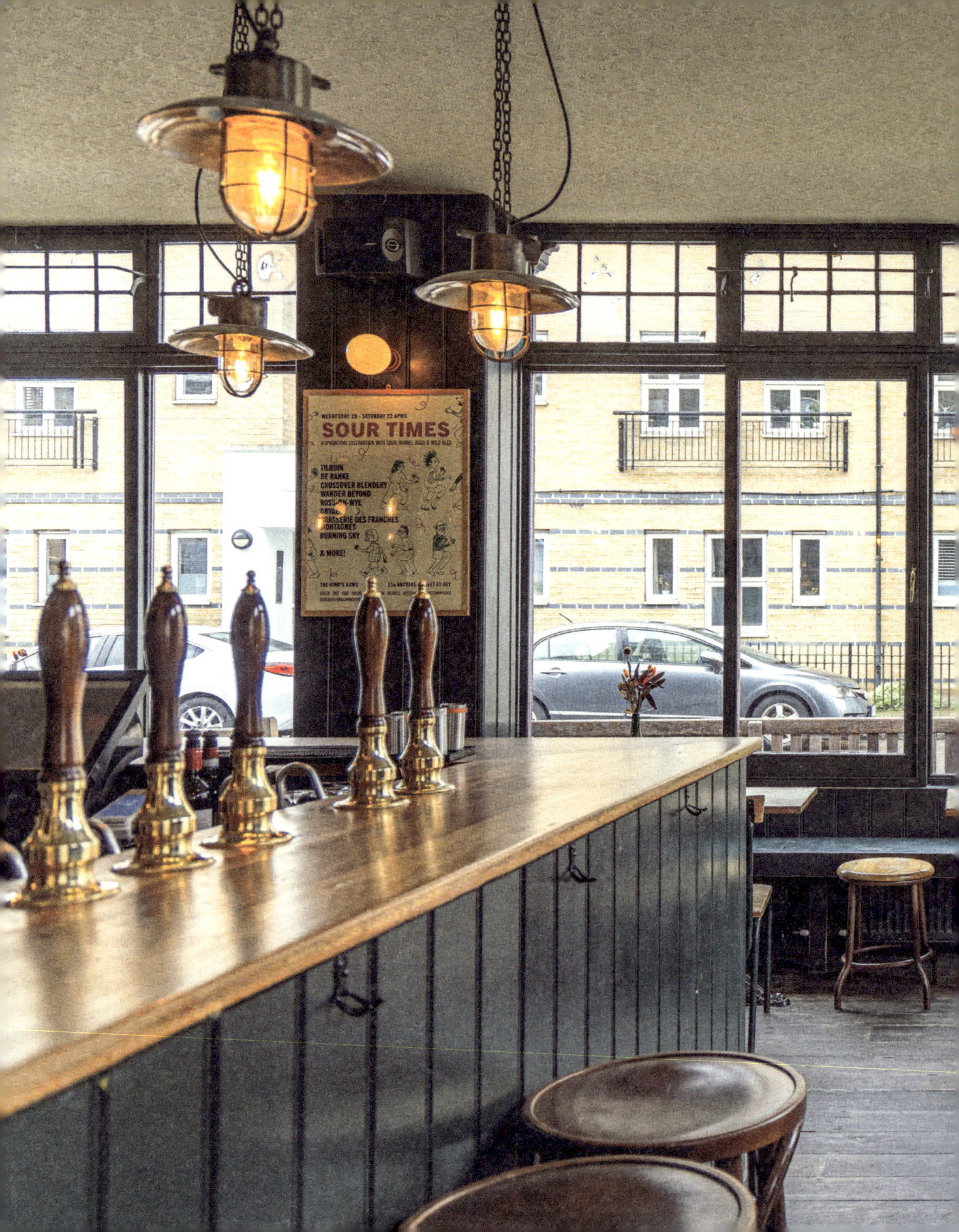
WEDNESDAY 19 - SATURDAY 22 APRIL
SOUR TIMES
A SPRINGTIME CELEBRATION WITH SOUR, BARREL AGED & WILD ALES
TILQUIN
DE RANKE
CROSSOVER BLENDERY
WANDER BEYOND
ROSS-ON-WYE
ORVAL
BRASSERIE DES FRANCHES MONTAGNES
BURNING SKY
& MORE!
THE KING'S ARMS
11a BUCKFAST STREET E2 6EY

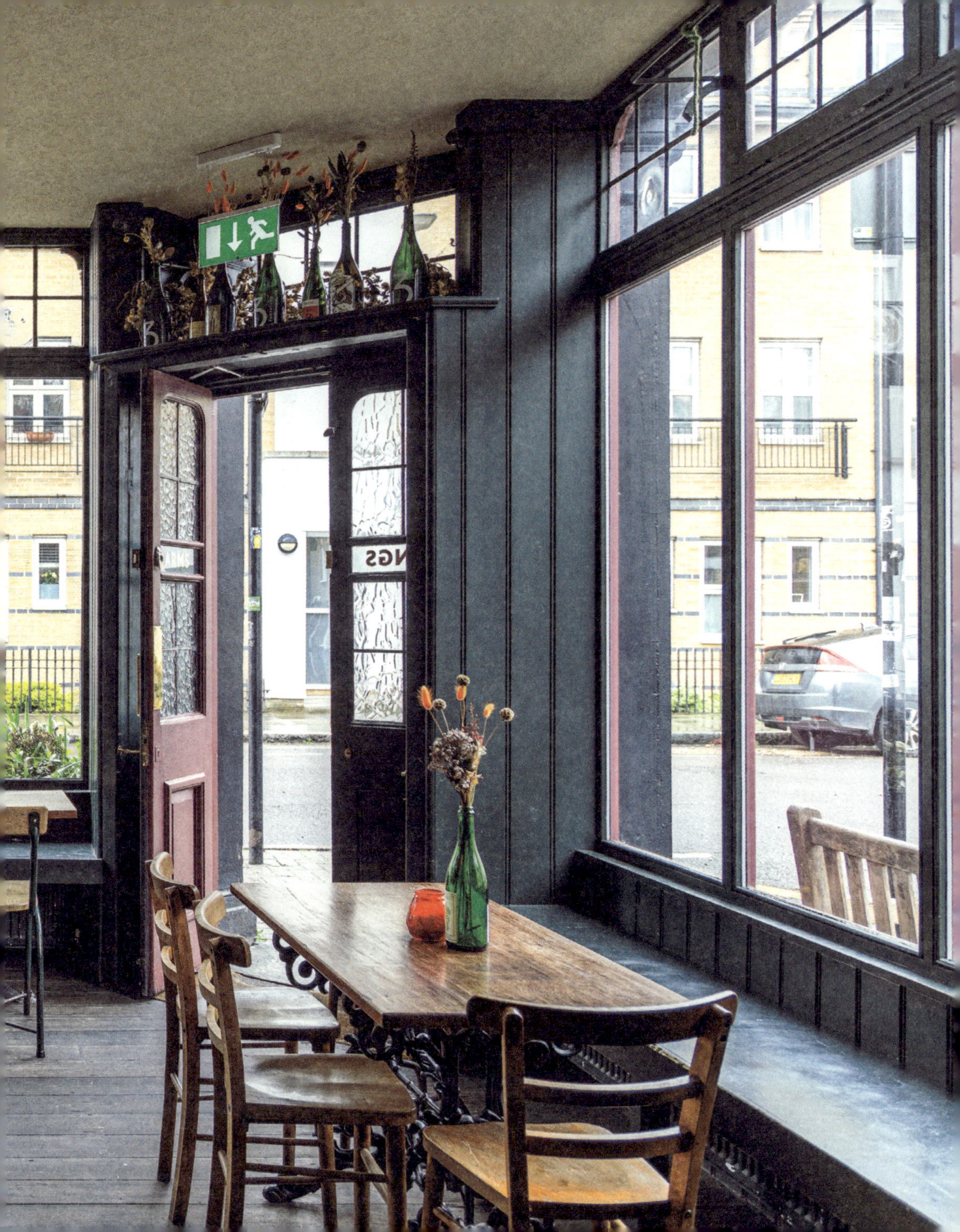

The Florist Arms

The Florist Arms has been cherished since it first opened its doors in the 18th century. Having survived a wave of pub closures in the last 40 years, it's remained a notable constant, along with its near neighbour The Camel (p.40). Open from midday, alongside its beloved barstools (where the true regulars sit) and old-school sociability, there are now craft beers, cocktails and stone-baked pizza. It's a place where visitors and locals drink together, making it one of Tower Hamlets' truly diverse and inclusive hostelries.

A large part of the pub's success is due to the infectious élan of third-generation Cockney landlady Emma Tarbard who is carrying the mantle for her proud East End family. Emma grew up in The Ferry House (p.170) on the Isle of Dogs where her parents, Eliza and Reg, were publicans until 2000. Her grandparents also ran pubs: The Rose and Crown, and then later The George (p.234).

Directing operations while regaling drinkers with tales from her pub-going past, there is no doubt that the Guv'nor of this establishment is exactly where she's meant to be. Emma's assured, no-nonsense management – matched by a strong community outlook – ensures social harmony even on the liveliest nights.

Tarbard rightly believes that pubs are de facto community centres and that people from all walks of life – in particular, women drinking alone – should feel comfortable and welcome. Luckily, a friendly environment comes effortlessly to this cheery red-brick corner boozer. The Florist Arms is a classic Bethnal Green establishment that has stood the test of time by keeping one eye respectfully on the past and another looking towards the future – there's no finer East End welcome around.

255 Globe Road, E2 0JD

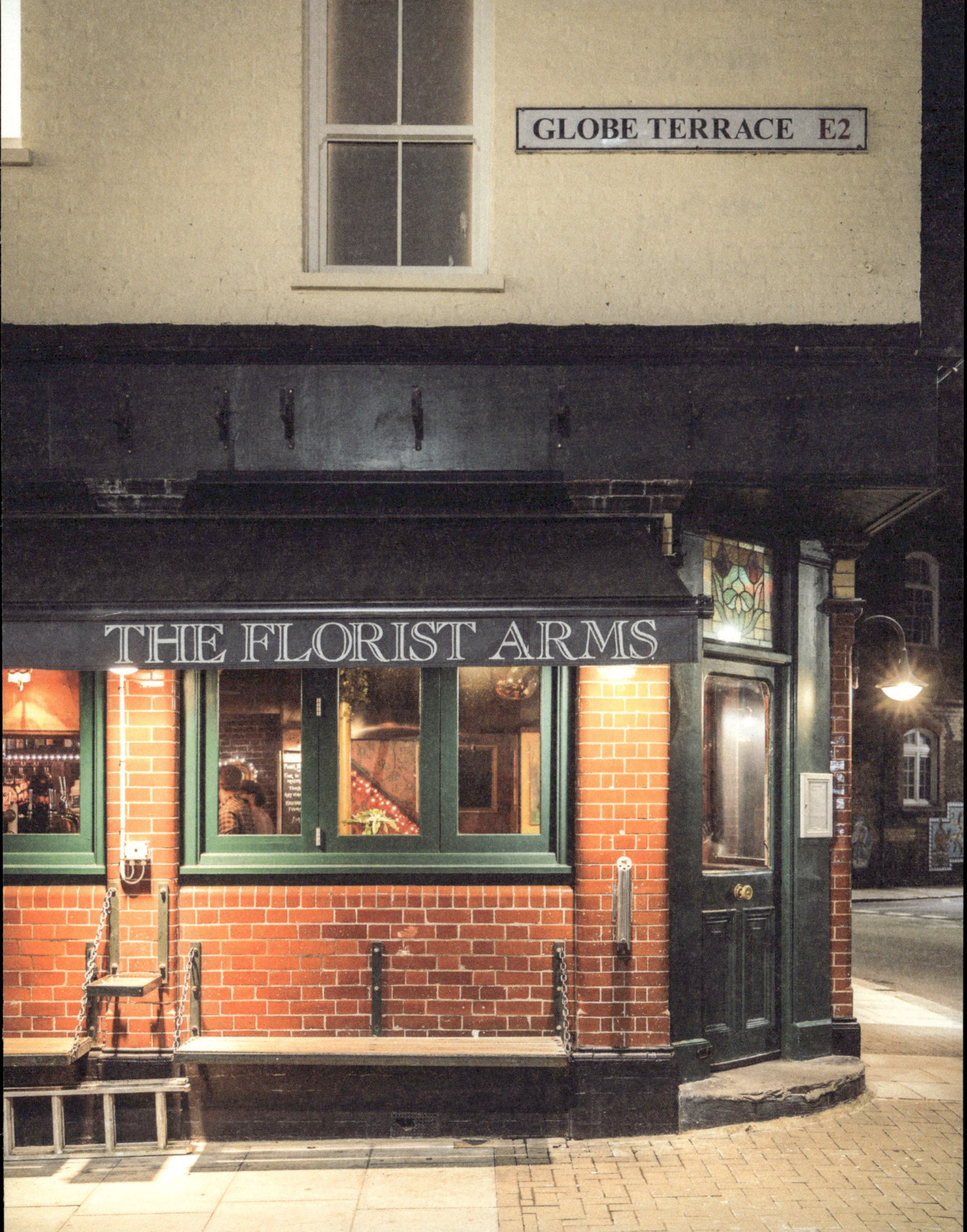

GLOBE TERRACE E2
THE FLORIST ARMS

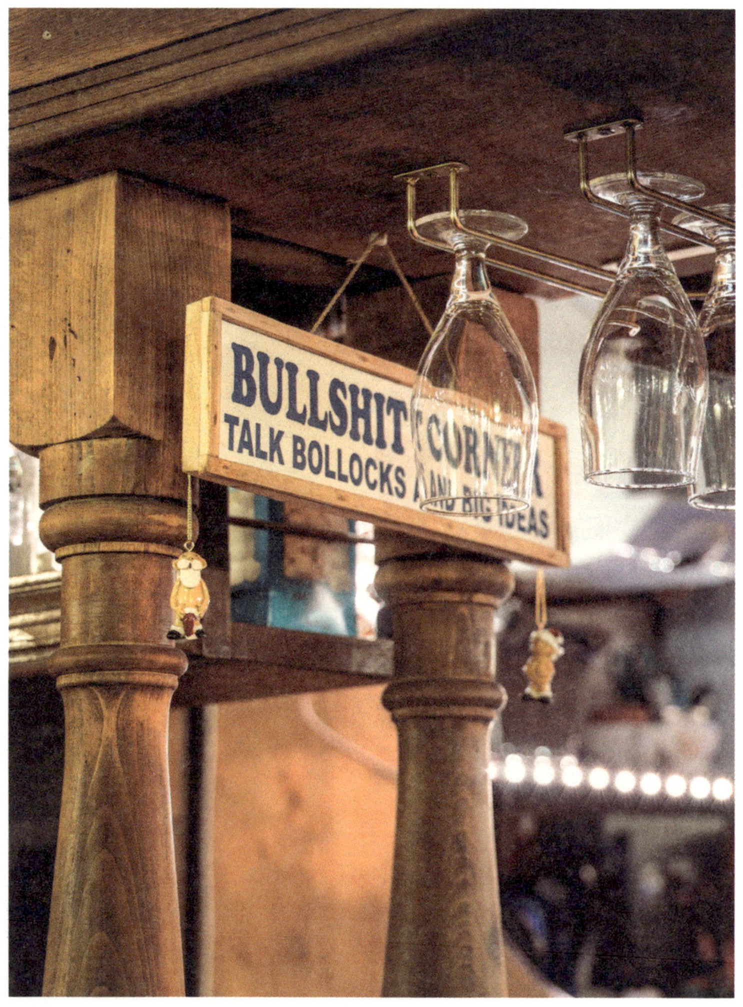

Landlady Emma Tarbard is passionate about creating a safe environment for women who want to have a quiet drink by themselves.

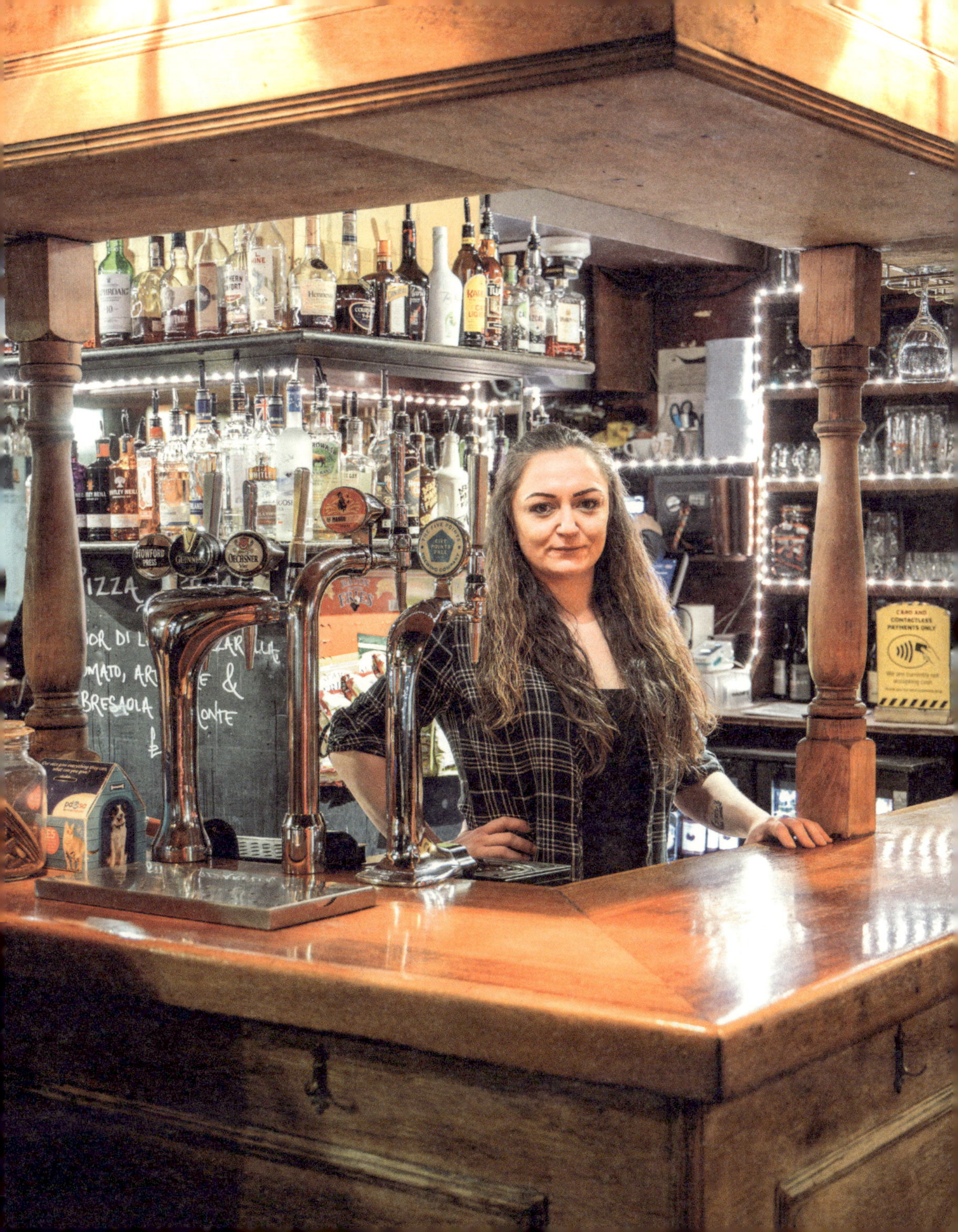

The Owl & Pussycat

A PUB THAT SERVES THE NEW SHOREDITCH

There are not many pub chains in the East End. This is because the 'Big Four' local breweries that dominated the area all closed in the 20th century, leaving most pubs in the hands of private landlords.

The Owl & Pussycat, run by Young's of Wandsworth, is one of the few remaining brewery-owned pubs. It has changed along with the community and customers it serves but at one time it was a warts 'n' all proper boozer where Cockneys would come to knock back a few pints of porter and smoke a Woodbine. Considering its low ceilings and gloomy interior warmed by roaring fires, it isn't hard to picture gangs of Dickensian rascals letting off steam here after a day in the markets.

From the 1990s onwards the arrival of artists and bohemians enticed by cheap warehouses and lofts saw the first change in clientele. They were replaced with corporate creative types as the area became a hub for start-ups and tech companies and, more recently, with weekend warriors arriving in London to sample a slice of urban life.

The pub's carefree atmosphere comes from the assured swagger of young people who come to let loose. Along with Young's signature ales and cocktails, high jinks and merriment flow freely whether night or day. An upstairs restaurant keeps the revellers fed and the outside courtyard bar attracts many thirsty patrons in the summer months. Although scores of its contemporaries have been demolished, fortunately The Owl & Pussycat is perpetually busy and in no danger of falling out of fashion.

34 Redchurch Street, E2 7DP

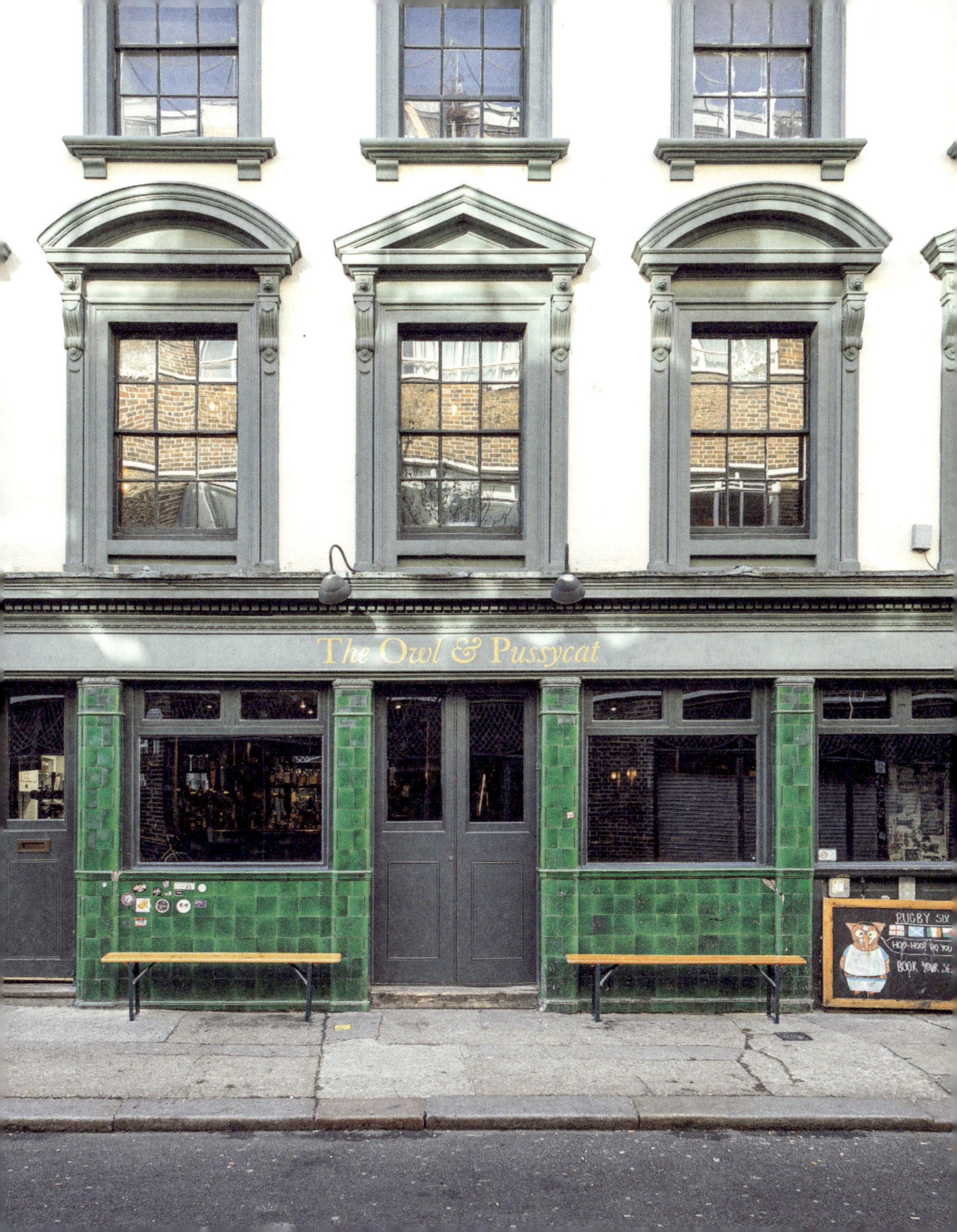
The Owl & Pussycat
RUGBY SIX
HOO·HOOT DO YOU
BOOK YOUR SE

The Lord Tredegar

Although the gentrification of the East End is largely associated with the end of the 20th century, its roots can be traced back to the early 1830s, when a series of grand squares were constructed as an attempt to draw the monied and genteel classes further east. These stucco-fronted and sash-windowed terraces with purposeful wrought-iron railings were the epitome of elegance. The fact that such terraces survived the Blitz is a miracle. Indeed, during the aerial bombardment resolute East Enders took refuge in hastily constructed shelters in the middle of the square.

Tredegar Square and this marvellous public house take their name, as is so often the case, from the local landowner. The lord of the manor here was Sir Charles Morgan, 2nd Baronet of Tredegar, for whom the nearby Morgan Arms (p.230) is also named.

Although the square was completed in 1847, this inviting boozer wasn't built until the 1850s. Bucking the trend of corner pubs fashionable at the time, The Lord Tredegar is wedged into a compact terrace of two-up-two-down houses.

For most of its life, the pub hardly changed, although it did acquire mock Tudor beams at some point in the 20th century, but thankfully these were removed during its refurbishment in 2012. This recent update was overseen by Remarkable Pubs, who have executed a stylish renovation that also humbly respects the pub's history.

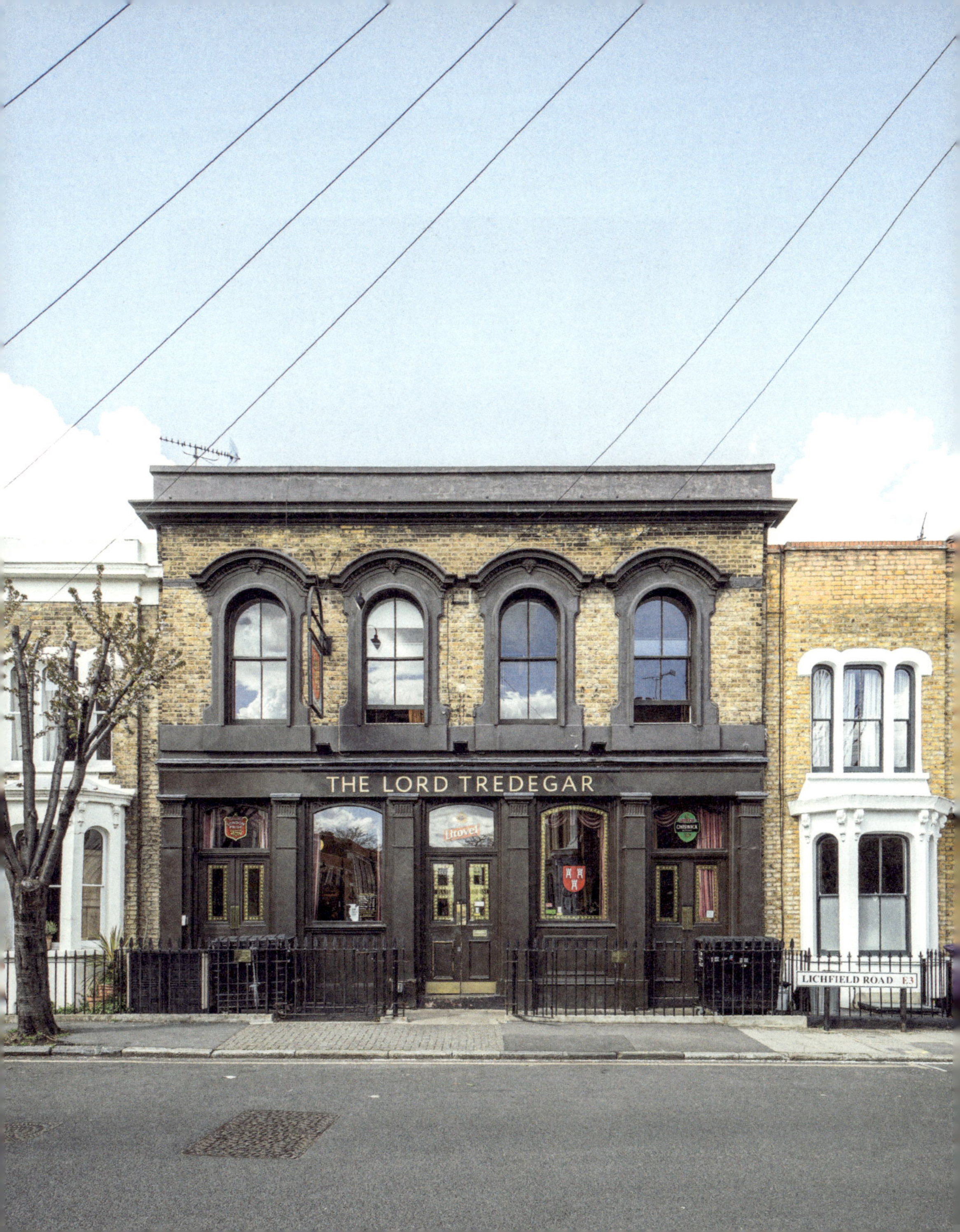

THE LORD TREDEGAR
LICHFIELD ROAD E3

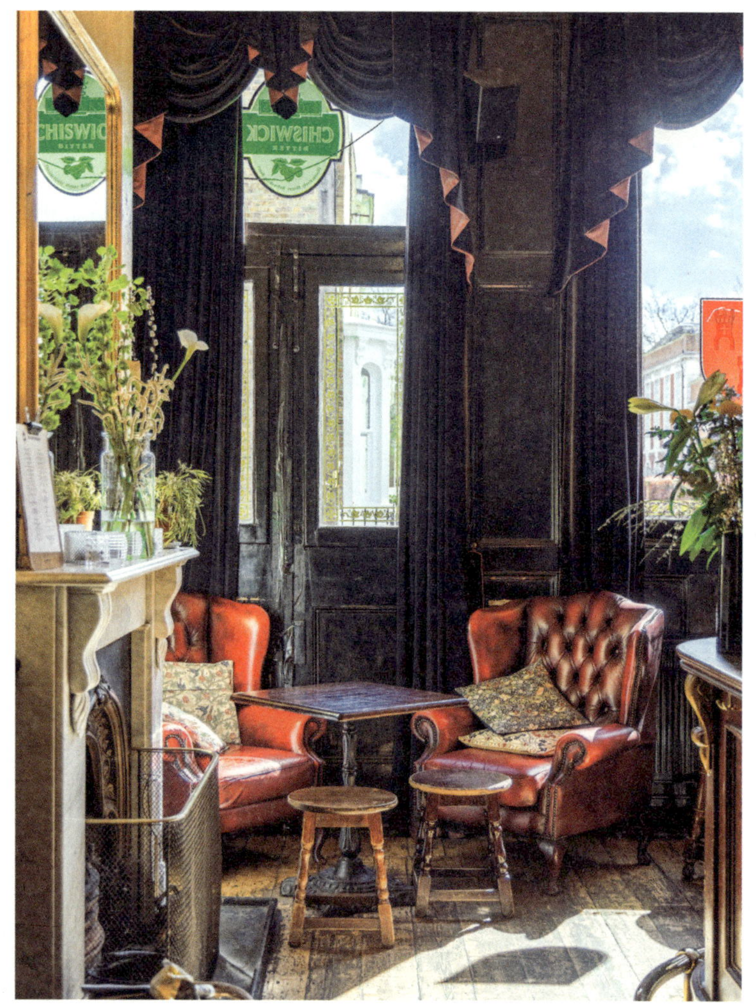

The Lord Tredegar is small but elegant, with high ceilings, an imposingly grand bar and plenty of nooks and crannies to hole up in. Being able to sit down with a pint after a long day is an important East End tradition and this age-old custom continues here at The Tredegar, where punters can rest with the heat from the two fires warming their backs and put the world to rights. This cornerstone of local pub life is very much respected by the team at Remarkable, as is the comforting presence of a free jukebox.

Some believe that certain East End pubs have been ruined by desperate attempts to attract diners – turning into restaurants, rather than proper pubs – but not so the Tredegar. In what feels like a textbook example of how a boozer and a gastropub can coexist in the same building, Remarkable Pubs have found an ideal solution. While the front of the pub is very much set up for drinkers, the rear extension at the back houses any patrons looking for an excellent meal. The open kitchen set on a flagstone floor under an atrium roof emits the enticing smell of risotto and burgers along with traditional pie and mash.

In the summer, the charming garden (complete with resident feline Beyoncé) is an idyllic spot to while away an afternoon with friends. Whether sharing a bottle of wine in the leather wingbacks by the fire, scoffing a Sunday Roast or enjoying a spritz on a baking hot day, The Lord Tredegar is an East End pub for all seasons with few rivals.

50 Lichfield Road, E3 5AL

The Lord Tredegar has two working fireplaces, a rarity in pubs these days.

The Manor Arms (Bum Daddy's)

People disagree about what constitutes a proper boozer. But anyone seeking to patronise an establishment that can unquestionably be awarded that revered moniker need look no further than The Manor Arms – or Bum Daddy's, as it's known locally. It maintains the cherished air of an ungentrified, working-class public house. In the East End, there were once hundreds of such pubs but today few exist.

The most plausible theory as to how The Manor Arms earned its nickname is that it references the 'bum boats' (barges) in the docks, as their captains, who were called 'daddies', frequented the pub. But it might also reference a former Guv'nor known to loan money to merchant seamen. Legend has it that if the Guv'nor's son was asked for a loan, he would say, 'Don't bum me, bum daddy.' In this case, 'bum' is a corruption of 'bung', a slang term for loan or bribe.

Kev Mallinson and Keeley Sharpe have been the pub's proud custodians for 15 years. They took on the licence from Keeley's dad, Terry, who passed away in 2009, and have kept his vision alive. Once, there were 14 pubs on East India Dock Road, but the Manor is the only survivor. Pictures of long-dead Guv'nors sit above the bar and there are always plenty of silver-haired campaigners happy to tell tales of the old East End. The Manor Arms is a community pub, with a strong focus on live music, in which joys and sorrows are shared. For a warm Cockney welcome in a proper boozer, there's no better place.

150 East India Dock Road, E14 0BP

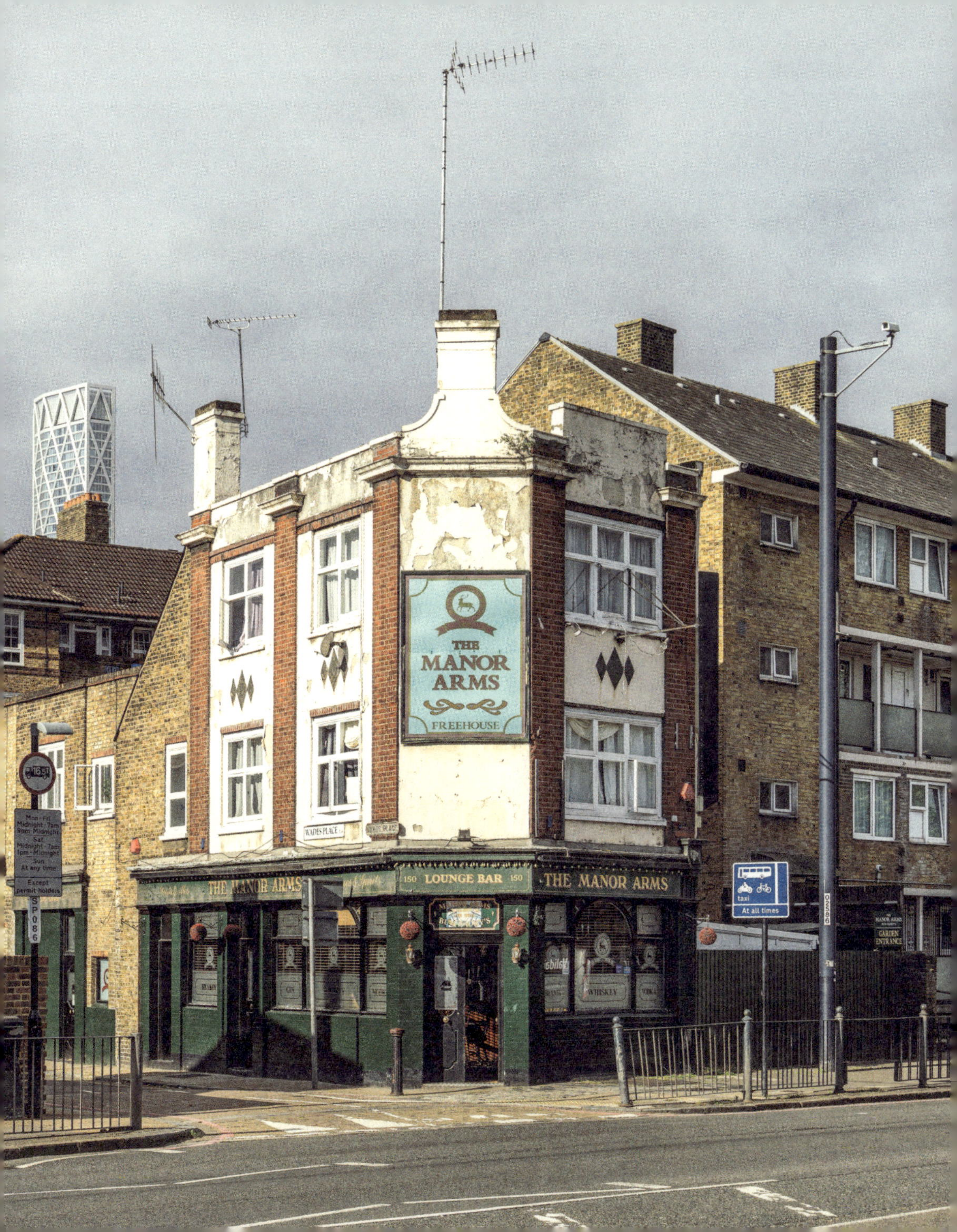

THE
MANOR
ARMS
FREEHOUSE
THE MANOR ARMS
LOUNGE BAR 150
150
THE MANOR ARMS
WHISKEY
WADES PLACE
MANOR ARMS
GARDEN
ENTRANCE
taxi
At all times
SP086
Mon - Fri
Midnight - 7am
9am - Midnight
Sat
Midnight - 7am
7pm - Midnight
Sun
At any time
Except
permit holders

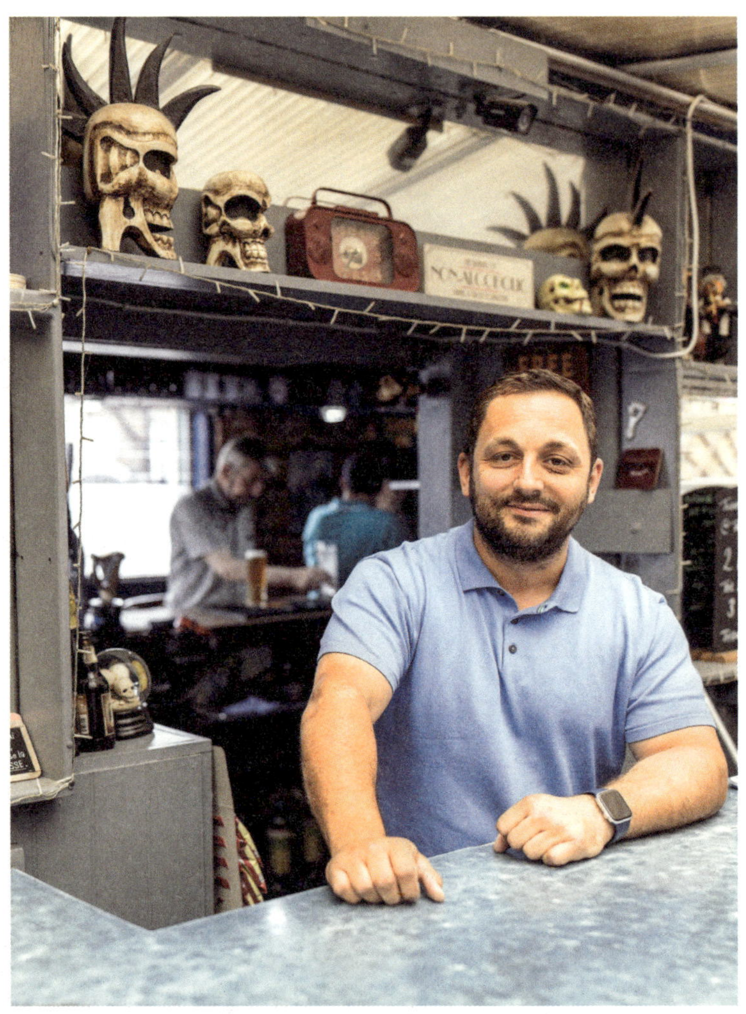

Kev Mallinson and Keeley Sharpe have been Guv'nors of The Manor Arms for 15 years.

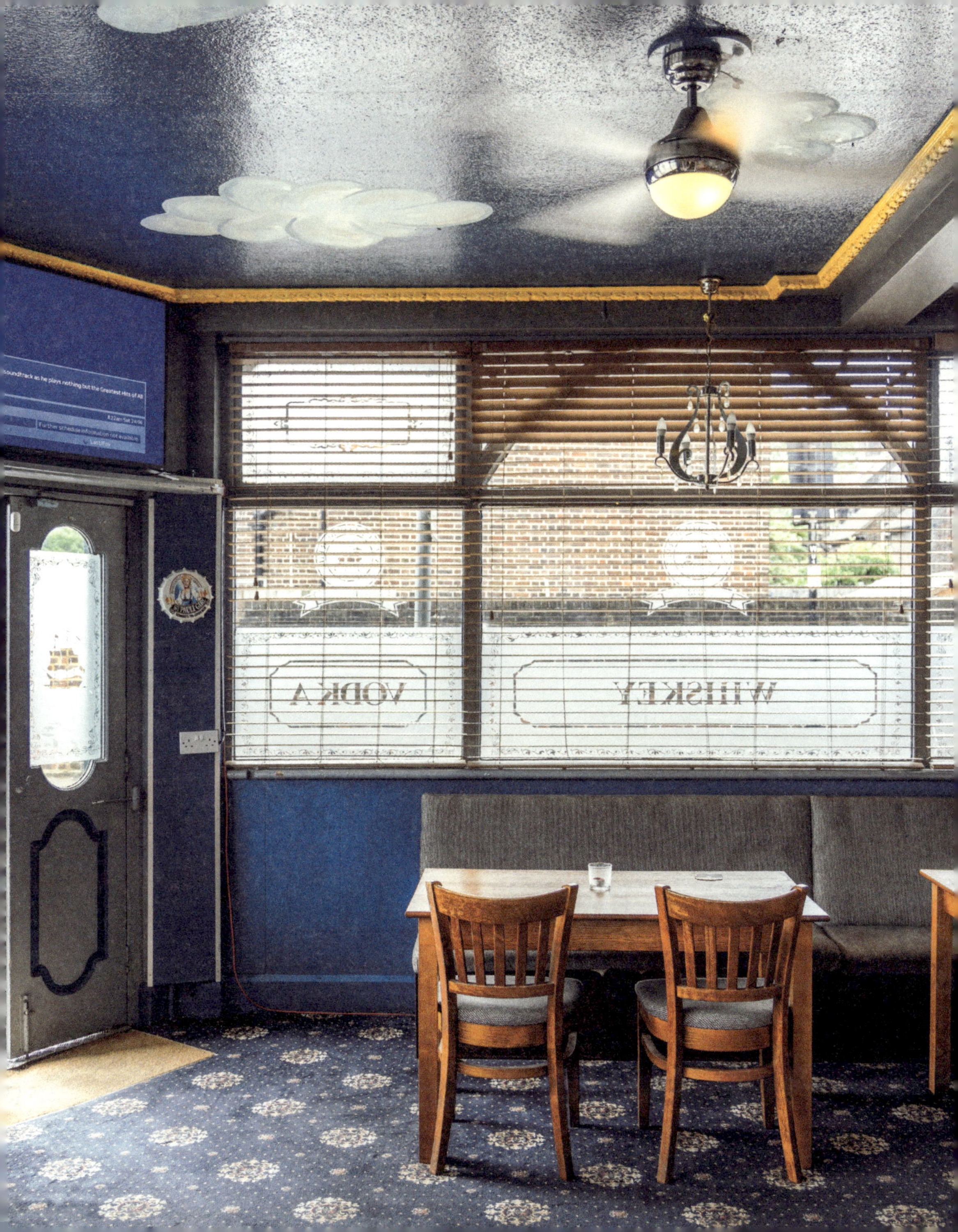
soundtrack as he plays nothing but the Greatest Hits of All
8.22 am Sat 24/06
Further schedule information not available
Last Pay
VODKA
WHISKEY

The Green Goose

OLD SANCTUARY WITH A NEW NAME

In a pub landscape that has shrunk massively in the last 20 years, the Green Goose has ensured its survival by reinventing itself for a new customer base. Located around the corner from Roman Road, it is owned by Mosaic Pub & Dining, and mainly serves the affluent professionals who are the area's most recent arrivals. It is a far cry from the spit 'n' sawdust wet-led boozer it was when it first opened in 1863 as The Lord Cardigan.

The pub was originally named after the seventh Earl of Cardigan who disastrously led the Light Brigade into slaughter at the Battle of Balaclava during the Crimean War. Its new name has much older roots. From the 17th century until its closure at the hand of local authorities in the 19th century, the Green Goose fair was a notoriously unruly festival held the week after Pentecost. After an extensive refurbishment in 2015, the pub has had a new lease of life. It now includes a spacious dining area in the rear and the beer garden, where once the old Guv'nor would park his car, has benefitted from much-needed attention.

What is most appealing about this backstreet sanctuary is that it coexists as pub and restaurant. The front of the building is still a traditional hostelry, while the rear is set up for those eating. Despite a different name and customer base, the Green Goose is in rude health and a most valued asset for both new and old faces of the manor.

112 Anglo Road, E3 5HD

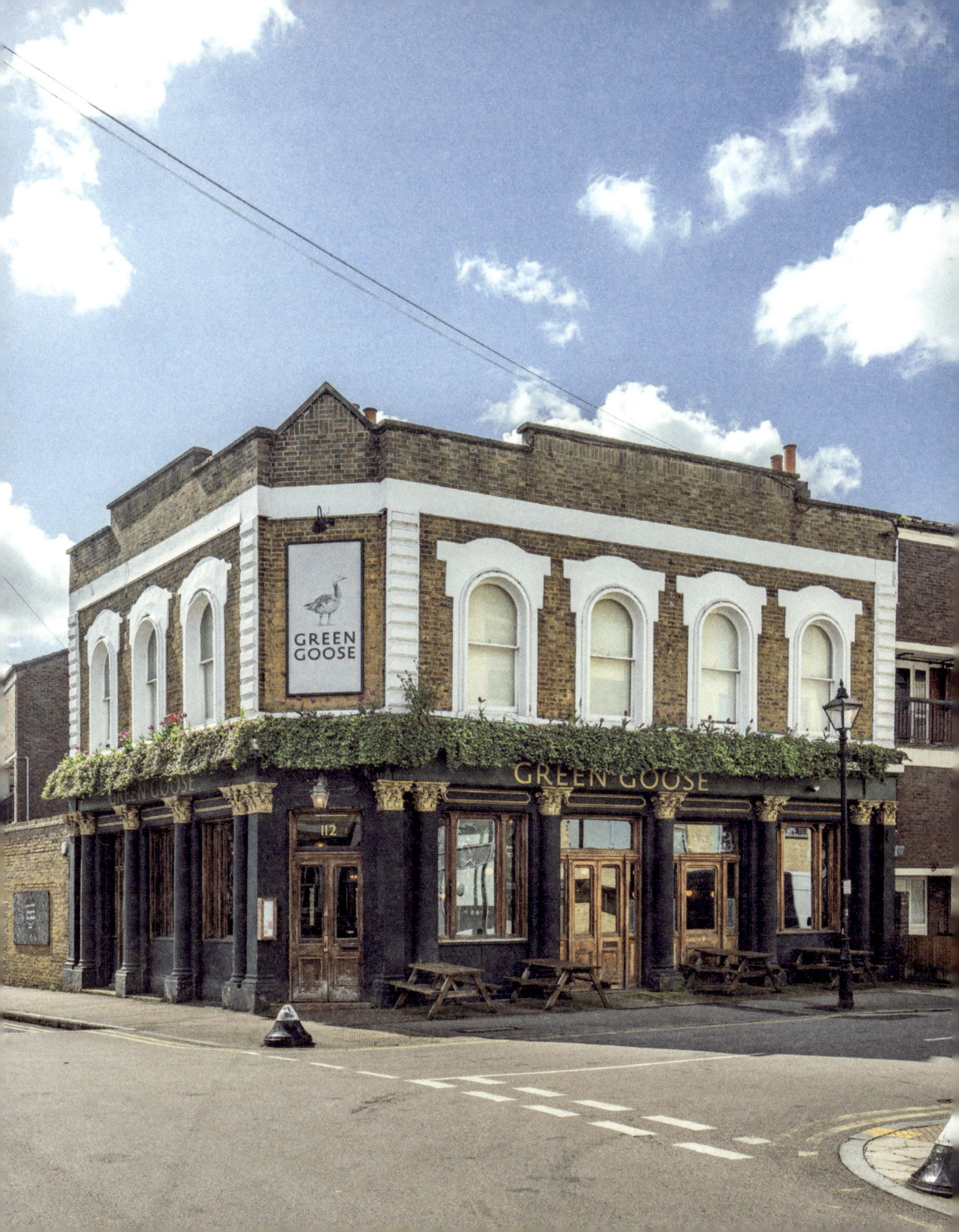

The Bow Bells

COCKNEY LEGEND WITH A BRIGHT FUTURE

This bright orange boozer on Bow Road holds a place in the hearts of Cockneys far and wide. The origin of its name is also what defines them. Folklore dictates that all Cockneys must be born within earshot of the bells of St Mary-le-Bow church on Cheapside, which could once be heard from Southwark to the Hackney Marshes. The original church was destroyed by the Great Fire of London in 1666 and was rebuilt by Sir Christopher Wren, though like much of the city it was damaged during the Blitz in 1941. The bells came crashing to the ground and fell silent until the church was restored in 1961 – leading to a much-disputed claim that for 20 years no Cockneys were born.

Anyone enthused by Cockney culture will feel at home at The Bow Bells. Luxurious wallpaper, high ceilings, a mahogany bar fronted with latticed glass, banquette seating and a proper pub carpet make it a classic.

A new generation of punters is welcomed at this inclusive community pub, which now serves pizza and craft beer and shows live sports. But you can still rest a pint on the mantlepiece to take up a pool cue, an age-old pleasure no doubt enjoyed by the many long-forgotten East Enders gazing down from the photographs on the walls.

The Bow Bells is at its best when football fans converge for match day at the London Stadium. An allegiance to West Ham United runs deep in the borough and among the Cockney diaspora, so when the Irons are playing at home, the pub is heaving. Spending just five minutes in the pub on a day like that and you'll be assured that the vibrant culture of the East End will continue for decades to come, whether those bells keep ringing or not.

116 Bow Road, E3 3AA

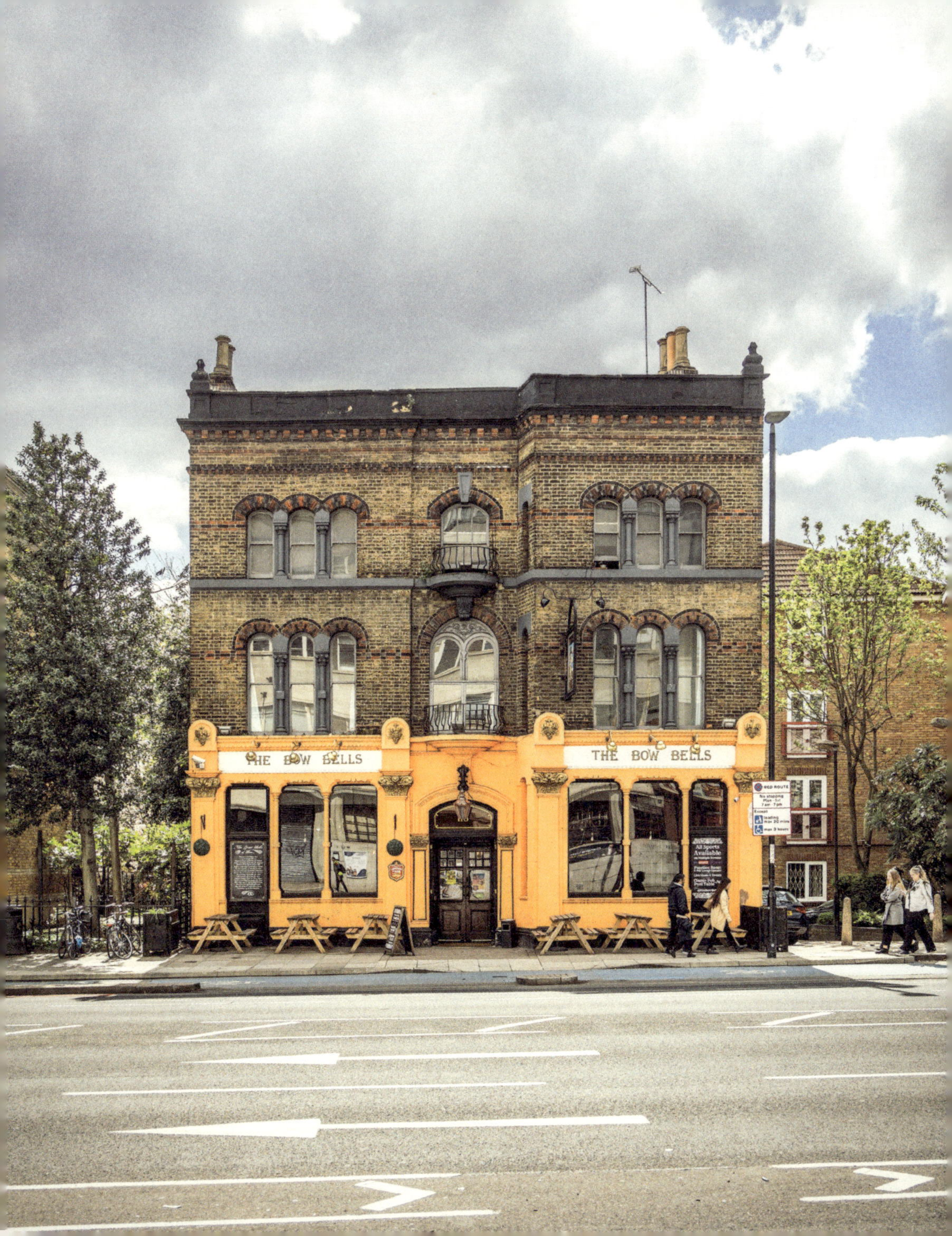

THE BOW BELLS
THE BOW BELLS
All Sports
Available
RED ROUTE

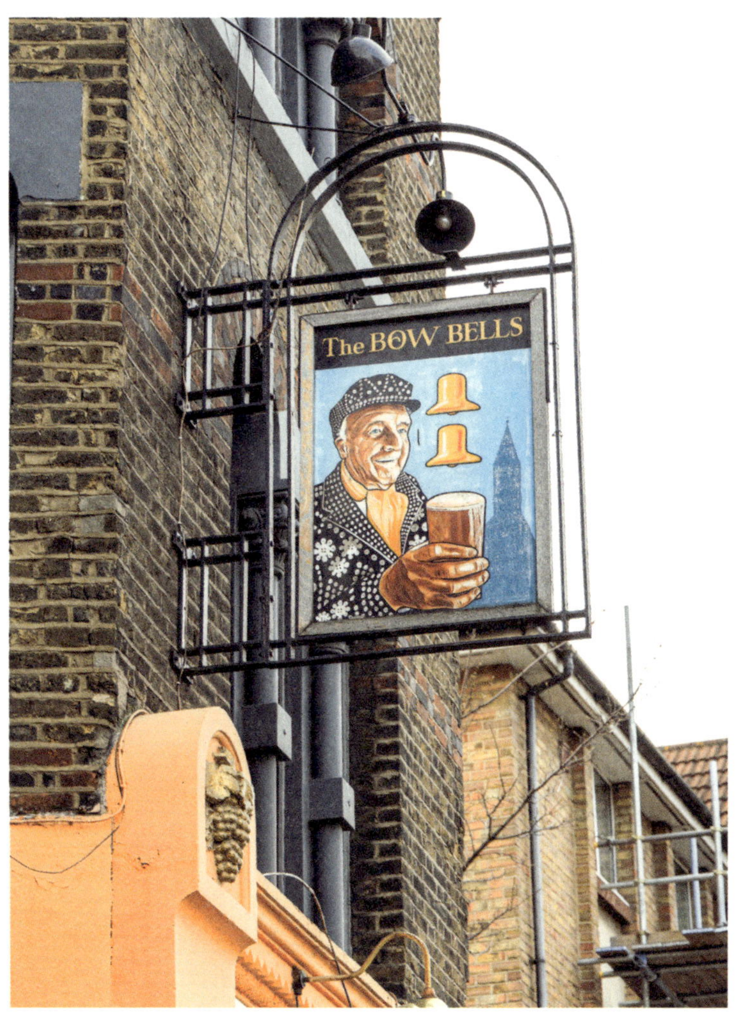

(Opposite) *The traditional patterned pub carpet, so excellent
at hiding stains, can still be enjoyed at The Bow Bells.*

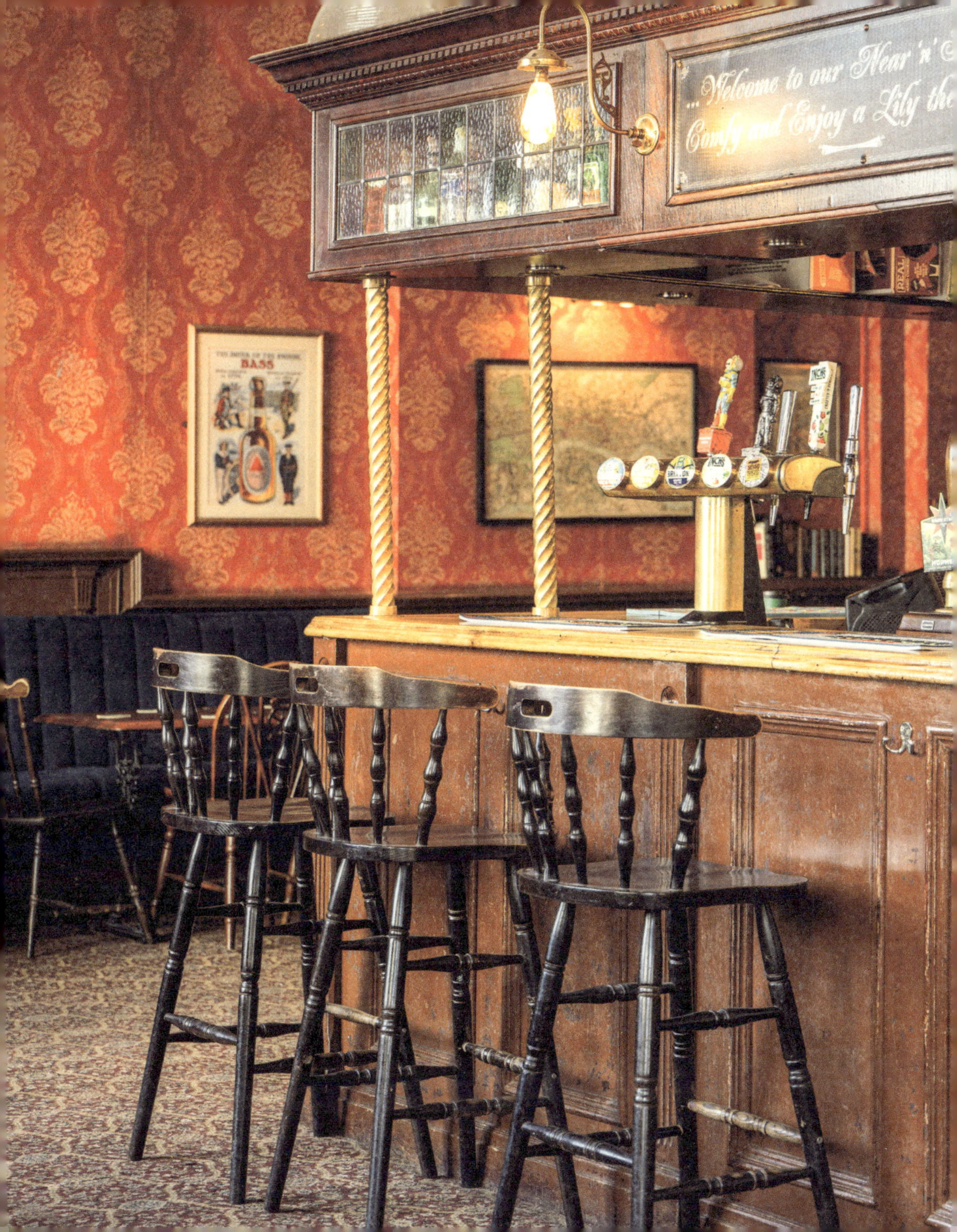
BASS
...Welcome to our Near 'n'
Comfy and Enjoy a Lily the

The Beehive

AN INTERWAR MUSICAL PUB

A little-known pub, The Beehive is not the kind of establishment that you'll stumble across, so it's had to diversify to stay relevant and profitable in an ever-changing East End.

Replacing a pub of the same name (situated slightly further down the street), it sits in the shadow of what was once St Andrew's Hospital. The hospital was founded in 1868 as the Poplar and Stepney Sick Asylum and it oversaw the arrival of new generations of Cockneys in its maternity ward until it closed in 2006. One can picture nervous fathers nursing a pint at The Beehive in days gone by, while mothers at St Andrew's had the infinitely more difficult task of giving birth.

The Beehive now sits among the quiet residential backstreets and light industry, built on the remains of the old hospital. Its all-female team is run by Lina Tomkeviciene, an affable landlady from Lithuania, who also manages alternative rock bands out of the pub's function room throughout the week. While regulars sup pints in the cheery traditional pub, the crash of cymbals and rumbling basslines can be heard with gusto as melodies mix with the back-and-forth banter at the main bar.

The new crowd who come for the music not only put money into the till, but they also create a lively environment, mixing harmoniously with the more seasoned customers.

As well as live music, this hidden gem has a pool table, darts, two generous outside areas, cheap pints and one of only three fish tanks in East End pubs. Thanks to its new lease of life, The Beehive will be on the pub map for many years to come.

104 Empson Street, E3 3LT

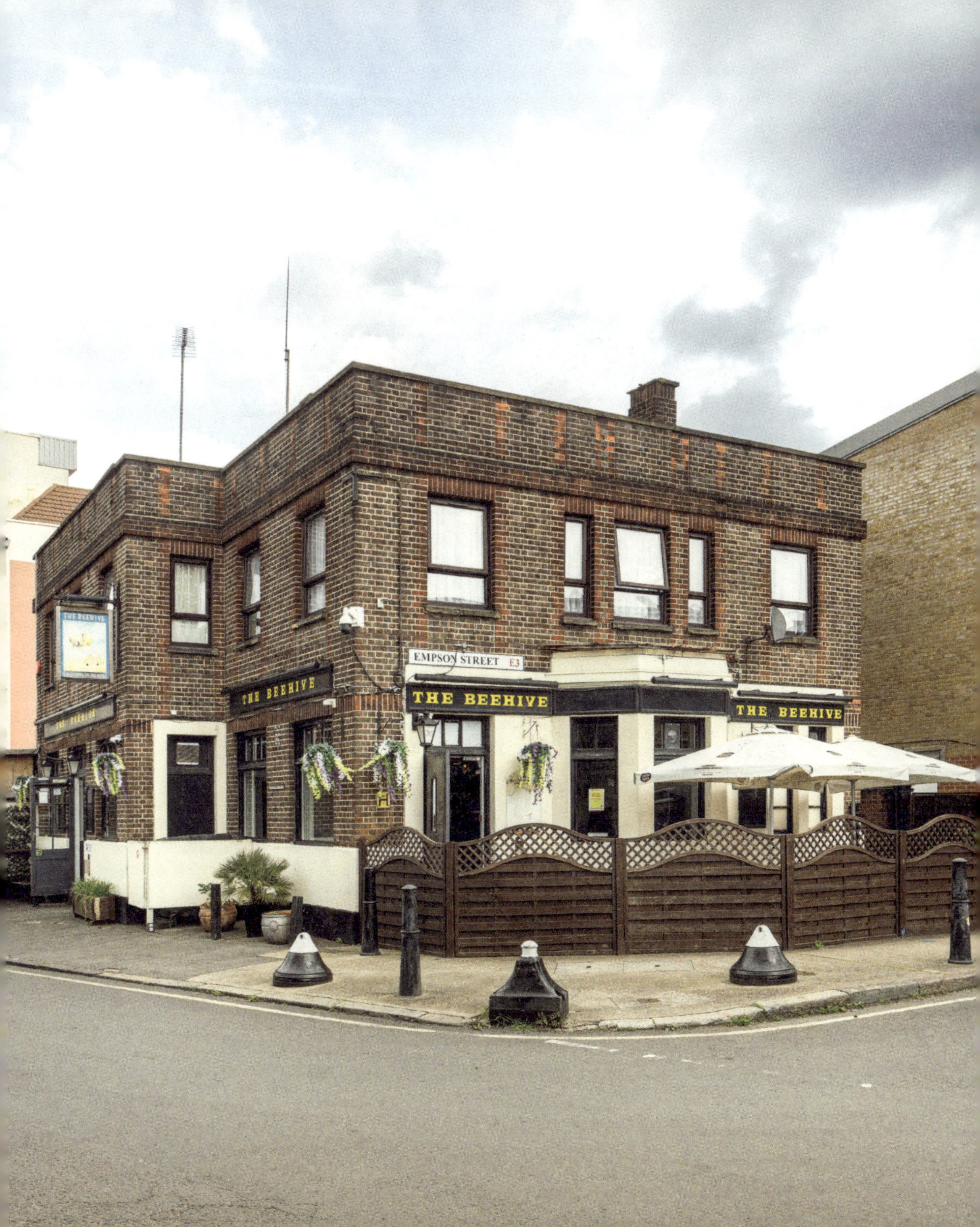
THE BEEHIVE
EMPSON STREET E3
THE BEEHIVE
THE BEEHIVE
THE BEEHIVE

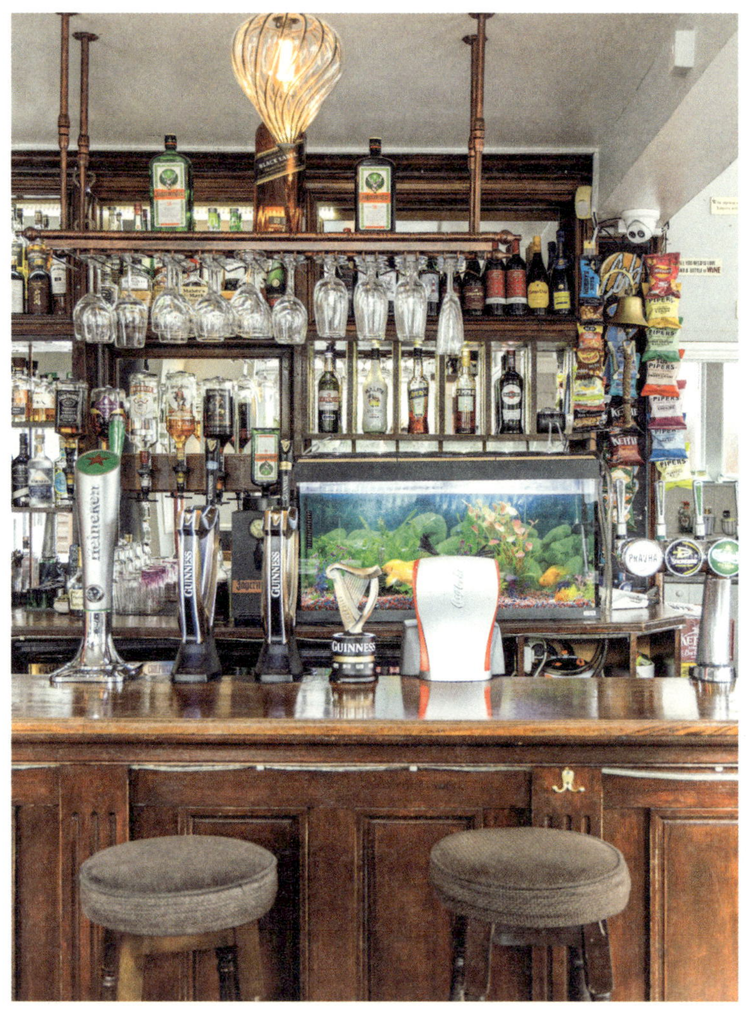

(Opposite) Lina Tomkeviciene, the landlady of The Beehive,
has kept the East End tradition of live music going strong.

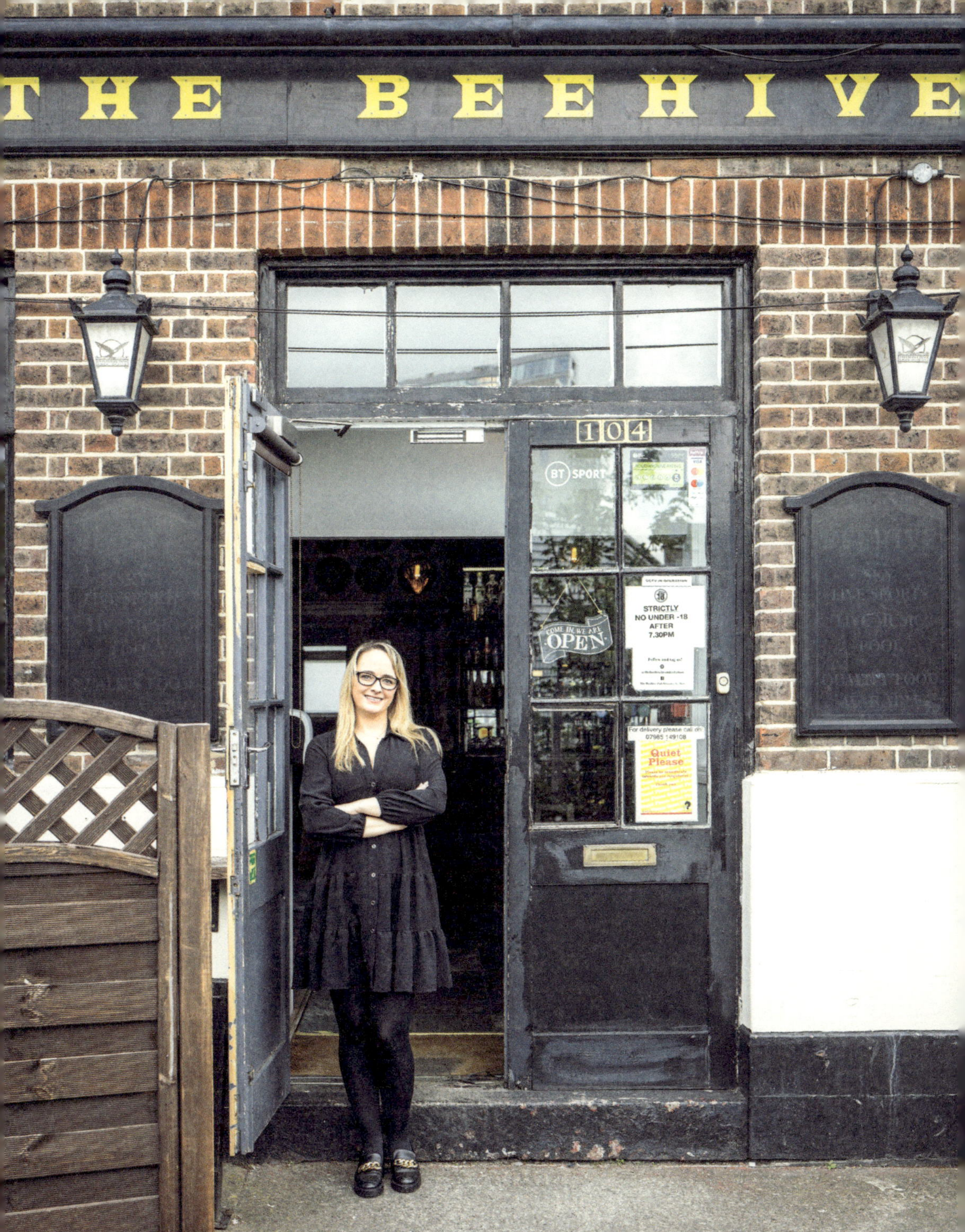

THE BEEHIVE
104
BT SPORT
COME IN, WE ARE OPEN
STRICTLY
NO UNDER -18
AFTER
7.30PM
For delivery please call on
07985 149108
Quiet Please

The Prince Regent

A BONA FIDE COCKNEY STRONGHOLD

With its weathered exterior, The Prince Regent is an unwavering stalwart situated on Salmon Lane. Standing between a former pub (the fallen Rose & Crown) and a tyre yard, The Prince Regent harks back to a time when everyone knew their neighbours.

Pubs that manage to survive must be well run, but they also need to have a desire to serve the community. Publicans are as important a vocation on these manors as local councillors, doctors or any other public servant. Micky Quinn, the Guv'nor of The Regent, is a veteran East End publican. Having run eight boozers since 1984, there isn't much he hasn't seen.

Micky moved into the licensed trade after a sporting career. In the 1970s, he was a successful boxer and represented England at multiple levels. Having only lost 13 in over 100 fights, he was well placed, after hanging up his gloves, to manage the rough and tumble of a boozer. He has the firm handshake of someone with a bouting past, and souvenirs of his time in the ring adorn the wall.

Since taking over the pub from fellow long-standing Guv'nor Joe Hennessey, who also ran The Ancient Briton in Bow, Micky has repainted the facade, removed the net curtains, put in new banquette seating and installed a jukebox. The original tiling on the exterior has been retained, as have many old features, such as the mock Tudor beams and horse brass – neither of which would look out of place in a country pub.

While The Copenhagen, Freemason's, Crow's Nest and many other pubs on Salmon Lane are long gone, The Regent remains a place where burdens can be shared with Cockney bonhomie and wit.

81 Salmon Lane, E14 7PR

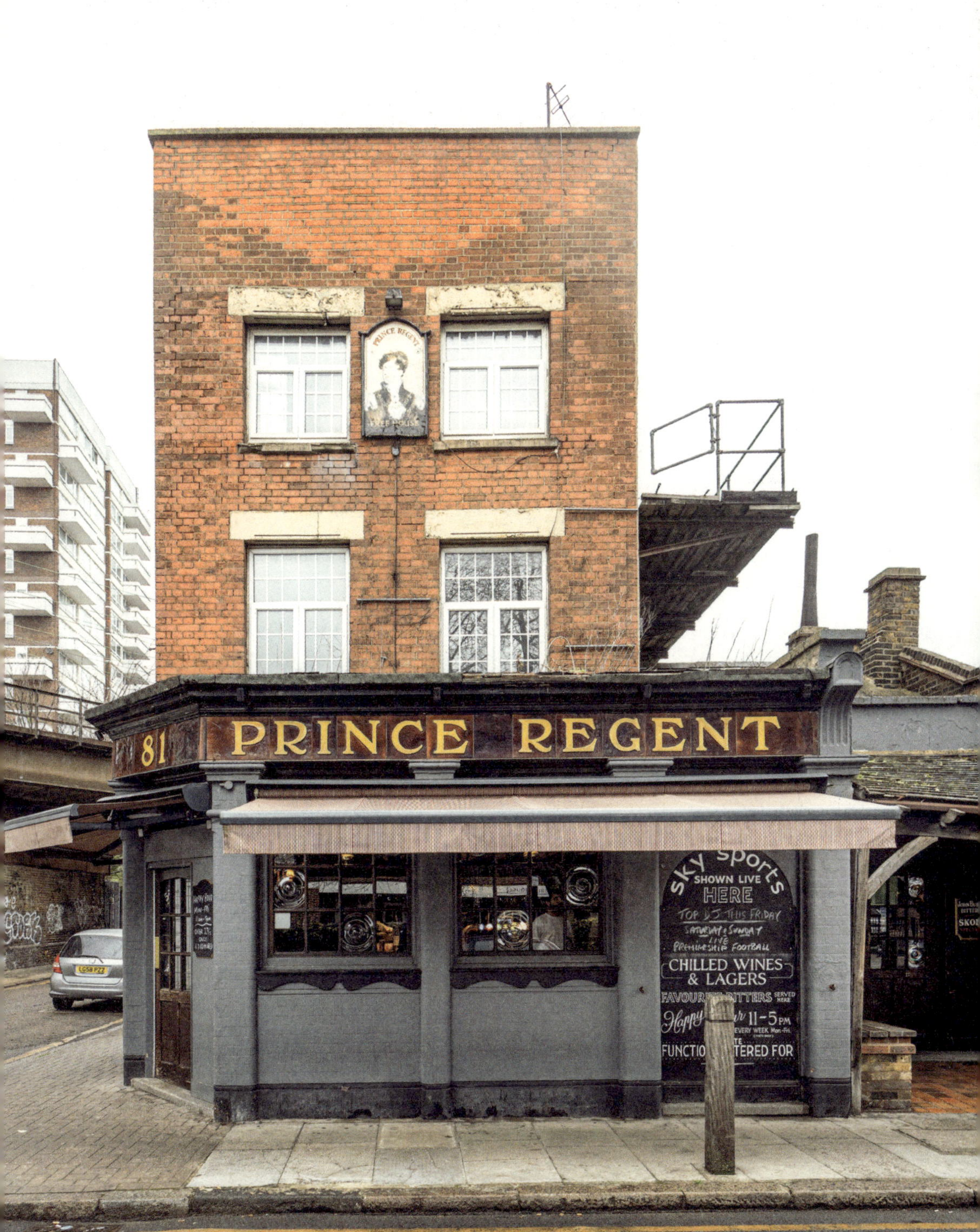
PRINCE REGENT
FREE HOUSE
81
PRINCE REGENT
SKY Sports
SHOWN LIVE
HERE
TOP DJ THIS FRIDAY
SATURDAY & SUNDAY
LIVE
PREMIERSHIP FOOTBALL
CHILLED WINES
& LAGERS
FAVOURITE BITTERS SERVED HERE
Happy HOUR 11–5 PM
EVERY WEEK Mon–Fri
FUNCTIONS CATERED FOR

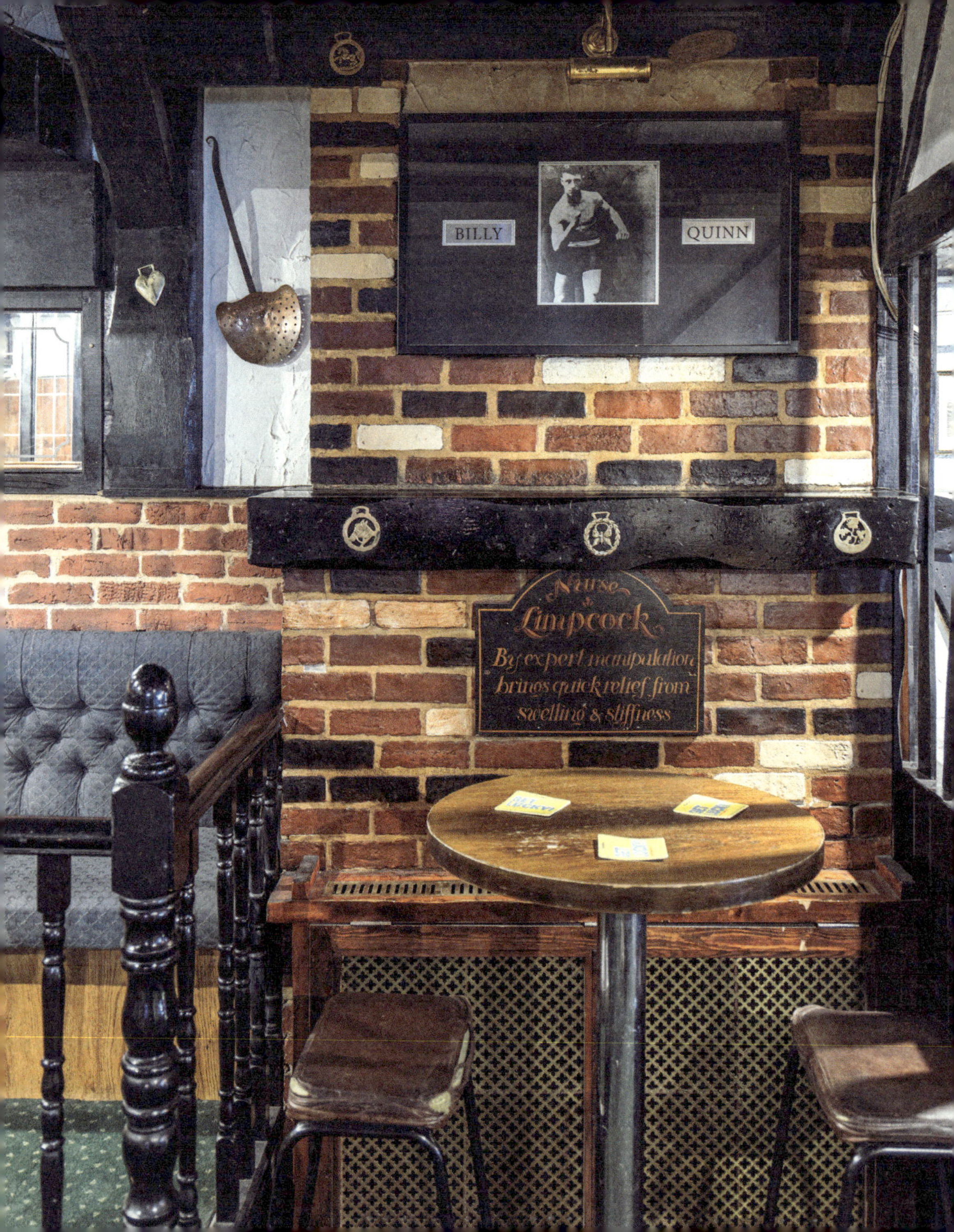

BILLY
QUINN
Nurse
Limpcock
By expert manipulation
brings quick relief from
swelling & stiffness

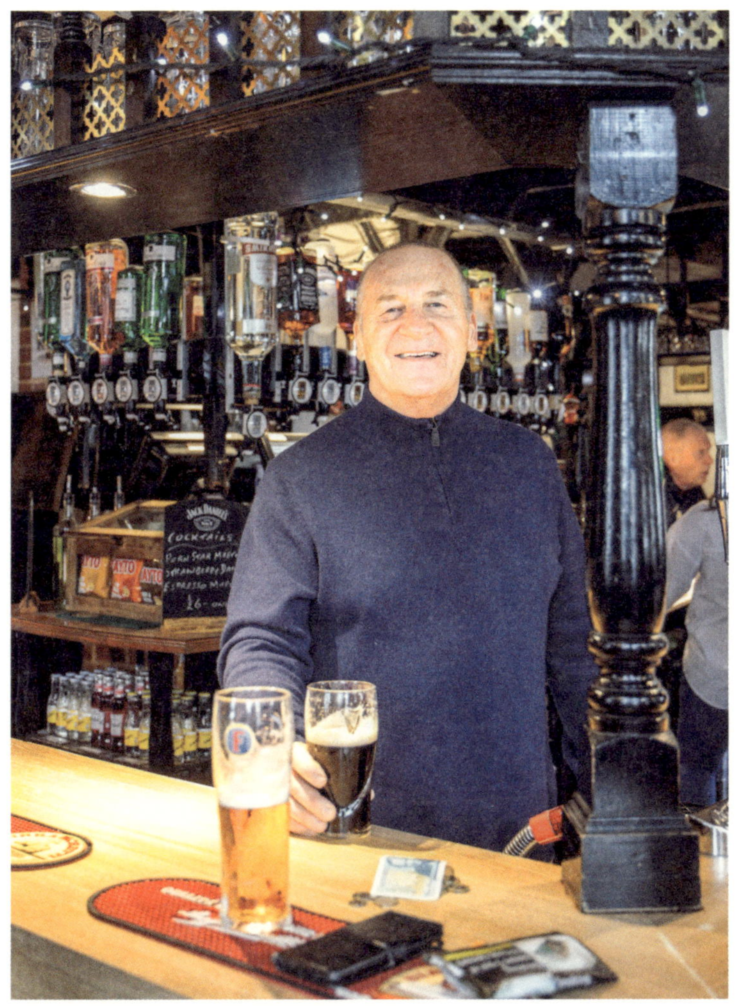

*Ex-boxing champion Micky Quinn, the Guv'nor of The Prince Regent,
has a wealth of stories about his time in the ring.*

The Hungerford Arms

After a long, back-breaking day labouring on railways, canals and in factories, East End grafters relied on the simple pleasure of a rewarding soak in a fine hostelry. The Hungerford Arms still serves a similar purpose: a place to relax, recharge and forget the daily grind for a few hours. Many drinkers are in the autumn of their lives and, if people take the time to listen, have a wealth of stories to tell.

Those pubs that remain in the East End are sadly clinging on amid a changing world, standing proud but often looking battle-worn. It is a raw London, far removed from the Palace of Westminster, but sanctuary and solace can still be found in the traditional boozer.

For many punters, The Hungerford is an extension of their living rooms and provides the vital public service of a community check-in. Open from 10am for the early risers, its beauty is in its simplicity: a long wooden bar, stripped flooring and pool table do famously for its hearty loyal band of old faces.

It is a familiar setting to share the sacrament of a decent pint and good conversation. For many who live on their own it is a lifeline, and the bar staff might be the only people they speak to all day. The Hungerford will hopefully remain for many years to come to service those who rely on it for pastoral support.

240 Commercial Road, E1 2NB

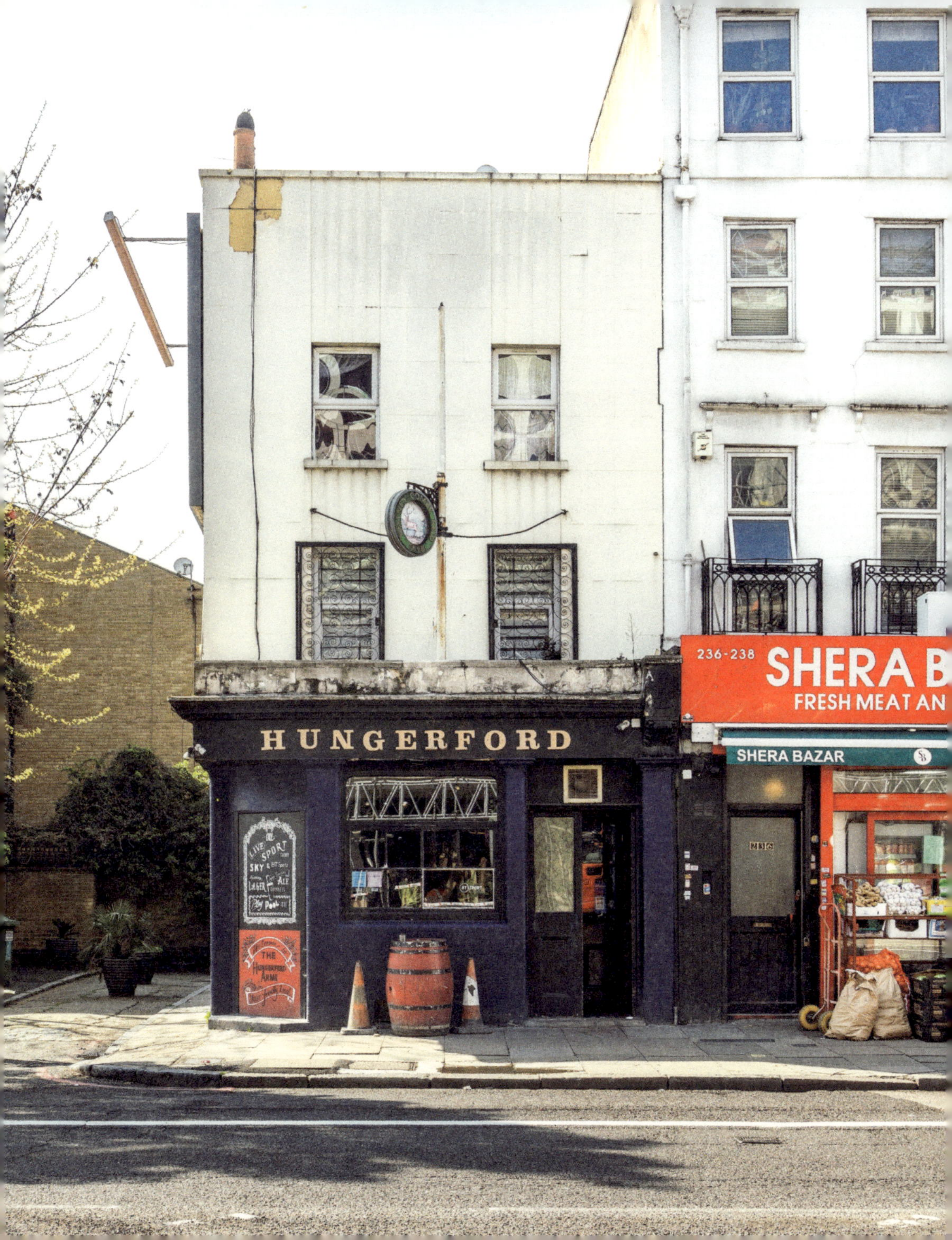
HUNGERFORD
LIVE SPORT
SKY & BT Sport
LAGER ALE
Big Pub
THE
Hungerford
Arms
236-238 SHERA B
FRESH MEAT AN
SHERA BAZAR

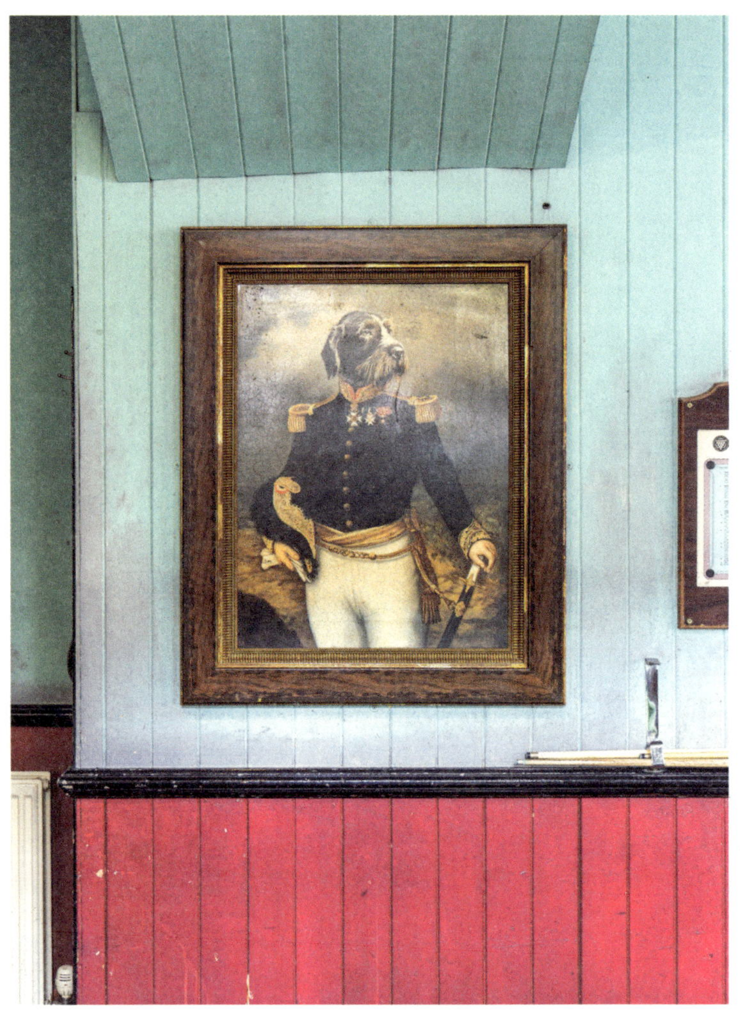

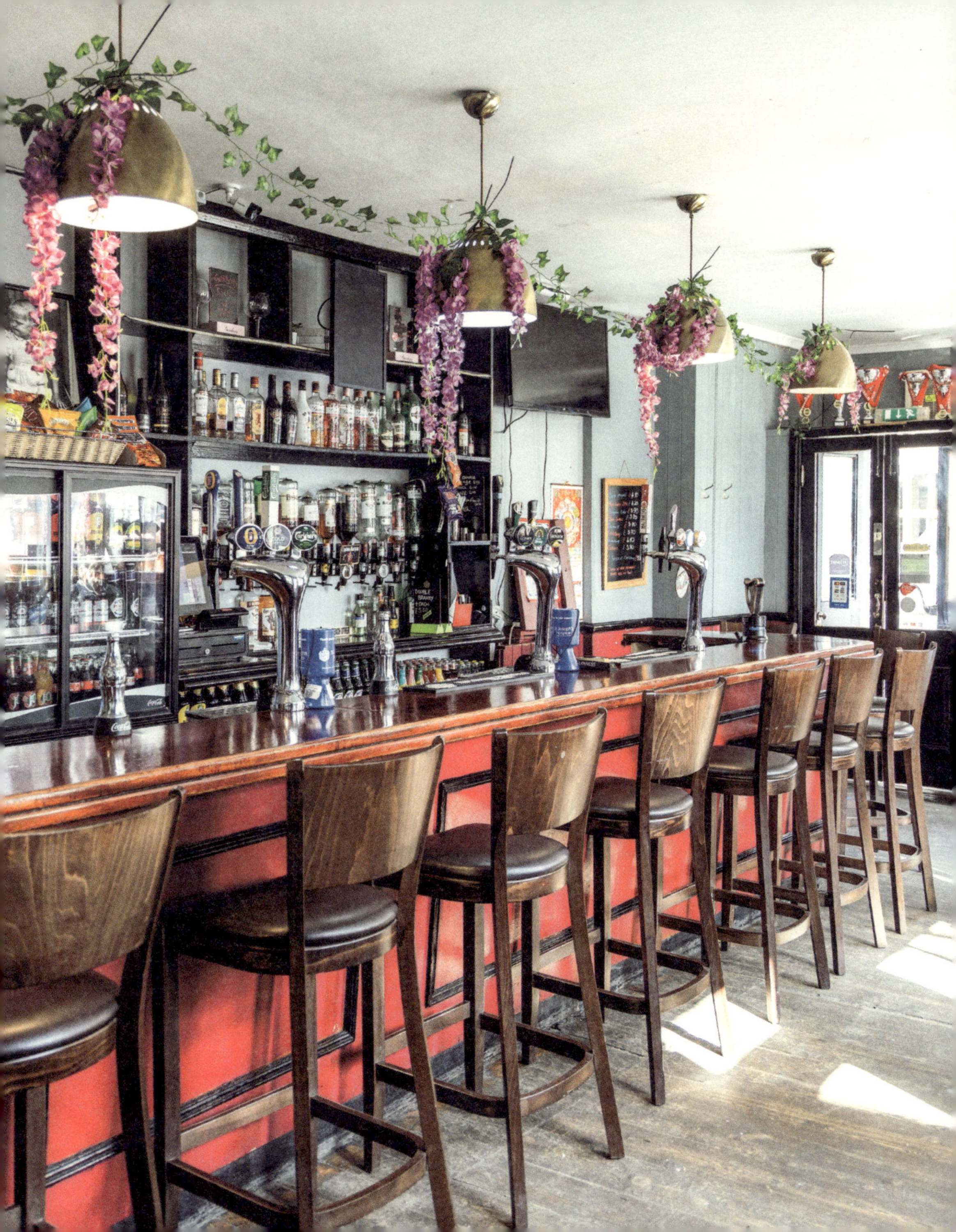

The Queen's Head

This Grade II-listed public house was blessed with royal patronage when it hosted the Queen Mother in 1987. A popular figure in east London, when Buckingham Palace was struck during the Blitz, Her Majesty was reported to have said, 'I'm glad we've been hit, as now I can look the East End in the face.'

As someone who enjoyed a stiff drink, the Queen Mother further endeared herself when she made her way behind the bar at The Queen's Head. Her Majesty poured a pint of bitter and proceeded to drain most of her glass. The exclamation of, 'It tastes better than champagne!' received rapturous applause and, until 2020, photographs of the visit (p.2) adorned the pub's walls. Sadly, they were lost during the pub's recent renovation.

The pub almost closed forever in 2020, when it lost its alcohol licence due to complaints about after-hours parties during lockdown. Thankfully, an Asset of Community Value (ACV) had already been secured to protect the pub and five investors planned a rescue bid in 2022.

After a six-month refurbishment, they reopened its doors in 2023. While the quaint sandwich counter that sat in the public bar in days of yore is no more, The Queen's Head has been sympathetically furnished. Now customers can enjoy the craft delights of Walthamstow's Pillars Brewery and Siren Craft Brew from Wokingham, along with familiar stout and lagers.

Red banquette seats and brass taps gleam, as do the lovingly varnished wooden floors, but it's the warm welcome from the team that makes this pub such a noteworthy sanctuary.

8 Flamborough Street, E14 7LS

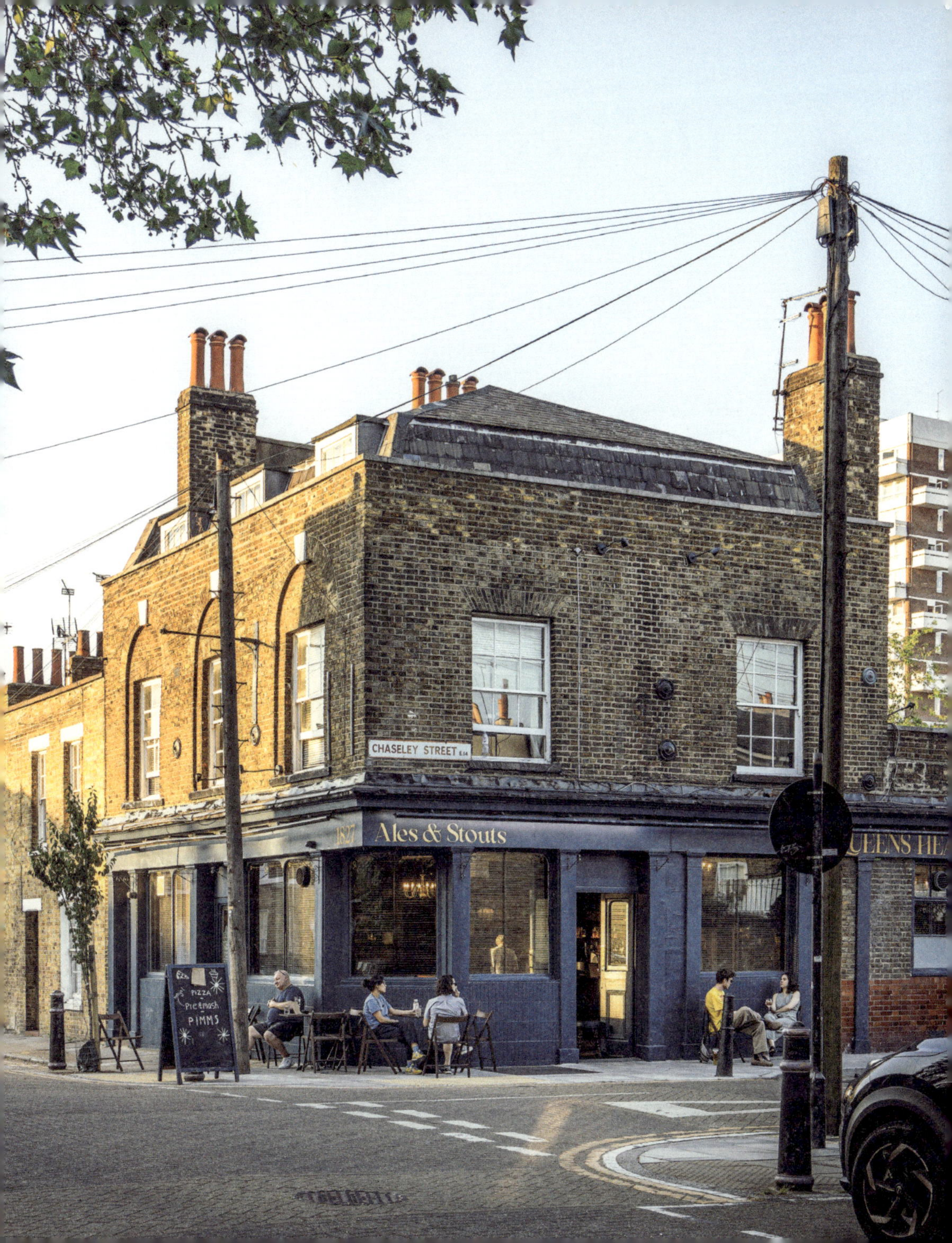
CHASELEY STREET E14
1827
Ales & Stouts
QUEENS HEAD
PIZZA
Pie&mash
PIMMS

The George Tavern

ICONIC PUB FIGHTING THE GOOD FIGHT

Shadwell and Stepney have endured scores of pub closures since the 1980s. Street corners once bursting with life are now silent, but one survivor still stands proud with its golden signage, striking brickwork and neon sign: The George Tavern. A treasured asset to London's music scene, it has been under almost constant threat of closure for the last ten years.

Landlady and artist Pauline Forster has owned the Grade II-listed pub since 2002, and has fought diligently for its survival. As a late-night music venue, it relies heavily on events to remain solvent, but a recent rise in neighbouring residential flats has led to an increasing number of noise complaints. Luckily, in 2019, the local authority recognised the pub's unique value and protected it against unnecessary complaints.

In 2022, The George was again in danger when the adjacent Stepney's Nightclub was on the brink of being demolished and replaced with new flats. But the local council rejected the developer's proposal and again saved the much-loved pub. There is always the risk that the developers might come again, but Pauline and her many supporters (including Kate Moss and fellow local publican Sir Ian McKellen) are ready for the fight.

For now, music from up-and-coming musicians still echoes off the high ceilings. And long may we continue to sit back with a pint of ale and take in the stunning tiled mural illuminated by flickering candlelight. If Pauline has anything to say about it, people will be able to sit at the bar and hear her colourful stories about The George Tavern for many years to come, as the rumble of a bass line continues to blast out into the night.

373 Commercial Road, E1 0LA

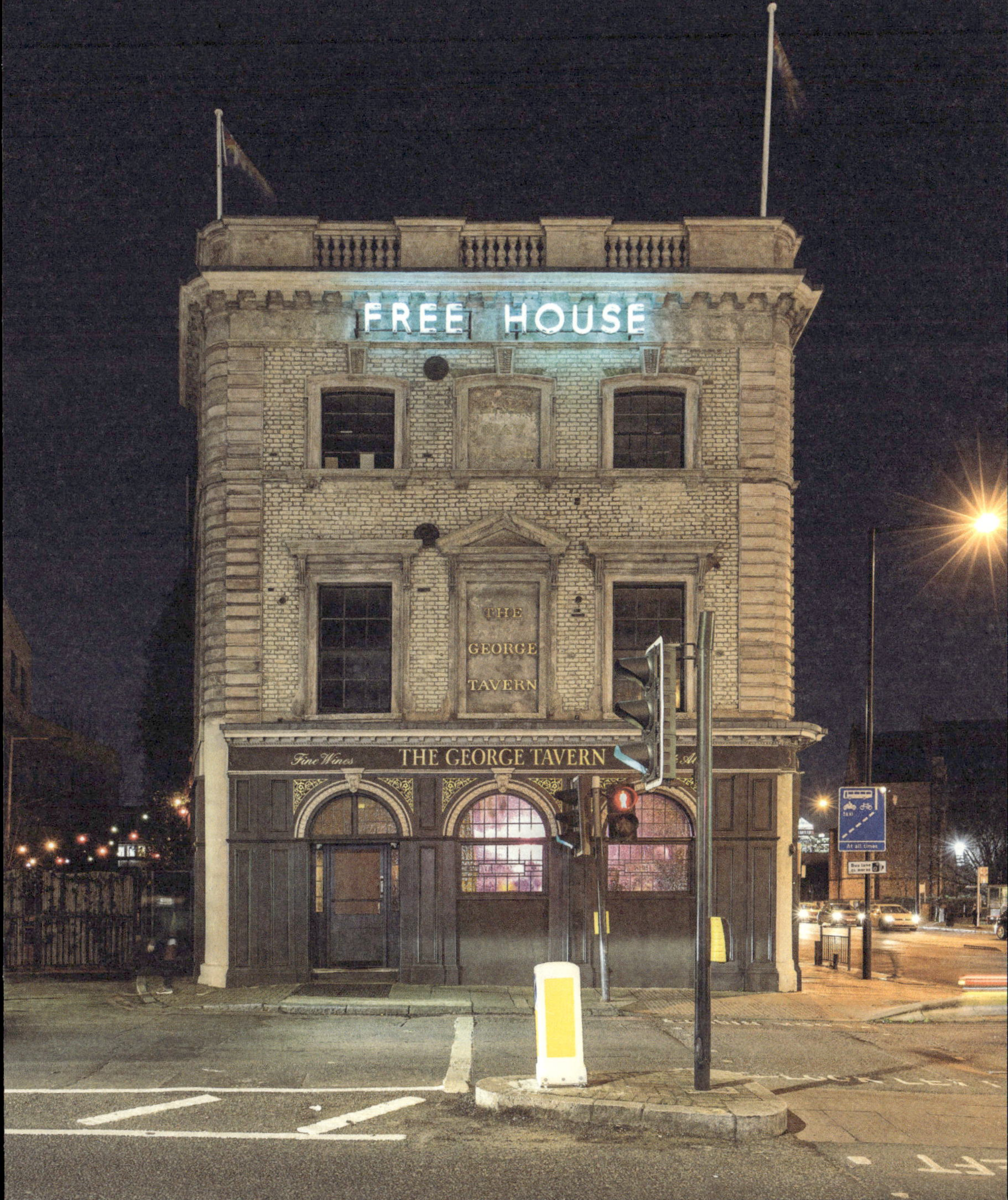

FREE HOUSE
THE GEORGE TAVERN
Fine Wines
THE GEORGE TAVERN

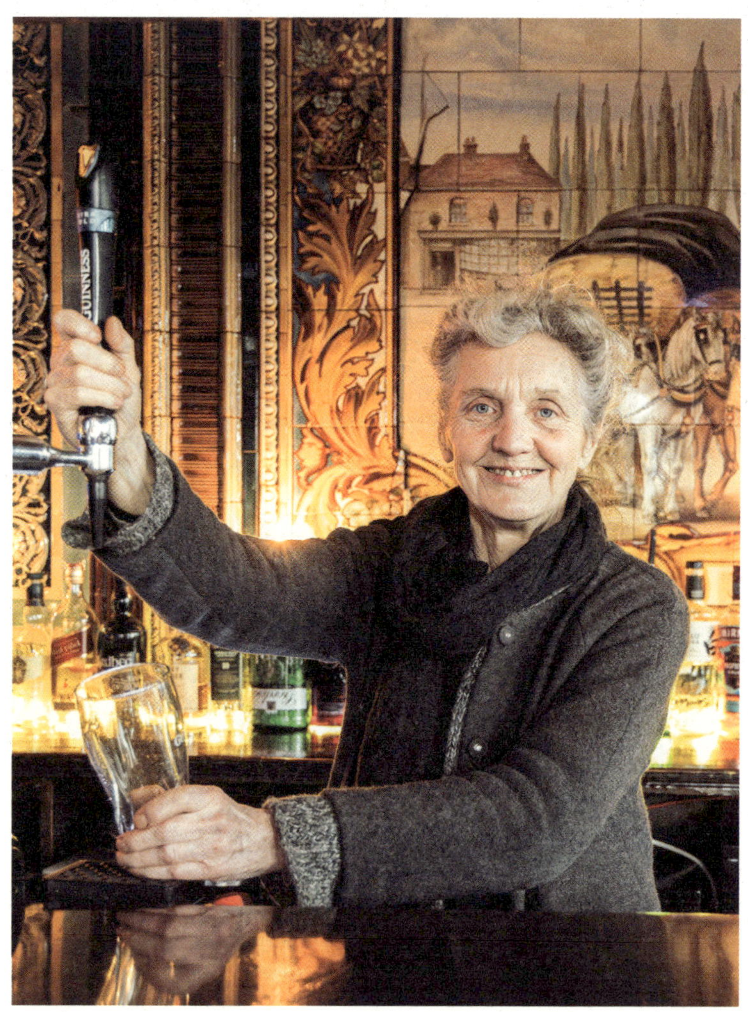

*Having an artist like Pauline Forster in charge to curate
The George Tavern's historic interiors has served the grand boozer well.*

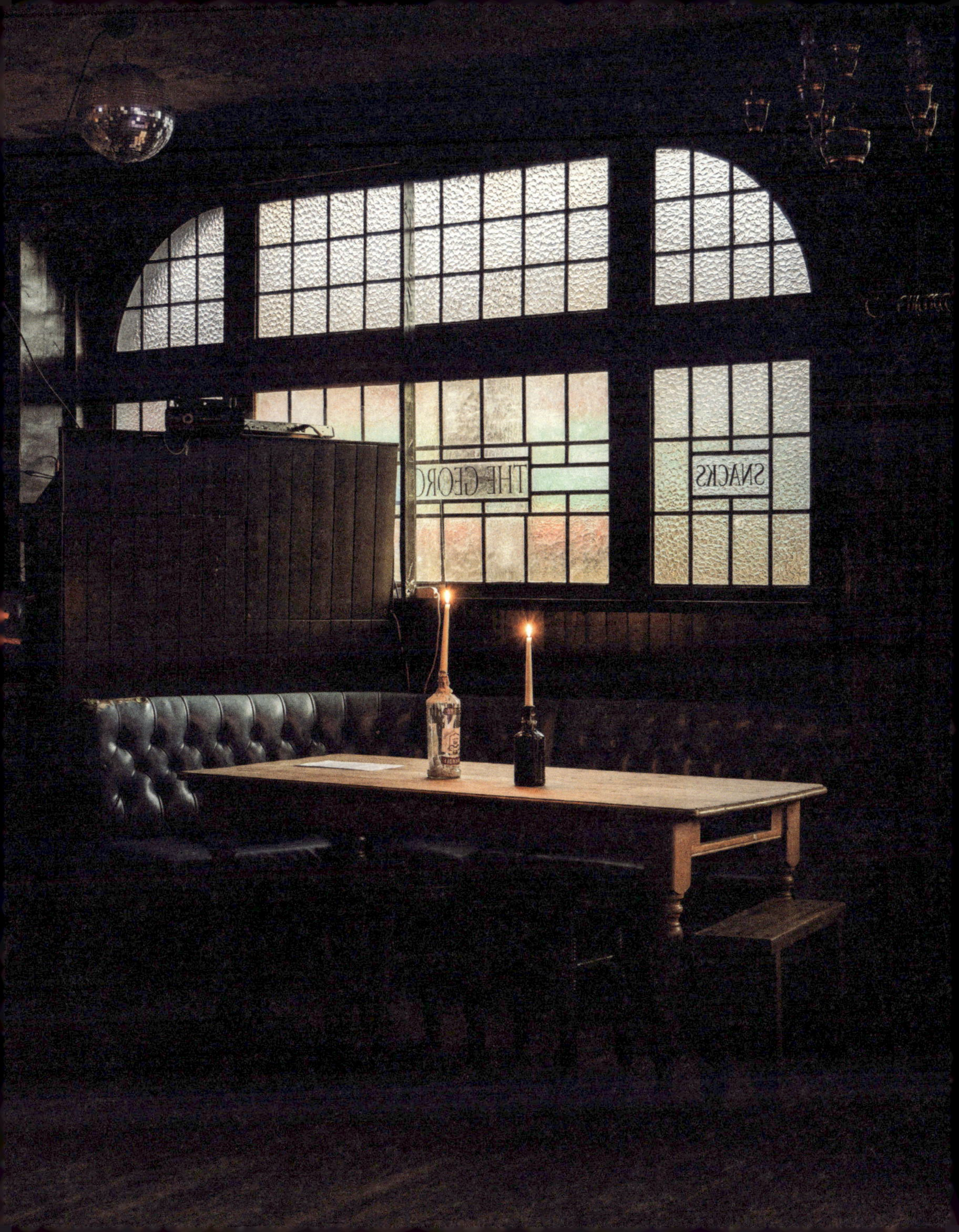

Turner's Old Star

A TIMELESS CLASSIC WITH AN ARTISTIC TALE

Since the turn of the millennium, the volume of traditional East End pubs has dwindled. Tastes and demographics are changing, people lead healthier lifestyles and the days of the backstreet local are almost over in some neighbourhoods. But the odd cosy inn remains, loyal to the old ways of life. Turner's Old Star is one such pub, affording those who stray from Wapping's well-trodden tourist path a nostalgic window into a bygone era.

There is a legend that the pub was founded by Romantic painter J.M.W. Turner when he inherited two cottages and converted them into a tavern. Allegedly, his lover Sophia Booth, a widow from Margate, moved in and they named the pub The Old Star. The story goes that, among locals, Turner was known by Sophia's surname and earned the nickname 'Puggy Booth' thanks to his portly stature. In 1987, the pub changed its name to Turner's Old Star as a tribute to the artist who stars in the local tale.

Its Guv'nors today are Bernice and Paul Drew. Both have strong connections to the area. Bernice's family have lived here for five generations and her uncle ran Turner's Old Star in the 1970s – she worked the bar herself as an 18-year-old. She met future husband Paul on the Stepney pub circuit in the 1970s, which was centred around the famous landlady Kate Hodder's pub, The Prince of Wales on Duckett Street. It was Paul who ended up surprising his wife by taking on the lease for Turner's Old Star, her family's much-loved boozer, in 2006.

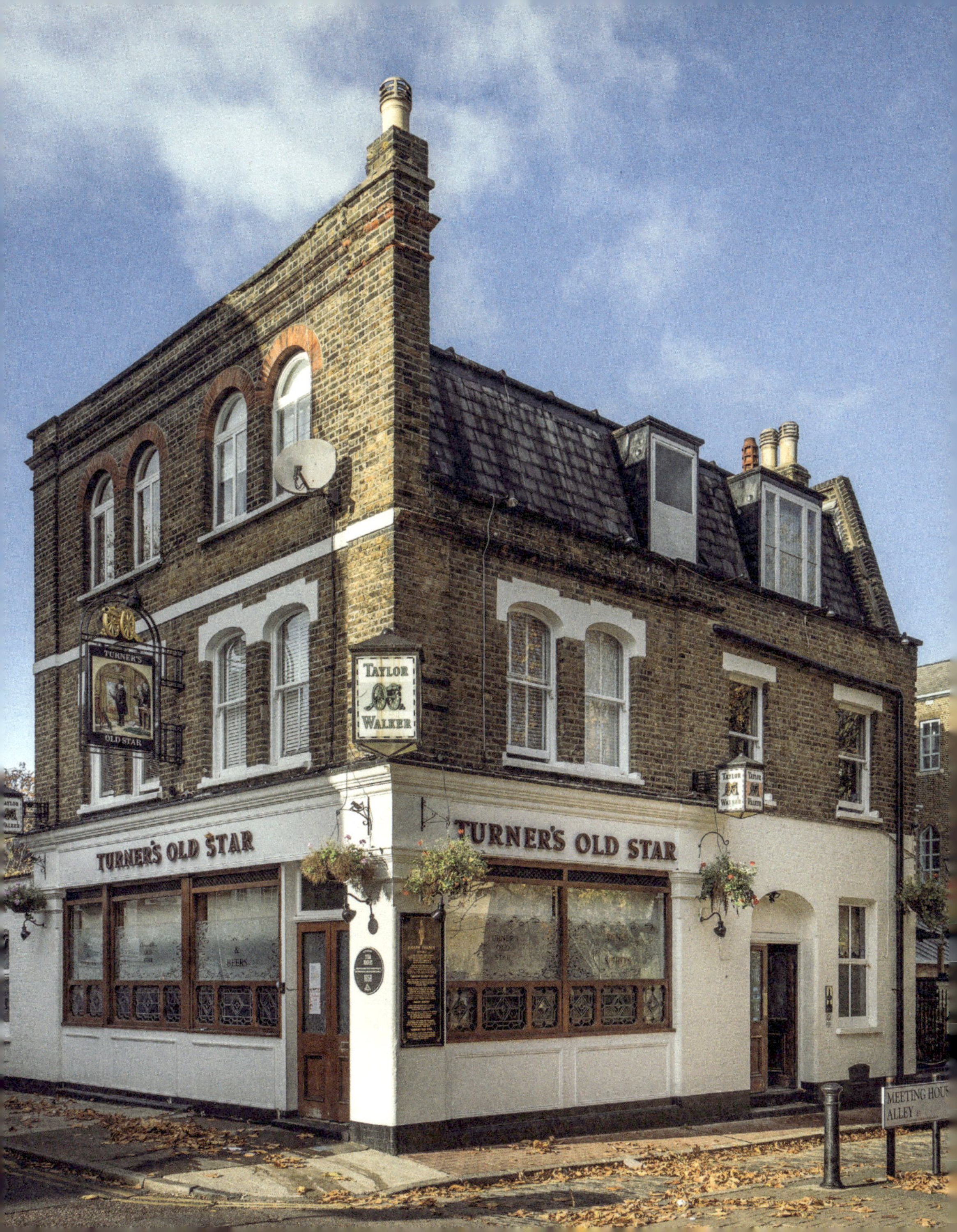

TURNER'S
OLD STAR
TAYLOR
WALKER
TURNER'S OLD STAR
TURNER'S OLD STAR
TAYLOR
WALKER
& BEERS
MEETING HOUSE
ALLEY

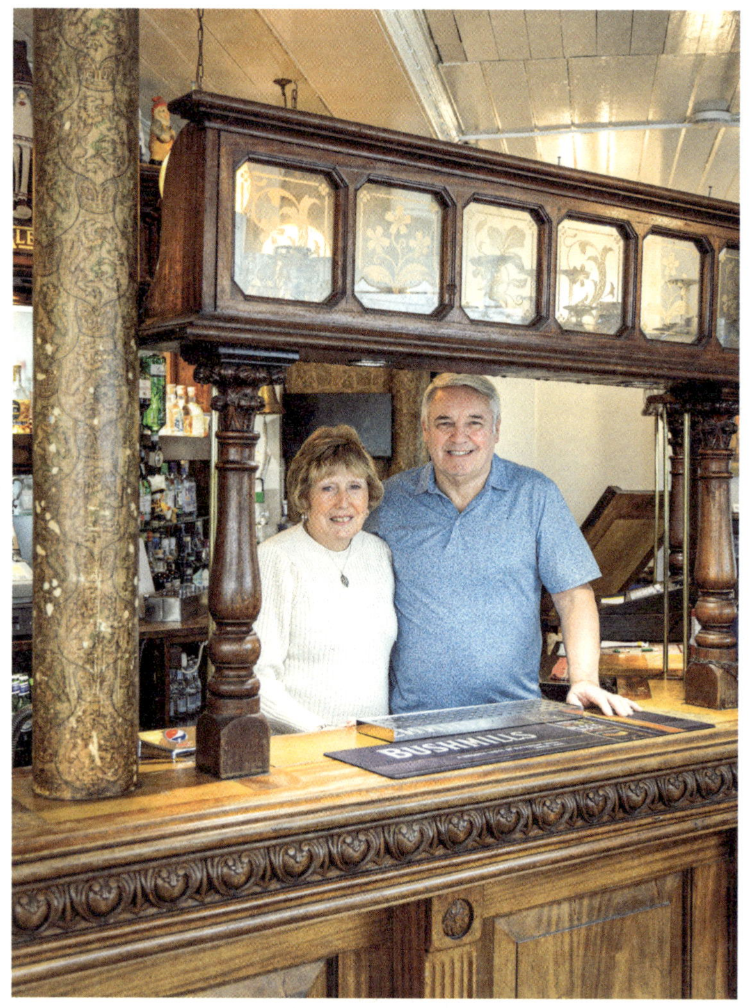

Bernice and Paul call Turner's Old Star their 'pub pub', due to it being true to the kind of proper East End pubs they patronised when they were young. It's taken a great deal of time, love and investment to maintain the pub's traditional atmosphere and legacy.

So authentic is its distinctive bar with glass panelling (left) that it looks like it belongs in a period drama. It's the beating heart of a pub where not only are drinks poured but stories are shared and wisdom imparted.

Maintaining a link with the past is not just important, it's essential to Bernice and Paul's vision of the pub. While many houses removed their pool tables and dart boards to free up space for dining, Turner's still participates in an East End pool league, which helps it to forge bonds with other boozers of its ilk.

When the crack of the white cue ball on the table falls silent there is a tranquillity which runs through the pub, created by locals and staff alike. The Drew family wish to ensure the pub is welcoming to all; televised live sports are a big focus along with a beautifully maintained beer garden, weekly quiz and monthly karaoke knees-up.

While most pubs with a convivial atmosphere and family link have disappeared across the East End, Turner's manages to keep visitors old and new coming back. Whether cheerily served by Bernice or her daughter Katie, or listening to raconteur Paul tell the tale of where the bullet holes in the woodwork come from with a pint of quality cask-conditioned ale in hand, Turner's treats new faces like old friends. It is a true London gem and a must-visit for anyone wishing to wet their whistle in a timeless East End tavern.

14 Watts Street, E1W 2QG

Bernice and Paul Drew are fully invested in the life of the local community, and always make sure the pub is involved in street parties and summer fêtes.

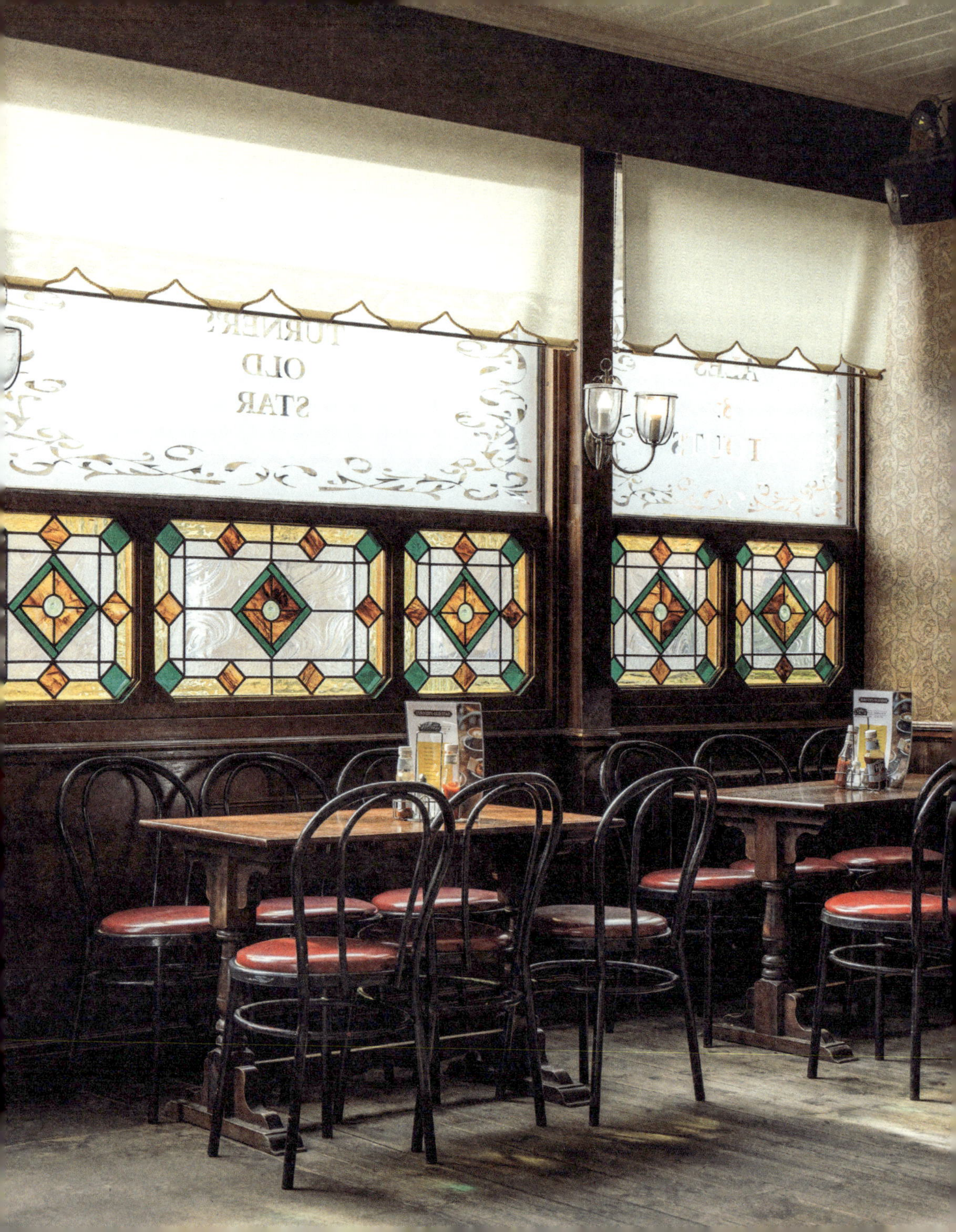
TURNER'S
OLD
STAR

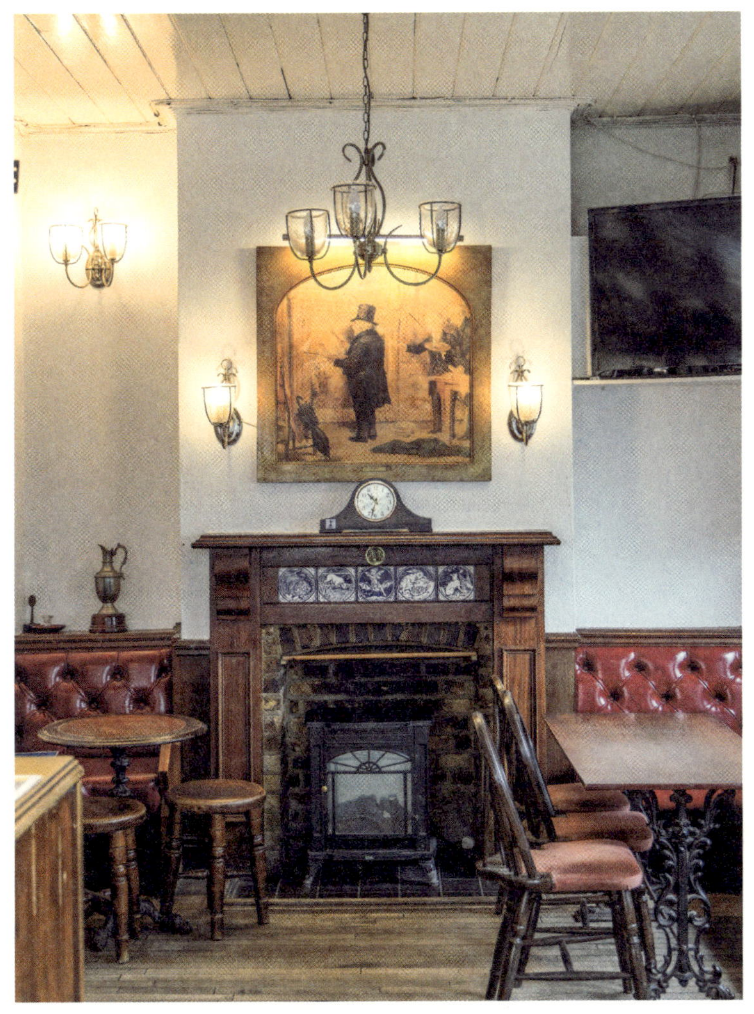

The Sebright Arms

A MUSICAL BACKSTREET TREASURE

In past decades, residents of the East End popped into their local every night for a pint and to catch up on local life. Now, people are less inclined to go to the pub as often – choosing to work out at the gym or watch Netflix instead. It's hard for any pubs to get people through the door on quiet week-nights, but even more difficult for backstreet boozers.

One of the first pubs to diversify in order to draw in more drinkers was this Charrington's pub built in 1936. Named after William Sebright, a 16th-century philanthropist and Town Clerk of London, The Sebright Arms is a lesser-known, but very handsome, boozer.

It has staged live music ever since it opened, and in the 1970s it even briefly became a punk venue called Solly's. Over the years, it continued to adapt to changing tastes – hosting disco nights and heavy metal bands, and later cabaret. The pub has since reverted to its original name, but live music is still the primary entertainment on offer.

Down in the cellar, a 120-capacity venue sees the wordsmiths and musicians of London's creative scene perform most nights of the week, with the pub playing host to acts including Charli XCX and Courtney Barnett. If raucous rock 'n' roll or electric beats aren't your thing, the pub is still the perfect place to while away an afternoon imbibing fine craft beer in an intimate setting. The Sebright Arms is rising to the challenge of providing a community-oriented local that caters to everyone.

31–35 Coate Street, E2 9AG

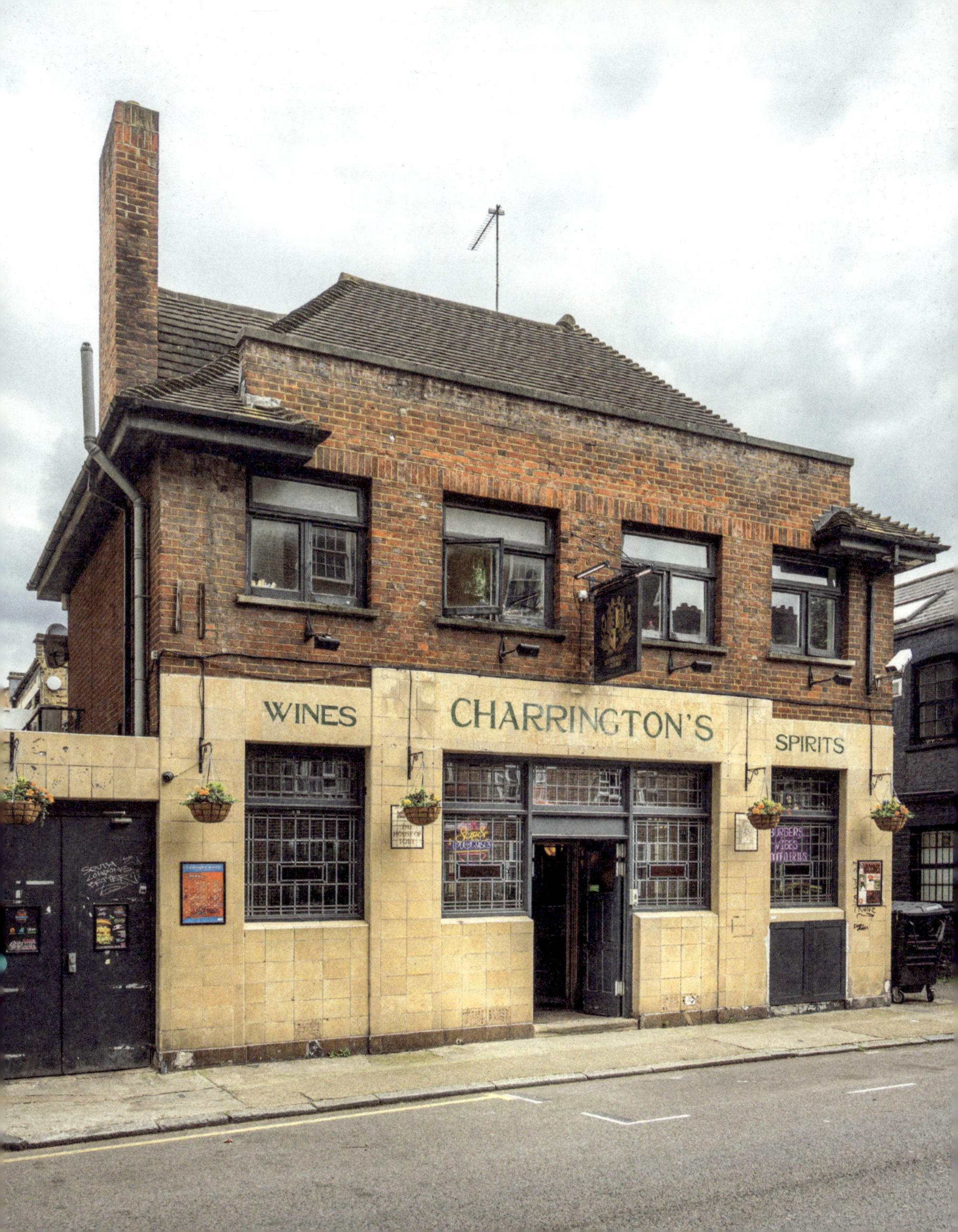

WINES
CHARRINGTON'S
SPIRITS

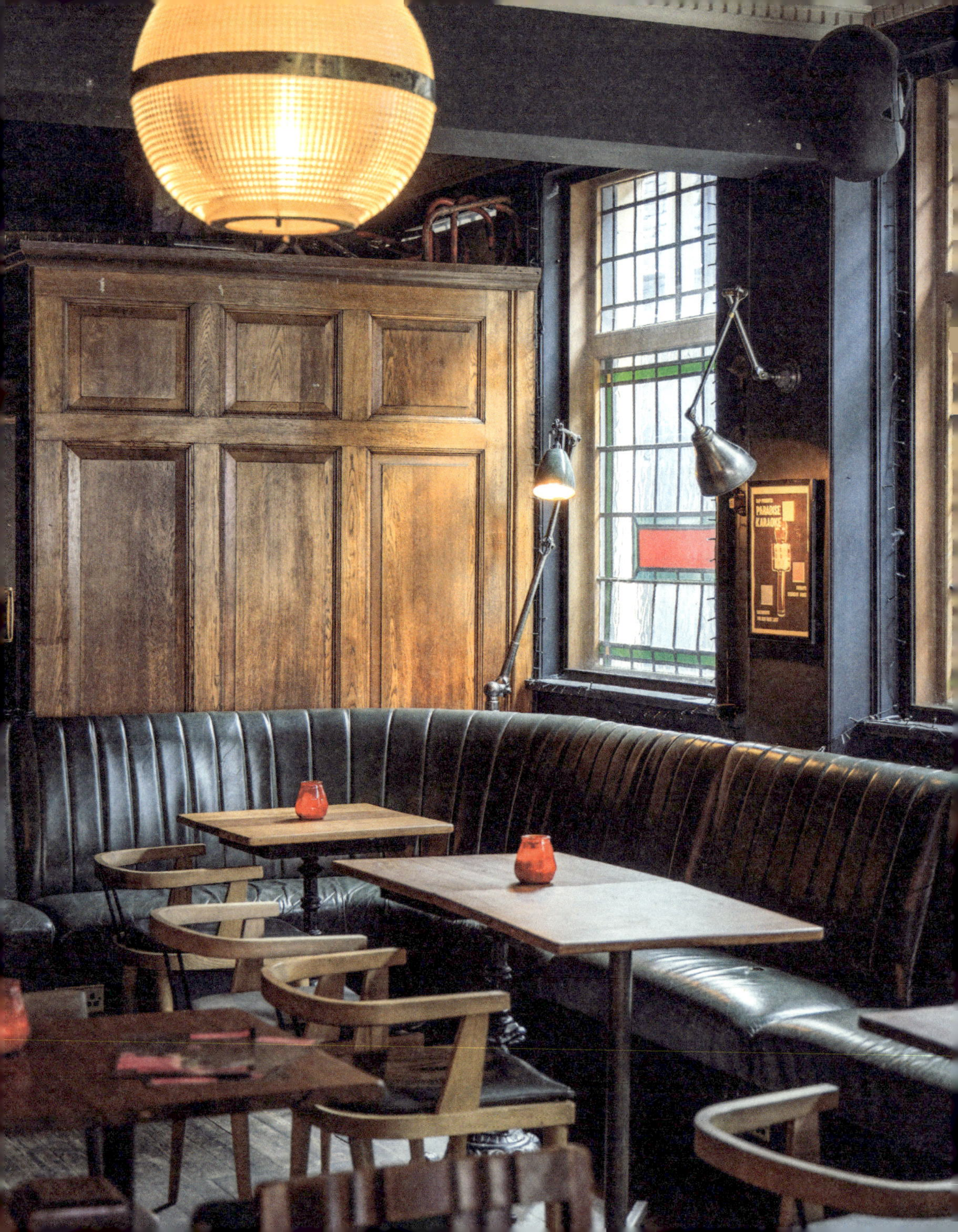

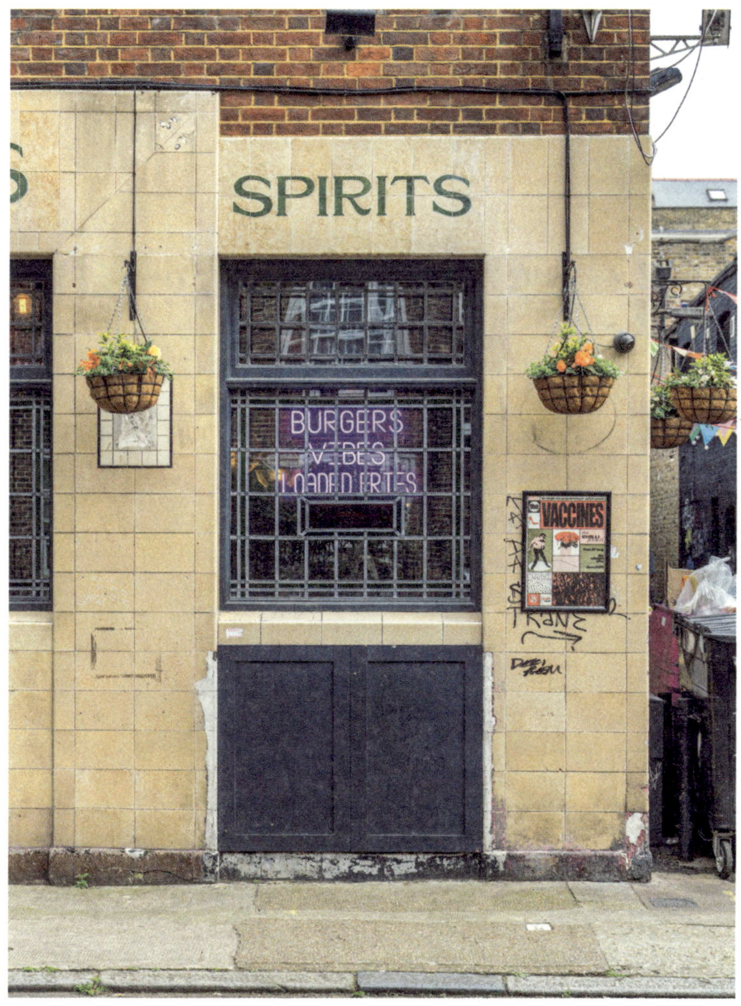

(Opposite) Traditional wood panelling and low-lighting creates
a cosy atmosphere for punters lingering over their drinks.

The Town of Ramsgate

RIVERSIDE INSTITUTION THAT HAS SEEN IT ALL

Sitting at the end of Wapping High Street's ancient and cobbled thoroughfare, the Town of Ramsgate has seen it all over the years. Believed to be among the oldest pubs on the Thames, with records dating back to 1545, it has been serving frothy tankards for almost half a millennium.

Down a narrow alley along the side of the pub lie the Wapping Old Stairs, once used by watermen to take their passengers to boats waiting to ferry them across the Thames. One of the most famous incidents to occur on the Wapping Old Stairs was the capture of the viciously cruel 'Hanging Judge' George Jeffreys in 1688, while he was attempting to flee the country after King James II was deposed. Fittingly, he was recognised by a man who'd narrowly escaped the noose. The pub was frequented by smugglers, and crime has long been a part of its history – nearby, Execution Dock saw men condemned by the naval courts hanged for crimes such as piracy and murder, and legend has it that the pub cellars were used to hold convicts awaiting transportation to the colonies.

The Town of Ramsgate is now a much-loved family-run business operated by Sonia and Bruno Cernecca. They took over from Sonia's parents, Janet and Peter Biddle, who ran the pub since 2005. The Ramsgate prides itself on offering first-class food and beverages at sensible prices, and fine ales from four handpumps are served alongside belt-loosening portions of fish and chips. Now that its gory days are behind it, the Ramsgate is an intimate riverside bolthole that's ideal for taking refuge from the elements to linger over some hearty sustenance and restorative refreshment.

62 Wapping High Street, E1W 2PN

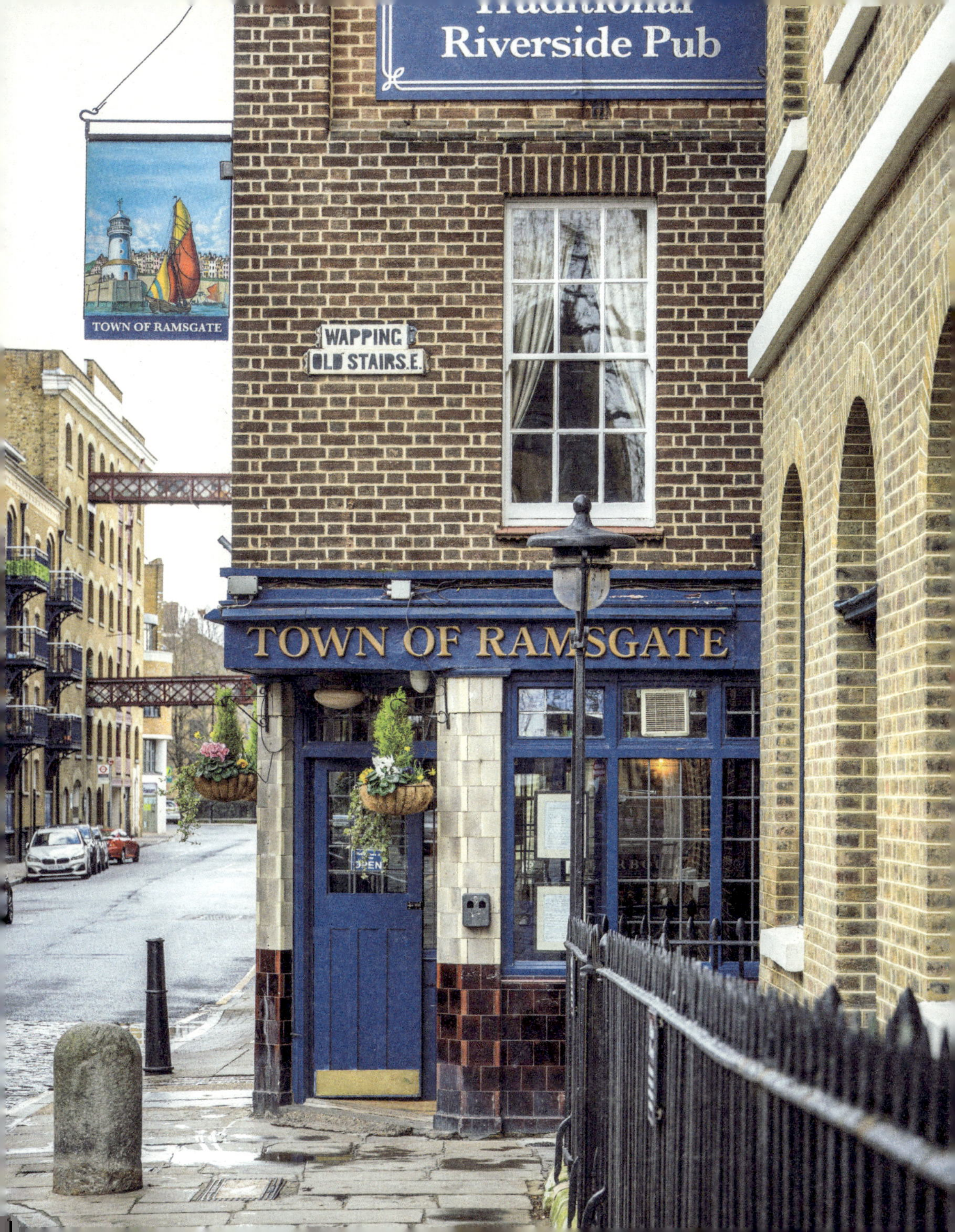

Traditional
Riverside Pub
TOWN OF RAMSGATE
WAPPING
OLD STAIRS.E.
TOWN OF RAMSGATE

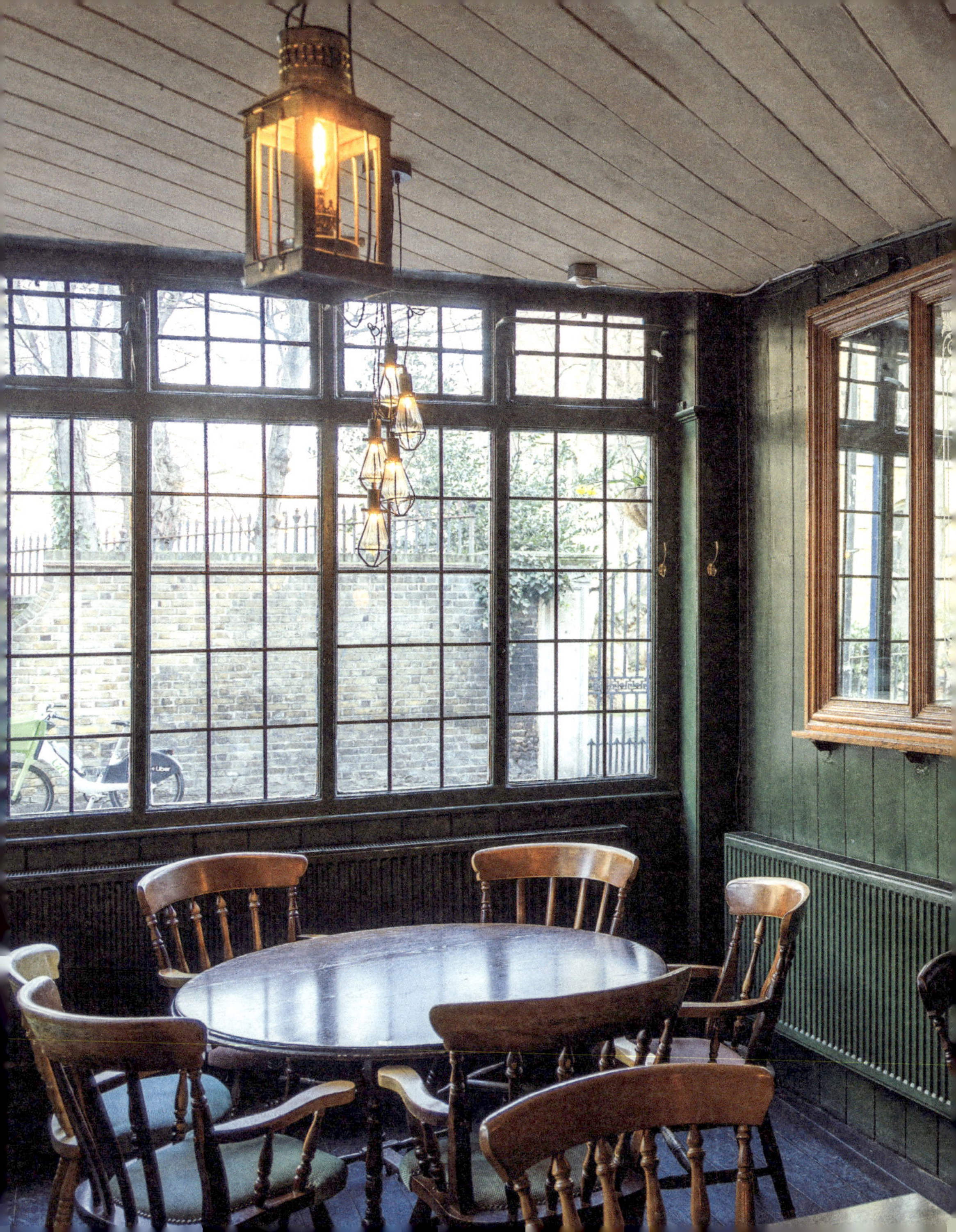

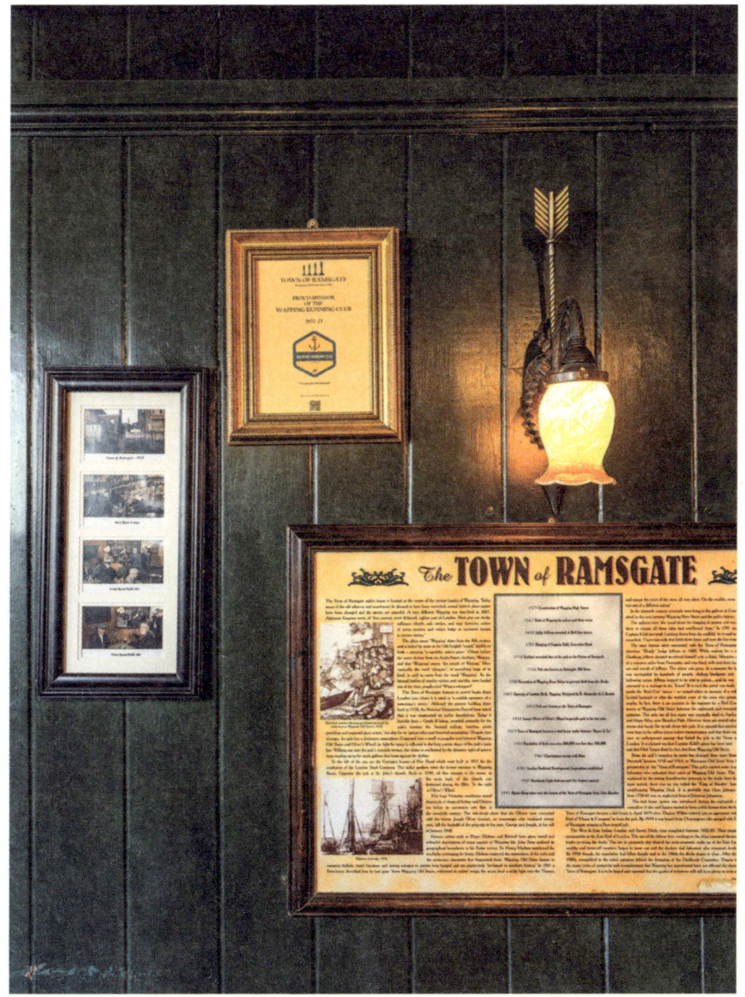

A history of *The Town of Ramsgate* sits alongside a certificate for sponsoring a local running club, showing that the pub is as invested in its area as ever.

The Lord Nelson

POPULAR COMMUNITY BOOZER ON THE ISLAND

In the distant past, sailors from all over the globe passed through London's Docklands. Some for just a short time, many for longer, while others never left – but most would have spent at least a few hours in the Thames-side taverns, squandering wages and swapping stories ahead of their next voyage. This would have been an everyday scene at the Lord Nelson, built in 1855. At one time a life-sized statue of Admiral Lord Nelson stood on the pub's roof, overlooking the entrance and welcoming sailors.

Visitors seeking to experience a relaxed old-school East End boozer can do no better than the Lord Nelson, the sister pub to The Ferry House (p.170), which is nearby. The Nelson pays homage to Millwall F.C., a football club founded on the Isle of Dogs in 1885 who originally played on the ground behind the pub. The collection of football scarves and memorabilia generates a homely warmth, but to maintain local harmony, the colours of West Ham United (originally founded as Thames Ironworks F.C., their stadium is now just outside the East End in Newham) are displayed alongside framed Millwall shirts.

Hosting live music or karaoke as well as their famous barbecues every summer, the Nelson is still a destination for revellers looking to blow off some steam. Although they no longer cater to the transient world of naval officers and buccaneers, they still welcome many locals who've moved to London from across the seas. Just as those sea farers did long ago.

1 Manchester Road, E14 3BD

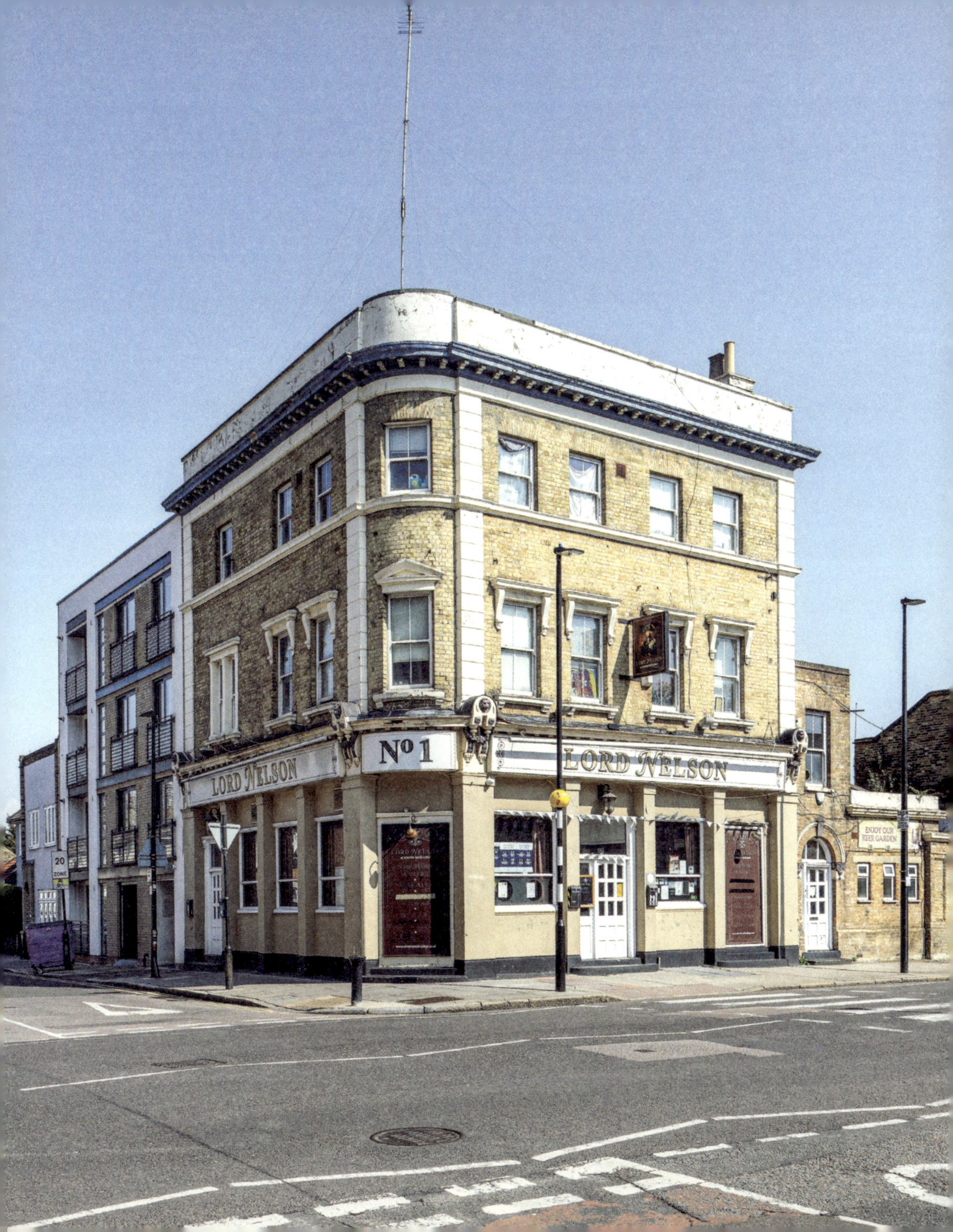

LORD NELSON
No 1
LORD NELSON
20 ZONE
ENJOY OUR BEER GARDEN

The Pride of Spitalfields

A SLICE OF EAST END PERFECTION

Hidden away from the hotel bars and small plates restaurants that now surround Old Spitalfields Market lies the East End's most unabashedly authentic boozer. Many refurbished London pubs are often described as 'pubs for people who don't actually like pubs' due to their sanitised and homogenised interiors, but The Pride is truly worthy of its name, as it epitomises everything great about the traditional London pub.

Beginning life as The Romford Arms in the early 1800s under the aegis of the Star Brewery, it has remained a consistently excellent boozer for centuries. In 1985, the current landlady Ann Butler and her late husband Kerry changed its name to The Pride of Spitalfields. Having moved from The Royal Saxon in Paddington, which they'd also renamed The Pride of the Canal, the prefix travelled with them.

Before the millennium, most pubs in the East End were like The Pride, so a visit allows younger punters a window into a bygone world of proper public houses: low ceilings, a tight bar with a generous number of cask ales on offer and walls decorated with old prints. On a raucous East End night, the sounds of ivories being tickled on an 'ol Joanna can still be heard, as the dulcet voices of suitably refreshed patrons belt out songs. It is an anchor to an older way of life that has slowly been eroded. And for some it can feel like the one constant in a changing world.

Whether ducking in for a livener or a sing-song while enjoying some of the many well-kept ales from Ann's partner Marc's cellar, this is unequivocally the perfect East End pub.

3 Heneage Street, E1 5LJ

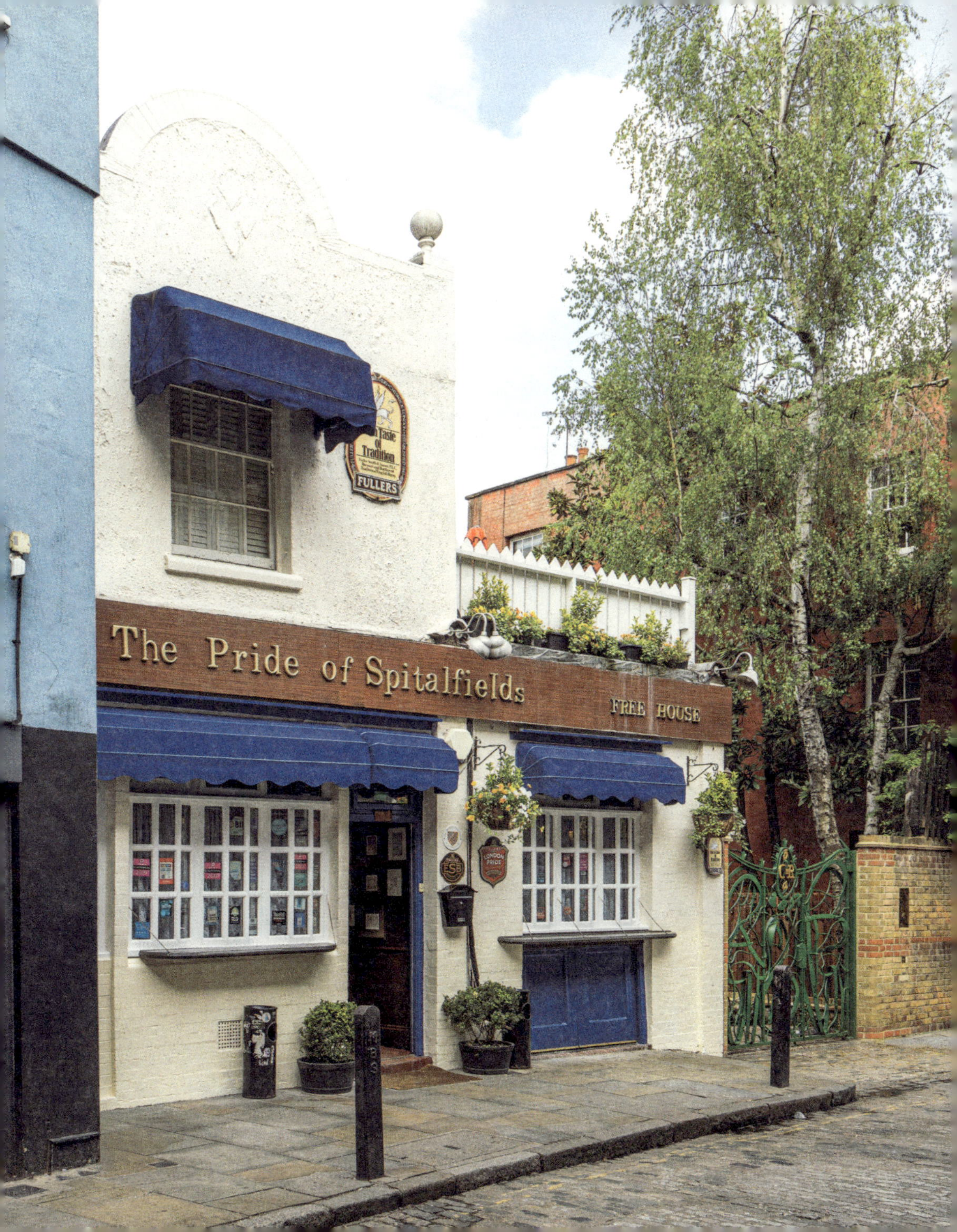
Taste
of
Tradition
FULLERS
The Pride of Spitalfields
FREE HOUSE
ESB
LONDON
PRIDE

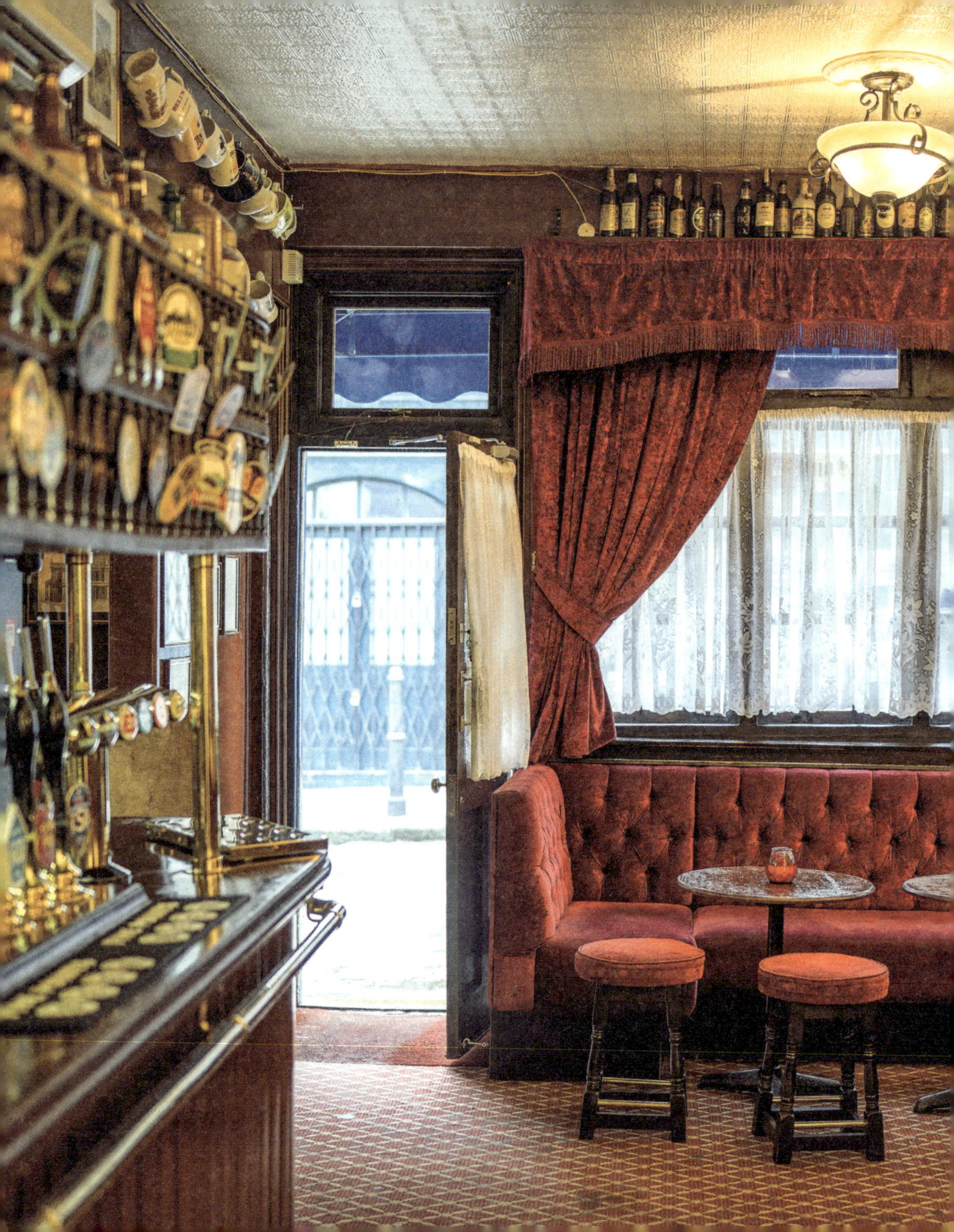

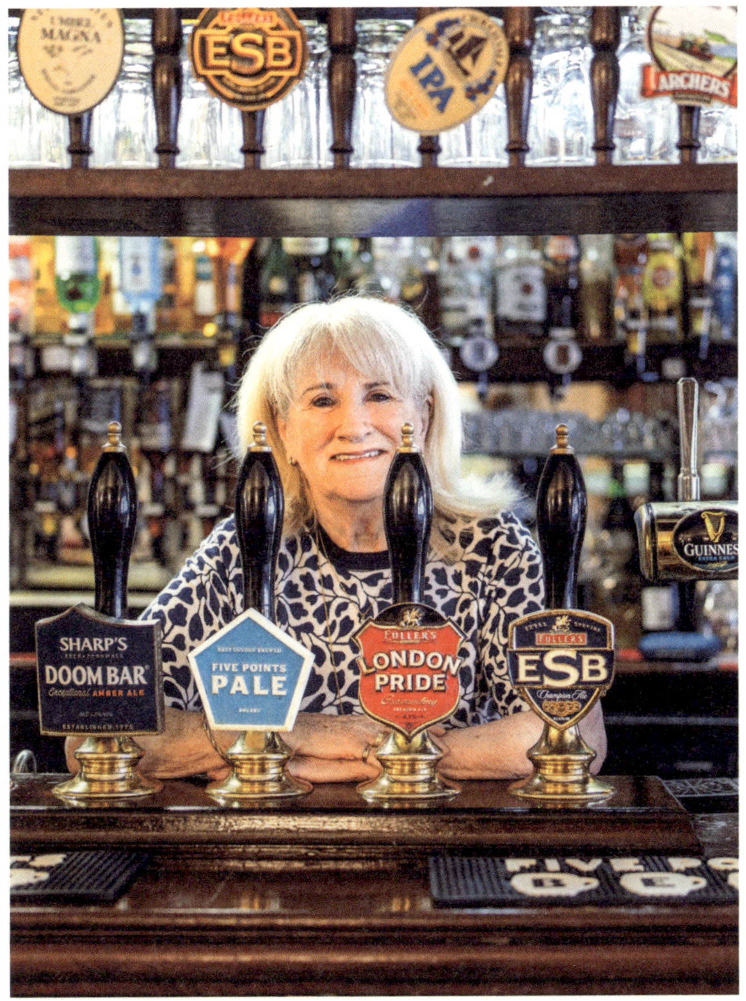

*Ann Butler has been the beloved
landlady of The Pride of Spitalfields since 1985.*

The Artful Dodger

A CHEERY ENCLAVE OF COCKNEY LIFE

Below the tracks of the Docklands Light Railway, thousands of trains pass by The Artful Dodger on their way to the City. It is one of London's most intriguing public houses and yet, bizarrely, remains an enigma to most of us.

While its striking exterior and unusual name catch the attention of many passengers, very few ever venture into its friendly confines. They are certainly poorer for it, as it is a treat for any traditional London pub aficionado. Formerly a warehouse, the first pub here was the Crown & Seven Stars, which opened in 1904, before it became The Artful Dodger in 1985. In today's world, it serves locals from the estate behind the pub and office workers from the City. A friendly welcome from staff, and the fact that no drinks are priced over five pounds, makes it a refreshingly jovial pub.

Many of the older customers who sit at the wooden bar are community stalwarts who have lived in the same area their whole lives. The same can be said for the Guv'nors Danny Corrigan and Georgiana Mercieca who have been at the helm since 2014. Both were raised in the area and have lived here for over 34 years.

The Dodger is the perfect spot to while away an afternoon or evening, whether playing pool or darts, chatting to firm friends quickly made or gazing up at the DLR tracks from the suntrap beer garden and wondering if the people looking down at the Grade II-listed boozer from the trains will one day visit this spot themselves.

47 Royal Mint Street, E1 8LG

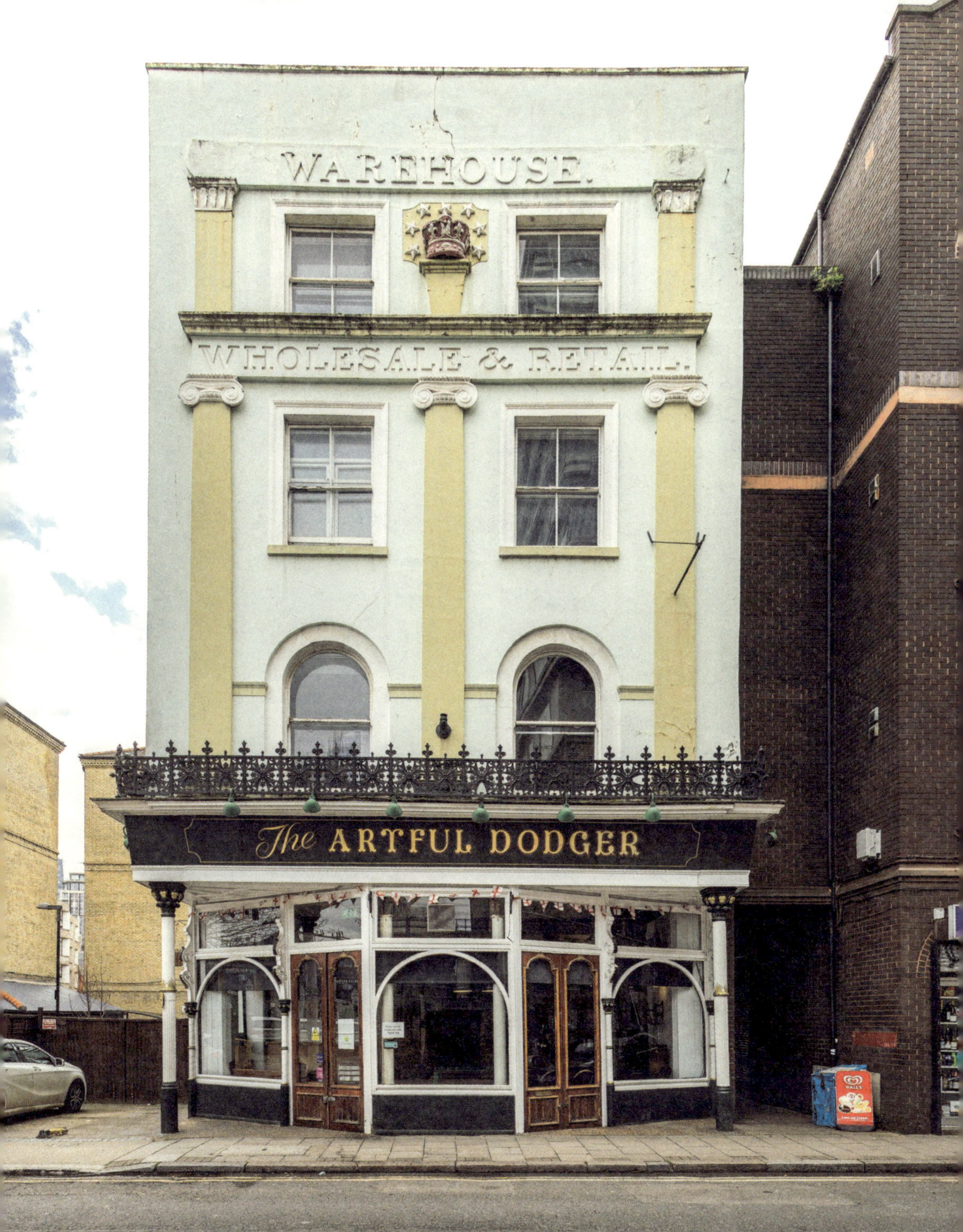

WAREHOUSE.
WHOLESALE & RETAIL.
The ARTFUL DODGER

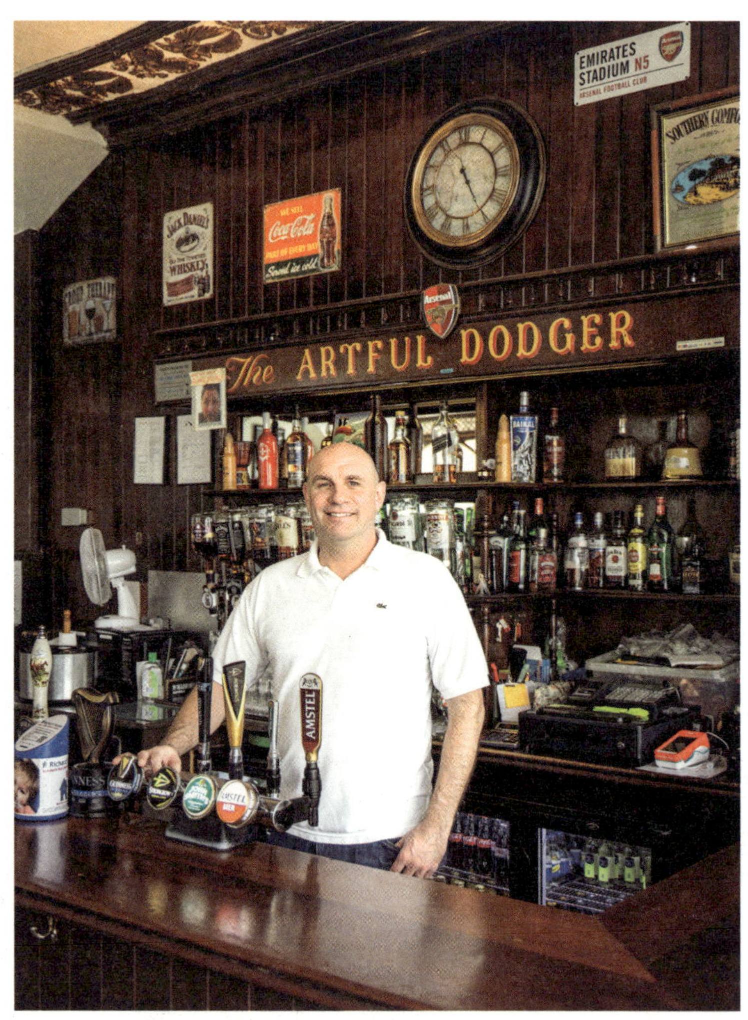

Danny Corrigan grew up in the area and has been
Guv'nor of The Artful Dodger since 2014.

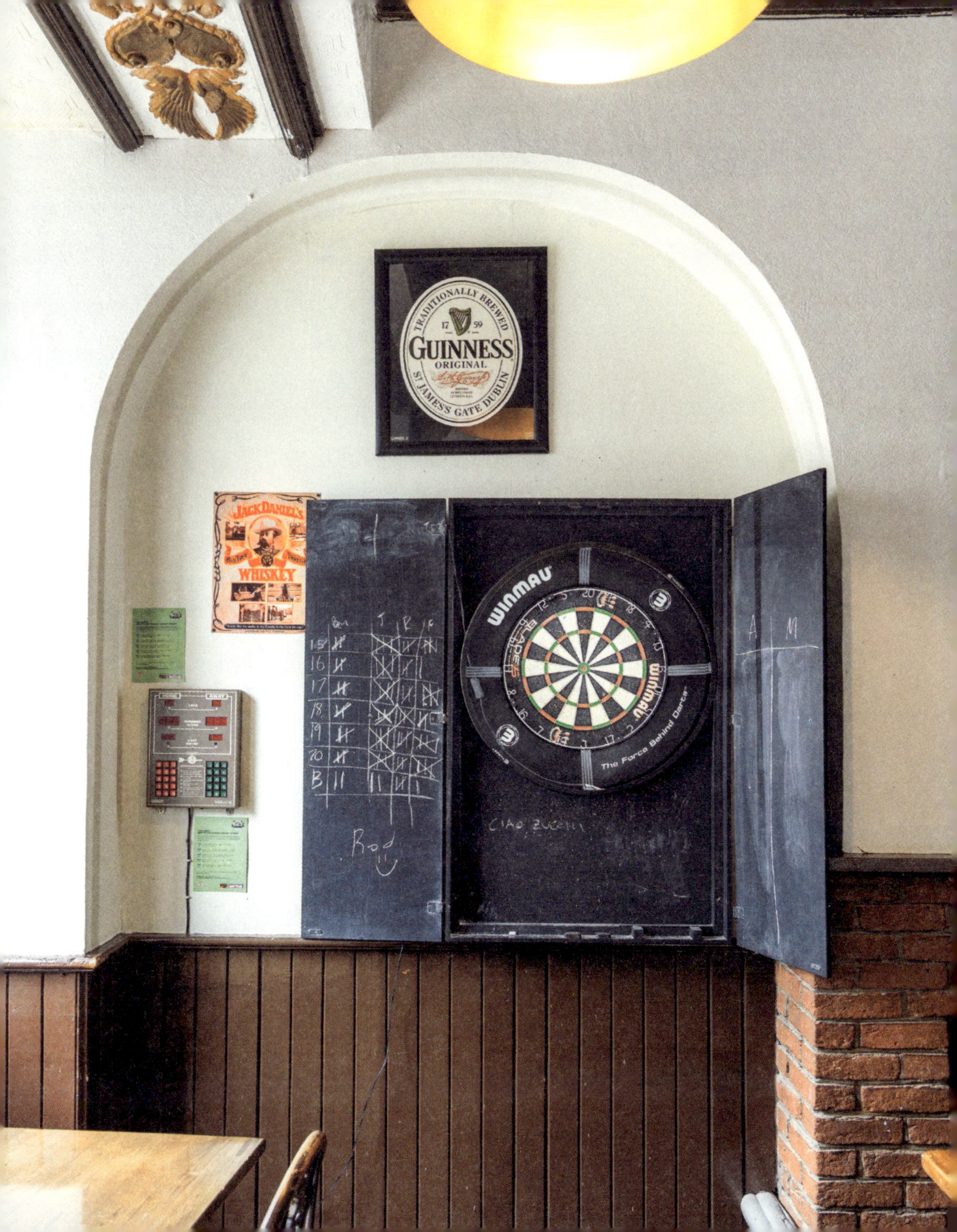

TRADITIONALLY BREWED
17 59
GUINNESS
ORIGINAL
ST JAMES'S GATE DUBLIN
JACK DANIEL'S
WHISKEY
WINMAU
The Force Behind Darts
CIAO ZUCCHI
Rod

The Marquis of Cornwallis

Situated on the corner of Bethnal Green Road, halfway between the Underground station and Shoreditch High Street, The Marquis of Cornwallis could be considered the geographical epicentre of the traditional Cockney's Bethnal Green. Just a short distance on foot from this corner pub lie most of the East End's lodestars. Columbia Road Flower Market, Repton Boxing Club, E Pellicci's cafe, St Matthew's Church and G Kelly's pie and mash shop have been constant staples for many families since time immemorial.

These landmarks have managed to retain their traditions, while sadly many of the local pubs have not. The Marquis of Cornwallis has pleasingly continues to appeal to traditionalists and elderly drinkers by keeping one eye on the past. Although the pub is run by the Craft Union Pub Company, it is thought of as a 'proper pub'. It has affordable pints, live music and opens at 11am (as all pubs once did), so older locals prop up the island bar early doors. The exchange at the barstools is always convivial with many tales shared of the neighbourhood's former glories. Returning to the old manor to call on relatives after moving away can be hard for many Cockneys due to the scale of change the area has seen over the decades, especially if their former local has become a gastro-pub or shifted its focus to craft beer and artisan spirits. But The Marquis remains a home away from home.

For those seeking a more down-to-earth pub experience reminiscent of the 1970s and 80s, filled with gassy continental lager, horses on the telly and pop music from the past, this pub is a landmark that never disappoints.

304 Bethnal Green Road, E2 0AG

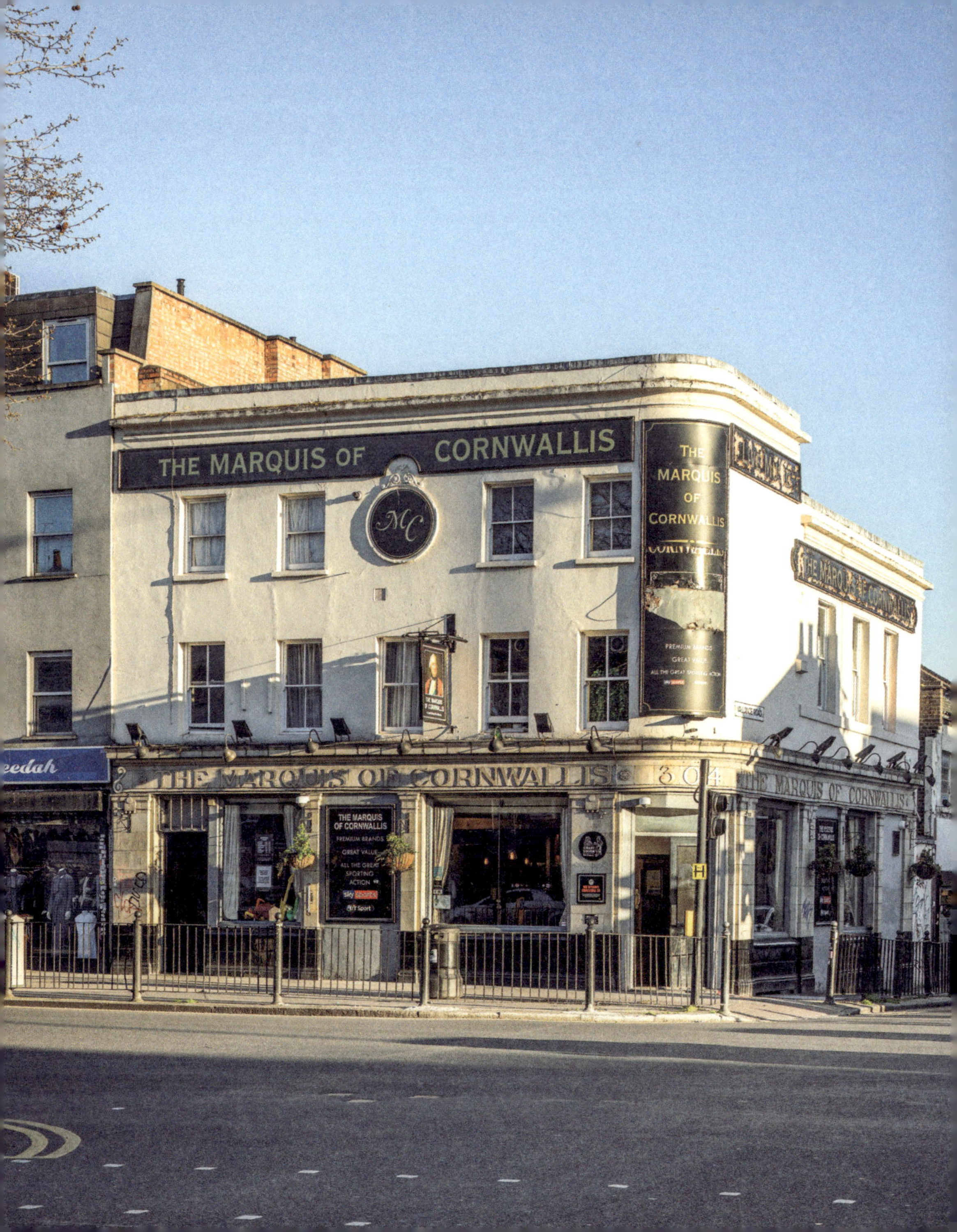
THE MARQUIS OF CORNWALLIS
MC
THE
MARQUIS
OF
Cornwallis
PREMIUM BRANDS
GREAT VALUE
ALL THE GREAT SPORTING ACTION
THE MARQUIS OF CORNWALLIS
304
THE MARQUIS OF CORNWALLIS
THE MARQUIS OF CORNWALLIS
PREMIUM BRANDS
GREAT VALUE
ALL THE GREAT SPORTING ACTION
sky SPORTS
BT Sport
eedah
H

The Wenlock Arms

A HISTORIC CASK ALE PUB RUN BY AN AFFABLE LANDLORD

Those who stray from City Road are sure to be impressed by The Wenlock Arms. Originally a tap room for the Wenlock Brewery, which closed in 1962, the pub now stands as a relic from another time. After it too temporarily closed in 2010, there were real fears that it might be demolished. Luckily, tenacious campaigning led by the local community and Campaign for Real Ale (CAMRA) won the day and it reopened in 2013.

Landlord Marcus Grant has overseen The Wenlock Arms since then. The gregarious Scot from Carnoustie is a quintessentially old-school Guv'nor. If Marcus is not keeping the ten cask ale lines in excellent condition or rustling up toasted sandwiches, you'll find him with a bar towel over his shoulder regaling punters with tales from his pub-going past.

The pub's unashamedly traditional interior is part of its honest charm: branded mirrors, old black-and-white photographs on the walls and stripped wooden floors beneath a tidy horseshoe bar afford guests the opportunity to drink in a slice of the past from their bar stool.

The Wenlock prides itself on being an inclusive pub where patrons come for a pint and a chat. Some of its most loyal punters are local nonagenarians who have lived in the area their whole lives and have rich tales to tell. For those of a nostalgic nature there isn't a finer location than this classic gem, which thankfully defied the odds and came back from the dead.

26 Wenlock Road, N1 7TA

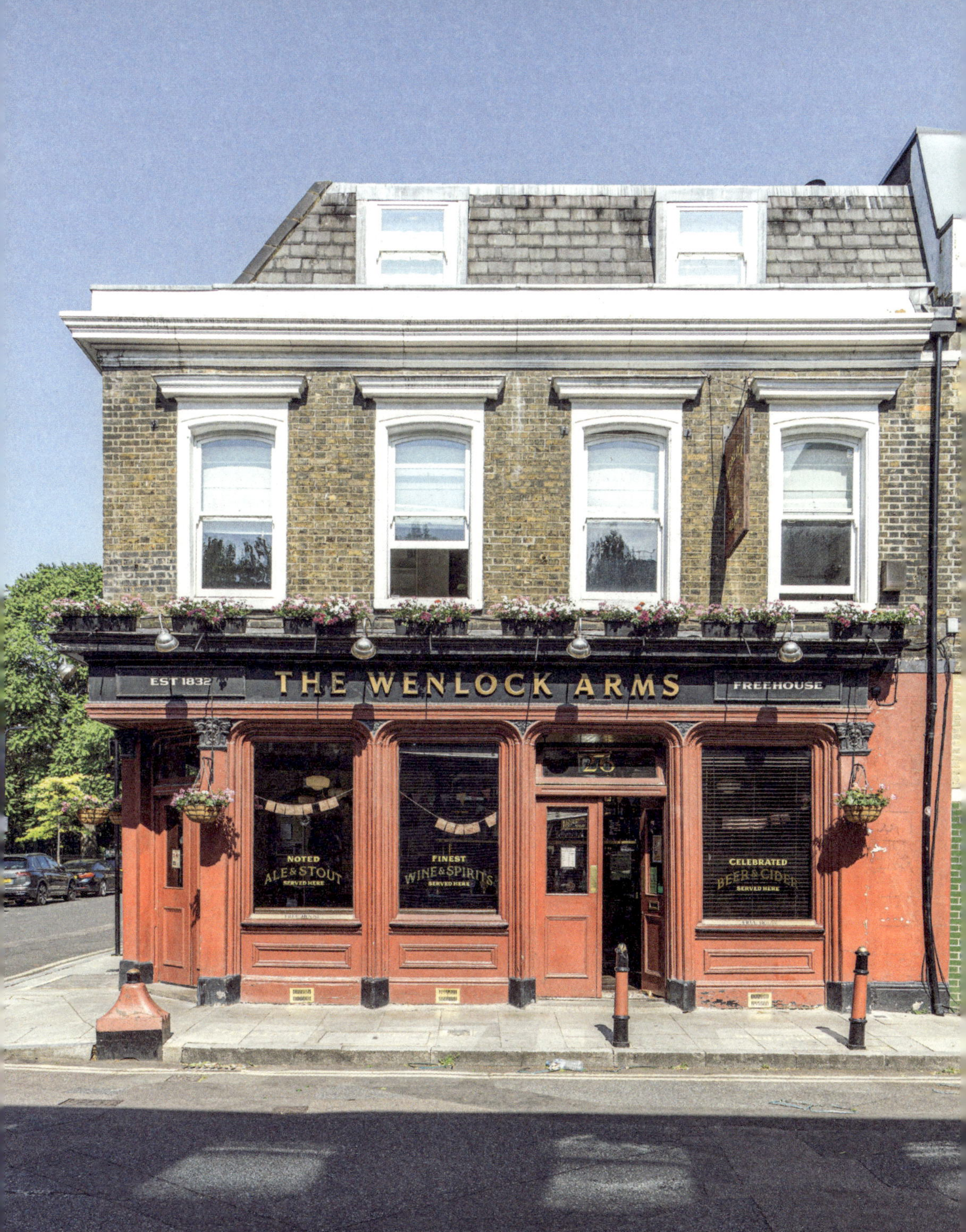
EST 1832
THE WENLOCK ARMS
FREEHOUSE
NOTED
ALE & STOUT
SERVED HERE
FINEST
WINE & SPIRITS
SERVED HERE
CELEBRATED
BEER & CIDER
SERVED HERE

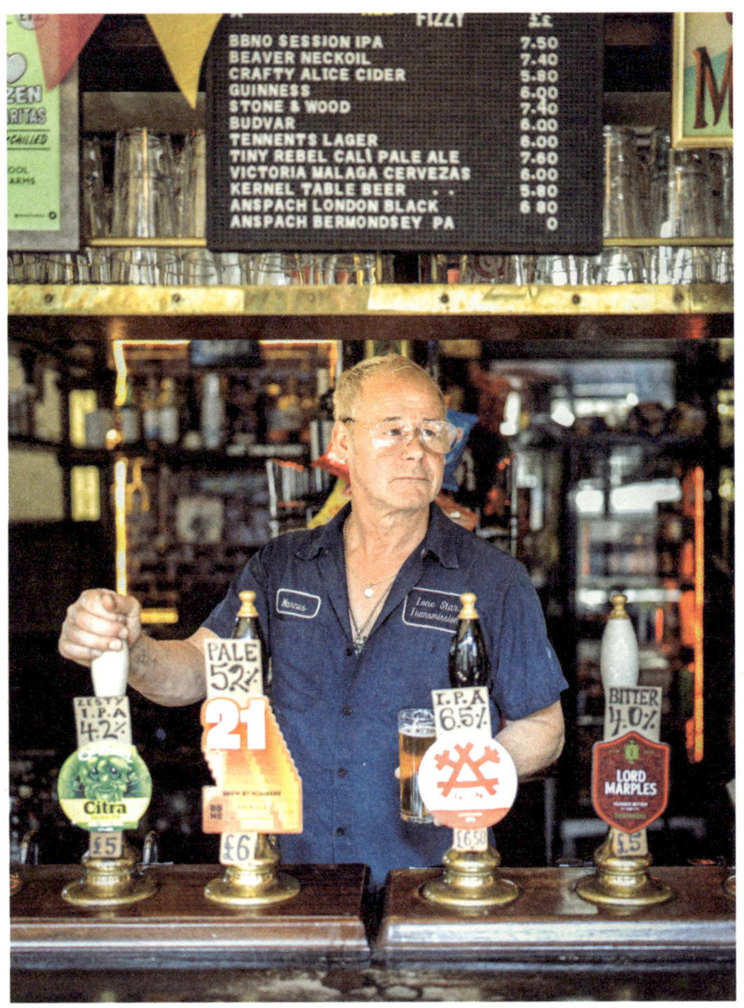

Landlord Marcus Grant takes exceptional pride in serving up quality cask ale to his thirsty loyal customers.

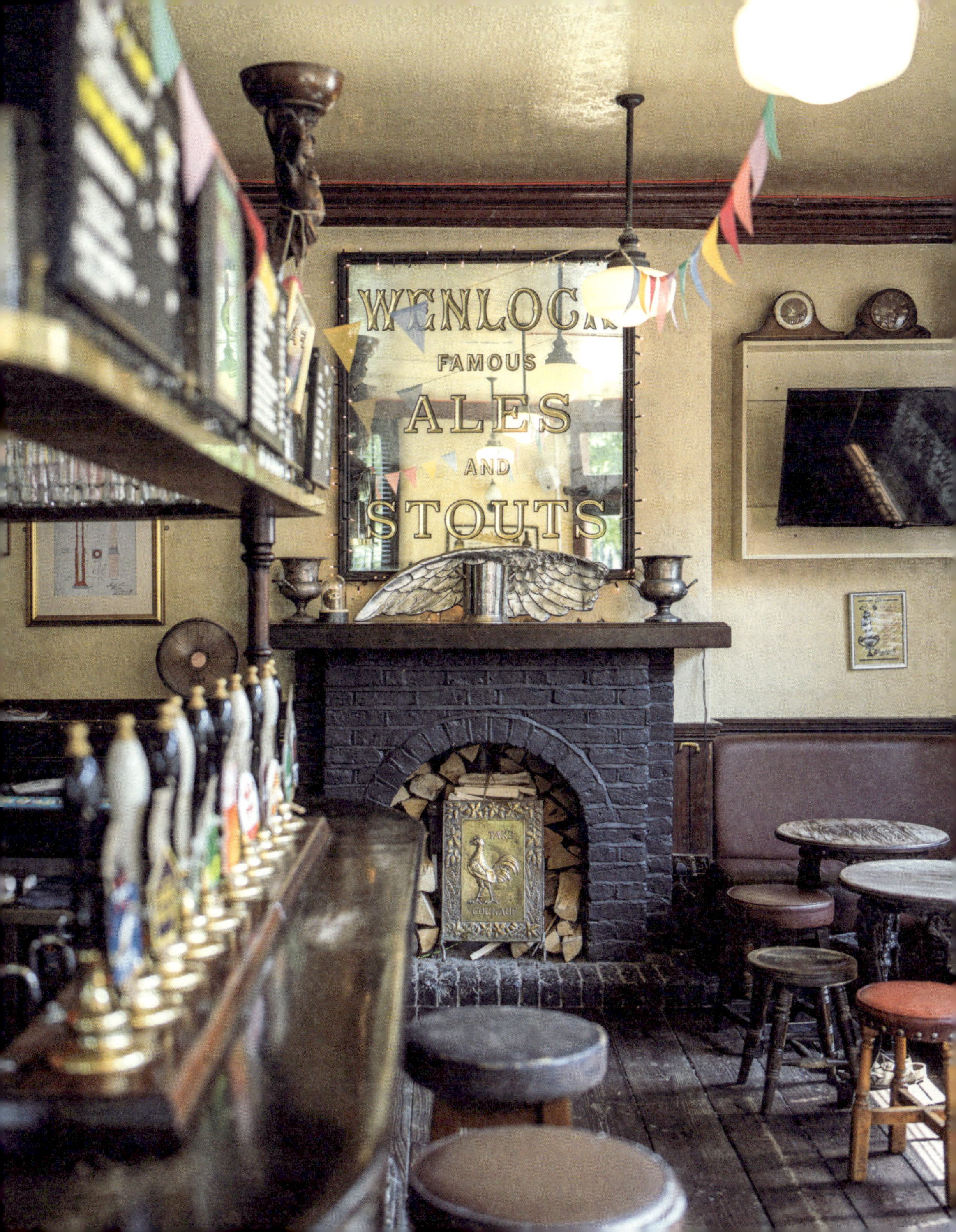
WENLOCK
FAMOUS
ALES
AND
STOUTS
TAKE
COURAGE

The Brown Bear

Squashed between two huge arterial roads lies a warren of compact streets where the social history of the East End oozes from the ground. Ancient churches, boxing gyms and the odd backstreet boozer cling on in a drastically different landscape, whose culture is always evolving. These pubs, once called dens of iniquity by social reformers such as Charles Booth, whose poverty maps of London traced the city's economic inequalities, are the beating heart of the old East End, offering sanctuary from the travails of a pertinacious life.

Today, the area around Leman Street has a handful of wet-led pubs that have managed to survive due to the abundance of office workers and their propensity to imbibe after (and during) a working day. One of their favourites is the Grade II-listed Brown Bear. It originally opened in 1793, but was rebuilt by Limehouse brewers Taylor Walker & Co. in 1830 and retains the brass rails and windowsills that give the pub its old-world charm. Its cheery blue facade, with Taylor Walker's branding proudly displayed above hanging flower baskets, lights up the monotonous grey of the surrounding streets.

Things never stay the same on the borders of the City, but the fact that many hostelries remain open is comforting. People can still find respite from their worries in a humble public house which hasn't changed too much over the years – even if only for an afternoon.

139 Leman Street, E1 8EY

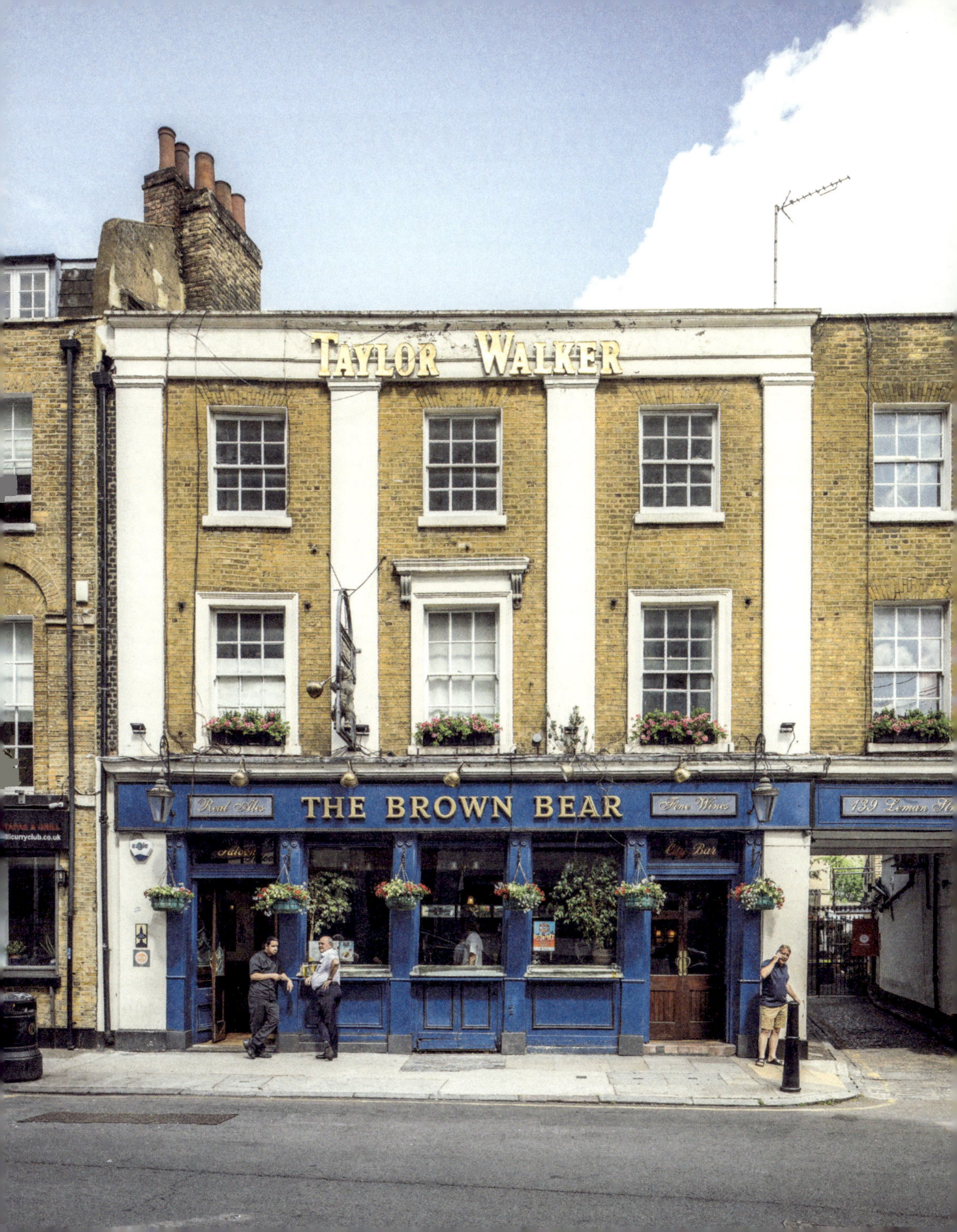
TAYLOR WALKER
Real Ales
THE BROWN BEAR
Fine Wines
139 Leman St

The Commercial Tavern

Wedged between Spitalfields Market and Shoreditch lies a welcoming example of a new East End hostelry. The Commercial Tavern, its unusual round-fronted facade instantly recognisable, sits in a part of the East End that now feels far from its Victorian heyday of bustling industry. Even before the artists' squats and start-ups moved in, bringing gentrification in their wake, the area contended with many intervening years of poverty and decline. Most of the pubs that opened to quench the thirst of manual workers in the 19th century have since closed. The Commercial Tavern's fallen comrades include The Norfolk Village, The Eagle, The King's Arms and The White Swan.

Despite a post-millennium boom, at times the area feels in transition. But for those who look for it, the legacy of its past lingers, if a little wearily. The cries of costermongers are long gone and the patrons of The Commercial Tavern today might not be the Cockneys of the past, but the building's soul remains.

Although the interior is artificially distressed, the wooden floorboards, subtle tiling and exposed brick are nods to the heritage of the Grade II-listed site. Late night revelry goes on here as it always has done, taking place to a soundtrack of eclectic beats. As the bell rings for last orders and patrons go out into the night, one wonders if they look up to the handsome stucco windows, which have witnessed the birth of a new London, and question how the pub will look when they too are gone.

142-4 Commercial Street, E1 6NU

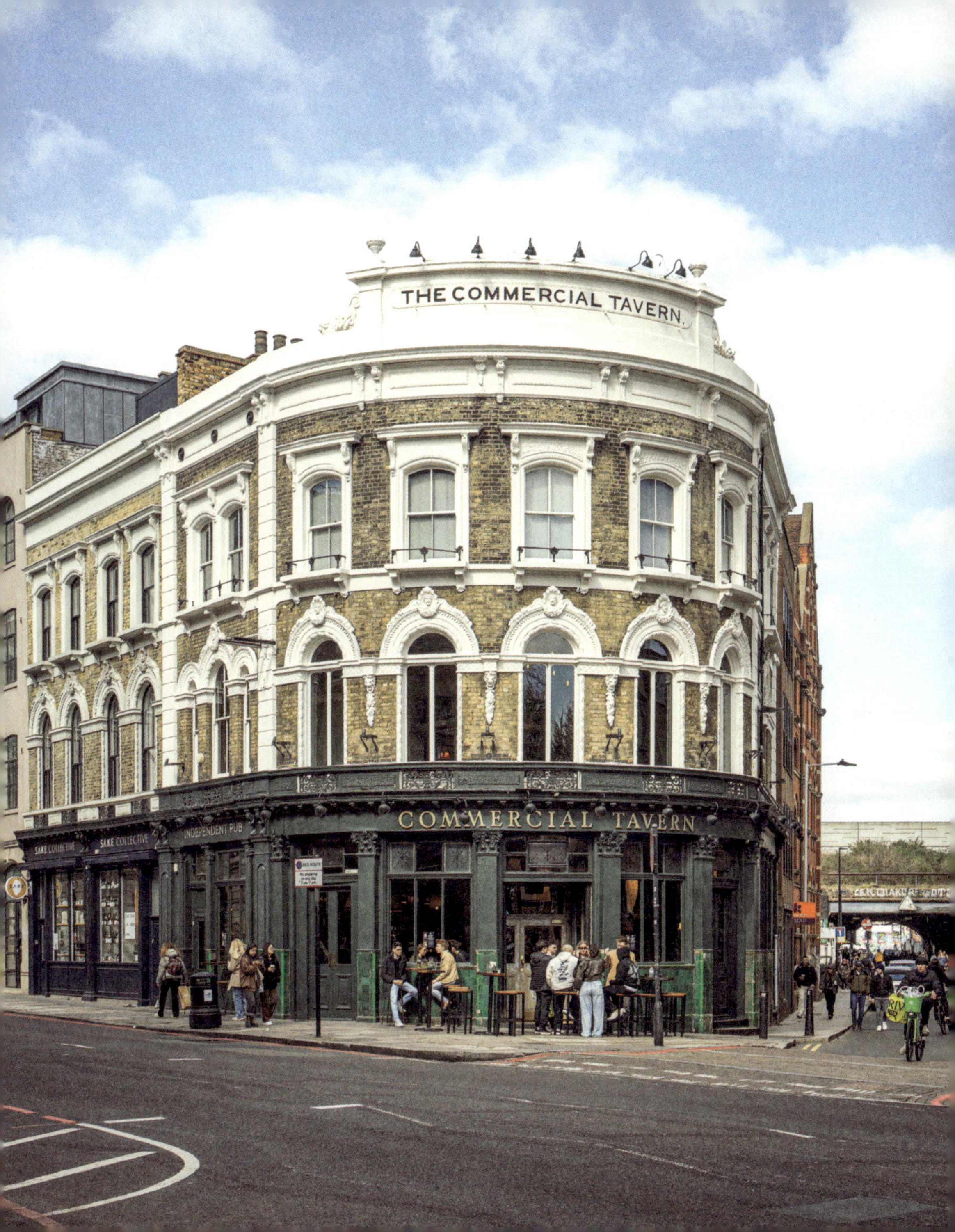

THE COMMERCIAL TAVERN.
COMMERCIAL TAVERN
SAKE COLLECTIVE
SAKE COLLECTIVE
INDEPENDENT PUB

The Gun

This pub had already been serving pints for well over a century when it was renamed The Gun in honour of the cannon fired to mark the opening of West India Docks in 1802. Once a notorious haunt for criminals, these days the out-of-the-way hostelry is known just as much for its fine hospitality as its mysterious history.

The past lingers, and nods to its nautical pedigree run through the waterside establishment. On foggy nights, it is possible to imagine foul deeds taking place within the warrens of neighbouring backstreets. The vista offers a window into an East End of compact thoroughfares, where working-class people lived, worked and died within a small radius. Over 200 years ago, the upstairs River Room, now reserved for private functions, was used by Admiral Lord Nelson to secretly meet with his lover, Lady Emma Hamilton, for illicit trysts. And though the smugglers are long gone, the spyhole they once used to look out for custom officers is still hidden on an old staircase.

The traditional oak-panelled pub does not feel too far from Nelson's time, as the low-lighting flickers off the pewter tankards hanging from the ceiling. But there are welcome modern additions, including a covered terrace and garden with a separate bar. It is a venue that has moved with the times. Today, the patrons are corporate white-collar workers from Canary Wharf rather than Cockney manual labourers from the docks, but it remains a huge asset to the Isle of Dogs' community, which can only benefit from thriving local businesses.

27 Coldharbour, E14 9NS

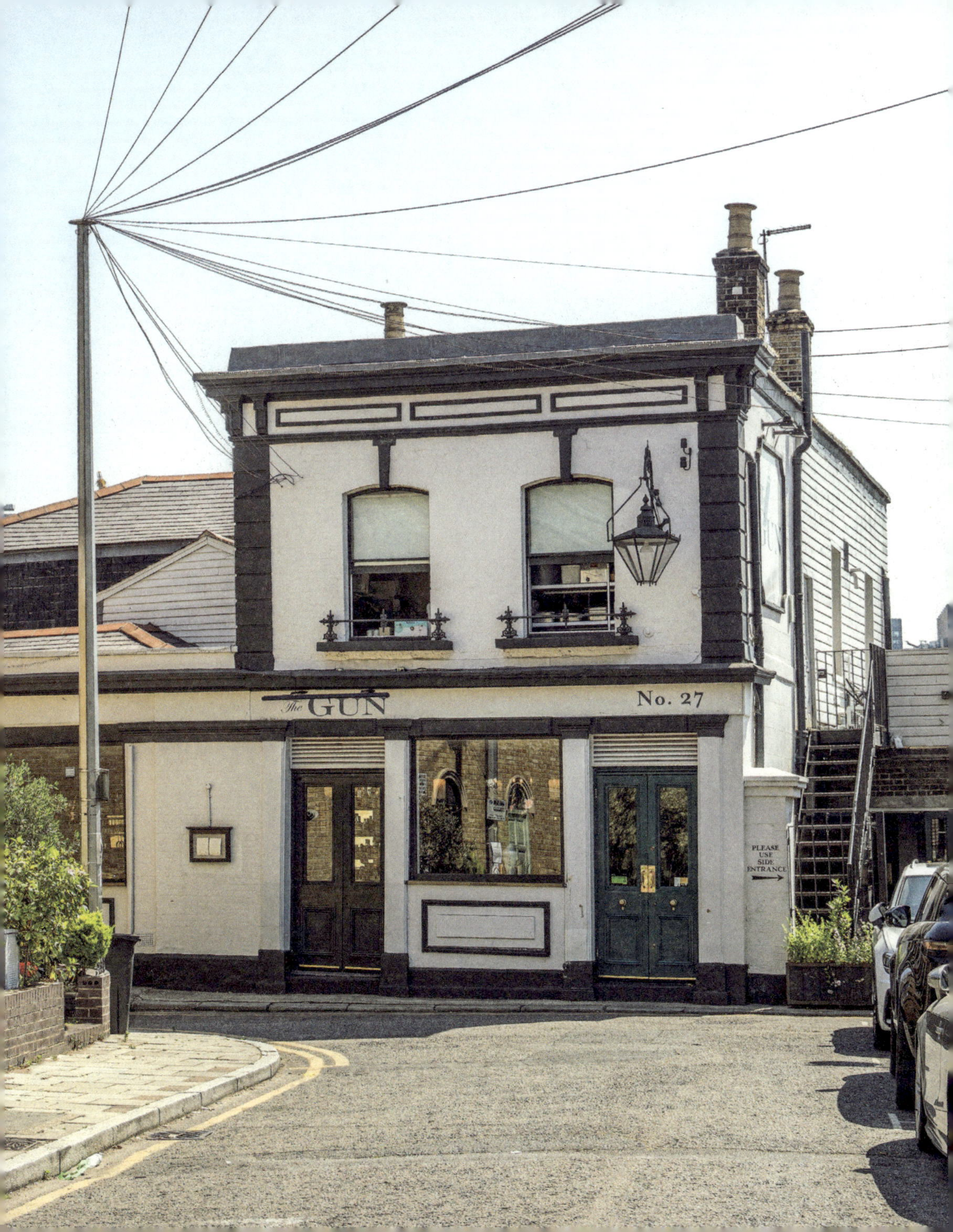

The GUN
No. 27
PLEASE
USE
SIDE
ENTRANCE

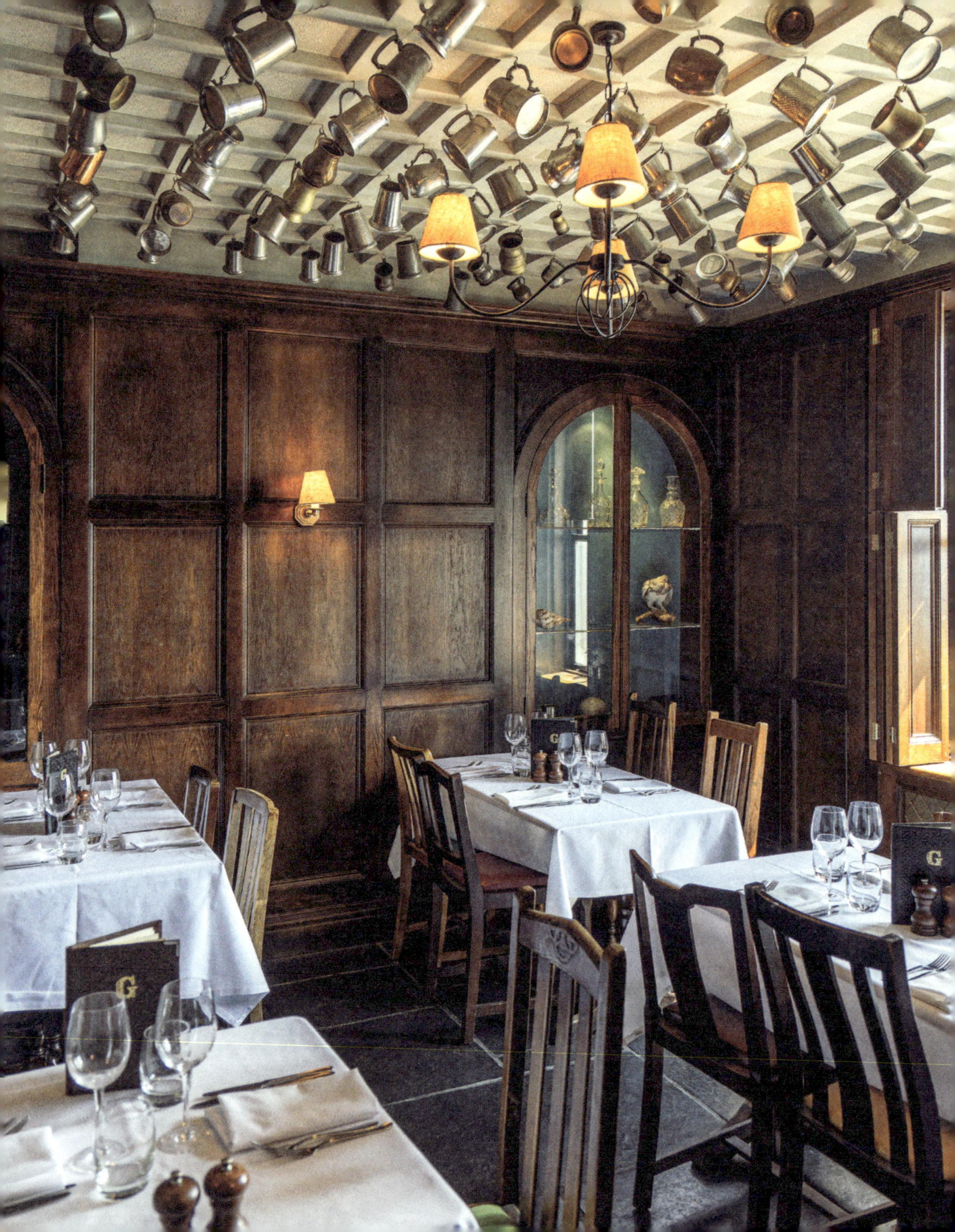

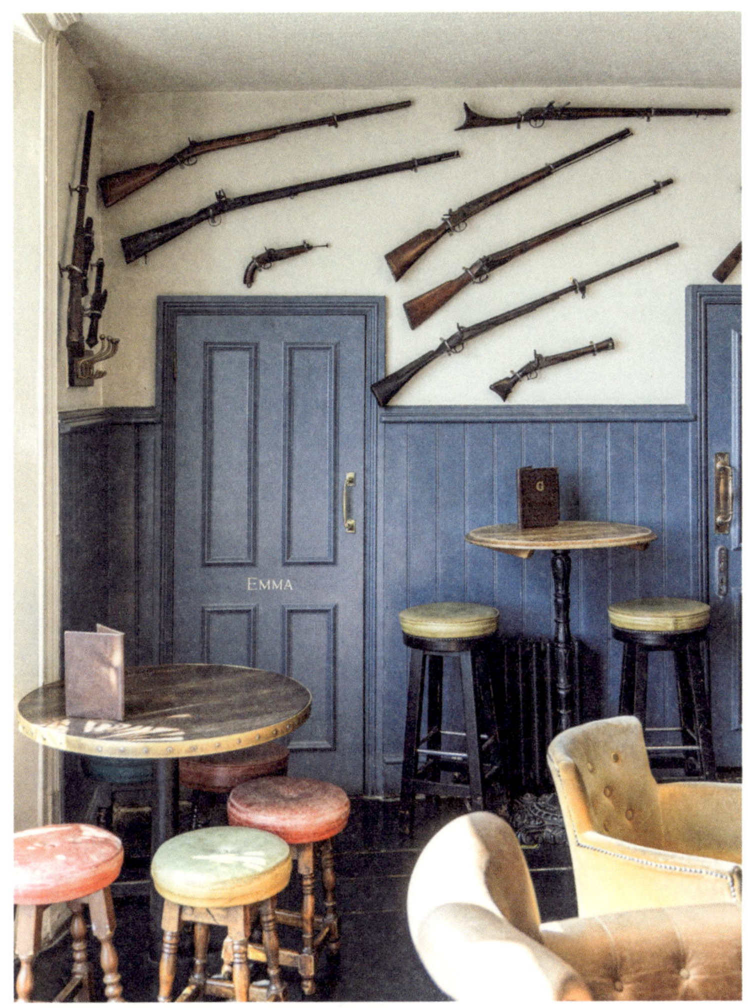

*The Gun was named after the cannon fired to open West India Docks,
and these decorative firearms serve as a nod to its naval past.*

Ye Olde Axe

A BAWDY PUB WITH AN UNCERTAIN FUTURE

Ye Olde Axe's majesty speaks for itself, with a forbidding facade, neo-gothic turret and intricately detailed ceramic fruit garlands interwoven with glazed tiling. In grim weather, it takes on a slightly eerie aspect. When the pub was being refurbished in the 1970s, two bodies were found in the cellar and are said to haunt the building, though to this day they have not been identified.

It was one of the last surviving 'pound in a pint' strip pubs in the East End, in which a pint glass would be passed around for everyone to put a pound coin in for the dancers. In the days of boozy City lunches, it was once common practice for office workers to head to strip pubs during the day. As attitudes began to change in the 1990s, these erotic establishments steadily disappeared from residential areas. However, in Soho and Shoreditch, they continued throughout the noughties and beyond.

Time was called at Ye Olde Axe in 2022 when its licence was not renewed after opposition from residents who complained about lockdown breaches and noise. The shabby but charming interior – which had a late-Victorian feel, boasting an ornate ceiling, traditional pub bar and old-school carpet – is now empty.

Although it is unlikely that dancers will ever tread the stage again, perhaps one day Ye Olde Axe will reopen as a pub that can serve its community both new and old.

69 Hackney Road, E2 8ET

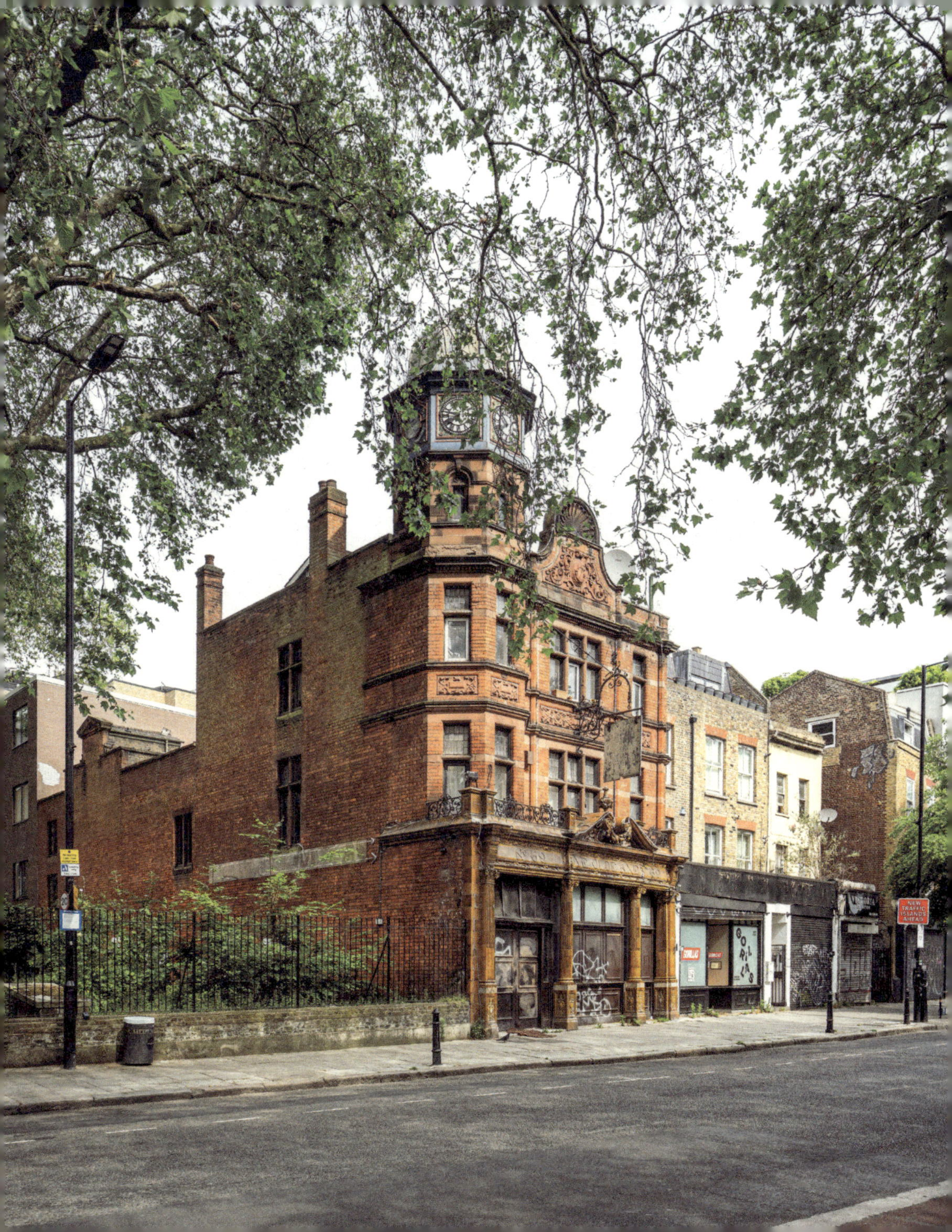

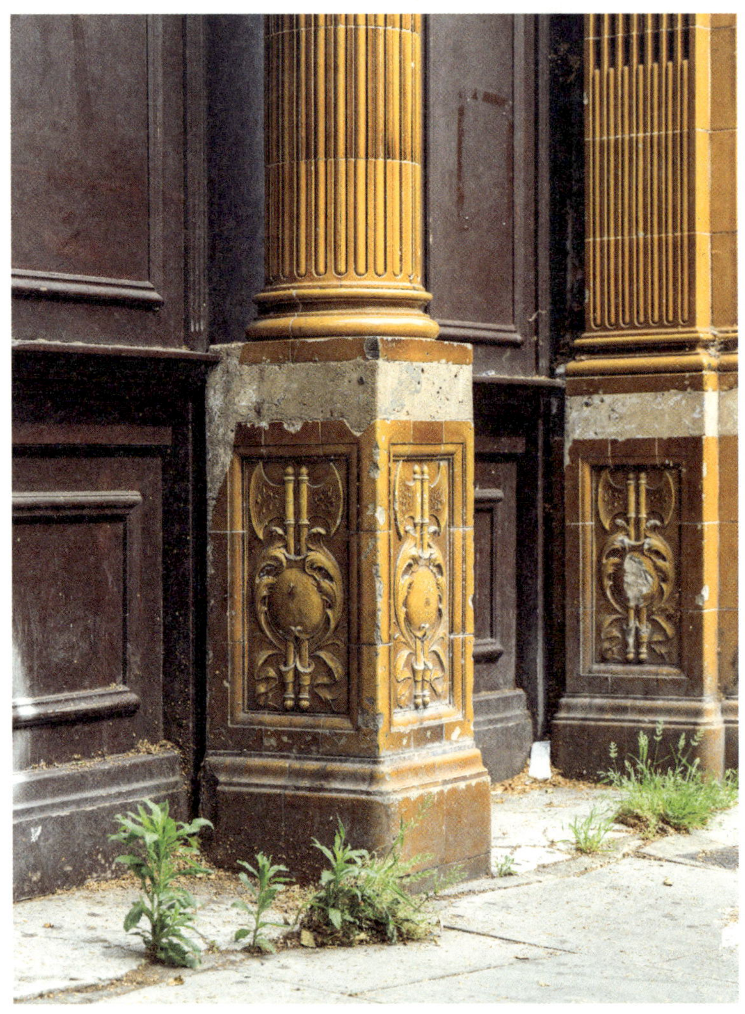

*For now, the magnificent Olde Axe remains
closed and shuttered, awaiting its new purpose.*

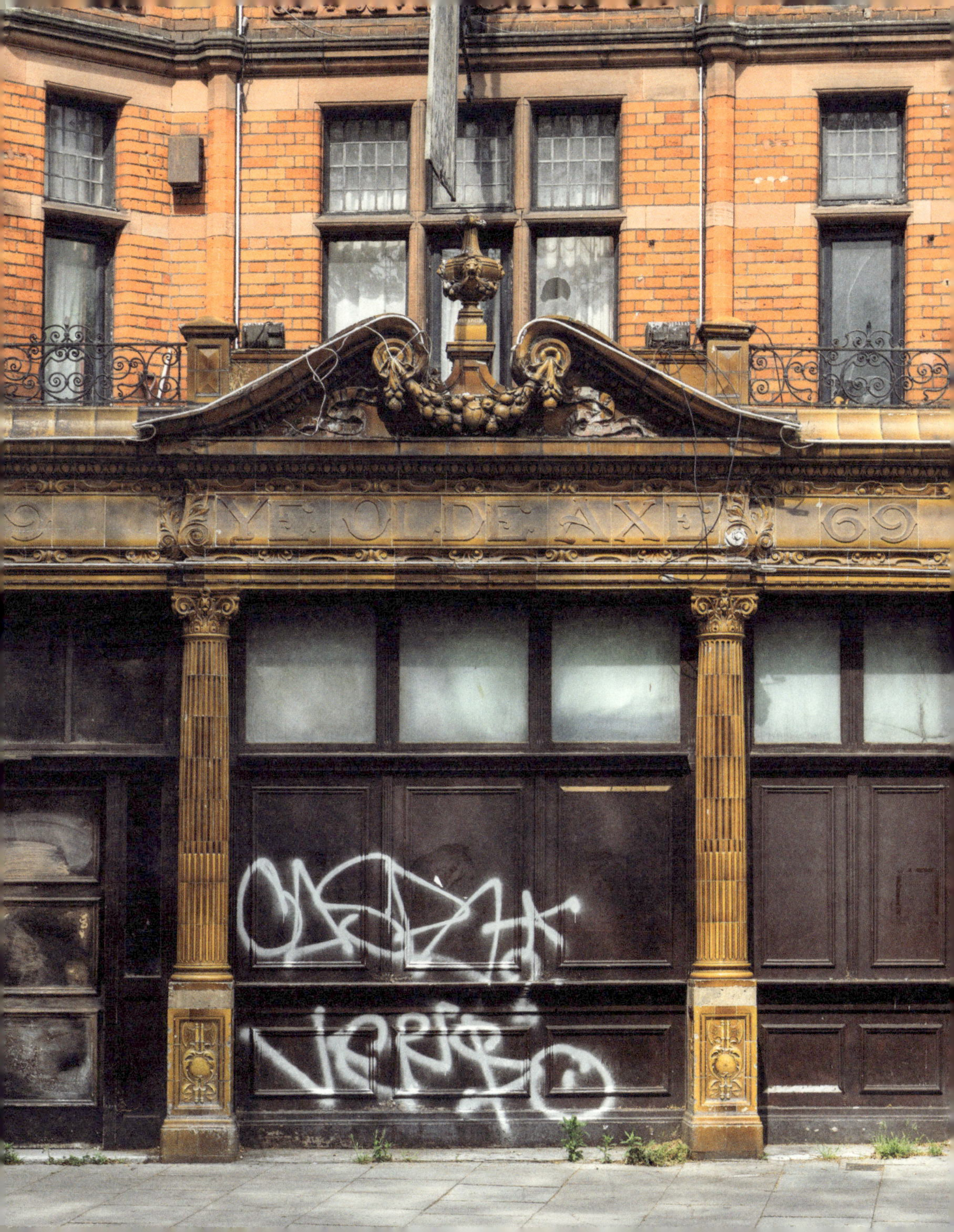

9
YE OLDE AXE
69

The Grapes

One of the oldest pubs on the Thames, The Grapes is a seasoned champion of tradition. Serving all walks of life, from cut-throat pirates to wealthy merchants, dockers and printers it features in Samuel Pepys' 1661 diary, as well as being a haunt of Charles Dickens in the 1820s. While the pub has changed since then, it still affords modern visitors a window into the comings and goings of a traditional riverside inn.

A stone's throw from Limehouse brewers Taylor Walker's old Barley Mow Brewery, the current building dates from the 1720s. The hostelries glorious facade is resplendent year-round, enticing inquisitive explorers inside after a brisk walk along the Thames Path. Inside, the wood panelling and threadbare rugs conjure an image of how the tavern might have been for thirsty mariners in the distant past.

In a room upstairs, punters can sit at bar stools around large barrels, which reference the area's brewing and nautical history. It is from here that fine views of the Thames can be enjoyed with a glass of claret on an unforgiving winter's day, when the elements are raging and the only option is to hunker down at what is much more than just any port in a storm. Famous patrons of the past who also shared this experience included distinguished painters Francis Bacon and Edward Wolfe, who both lived on the same street as The Grapes.

Great reverence is paid to the past by the current owners, so while the calibre of food and beverage will certainly have improved over the last five centuries, The Grapes is still a timeless riverside classic.

76 Narrow Street, E14 8BP

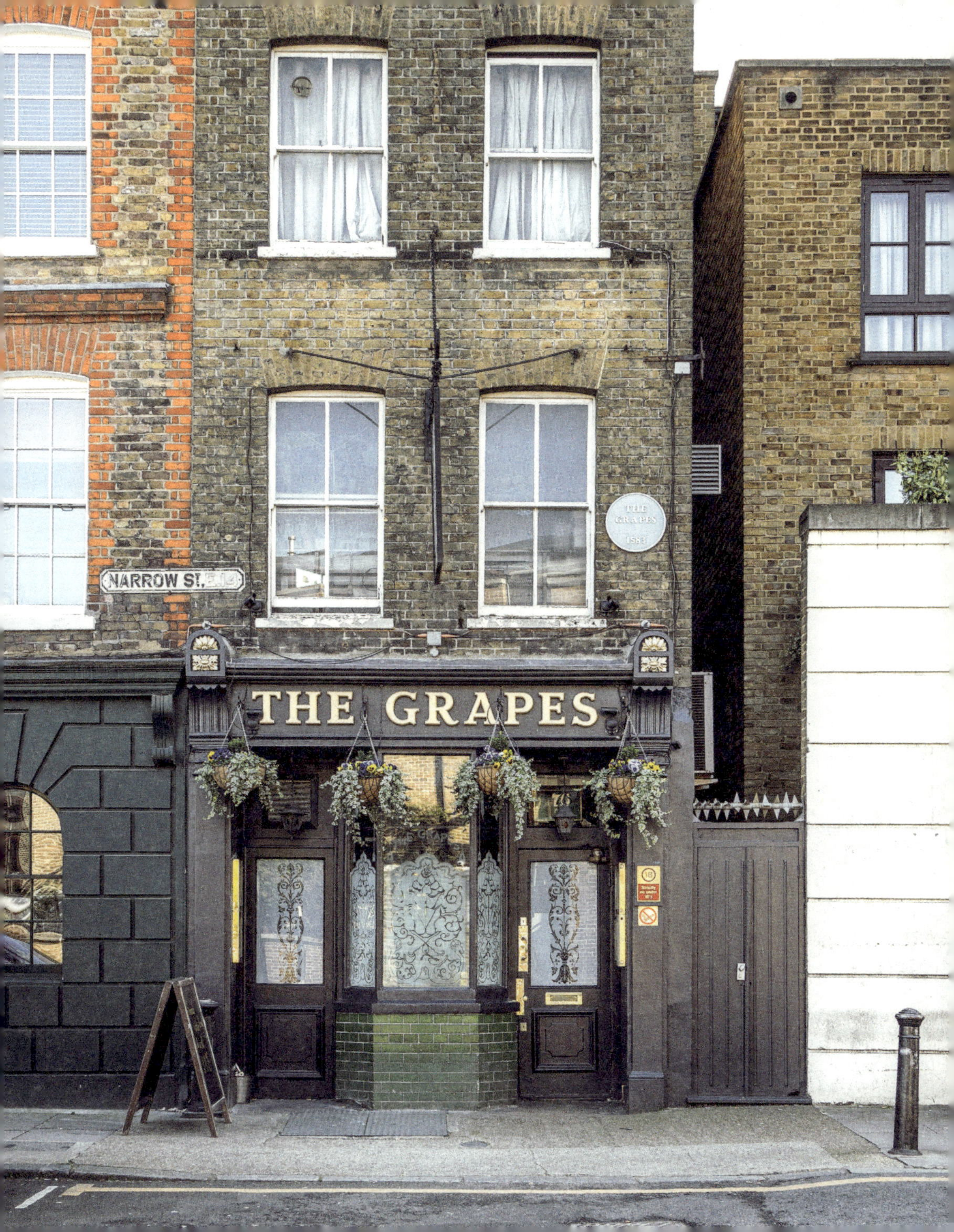

NARROW St, E.14
THE GRAPES
THE GRAPES
THE GRAPES
1863

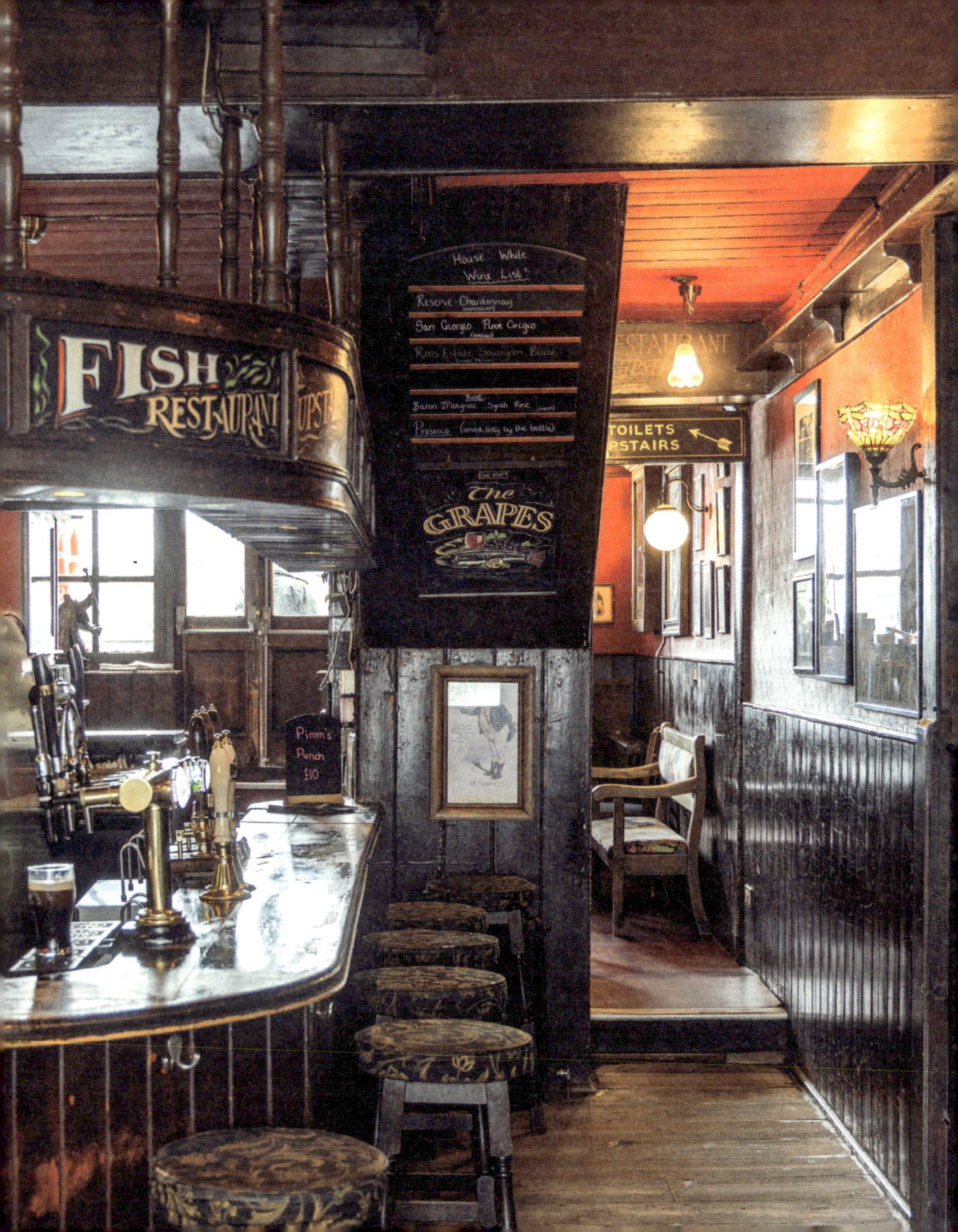
FISH
RESTAURANT UPSTAIRS
House White Wine List
Reserve Chardonnay
San Giorgio Pinot Grigio
Roos Estate Sauvignon Blanc
Rosé
Baron D'arignac Syrah Rosé
Prosecco (served only by the bottle)
Est 1867
The GRAPES
RESTAURANT UPSTAIRS
TOILETS UPSTAIRS
Pimm's Punch £10

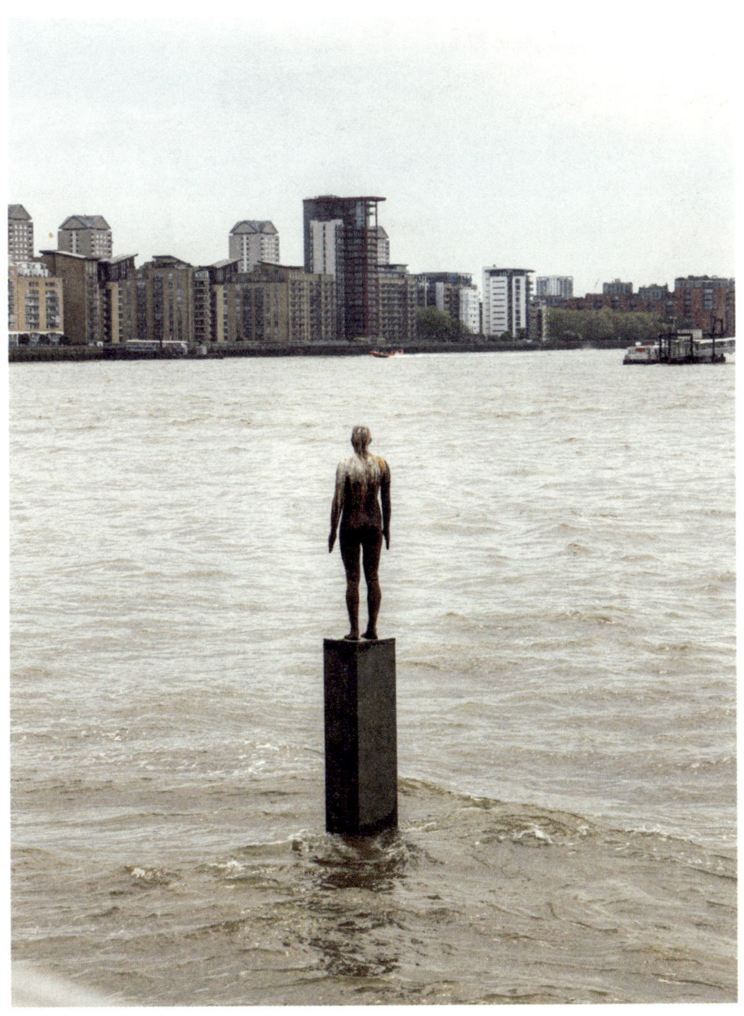

Antony Gormley's Another Time (2013) can be seen from the pub.
At high tide it looks as if the sculpture is standing on water.

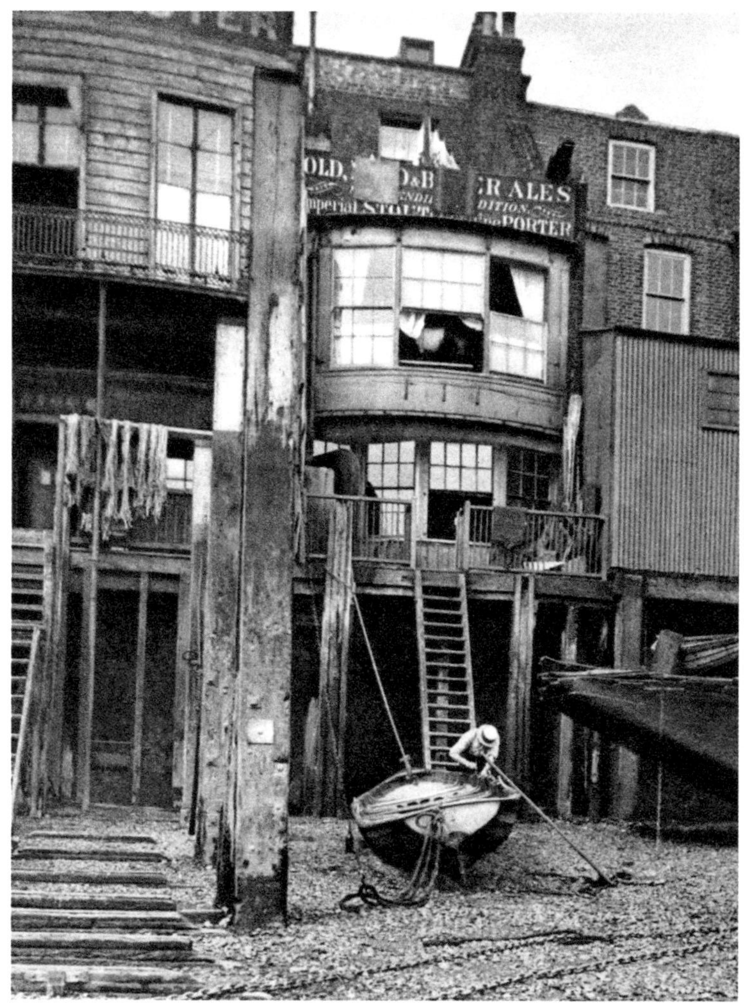

The Grapes would have served the workers who toiled in London's docks.
Today, it is the last adults-only hostelry (as all pubs once were) in the East End.

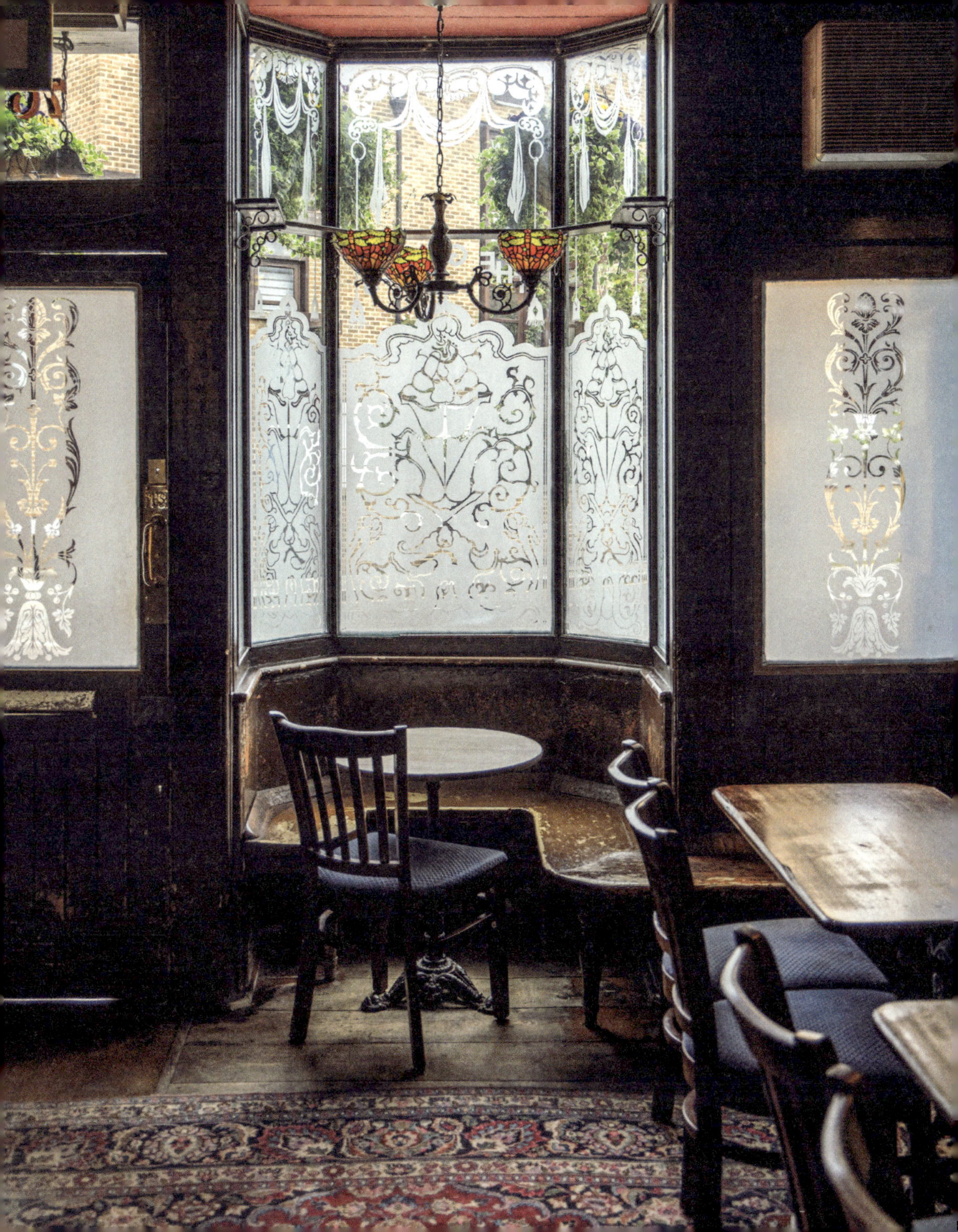

The Ferry House

THE ISLE OF DOG'S MOST SENIOR HOSTELRY

The Isle of Dogs once boasted 42 pubs to water thousands of dockers and sailors. In 2023, only seven remain. The Ferry House is the Island's oldest pub, and for many who live there it is also its dearest. Located a few yards of ale from the Greenwich Foot Tunnel, it has played a prominent role in Island life since at least 1722. Although at one time the Isle of Dogs was home to the busiest docks in the world, industry started to decline in the 20th century. It had a tight-knit community on account of poor transport links (there were no trains on the Island from 1926–87) and its separation from the rest of London, making residents historically wary of outsiders.

Originally owned by south London brewers Barclays Perkins, The Ferry later became a Courage house. But other than the removal of some ornate balcony railings, little has changed since the 1890s. It might have easily been otherwise; one night of the Blitz saw almost every building on its street destroyed.

The interior delivers a warm atmosphere with a compact horseshoe bar and wood-panelled walls that make for a snug drinking den. Small rooms lead off into what would have, at one time, been a saloon and a public bar. Deciding to move with the times, the pub has hosted a curry kitchen and done up the sunken garden. During the London Marathon, the old boozer bursts at the seams with the friends and family of runners embracing the carnival atmosphere. Or, if so inclined, visitors can pop into the pub on a quiet weekday for a few pints and sit by one of only three pub fish tanks in the East End.

26 Ferry Street, E14 3DT

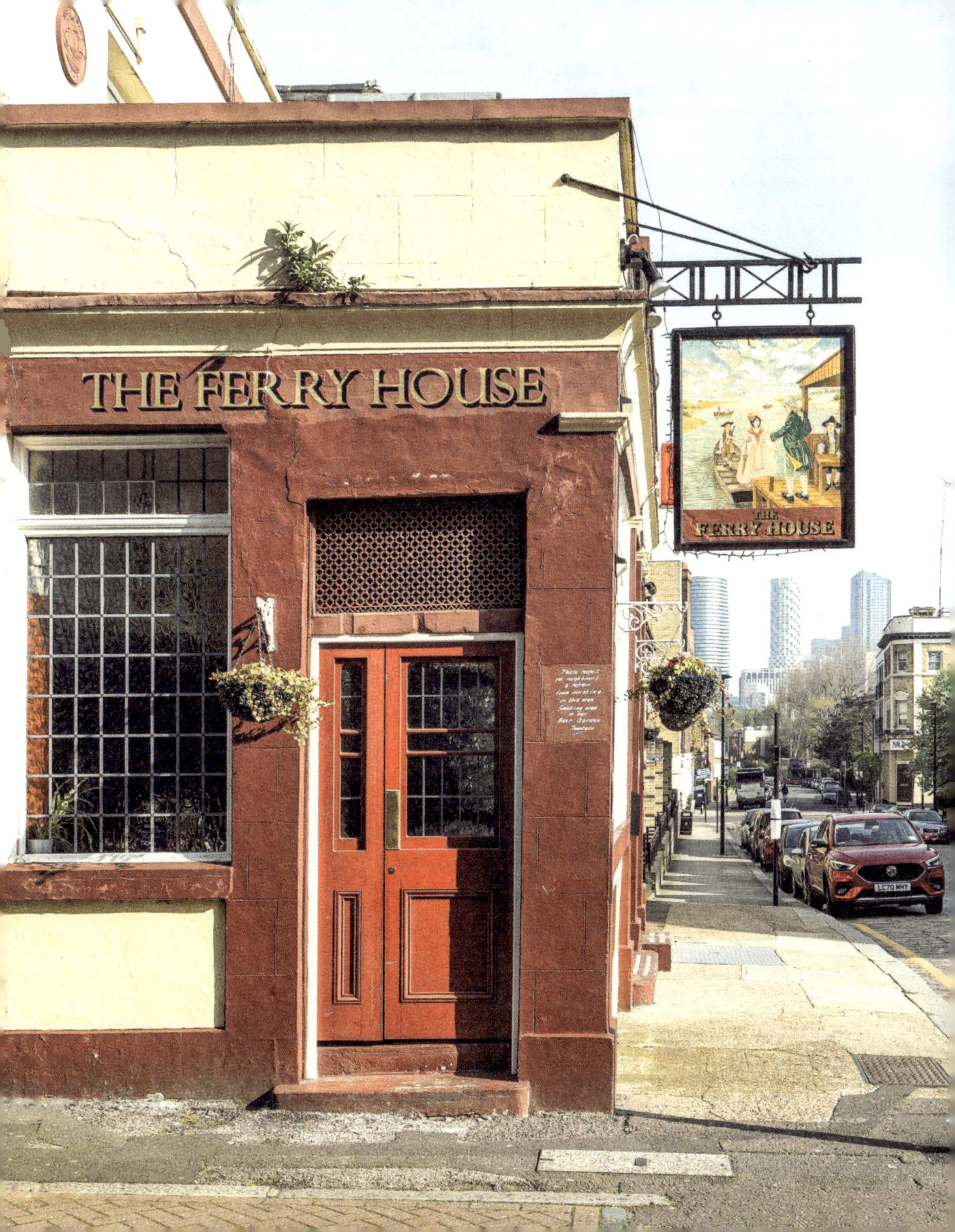
THE FERRY HOUSE
THE
FERRY HOUSE

The Old Ship

Limehouse has long been a destination for London's queer community, with pubs such as The White Swan hosting LGBTQ+ night-life since 1985. Another famous location, tucked behind Limehouse station on the quaint Georgian York Square, is The Old Ship. Built on land owned by the Mercer's Company (the guild for dealers in textile fabric), the ancient company's heraldic symbol of a crowned maiden with flowing hair is embedded in the pub's facade. York Square was designated a conservation area in 1973, and the open streets and squares retain a rich history as well as significant 19th-century architecture, which delights first-time visitors.

There are two community pubs on York Square which still act as the cornerstones of this serene neighbourhood. Directly opposite one another, both The Old Ship and Grade II-listed The Queen's Head (p.116) – although welcoming contrasting types of drinkers and different kinds of hospitality – reflect a time when the modest corner pub was the beating heart of every local area.

While The Queens Head is the modern face of a changing East End offering craft beer and more refined pub grub, The Old Ship is a simpler operation that attracts all kinds of visitors. These people are not just local faces but flock from all over the city for lively revelry – and the pub's treasured £2 filled rolls.

With its green-tiled facade set among rows of terraces, little has changed

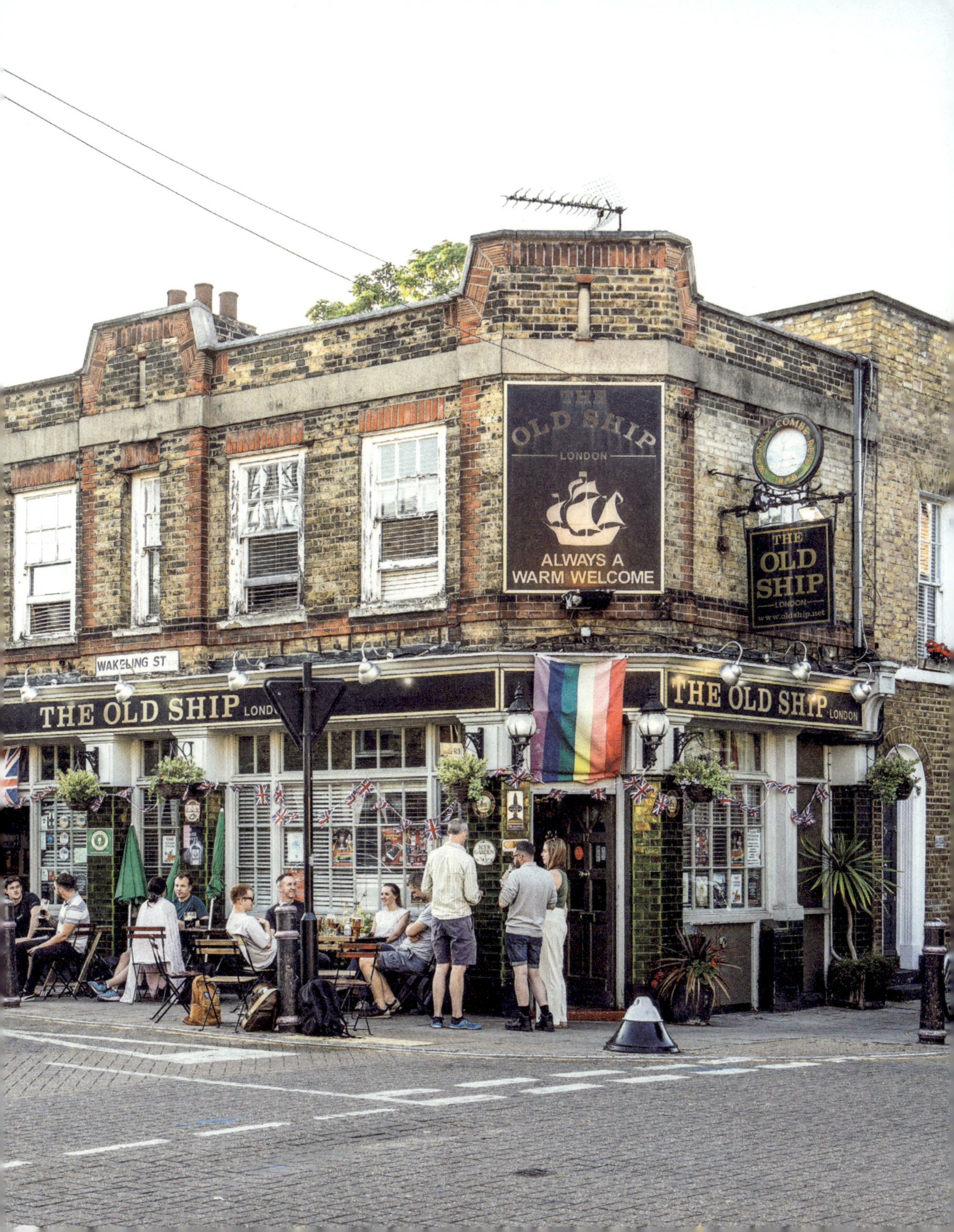
THE
OLD SHIP
LONDON
ALWAYS A
WARM WELCOME
THE
OLD SHIP
LONDON
www.oldship.net
WAKELING ST
THE OLD SHIP LONDON
THE OLD SHIP LONDON

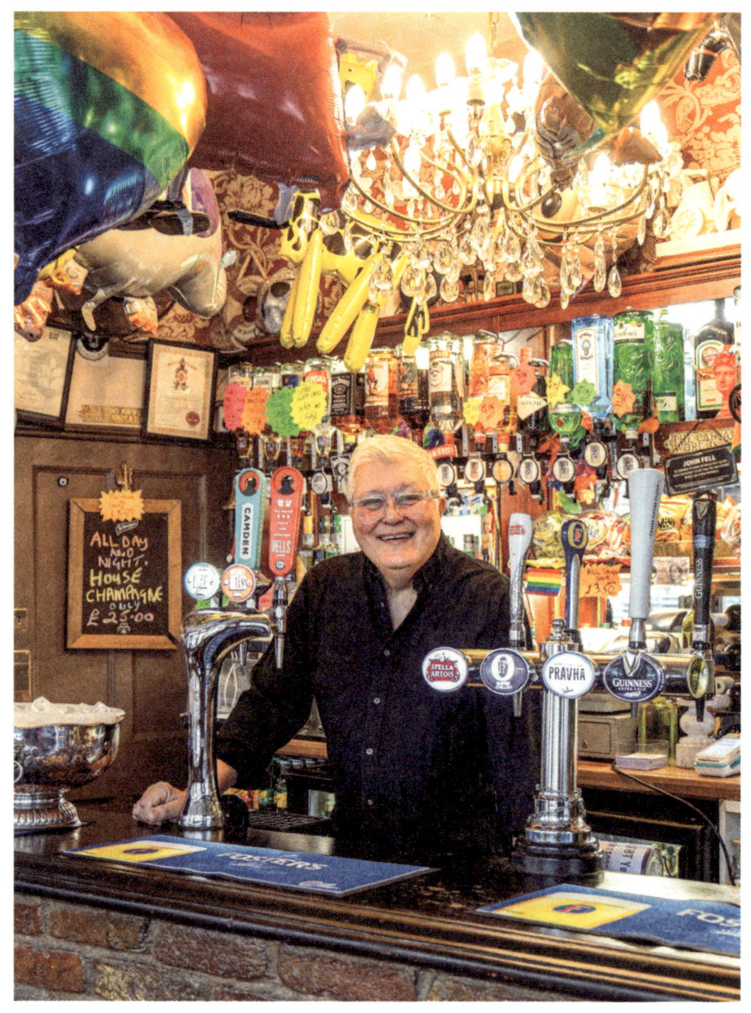

CAMDEN
HELLS
ALL DAY AND NIGHT. HOUSE CHAMPAGNE ONLY £25.00
JOHN FELL
STELLA ARTOIS
PRAVHA
GUINNESS
FOSTERS

aesthetically since The Old Ship first opened – even the traditional knees-up singalong from yesteryear is still in rude health thanks to the pub being a lively LGBTQ+ venue.

Under the bright lights of chandeliers and the odd disco ball, The Old Ship continues the East End's long love affair with drag – stretching back over 60 years when drag artists such as Gay Travers would tread the boards. That musical tradition is going strong within the inclusive walls of landlord John Fell's wonderful hostelry as, every weekend, first-class cabaret drag is performed on the tiny stage, including riotous performances from Sissy Lea and Miss Moppe that draw rapturous applause from the crowd.

In a small room at the back of the pub, John has a collection of hundreds of vintage photographs, old maps and paintings of Limehouse that celebrate the local history of the docks and the East End. This unexpected gallery contrasts with the merriment out in the main body of the pub and offers a welcome retreat to anyone who needs a break from the party.

On a quiet afternoon, The Old Ship is the perfect spot to enjoy a quiet pint of well-conditioned cask ale and a delicious roll from the sandwich counter, made fresh each morning. While the area has changed many times over the centuries – from land once used for market gardening, to homes for dockers, industrialists and later ravaged in the Blitz – it retains an air of old London unaltered by time.

17 Barnes Street, E14 7NW

Born in Stepney, Guv'nor John Fell previously ran Booty's Riverside Bar in Limehouse and The Norfolk Village in Shoreditch.

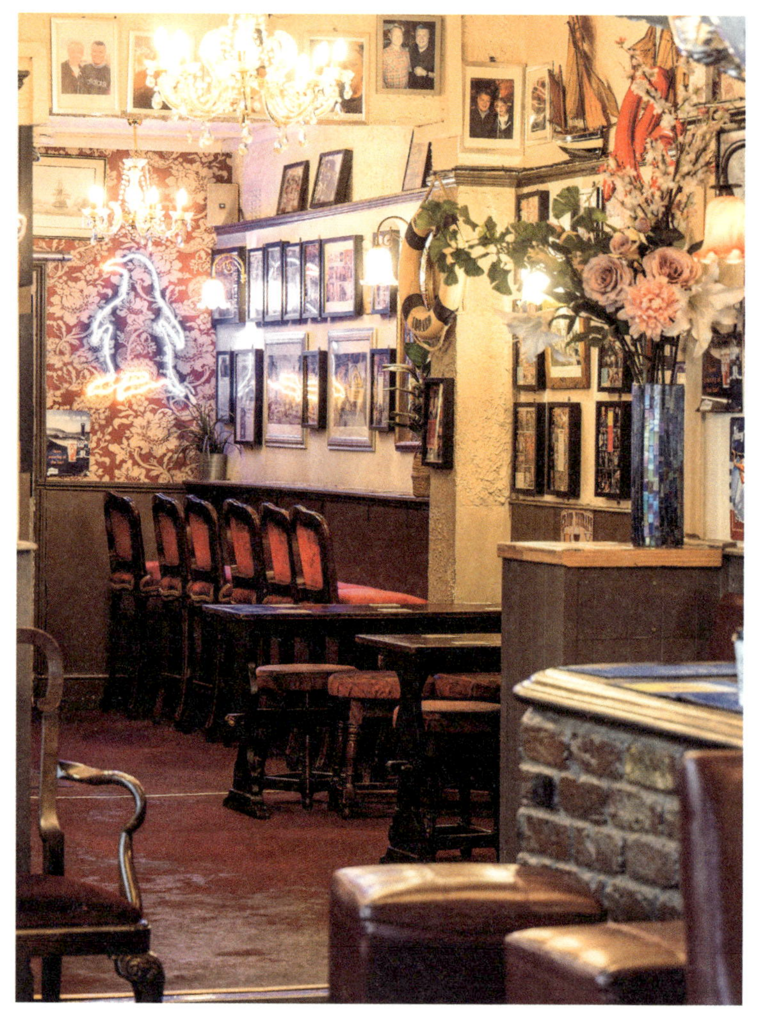

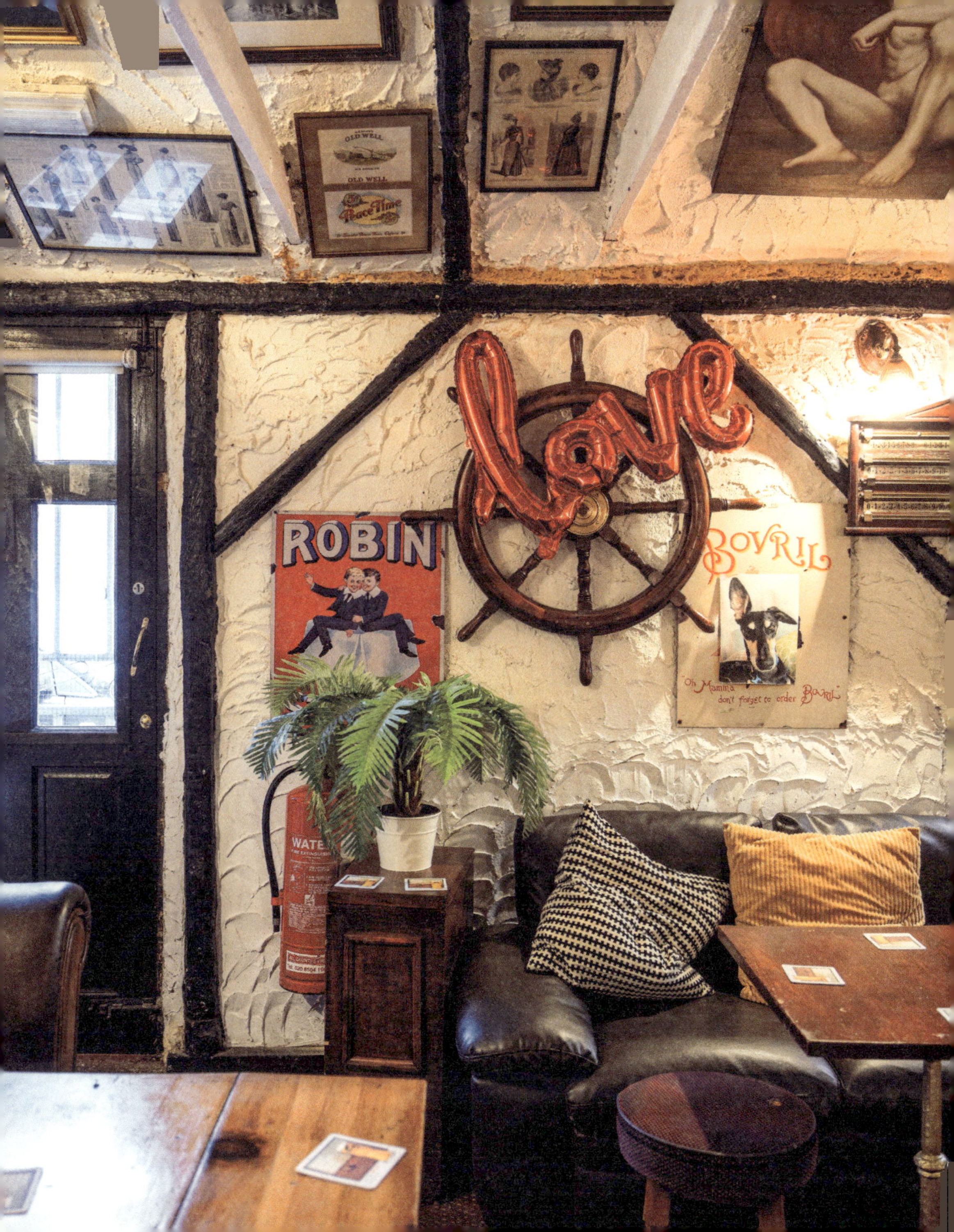

OLD WELL
OLD WELL
Peace Time
ROBIN
love
BOVRIL
Oh Mamma
don't forget to order Bovril
WATER
FIRE EXTINGUISHER

The Greenwich Pensioner

A MODERN EATERY INSIDE A HISTORIC LOCAL

The streets around The Greenwich Pensioner depict an East End scarred by a past of aerial bombardment and austerity. This old pub, believed to have been built in 1827, is one of the few beautiful old buildings that remain. It was once tucked within a terrace, which was sadly flattened in the Blitz and replaced with postwar social housing. The denizens of Poplar are fortunate that The Greenwich Pensioner managed to survive.

The pub is named after the retired sailors who lived at the Royal Hospital for Seamen just across the river in Greenwich. The Royal Hospital was built between 1694 and 1751 for sailors who had been injured or retired from old age, and at at its peak around 2,700 naval pensioners lived there. These ex-sailors wore a similar uniform (with the famous tricorne hats) to the Chelsea Pensioners at the Royal Hospital Chelsea, only with a naval blue coat instead of red.

The green Taylor Walker tiling on the pub's Grade II-listed exterior gleams in the sun on summer days, though, unfortunately, the interior does not deliver the expected hit of old London pub nostalgia. No original fixtures or fittings remain and the modern design is perhaps better suited to a restaurant than a traditional pub.

However, in an area where pubs are closing at an alarming rate, it is heartwarming to witness a remnant of the area's historic past extending a warm welcome to the thirsty and hungry of an ever-evolving Poplar.

28 Bazely Street, E14 0ES

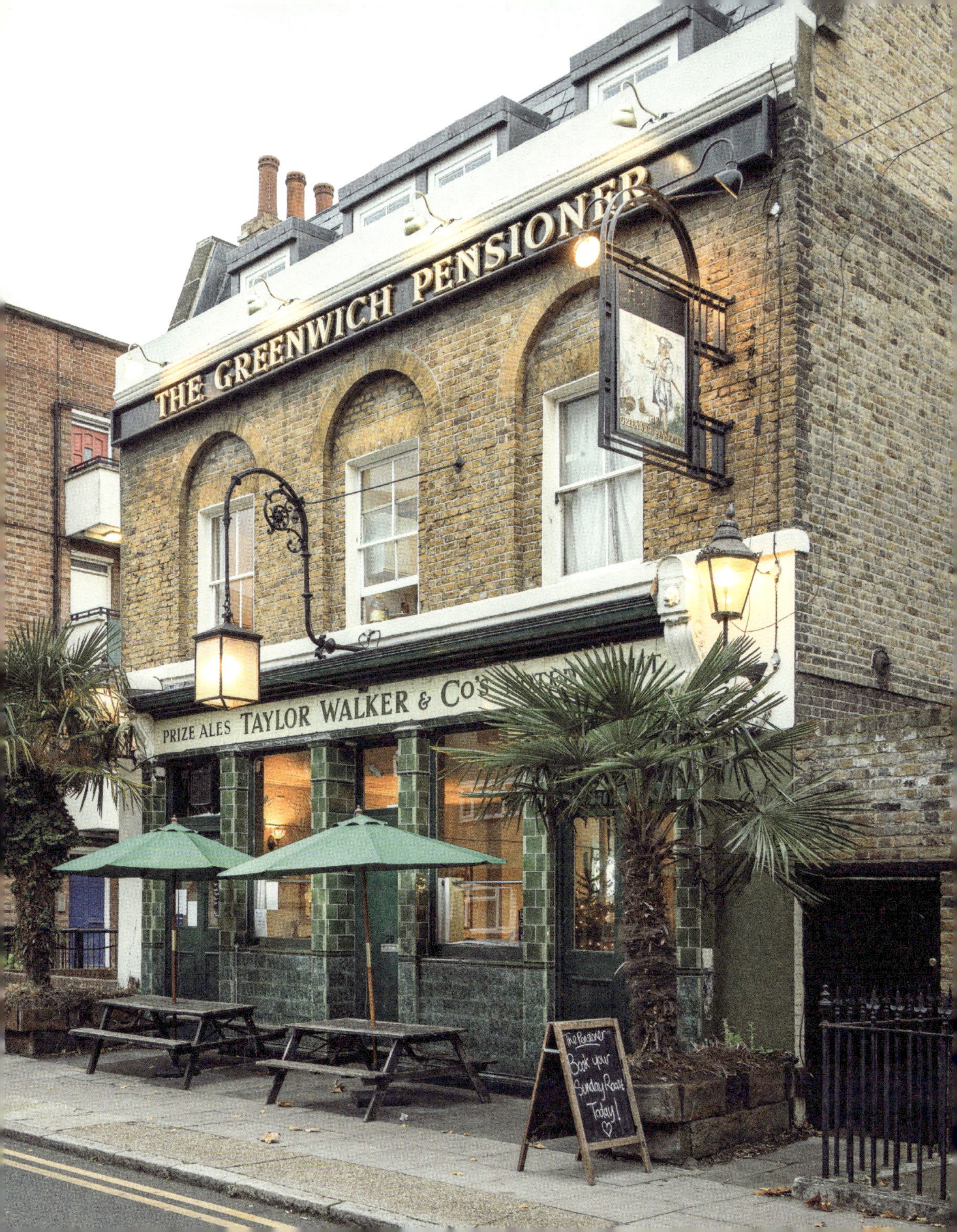
THE GREENWICH PENSIONER
THE GREENWICH PENSIONER
PRIZE ALES TAYLOR WALKER & Co's
The Pensioner
Book your
Sunday Roast
Today!

The Culpeper

Nowhere can remain the same forever, especially in the East End; old faces inevitably move on and a new crowd moves in. One pub that has creatively diversified and gained a new lease on life is The Culpeper, where contemporary style is embedded within the body of the past. The hostelry has arguably become the ultimate Spitalfields destination pub.

The Culpeper, which changed its name from Princess Alice (first opened in 1883, it was named after Queen Victoria's second eldest daughter), has moved with the times. Some believe that changing a pub's name brings bad luck, however this handsome structure, formerly owned by Truman's, bucks that trend and is busy from first opening until the time bell rings.

It's unlikely that any of the old punters who frequented the Princess Alice now head to The Culpeper, but it is always better for a pub to be open rather than closed. The bustling Culpeper animates the corner with its stylish, colourful tiling and Truman's legacy signage, and its interior has been transformed into a lofty and fresh open-plan space. There's a bar boasting exposed brickwork and sharp fixtures on the ground floor, while the first floor is occupied by a high-end restaurant with their five-bedroom boutique hotel tucked away on the upper floors. The whole operation is devoted to sustainability, with an impressive garden on the rooftop that grows produce to be served in the restaurant below. This, in the shadow of Old Spitalfields Market where fruit and vegetables were once sold, is a welcome enterprise.

40 Commercial Street, E1 6LP

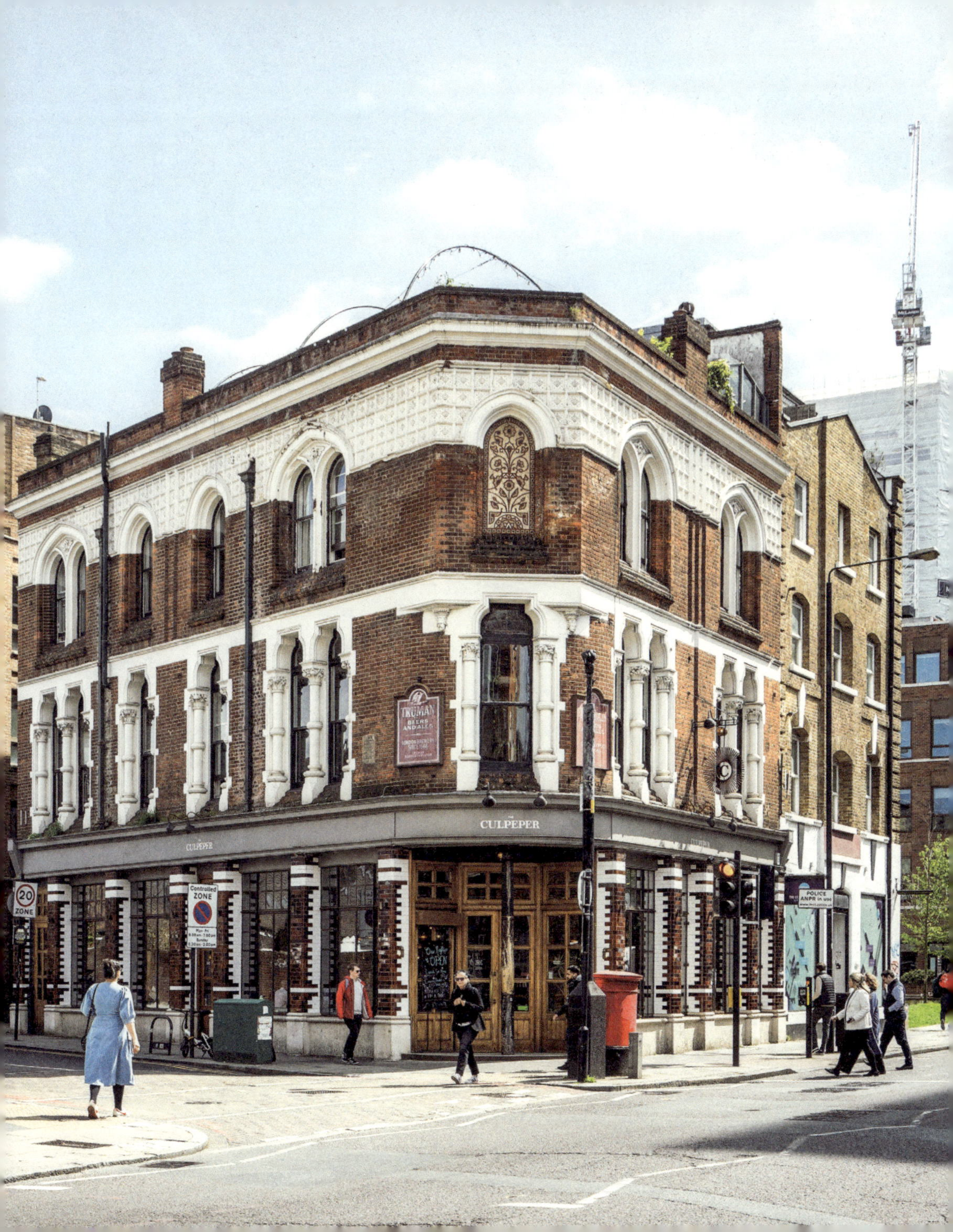

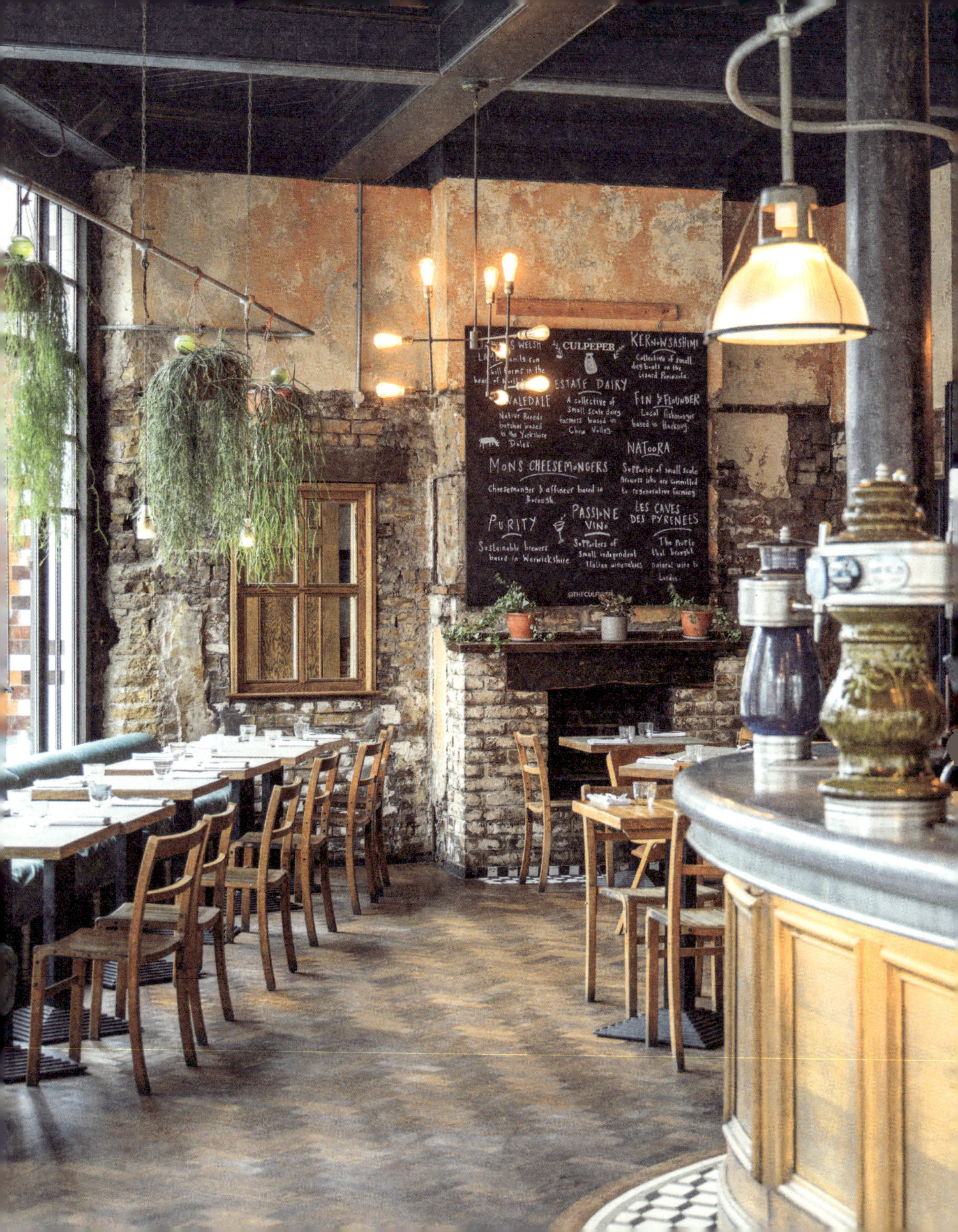
WELSH LAMB
Families run hill farms in the heart of North Wales.

CULPEPER

KERNOW SASHIMI
Collective of small day boats on the Lizard Peninsula.

ESTATE DAIRY
A collective of small scale dairy farmers based in Chew Valley.

VALEDALE
Native Breeds butcher based in the Yorkshire Dales.

FIN & FLOUNDER
Local fishmonger based in Hackney.

NATOORA
Supporter of small scale growers who are committed to regenerative farming.

MONS CHEESEMONGERS
Cheesemonger & affineur based in Borough.

PURITY
Sustainable brewers based in Warwickshire.

PASSIONE VINO
Supporters of small independent Italian winemakers.

LES CAVES DES PYRENEES
The people that brought natural wine to London.

@THECULPEPER

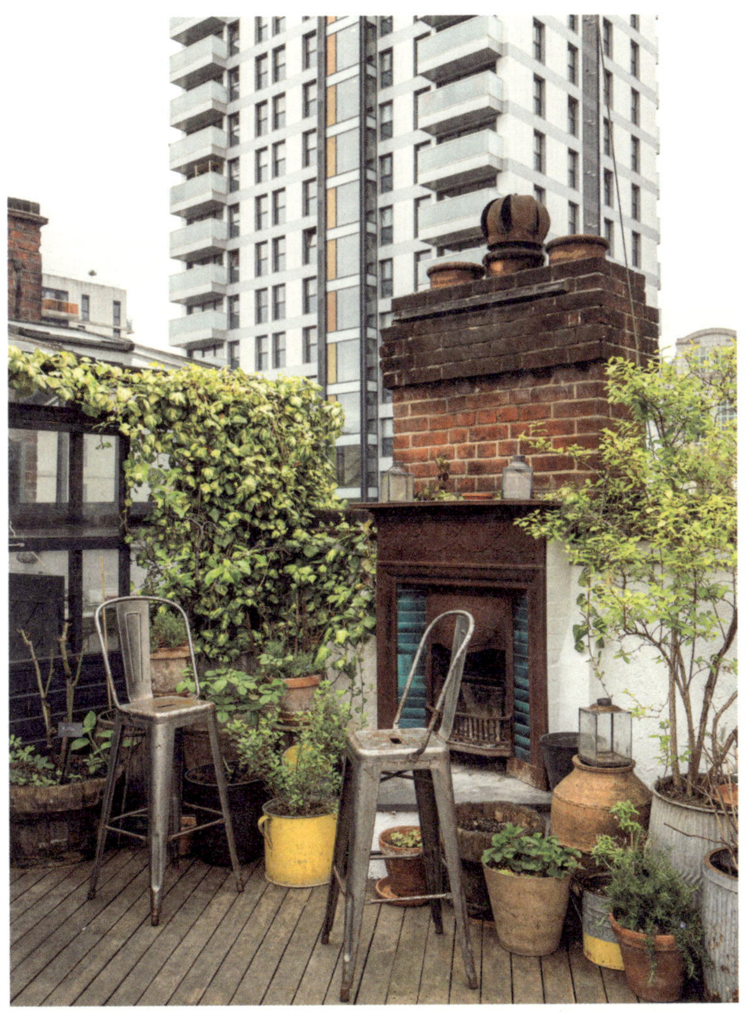

The pub is named after Nicholas Culpeper, a 17th-century herbalist who once
lived round the corner, so it's fitting that they have a flourishing rooftop garden.

The Tooke Arms

A VITAL COMMUNITY PUB ON THE ISLE OF DOGS

The original Victorian Tooke Arms was demolished and rebuilt in the 1960s during the construction of the Barkantine Estate, an ambitious social housing scheme intended to replace the Isle of Dog's Luftwaffe-ravaged slums. The upgrade in living standards, from outdoor toilets to mod-cons, would have been quite the talking point in both the old pub and the new.

The Tooke Arms still predominantly serves long-term residents of the estate or the odd explorer who stumbles across the pub. Its interior offers a warm atmosphere, akin to a working men's club, with affordable pints purchased by cash only. Many of the older drinkers who imbibe here recall the area before the glass and steel of the Canary Wharf estate started going up in 1988. They have had a front-row seat to the cultural and architectural change of the area as it happened.

These postwar estates aimed to provide a bright new future for their residents – and this included a good local pub. But most estate pubs have now been demolished, or seen change of use to retail or other community functions, which paints a picture of how East End working-class communities and their drinking habits have changed in recent generations. In the days of dockers and stevedores, the Island was teeming with life and The Tooke was one of 15 pubs on its western side. Today, it is the only survivor and arguably the last slice of old life that clings on in a changing world.

165 Westferry Road, E14 8NH

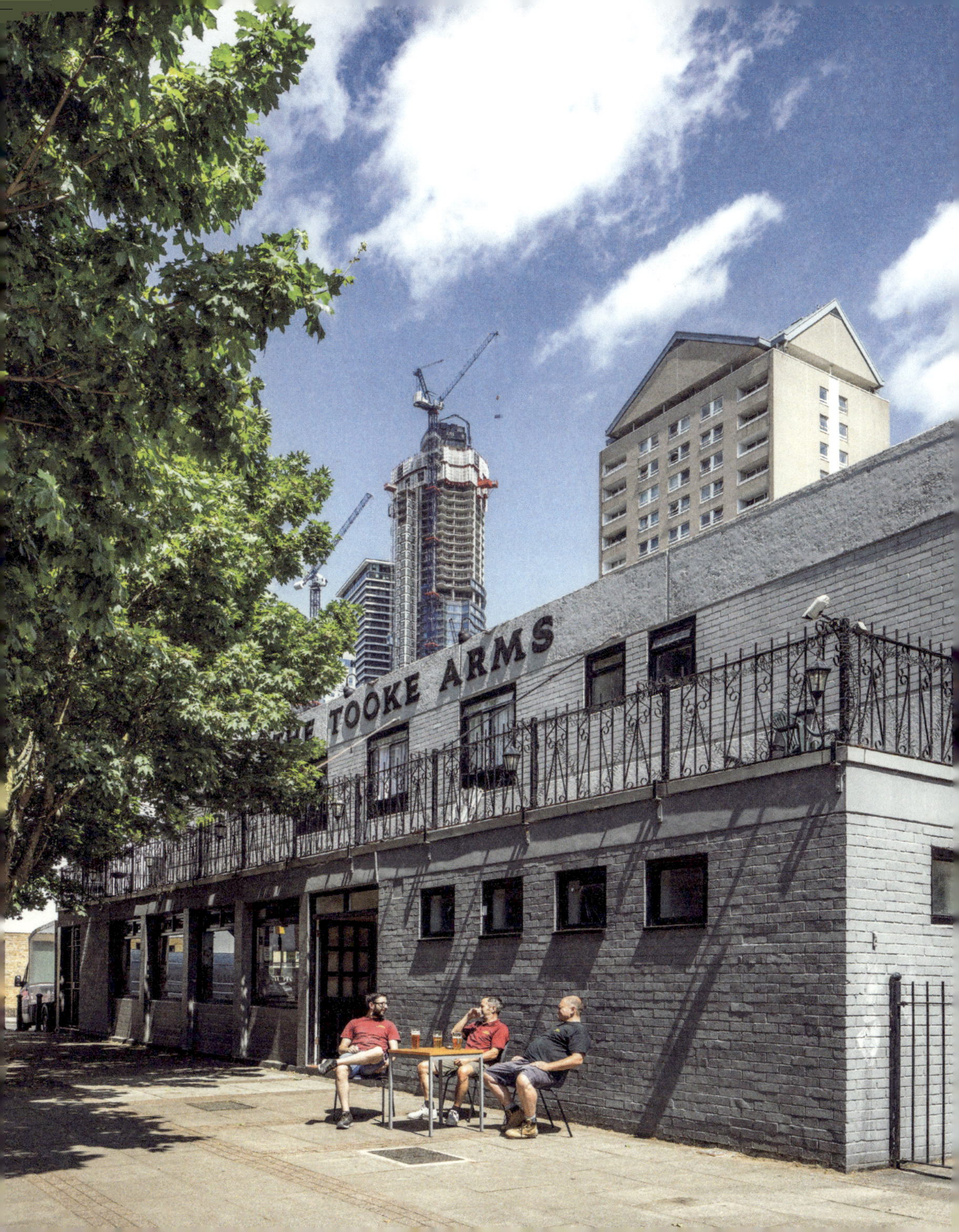
TOOKE ARMS

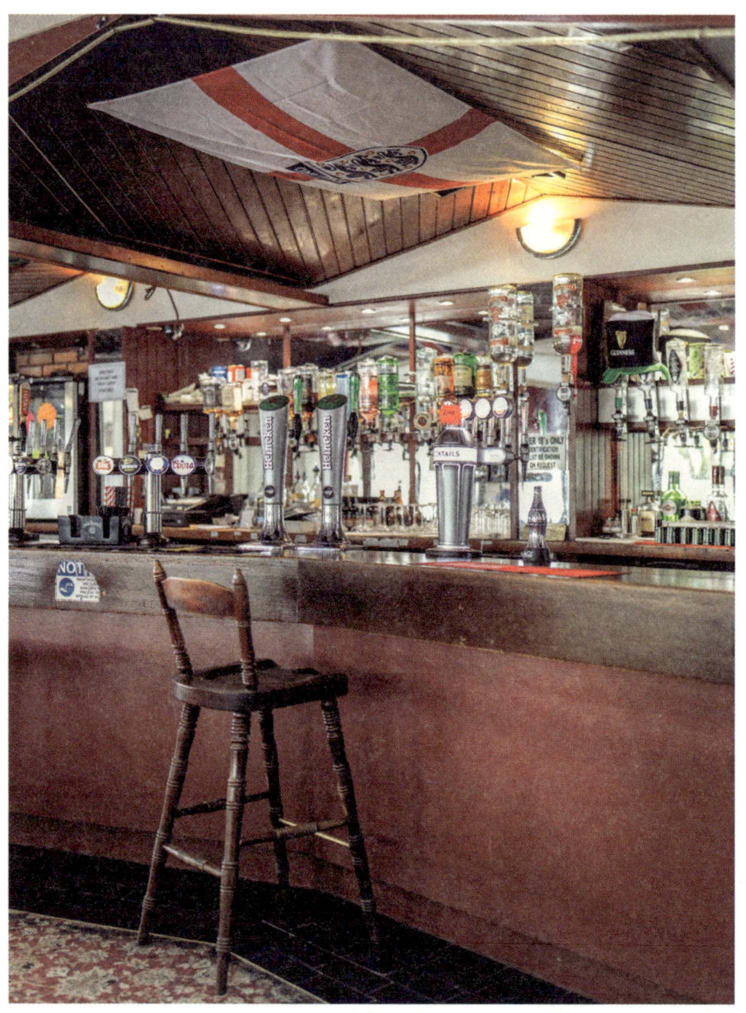

The Tooke Arms has all the markers of an authentic pub, from the patterened carpet to the pool table and party-ready disco lights.

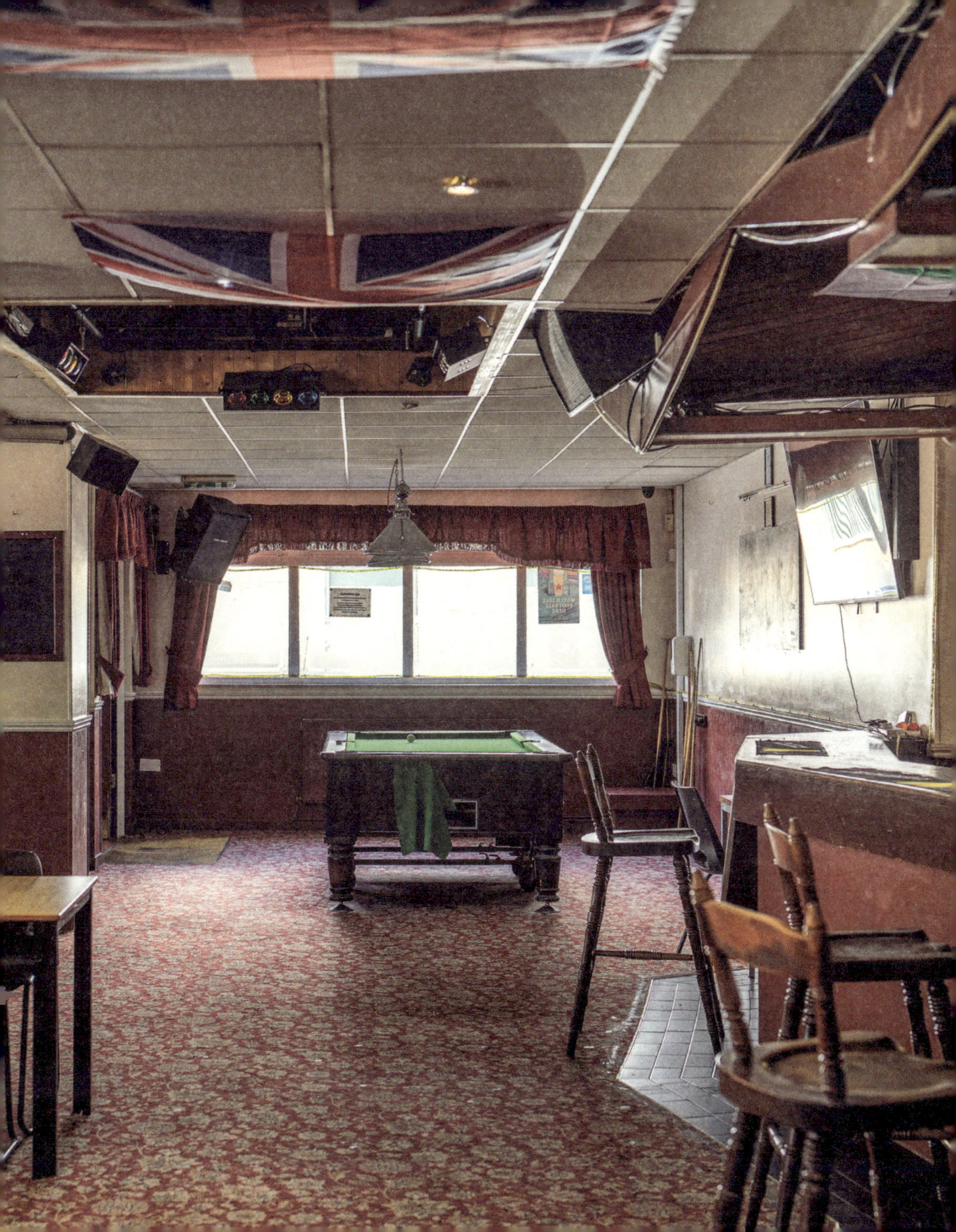

The Bancroft Arms

THE LANDLADY UPHOLDING EAST END TRADITIONS

This handsome interwar boozer once stood across from the People's Palace, a vast public building, which opened in the 19th century to provide facilities and entertainment to the working-class area, rivalling other great philanthropic edifices like Alexandra Palace in north London. Today, the People's Palace is part of the campus of Queen Mary University of London, and so their students have joined the eclectic but loyal band of customers who call The Bancroft Arms their local.

Rebuilt by brewing giant Truman's during the interwar period, The Bancroft Arms is a bellicose survivor, which has stood defiantly while many of its neighbours have been demolished. The striking exterior, with its eye-catching floral displays and bold, sombre brickwork, is both a hallmark and a reminder of a period when the brewing industry invested significantly in their pubs. The signature Truman's typography has a definitive punch, the letters so fresh and vibrant they could have been removed from the kiln just yesterday.

When illuminated at night, the gigantic orange signage on the eastern side of the pub makes it a notable landmark – as would have been the case for all hostelries when they were still used as markers for travellers seeking directions.

Although no original Truman's features remain inside, some traditions do die hard in this friendly establishment. After all, the

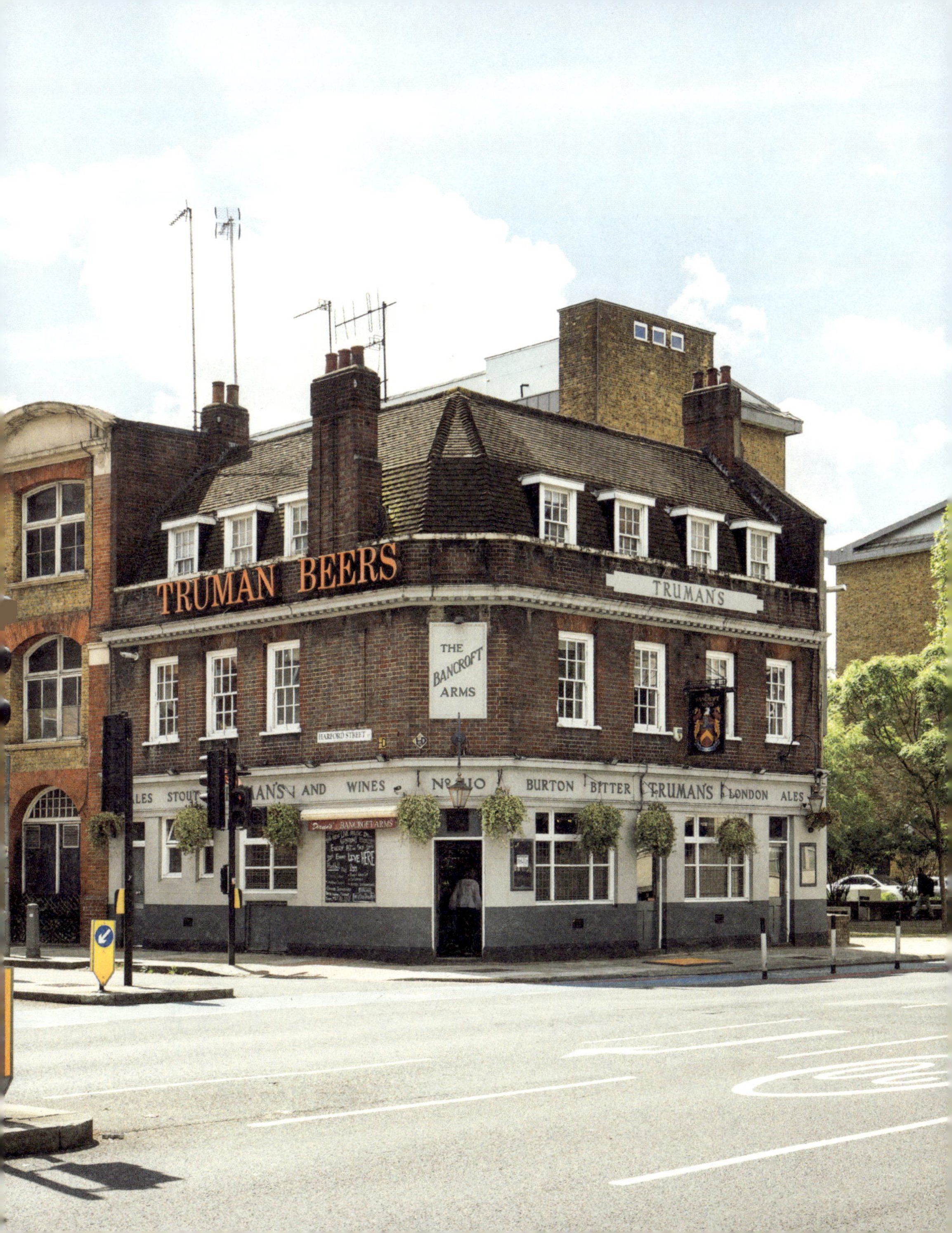

TRUMAN BEERS
TRUMANS
THE BANCROFT ARMS
HARFORD STREET
BANCROFT
Drews BANCROFT ARMS
LIVE MUSIC
EVERY
LIVE HERE
ALES STOUT MAN'S AND WINES No 110 BURTON BITTER TRUMAN'S LONDON ALES

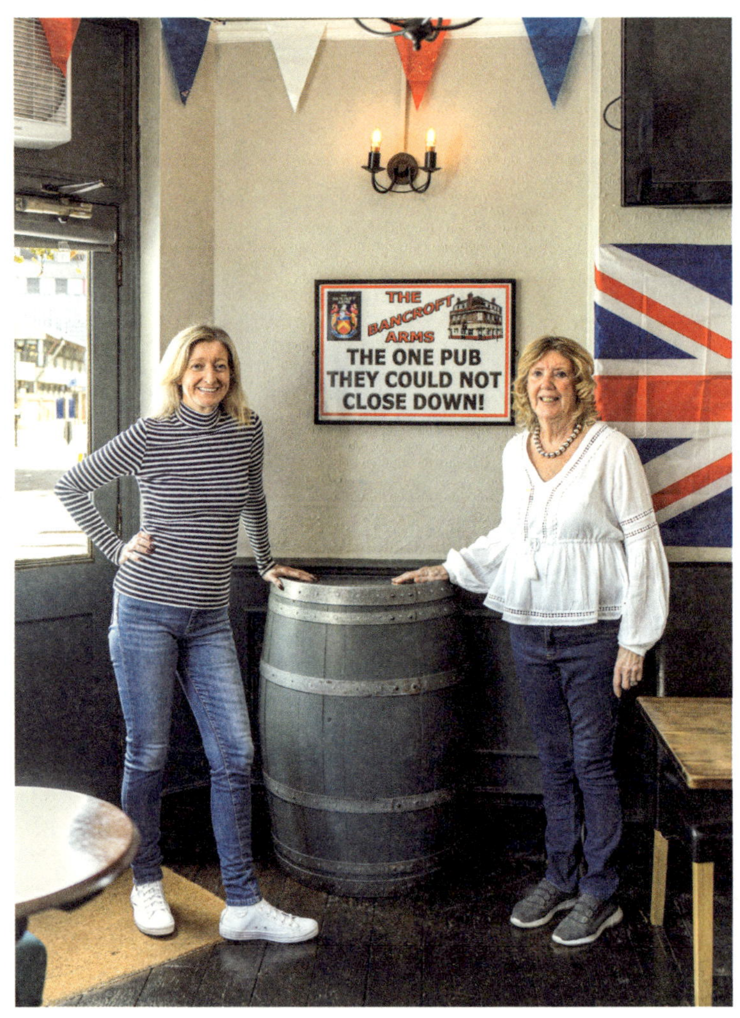

THE
BANCROFT
ARMS
THE ONE PUB
THEY COULD NOT
CLOSE DOWN!

landlady Doreen Martin has been welcoming old faces from Stepney's Ocean Estate for 30 years. Along with the live music and karaoke, it's one of the only places left where the old custom of putting complimentary hot roast potatoes or sandwiches on the bar for hungry punters to enjoy with their beer is still upheld. The genuine fondness that all its regulars have for the landlady is evident in its nickname – Doreen's pub.

Doreen worked as a cashier for Balls Brothers wine merchant for ten years then at the long-demolished Peasants' Revolt in Cleveland Way in Stepney, before taking on The Three Cranes (known locally as 45s) for three years while she waited for The Bancroft to be refurbished after a fire in the late 1980s.

Similar to Sandra Esquilant at The Golden Heart (p.250), Doreen has commanded her domain with an effortless finesse for the last three decades. As a landlady, she has witnessed much change but is unfazed by new surroundings and customers, and always stays true to the spirit of what makes a proper pub.

As a resolute local landlady who has seen it all and has successfully run 'the one pub they couldn't close down' (even after a fire and later battling the threat of developers), Doreen has no rival. Perhaps other than her daughter Mandy, who is very much a hands-on partner in the pub and will take on the reins when Doreen finally decides to hang up her bar towel.

410 Mile End Road, E1 4RQ

Doreen Martin and her daughter Mandy. Doreen has been Guv'nor of The Bancroft Arms for 30 years.

The Eleanor Arms

The sight of the 'Ele' homing into view is enough to warm the cockles of any pub adventurer. Built in the 1930s to replace a 19th-century pub, this independent house is leased from the Kent brewers Shepherd Neame and, simply put, it is everything a good local should be.

Frankie and Lesley Colclough, the husband-and-wife team at the helm of this elysian pub since 2007, previously ran pubs in Swansea and Hull before settling in the East End. The interior can only be described as an extension of the hosts' living room, and their personal taste in art, furnishing and music is stamped on the pub's soul. Old fashioned games such as Shove Ha'penny and Shut the Box are played by visitors enjoying some of the fine ales, which always make the CAMRA good beer guide. Whether cosying up by the fire or playing pool overlooked by Frankie's collection of prints, the setting is agreeable to all who enter the Colclough's home-from-home. Frankie's cranium-taxing quizzes, which have raised thousands for charity, draw people in from miles around. As do his DJ skills, when the Minestrone of Sound creates a rumbustious atmosphere with pre-2010 music. However, it is on Sunday nights when the pub really comes alive, as the dulcet sounds of the Old Ford Jazz Club linger on the air and the good times really begin to roll in the back bar.

At one time there were 11 pubs on Old Ford Road. Today, there are only two. Residents are blessed to have custodians who went above and beyond in the past few years to look after loyal locals who lived alone. Hidden gem is a cliche, but here it is as spot on as the frothy pints that Frankie and Lesley serve up seven days a week.

460 Old Ford Road, E3 5JP

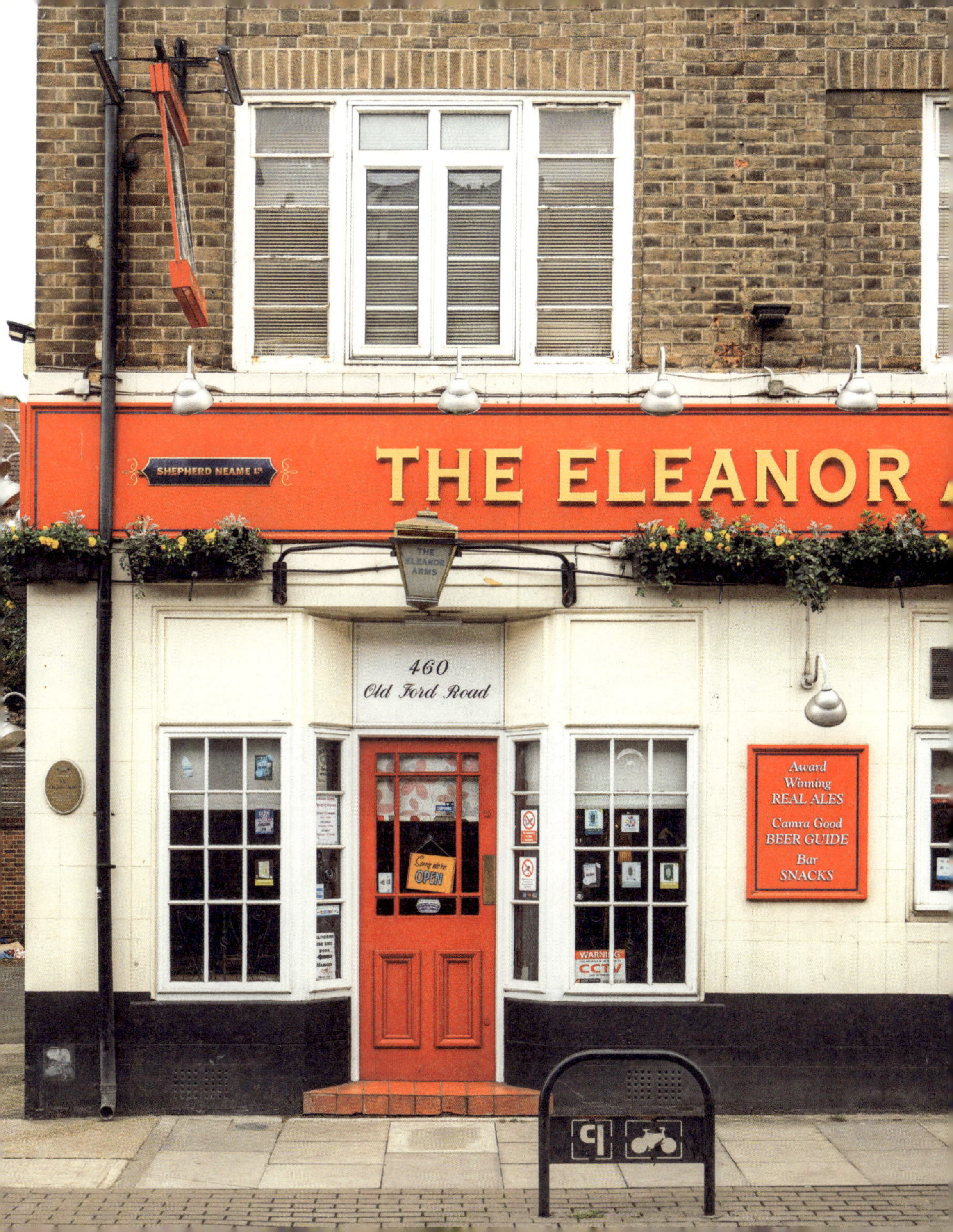

SHEPHERD NEAME LTD
THE ELEANOR A
THE ELEANOR ARMS
460
Old Ford Road
Sorry we're OPEN
WARNING CCTV
Award Winning REAL ALES
Camra Good BEER GUIDE
Bar SNACKS

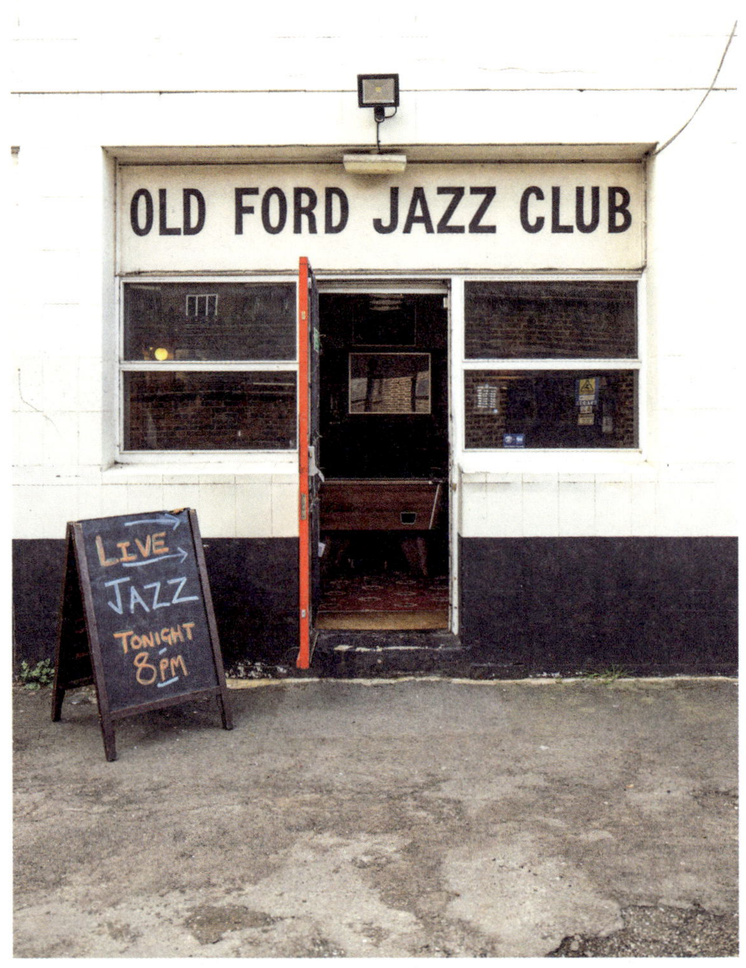

Frankie and Lesley Colclough ran pubs in Swansea and Hull before taking over The Eleanor Arms in 2007. Their passion for live jazz and superb real ale makes The Ele a must-visit.

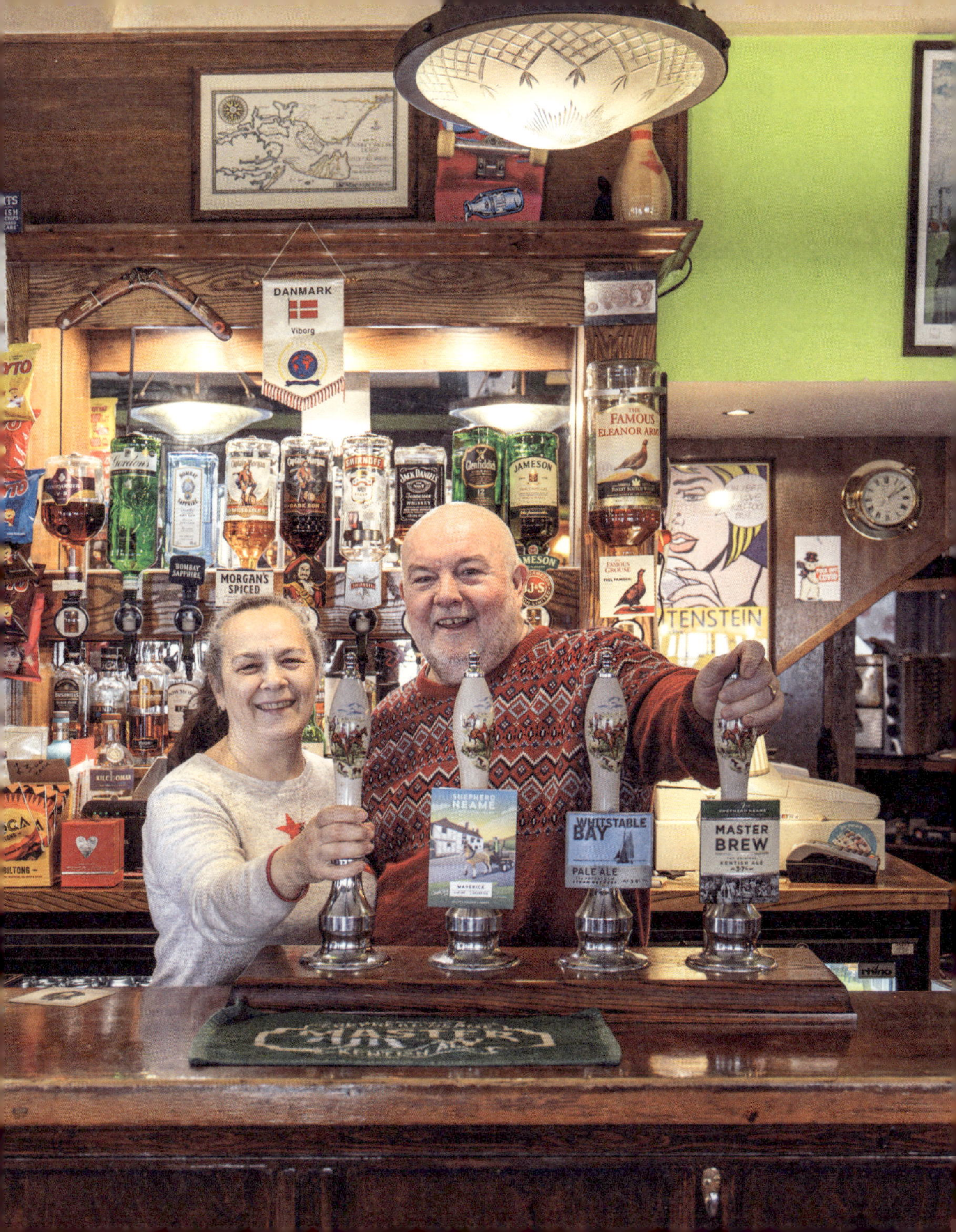

The Old Blue Last

AN IMPOSING BOOZER WITH A RAKISH PAST

Built on the site of an Elizabethan playhouse, this domineering boozer has had a colourful life. The first pub to occupy this corner of Shoreditch was The Last in 1700. But the hostelry you see today was built by Truman's in 1876, who renamed it The Old Blue Last. In the 1970s, the pub became a strip club and brothel, where gangsters ventured for illicit entertainment. Such was its notoriety that it was one of the only pubs not to feature in the 1983 East London and City Beer Guide, which listed over a thousand hostelries.

Shoreditch became popular with artists and students, and The Old Blue Last was bought by VICE Media Group in 2004. It is now one of the most loved music venues in London, where many pioneering musicians have performed, including The Artic Monkeys and Amy Winehouse.

The ground-floor public bar has been beautifully restored. A gilded Truman's mirror shimmers in the soft lighting as it surveys the large room – which once housed three separate bars – with its stripped floor and weathered furniture. Leather studded sofas add an air of 20th-century refinement to the Victorian pub, where it is believed porter was first served.

Porter is a hoppy, dark beer first brewed in London and named for its popularity with the porters of London's markets who guzzled down pint after pint at the end of a hard day's toil. Today, you're more likely to see creatives quenching their thirst with a craft beer, but both scenes depict the immense value of the pub to maintaining a vibrant London. Despite its troubled past, The Old Blue Last continues to do just that with both old-world grace and modern panache.

38 Great Eastern Street, EC2A 3ES

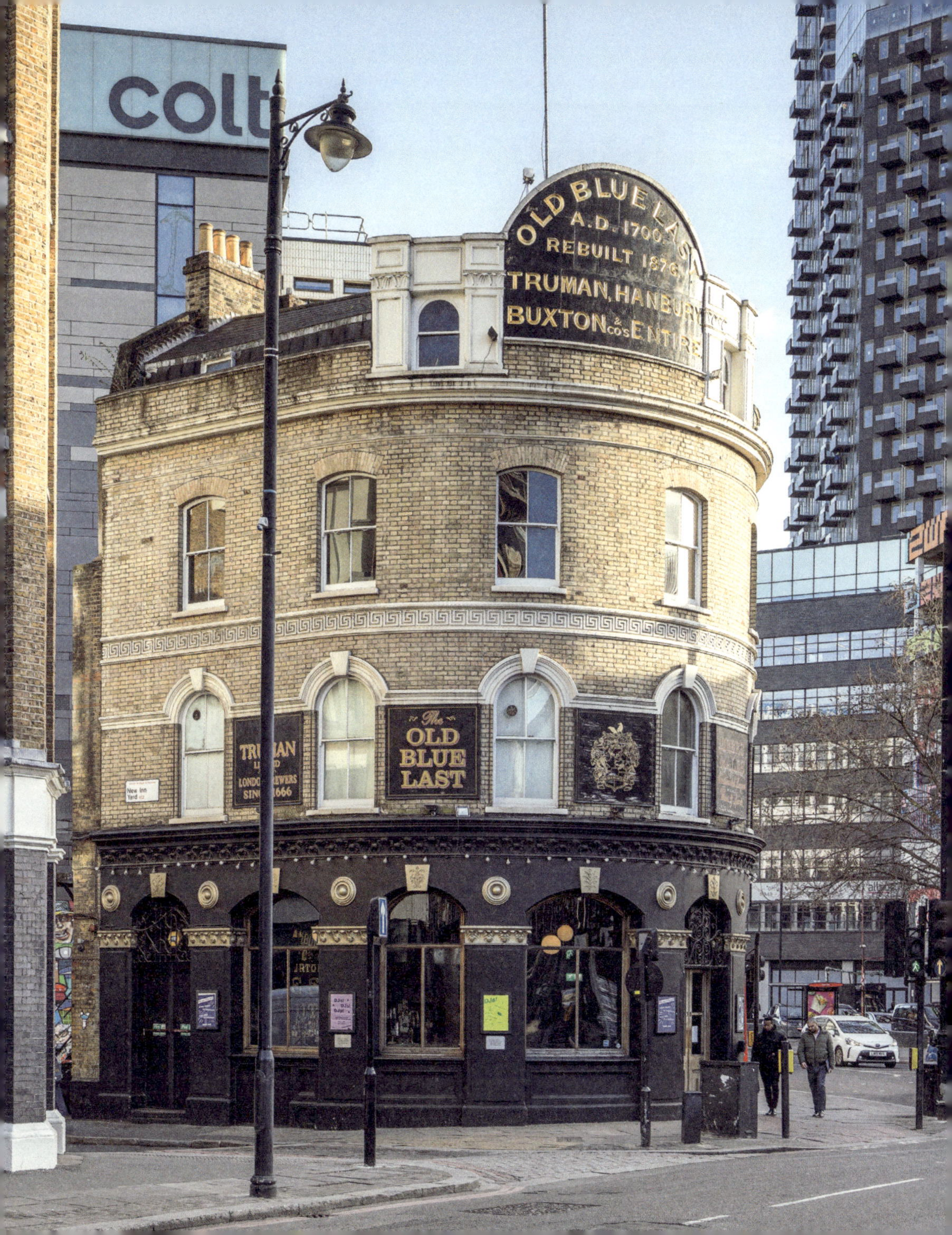

colt
OLD BLUE LAST
A.D. 1700
REBUILT 1876
TRUMAN, HANBURY
BUXTON & co's ENTIRE
TRUMAN
LONDON BREWERS
SINCE 1666
The
OLD
BLUE
LAST
New Inn Yard

The Angel of Bow

FORMER ESTATE PUB SERVING A CHANGING EAST END

In the last decade alone, the East End borough of Tower Hamlets has lost over 36 per cent of its pubs. On top of the high numbers that closed in preceding decades as rising rents and industrial decline pushed Cockneys out of the area, the death knell for many survivors came when the traffic-clogged A12 split the old manor of Bromley-by-Bow in two, dividing communities that had formed around many local pubs.

The streets around Bow are today predominantly residential and devoid of the pub signage that once illuminated every corner. Many older residents believe that without the pubs the area's identity has disappeared.

It is therefore to be celebrated when any hostelry comes back from the dead, as The Angel of Bow did in 2017. There has been a pub on the site since the 19th century, but it was demolished and rebuilt in the 1930s, first as the Bricklayers' Arms. The building enjoys all the exterior hallmarks of interwar architecture. It has the boxy structure, distinctive clay tiles and pitched roof common for the period.

Inside, people come to drink craft beer from the innumerable taps while playing board games around the wood burner on mismatched furniture. While in its past life the interior was bright red, the more neutral colouring today projects a feeling of effortless cool. With weekly events such as open mic nights and Salsa Saturdays, the bonhomie and revelry of the East End's glorious social past is being revived at The Angel of Bow, ensuring that this corner of London is full of life.

171 Devons Road, E3 3QX

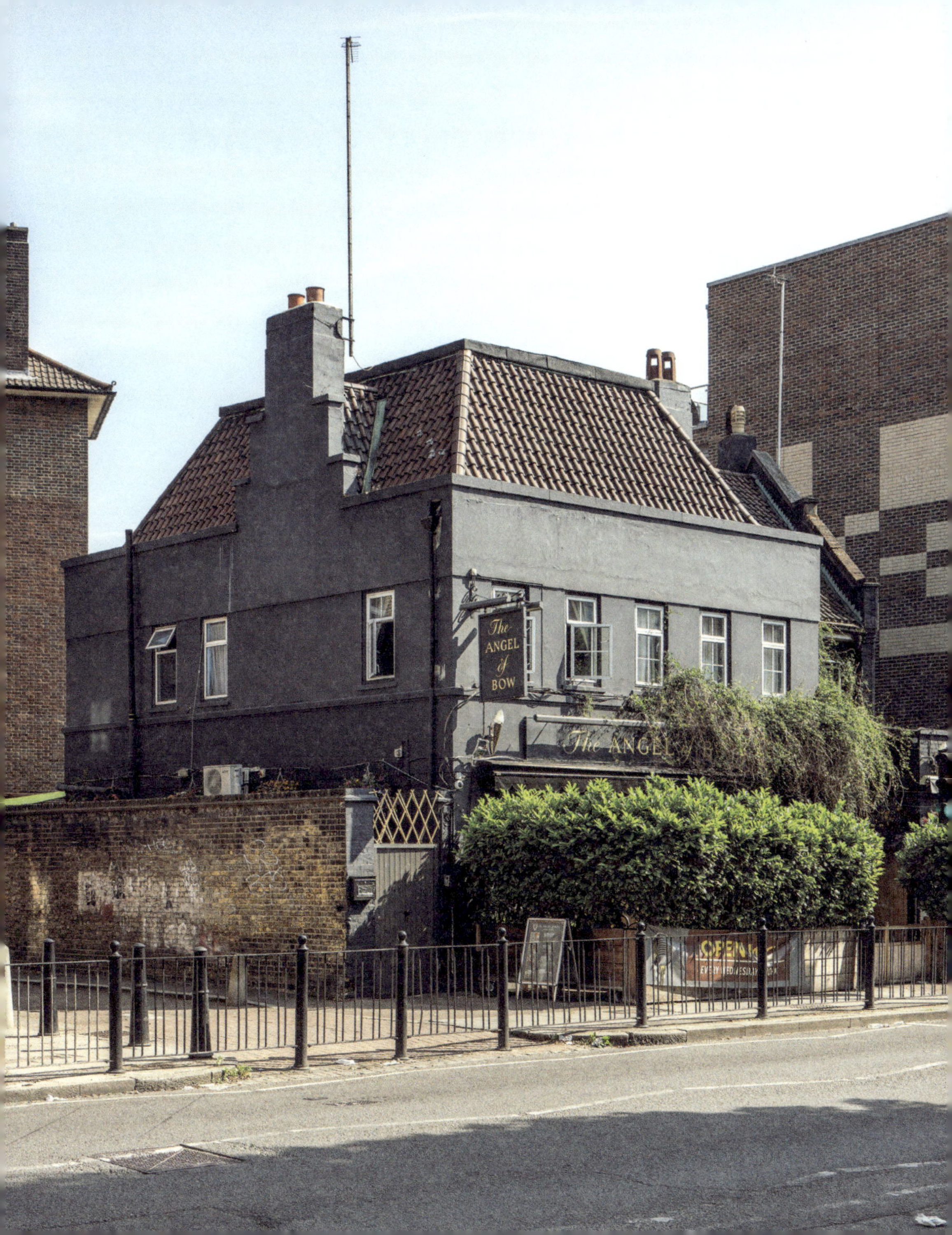
The
ANGEL
of
BOW
The ANGEL
OPEN
EVERY WEDNESDAY

The Old King's Head

A SHINING EXAMPLE OF A PROPER PUB

As a purveyor of good times since the mid-19th century, this tapered old-school boozer is a much-loved local treasure. Firmly planted on a fork in the road among the narrow backstreets of Shoreditch, its dazzling glazed tiles have no rival. It's not unusual for merry punters to spill out onto the street and benches to consume frothy pints with an enthusiasm that embodies the pub's perpetual spirit of bonhomie.

While many of its local contemporaries have transitioned into bars that cater to a younger, hipper denizen of Shoreditch, the Old King's Head retains the essence of a quintessential boozer. A seasoned carpet indicates the building is true to the old ways, as do the flashing fruit machines that light up the comfortingly gloomy interior. The wallet-friendly happy hour is also a welcome throwback to a time when all East End pubs offered one, not only to entice trade but also to fill up the pub during those quieter times of service.

The Turner family have been manning the pumps for 15 years, and work hard to make sure that all ages and tastes are catered for – serving belt-loosening full English breakfasts to old-timers as well as smashed avocado on toast to those who work in the nearby offices. For pubs to survive across the East End they need to diversify and be fully inclusive, which is something this stoic hostelry manages with aplomb.

28 Holywell Row, EC2A 4JB

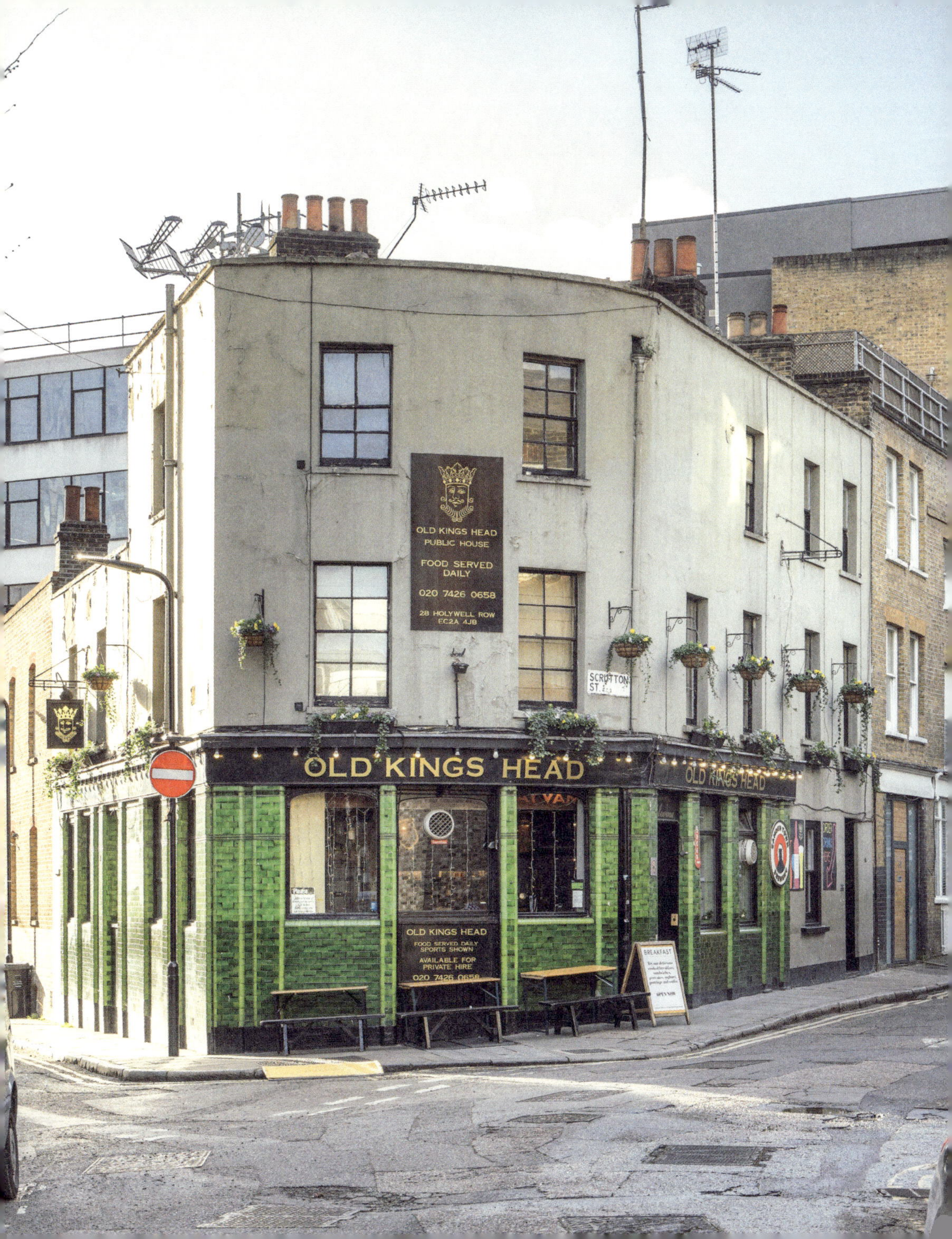

OLD KINGS HEAD
PUBLIC HOUSE
FOOD SERVED
DAILY
020 7426 0658
28 HOLYWELL ROW
EC2A 4JB
SCRUTTON
ST. EC2
OLD KINGS HEAD
OLD KINGS HEAD
OLD KINGS HEAD
FOOD SERVED DAILY
SPORTS SHOWN
AVAILABLE FOR
PRIVATE HIRE
020 7426 0658
BREAKFAST

Callaghann's

On the edge of Chrisp Street Market lies Callaghann's – or Cally's as it's fondly known – an estate pub built for the 1951 Festival of Britain and originally it was named the Festive Britain in its honour, replacing a hostelry on the same site called The Prince of Wales. It finally became Callaghann's around 1970, named after Guv'nor Cally Smith who ran the boozer until 1980. Like a neighbouring 'battle cruiser', the Grade II-listed Festival Inn, it is a market pub – a bare bones local where patrons go for a soak at the end of (and occasionally during) a hard day's graft.

While first-time visitors might describe Cally's as rough and ready, it has much charm. Most of its current patrons grew up together, forging bonds over affordable pints. Cally's is cash-only and has a menu dedicated to no-frills pub grub, like saveloys with pease pudding, at prices that would shame many trendier operators. Predominantly catering to more senior drinkers and market traders, Cally's opens early doors so they can wet their whistles from 10:30am each day.

The area is on the brink of seismic change with the regeneration of Chrisp Street Market well underway. While many Festival of Britain buildings like Cally's will be preserved for their architectural significance, much of the local estate will be demolished to make way for new homes. It is a good sign that the community value of the pub is being recognised in the midst of regeneration. It is a lifeline for the lonely and an affordable hostelry for working-class pensioners, many of whom are in danger of being left behind under the banner of progress.

55 Chrisp Street, E14 6LP

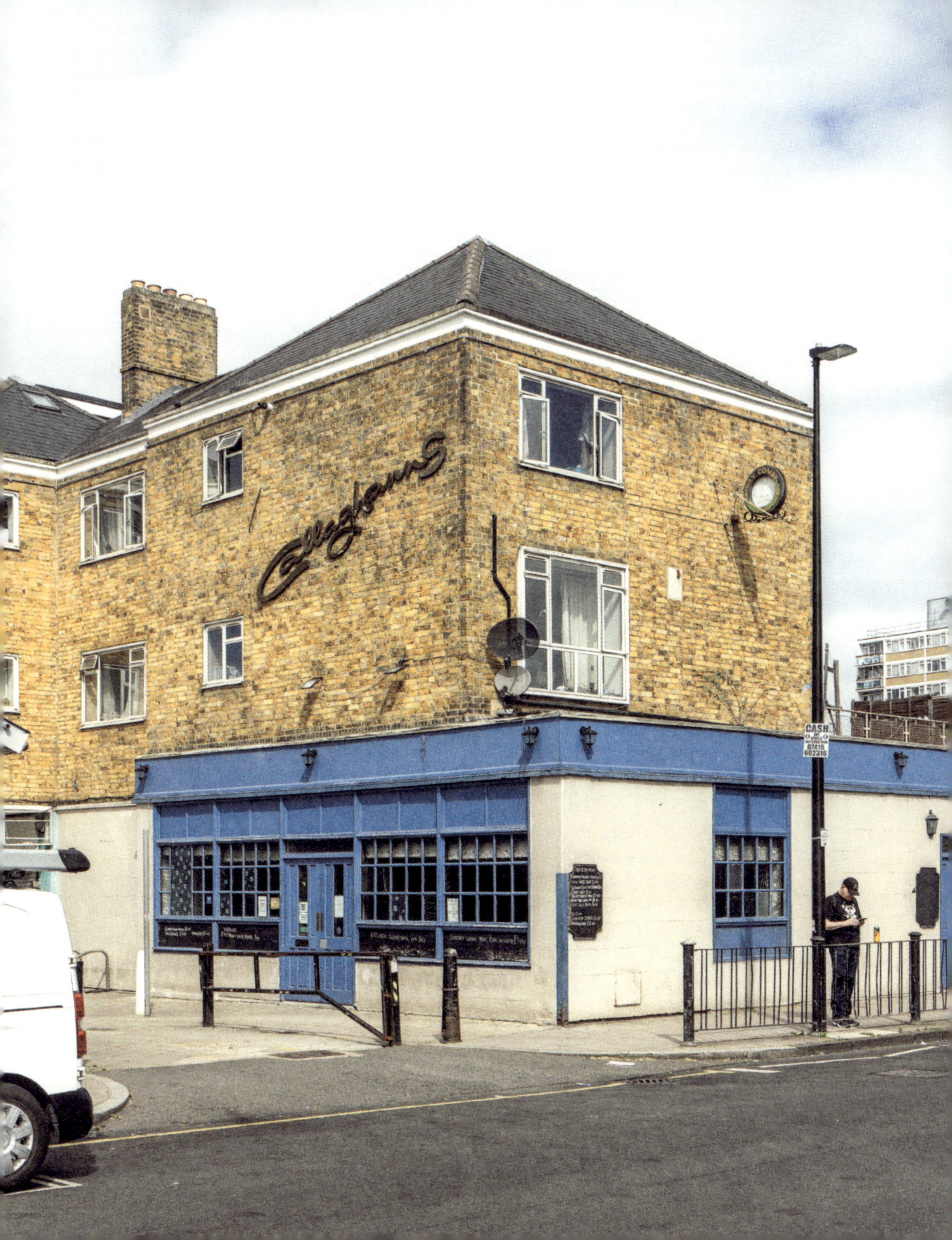

The Marksman

A HARMONIOUS BLEND OF PUB WITH FINE DINING

Moments from Shoreditch High Street lies a pub that encompasses the best of both worlds, thanks to the imagination of its chef-owners Jon Rotheram and Tom Harris. From the outside, the Marksman looks like a fairly typical grand old pub – resolutely commanding the corner of Horatio Street. But thanks to a thoughtful refurbishment in 2015, the ground floor is occupied by one of the most beautifully restored Victorian pubs in London – with a wood-panelled interior, green banquette seating, mushroom stools and a varnished bar with brass footrails and handpumps of locally sourced beer.

This traditional pub couldn't be more different to the restaurant on the first floor with its lively, contemporary design and adventurous menu of seasonal British cuisine. It's a fresh and modern dining room with coloured chairs, a kaleidoscopic floor and textured ceiling. It's not hard to see why the Marksman was the first pub in London to receive the coveted Michelin Pub of the Year award in 2017. Jon and Tom, who worked together at St John's in Clerkenwell, are blazing a trail with delicacies such as braised mutton with peas and guinea fowl with burnt apple jam.

Such variety makes the Marksman a destination pub and people travel great distances to sample the Sunday Roasts or enjoy a drink on the roof terrace overlooking the Hackney Road. But while Jon and Tom wanted to open a restaurant, they also wished to preserve a pub where some locals had been drinking for decades – that they managed to do both is a testament to their vision for the majestic building.

254 Hackney Road, E2 7SJ

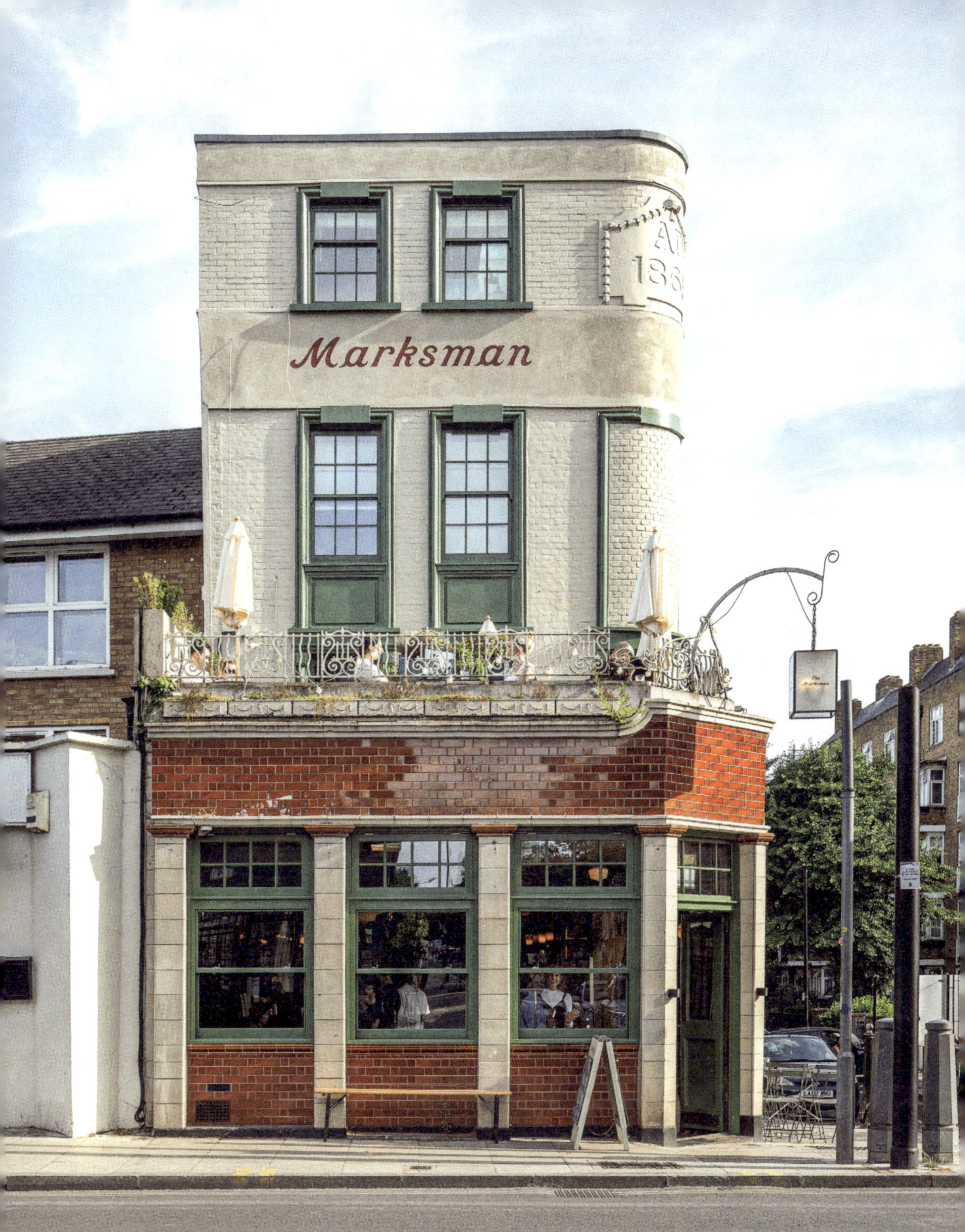
Marksman
A 186

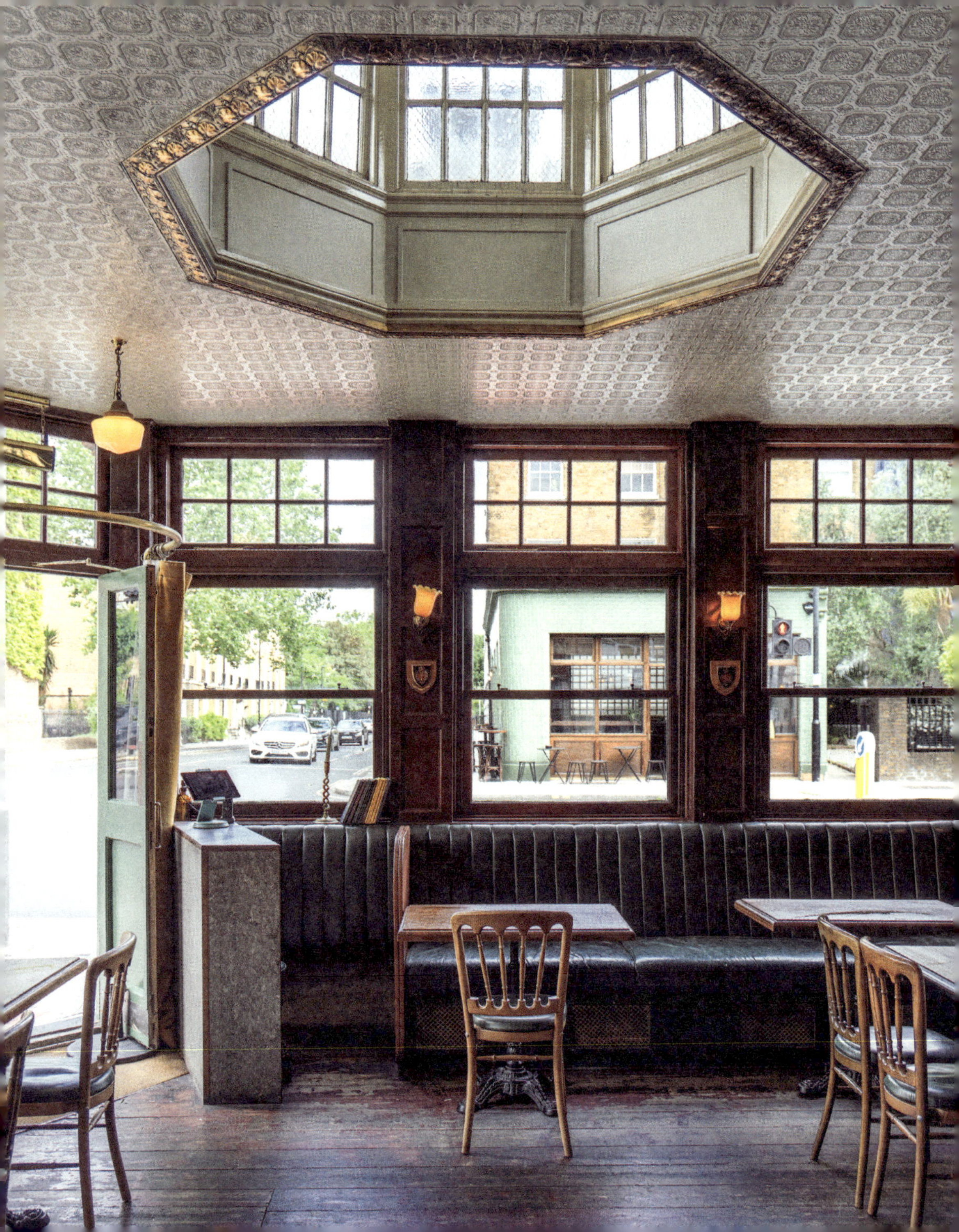

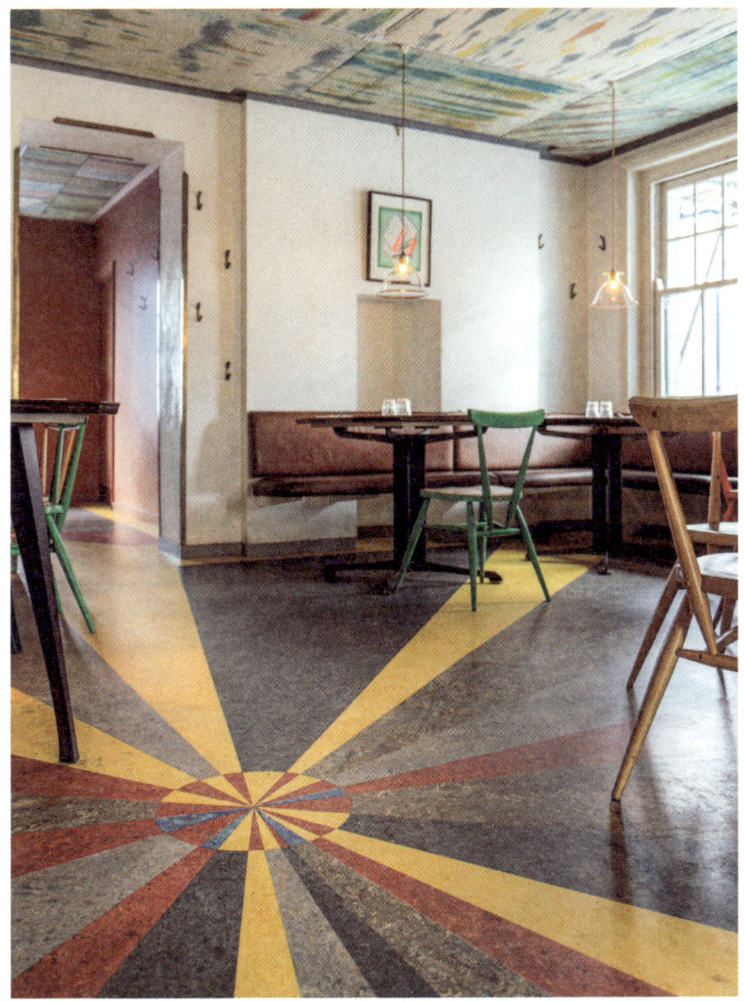

The upstairs dining room, designed by Martino Gamper, features a ceiling covered in a textured fabric produced by a small mill based in east London.

The Buxton

Once a battle-worn boozer, this red-brick pub reopened as a 15-roomed hotel and bistro in 2019. A sister site to the nearby Culpeper (p.180), most remnants of its former life have vanished. Gone are the green tiles, illuminated Truman's sign and net curtains; in their place are an understated pub sign and brightly painted window frames.

While name changes are usually considered bad luck, The Buxton's new moniker is rooted in the area's heritage. The pub stands in the shadow of Truman, Hanbury & Buxton's Black Eagle Brewery, and it is named after Sir Thomas Fowell Buxton, a brewer and politician who campaigned for improved living conditions in the East End. Until the pub was renamed, only Buxton Street paid homage to his life and achievements.

The pub's interior has also undergone a sleek redesign. Instead of raucous karaoke, the Buxton now entertains its guests with a seasonal menu of regional British and European dishes scrawled on chalkboards above the bar. With the few remaining Victorian features off-set by distressed walls, a white-tiled floor and a bar topped with red marble, The Buxton is a fresh and modern incarnation of a Spitalfields' inn.

Like The Culpeper, The Buxton has enjoyed much success since its rebirth and is popular with foodies and those looking for a special night out. That somewhere like Spitalfields, once synonymous with serial killers, abject poverty and organised crime, is now a destination that people travel from across the world to enjoy illustrates just how much the area has changed. The Buxton is very much at the forefront of the new East End.

42 Osborn Street, E1 6TD

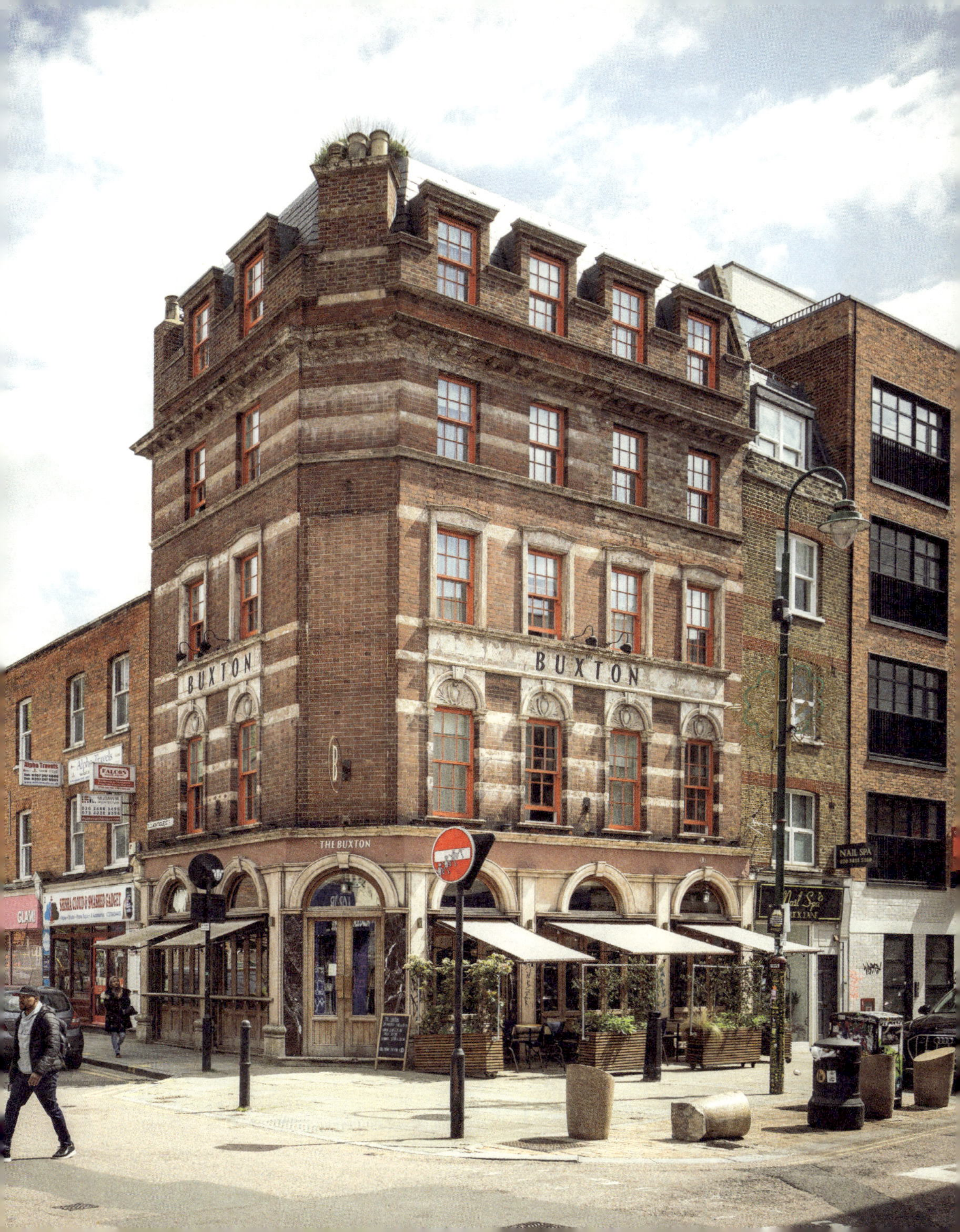

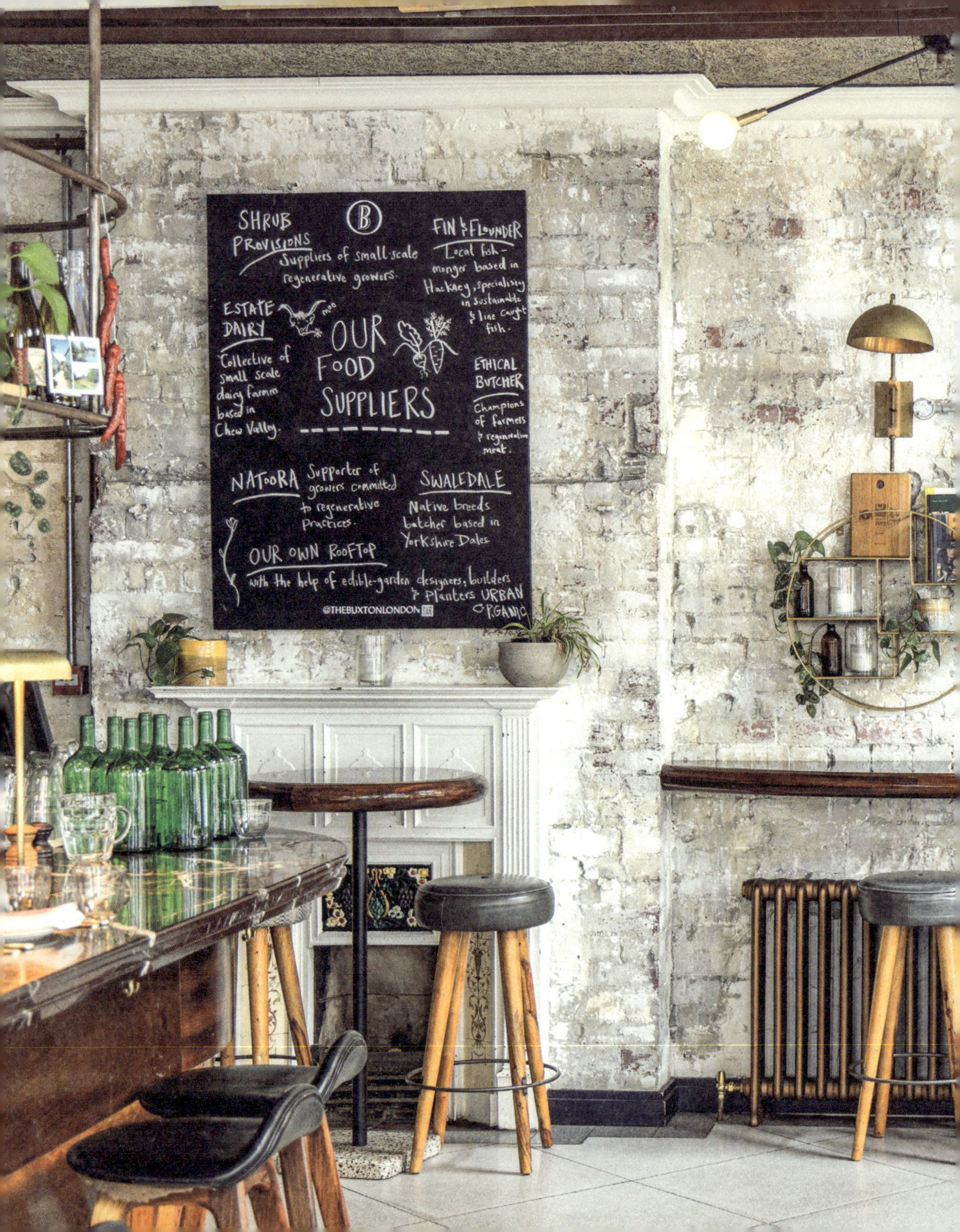

SHRUB PROVISIONS
Suppliers of small-scale regenerative growers.

FIN & FLOUNDER
Local fish-monger based in Hackney, specialising in sustainable & line caught fish.

ESTATE DAIRY
Collective of small scale dairy farmers based in Chew Valley.

OUR FOOD SUPPLIERS

ETHICAL BUTCHER
Champions of farmers & regenerative meat.

NATOORA
Supporter of growers committed to regenerative practices.

SWALEDALE
Native breeds butcher based in Yorkshire Dales

OUR OWN ROOFTOP
with the help of edible-garden designers, builders & planters URBAN ORGANIC

@THEBUXTONLONDON

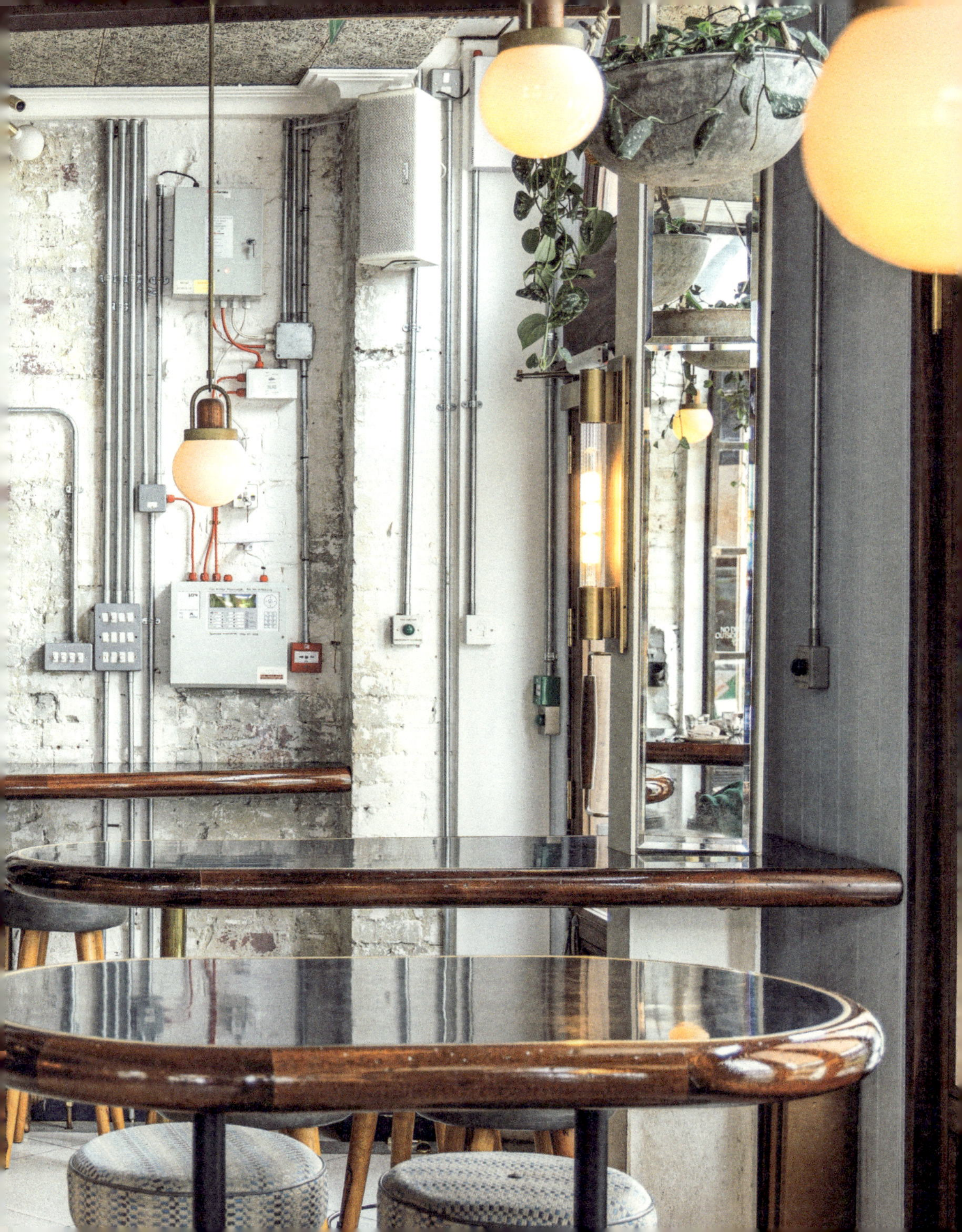

The Waterman's Arms

AN EAST END PUB WITH A SPRINKLE OF HOLLYWOOD GLAMOUR

The Grade II-listed Waterman's Arms has a storied past with many a tale to tell. Originally called The Newcastle Arms, the pub first drew fame when journalist and man-about-town Dan Farson purchased it in 1962. He was fascinated by the music hall traditions of the East End and so, after changing the pub's name to The Waterman's Arms, he persuaded a series of famous performers to grace its stage. Shirley Bassey, Queenie Watts and music hall star Ida Barr were among the many acts to perform for a crowd that included Hollywood royalty such as Groucho Marx and Clint Eastwood.

Sadly, Farson's bold venture did not last and he sold up, partly because of the logistical challenges punters had getting to the isolated Island. The pub soldiered on during the steady, terminal decline of the docks and it wasn't until 2020 that it returned to its former glory. Despite reopening just at the start of the pandemic, the pub is now flourishing under the stewardship of Laura Lythall, who was born on the Isle of Dogs.

Big windows welcome drinkers inside to imbibe at the long bar or dine where Farson's stage once lay. A menu boasting moreish small plates and classic pub fare is available throughout the day and, in the summer, can be enjoyed at leisure in the sunken garden. At one point in its long life, the upper floors had housed a backpackers' hostel. Now, there are seven boutique rooms, allowing out-of-towners to stay on the Island in style and comfort.

Although Farson's celebrity guests of yesteryear may no longer be regular customers, the Waterman's Arms is more than ready for its next role.

1 Glenaffric Avenue, E14 3BW

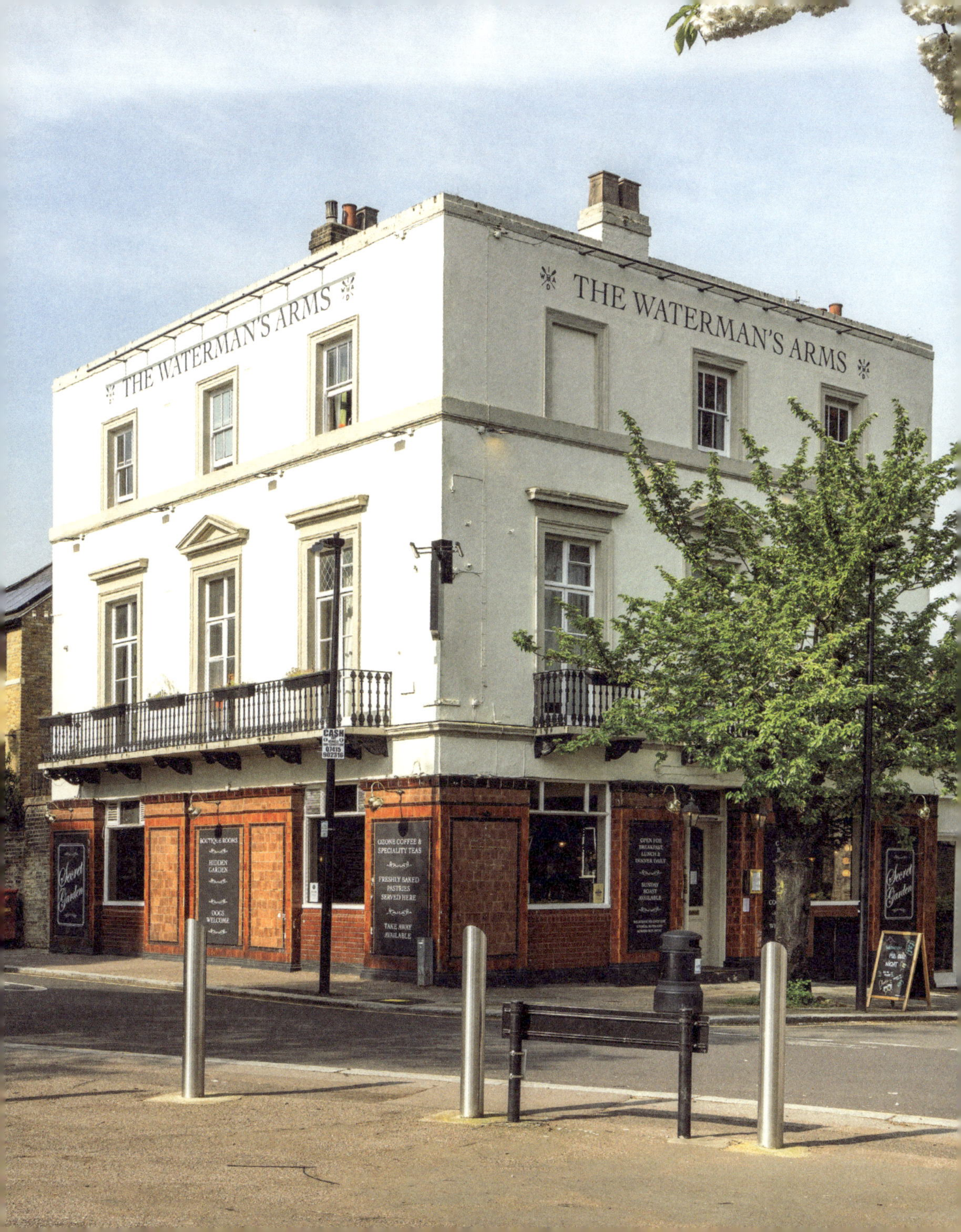

THE WATERMAN'S ARMS
THE WATERMAN'S ARMS
BOUTIQUE ROOMS
HIDDEN GARDEN
DOGS WELCOME
OZONE COFFEE & SPECIALITY TEAS
FRESHLY BAKED PASTRIES SERVED HERE
TAKE AWAY AVAILABLE
OPEN FOR BREAKFAST, LUNCH & DINNER DAILY
SUNDAY ROAST AVAILABLE
Secret Garden
Secret Garden
CASH

The Carpenters Arms

Construction began on the Collingwood Estate in the years following the First World War, but it wasn't until the 1960s that The Carpenters Arms was built to replace the original old pub that had dated back to the 19th century. Today, the estate pub cuts a stark and striking image against the block of flats it is embedded into, but passers-by unfamiliar with the area barely notice it as they rush to grab a pint at the famous Blind Beggar (p.32). While it might not seem as welcoming as a Victorian boozer, inside it is the most hospitable of Cockney enclaves.

Estate pubs were once at the heart of working-class communities. While most wouldn't win any architectural awards, these flat-roofed boozers (often unfairly represented in the media as dangerous and hostile to outsiders) were much more than just places to go for a drink. People often managed their lives from the public bar, whether buying a motor, sorting out an MOT or borrowing money from the pub's Christmas loan club. As one of the last remaining purpose-built estate pubs in the East End, The Carpenters Arms still offers a comfortable home away from home for many locals.

When the karaoke and live music kicks off at the weekend, the sight of the pub in full swing is something to behold. Whether an old regular or a curious newcomer, everyone who enters receives a pleasant reception from the staff, as well as cheap pints and some cheery camaraderie during a weekend Cockney knees-up.

135 Cambridge Heath Road, E1 5RN

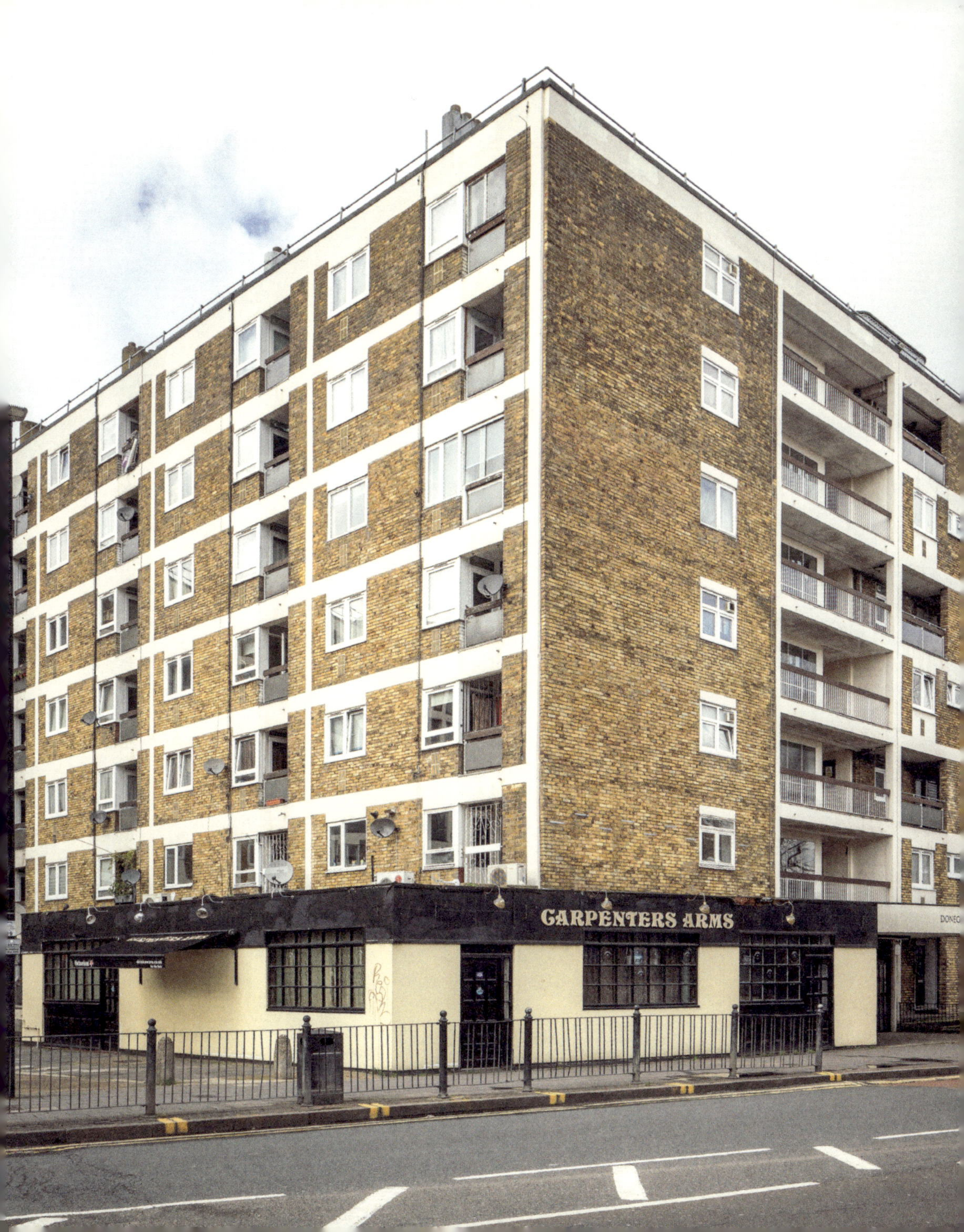
CARPENTERS ARMS

The Ship

There are some custodians of East End pubs who work hard to keep local history alive. One such publican is second-generation landlady and barkeep Laura Lythall. While her dad, Steve, only took on this cosy boozer on the edge of the Island in 2012, the family has run pubs in the East End for much longer. Steve and his partner Tracy Watkin ran a number of pubs, including the Isle of Dog's City Arms from 1985 until 2000. Laura grew up in the City Arms until she was five years old, and the values she learned there as a 'pub kid' have served her well at The Ship and its sister pub, which she also runs, The Waterman's Arms (p.212).

The pub was built in 1835 and named after the SS Great Eastern steamship designed by Isambard Kingdom Brunel, which makes one wonder if those who built the boat came to seek refreshment after toiling at Burrells Wharf. What is certain is that centuries later the honest Island boozer continues to offer warmth, shelter and sustenance to an appreciative crowd. Light ales and porters might have been replaced by craft beer, and pizza is now the culinary order of the day, but the value to local life is still priceless.

As a welcoming LGBTQ+ house with a regular poker night, the pub continues the East End's long tradition of hosting people from all walks of life. Perfect for a quiet pint and the paper, it's one of life's simple comforts to be able to sit at the bar and immerse oneself in a corner of Island life.

290 Westferry Road, E14 3AG

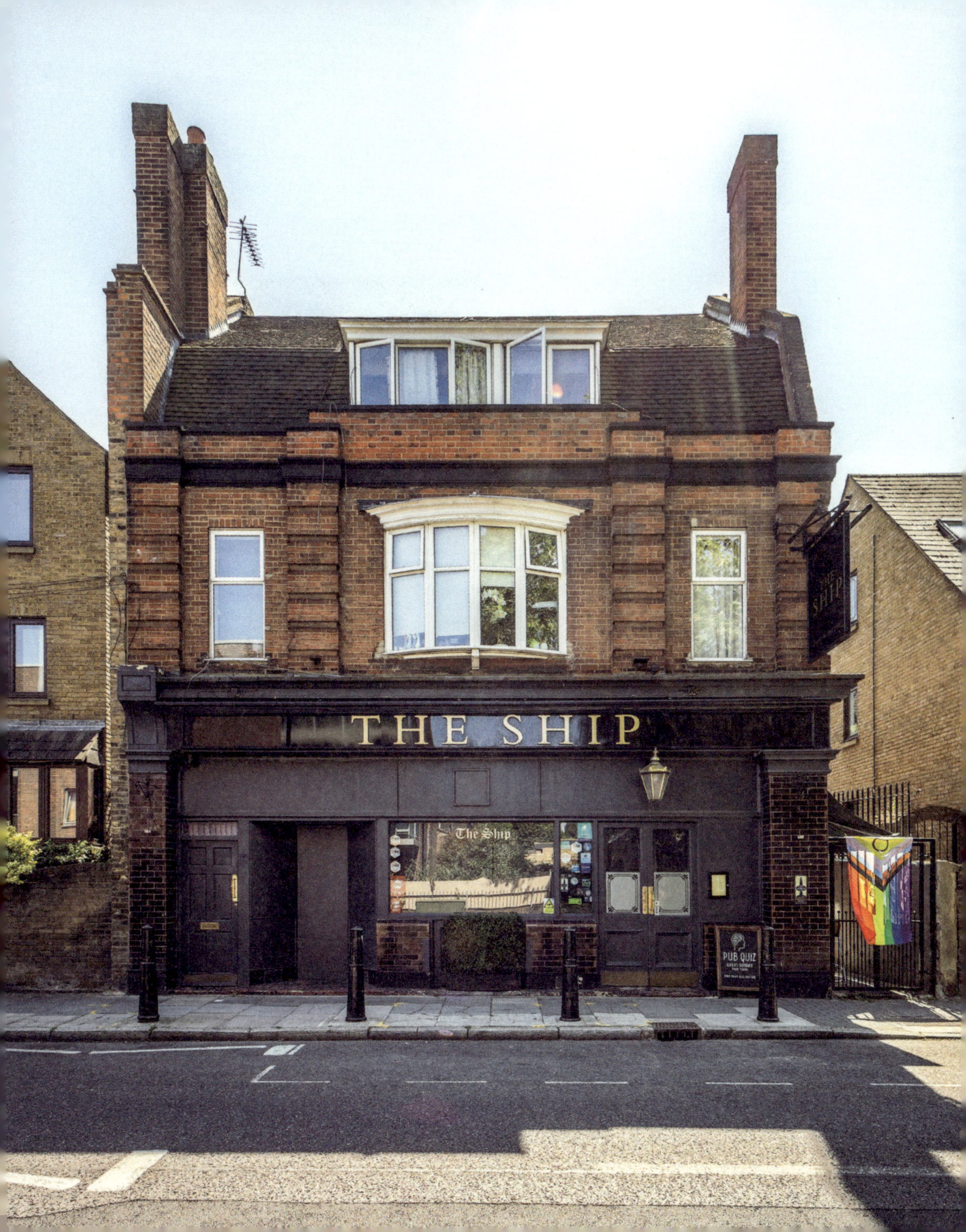

THE SHIP
The Ship
PUB QUIZ

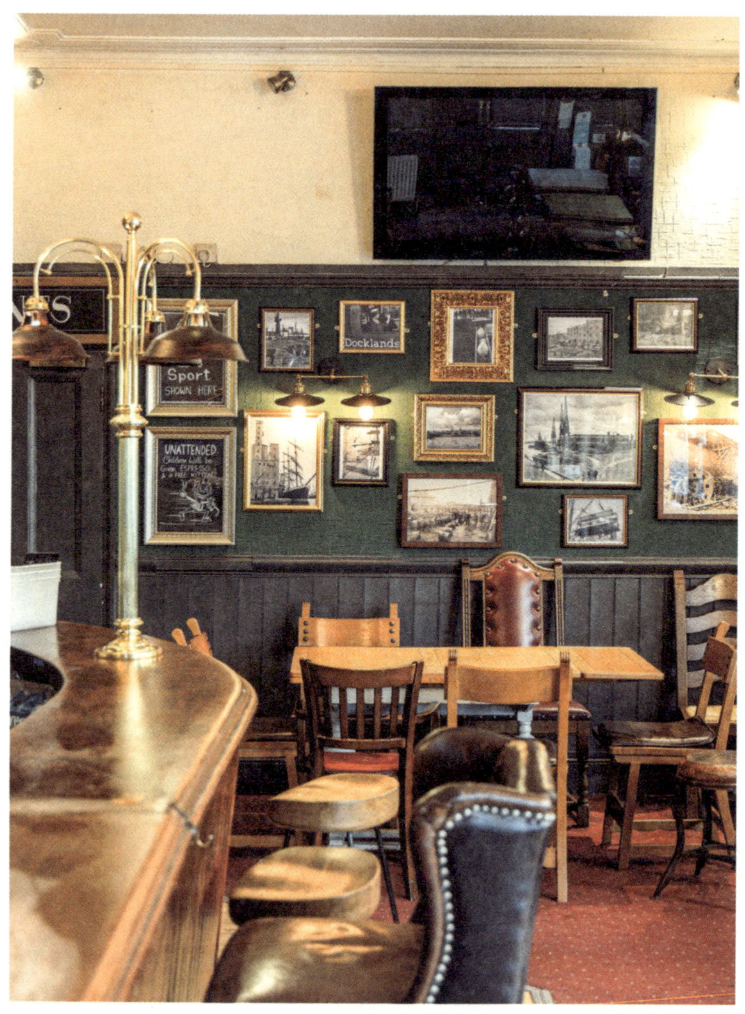

Friendly second-generation landlady Laura Lythall makes sure The Ship remains a welcoming and authentic pub. She also runs The Waterman's Arms (p.212).

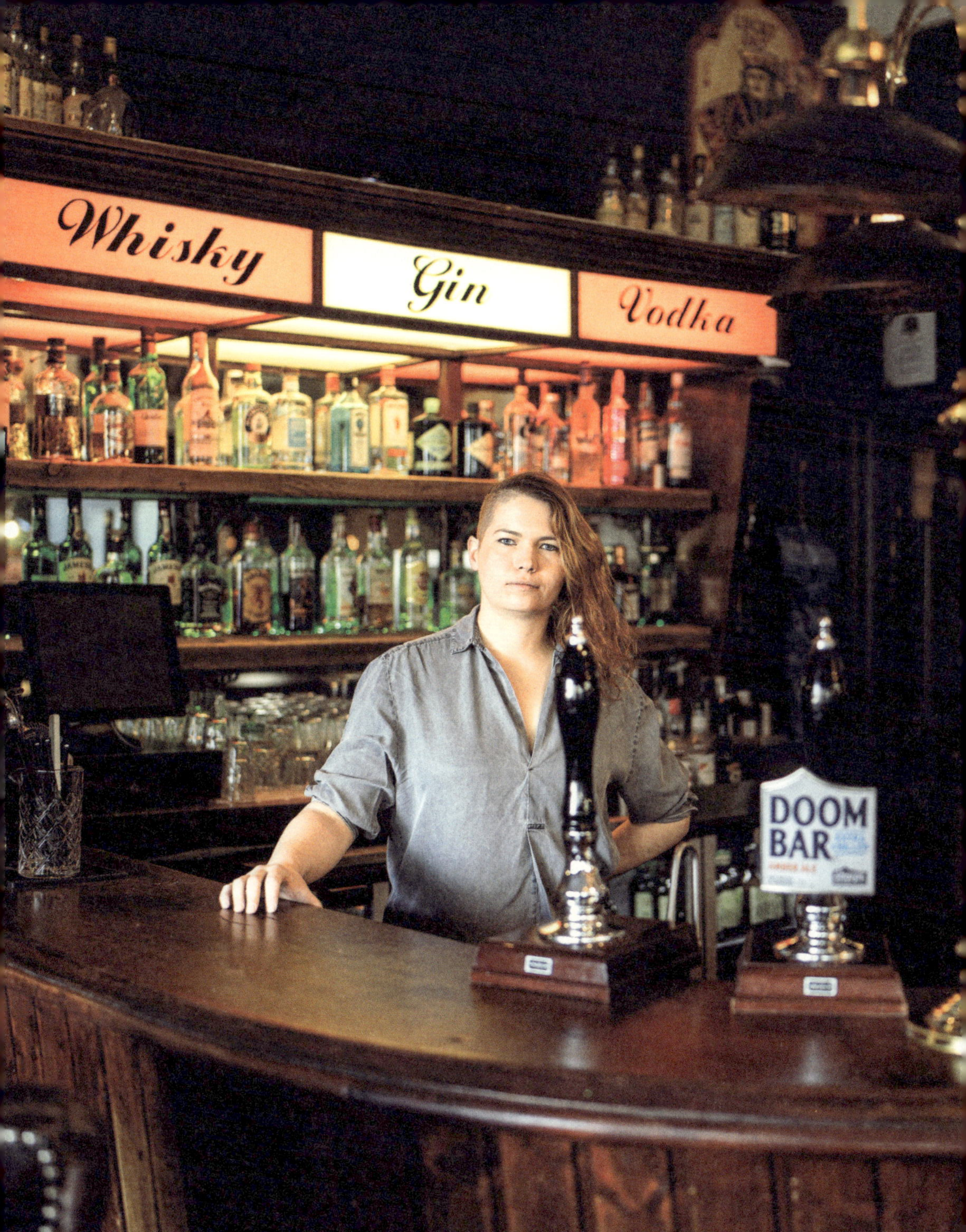
Whisky
Gin
Vodka
DOOM
BAR

The Queen Adelaide

PARTY PUB SERVING QUEER COMMUNITY

Hackney Road once boasted 12 public houses, but today there are only two left. One is the Marksman (p.204) while the other is a curious green-tiled pub built in 1834: The Queen Adelaide. A tenacious survivor, the Adelaide has gone through many changes since it first served Charrington's frothy pints. Over the last 40 years, it's been called The Hop Picker, Images, Keeley's and Tantrum's; existing as a gentleman's club, bistro, late night bar and, in the cellar, an illegal brothel. But in 2015, it finally reverted to its original name and purpose, although its facade retains the marks of its previous occupants.

In the present day, the pub is a vital venue for London's LGBTQ+ community amid the shrinking number of dedicated spaces in the capital. Much of The Queen Adelaide's success is down to the drive of trailblazing East End publican Richard Battye. Former landlord of The George & Dragon in Shoreditch, he was troubled by the diminishing number of queer venues. Around the same time that

Richard took on the lease of The Adelaide, another of Hackney Road's cherished gay venues, The Joiners Arms, called last orders. For many, the opening of The Queen Adelaide was a sign of resistance to be celebrated.

Richard transplanted pictures and knick-knacks from The George, collected over 25 years in the business, and dropped them into the Adelaide, giving this diverse and inclusive East End hostelry an immediately homely feel. With wooden floors, gold leaf pillars and an atmospheric bar, it's an enticing hideaway far from the strains of everyday life.

A 3am licence from Thursday to Saturday makes it a destination for partygoers. The fact that people from all walks of life can throw shapes together under the banner of love until the wee hours captures London's pub scene at its finest.

483 Hackney Road, E2 9ED

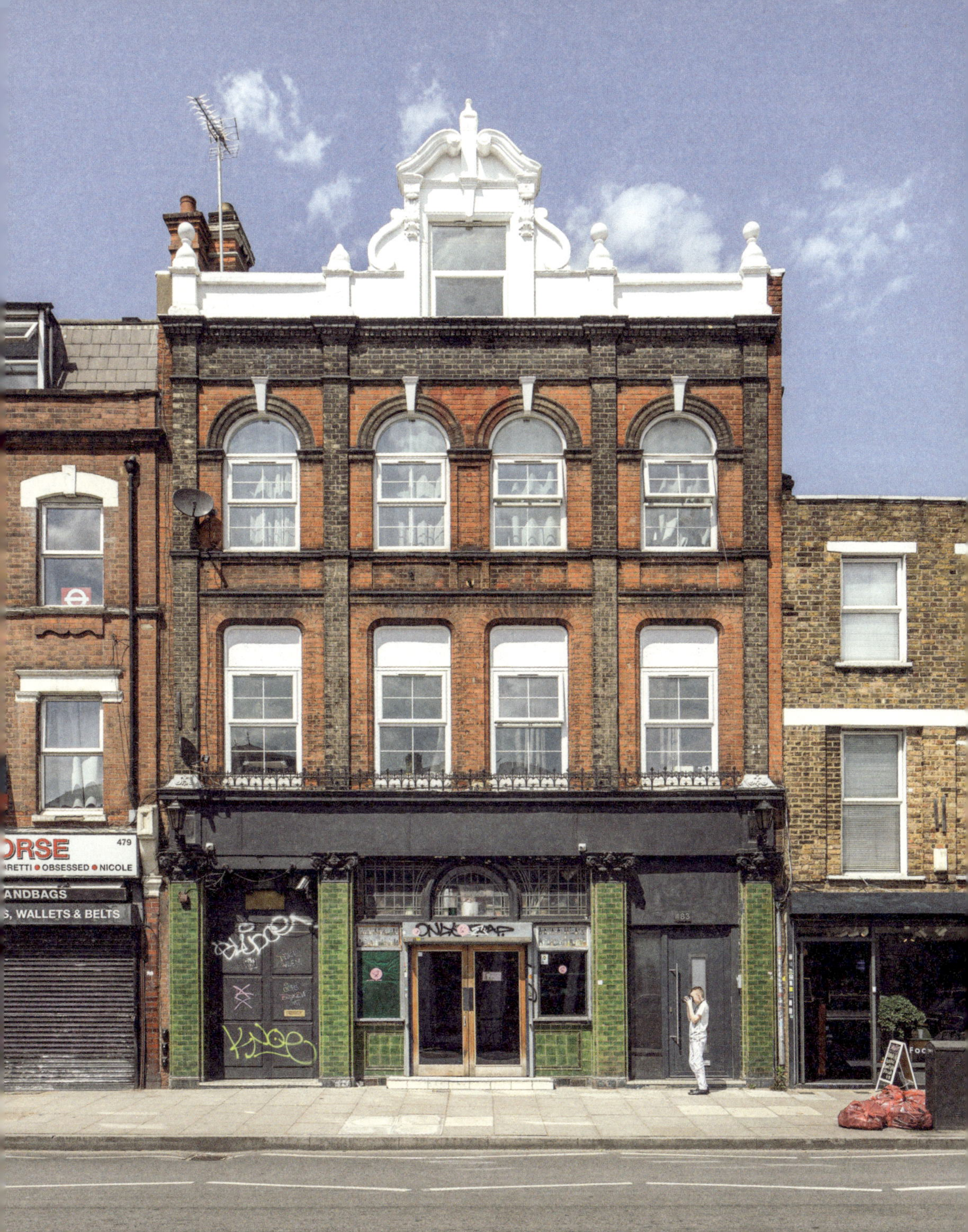
ORSE
479
RETTI ● OBSESSED ● NICOLE
ANDBAGS
S, WALLETS & BELTS
483

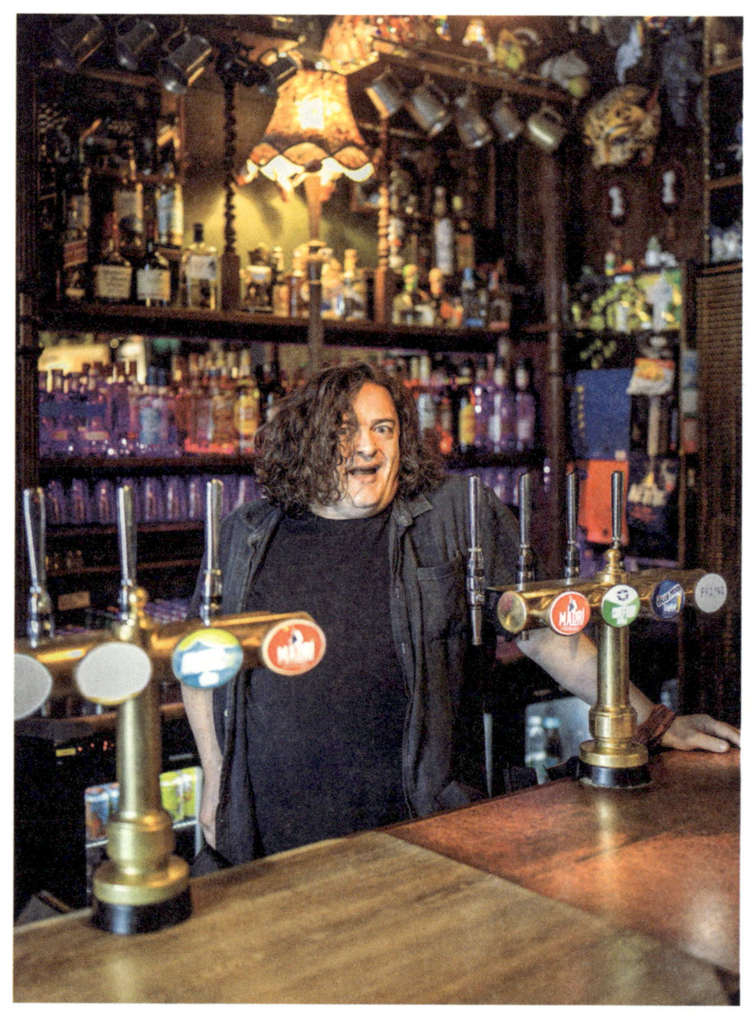

*Veteran East End publican Richard Battye took over
The Queen Adelaide in 2015 after he was forced to close
his previous pub, The George & Dragon, due to rising rents.*

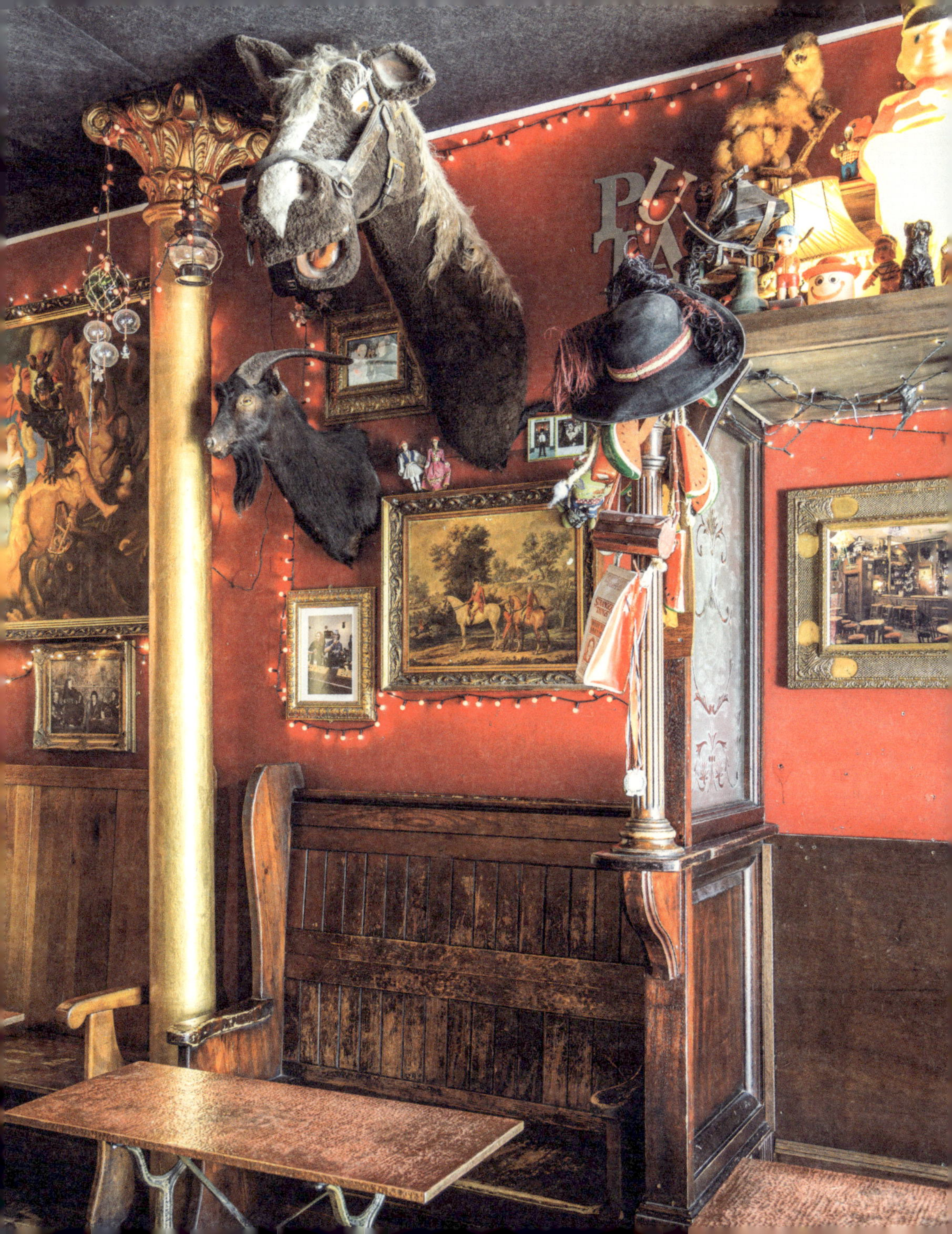

The Peacock

BELOVED LOCAL PUB BACK FROM THE DEAD

Backstreet locals were once the glue that held communities together. The Peacock was one such friendly East End hostelry serving as an anchor for the local area. However, the final time bell was rung under the stewardship of Patsy Pyne and her family in January 2022. They had taken over the 19th-century pub in 1976, when Patsy was just nine years old, but after nearly 50 years of service the family felt that it was time to move on.

There were fears that The Peacock would close for good when it was purchased by developers. The night before the Pyne's departure was an emotional evening as life-long friends celebrated the many drinks shared together there (p.16). However, Patsy was assured that only the top floors would be converted into flats and that the pub itself would reopen after the local authority made its retention part of the planning application.

After a substantial refurbishment, it reopened in 2023. Its wonderfully authentic atmosphere remains, harking back to a simple past of pints and good conversation. Tributes to the pub's heritage adorn the walls, including old prints of the building throughout its history. There is a new snug for dining, where the pool table was once housed, and live music in the main bar. However, older punters will be pleased to note that the same beers remain on tap and that the bar stools are unchanged.

The Peacock is a pub that welcomes customers for a drink, a Sunday roast or to tap their feet to the treble clefs hanging in the air. Its resurrection, amid the erosion of so much East End heritage, is nothing short of a pub miracle.

145–147 Aylward Street, E1 0QW

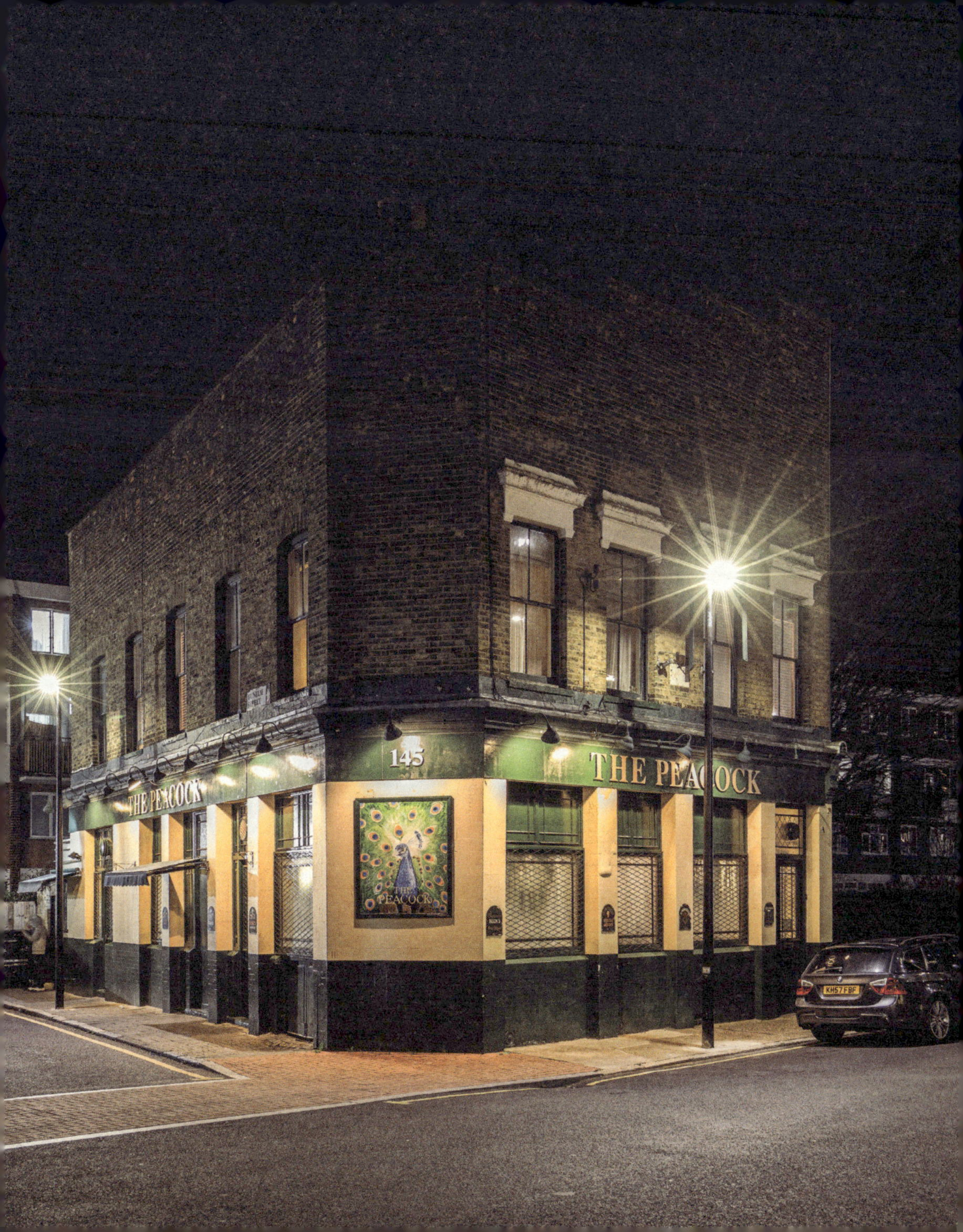
145
THE PEACOCK
THE PEACOCK
THE PEACOCK

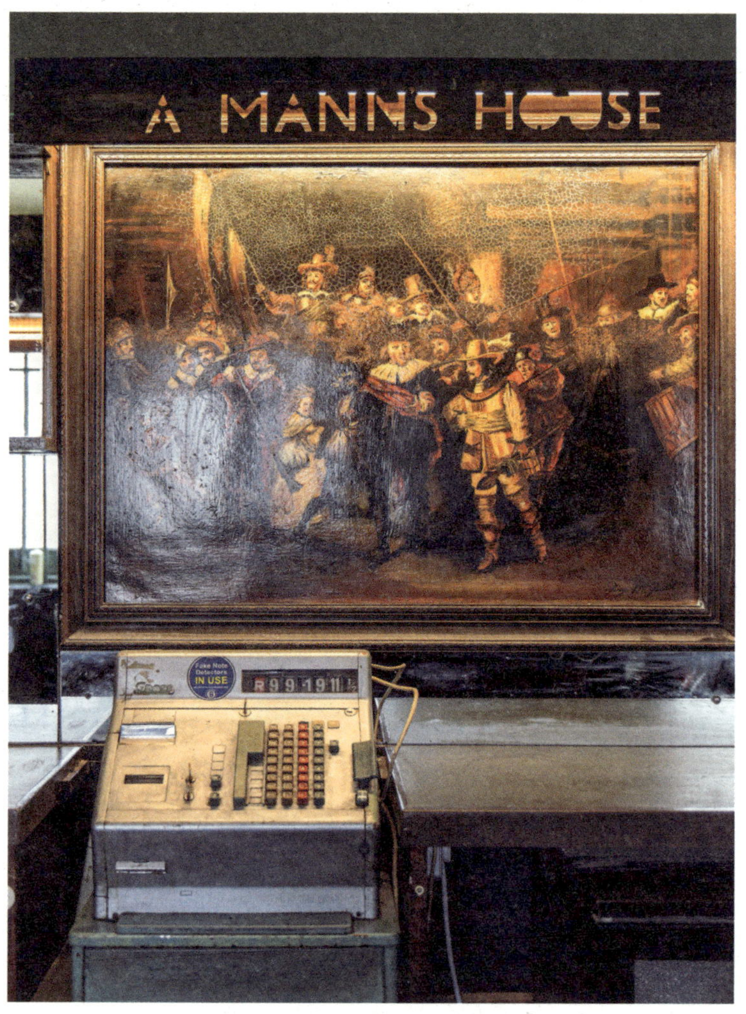

The Peacock contains many references to its heritage, from the old mechanical till to the ornamental peacocks that mean patrons can be in no doubt as to the retention of its much-admired name.

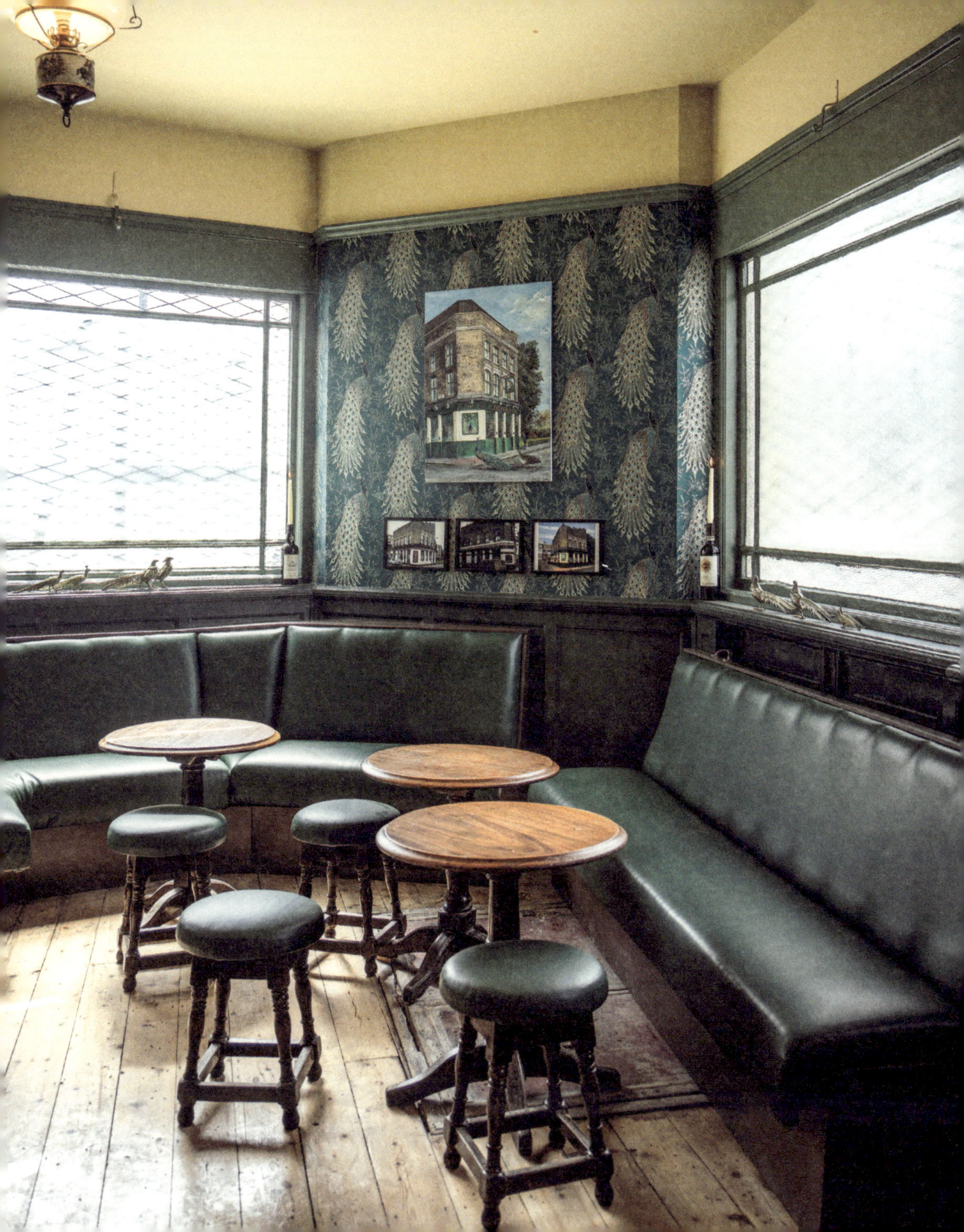

The Horn of Plenty

A ONCE TERRITORIAL PUB EXTENDING A WARM WELCOME

There is often a perception that the old manors and boozers of the East End are hostile to outsiders. While exaggerated, in some places it is true that frosted glass and net curtains in the window are unwritten warnings for strangers to keep out. No pub was more deserving of its territorial reputation than the Horns, a small backstreet pub on Globe Road. It was not for the faint-hearted and had a menacing reputation as a 'problem pub' infamous for its strippers and 5am lock-ins, so no one was surprised when it shut down without a whimper in 2014. Although there were fears that it would be converted into flats, as had already happened to five other hostelries on the same road, the new owners kept it on as a pub and carried out a sympathetic refurbishment, removing the thick drape curtains and splitting the interior into two rooms around a central bar.

The Horn of Plenty is now a cherished local favourite. With wood running throughout it feels cool and airy in the punishing summer heat and inviting in the dead of winter, when lights in the big windows draw thirsty patrons in out of the dark. It feels fresh and inclusive, and has a strong focus on selling local beers and produce.

Located 100 metres from Stepney Green station and the Mile End Road, it is no stranger to passing footfall. Hopefully the pub will have a long and healthy life pulling pints for a new generation of East Enders. It's perfect for a family Sunday roast, pub quiz or half-priced cocktails on Thursdays with friends and, with generous discounts for NHS workers, it clearly has a stake in the lives of its punters and their local area once more – just as all proper pubs have and always will.

36 Globe Road, E1 4DU

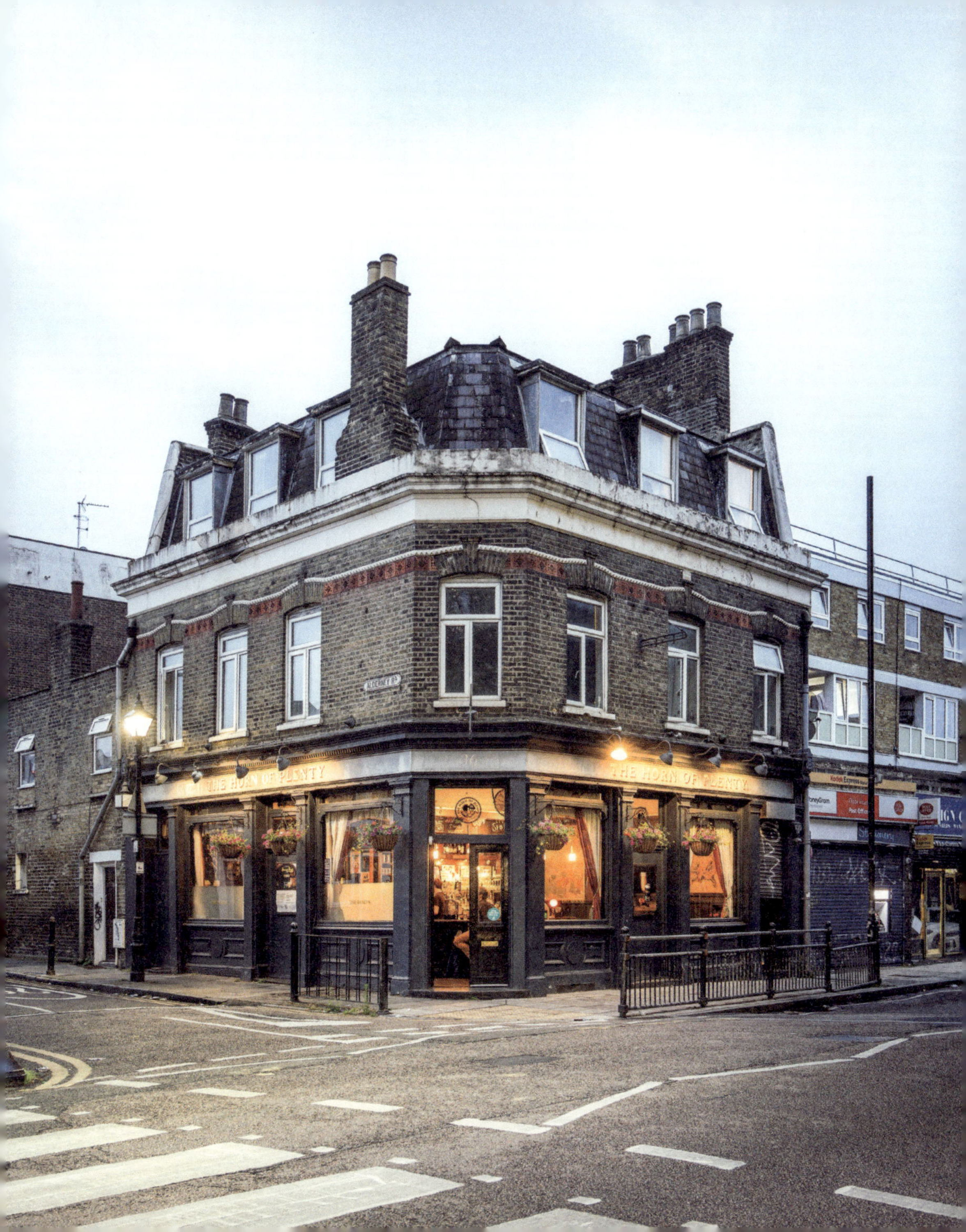
THE HORN OF PLENTY
THE HORN OF PLENTY

The Morgan Arms

A PUB FOR THE NEW EAST END

Like its neighbour The Lord Tredegar (p.90), this handsome corner pub was named after Sir Charles Morgan, 2nd Baronet of Tredegar. The current building was constructed in 1892, taking the place of an older pub of the same name. In recent times, The Morgan Arms has shifted from a working-class boozer to a gastropub, reflecting the changing demographics of the area as middle-class residents move in with different hospitality requirements to those who came before them.

It is an upmarket pub and restaurant that offers a changing menu of modern fare, but the front bar still possesses all the hallmarks of a proper East End boozer from yesteryear. Set within a conservation area, Victorian gas lamps can be viewed through the large plate-glass windows as they illuminate the perfectly aligned terraced streets. In the warmer months, sunlight cascades onto a truly remarkable carved wooden bar, which is the unrivalled centrepiece of the room. It is unique in a part of town where grand bars were understandably rare.

Its red brick facade contrasts with the mellow blue paint to project a cheery blend of both old and new. Dining is a key element that ensures the pub remains sustainable in a challenging climate, but just getting a drink at the bar, joining the pub quiz or enjoying some rays with a cold pint under the canopy as you watch the world trundle by is a life-affirming experience in a special part of London.

43 Morgan Street, E3 5AA

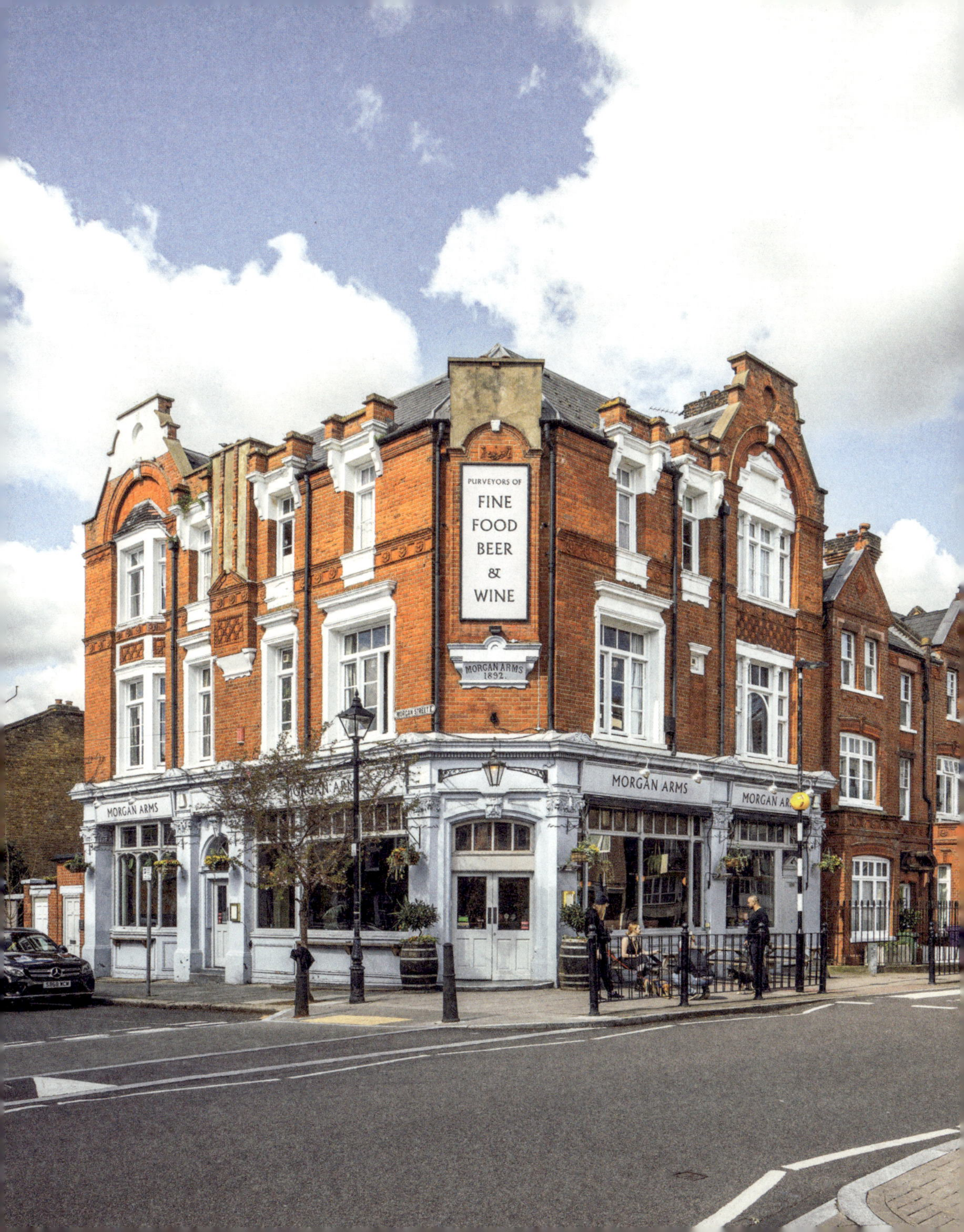
PURVEYORS OF
FINE
FOOD
BEER
&
WINE
MORGAN ARMS
1892
MORGAN STREET
MORGAN ARMS
MORGAN ARMS
MORGAN AR

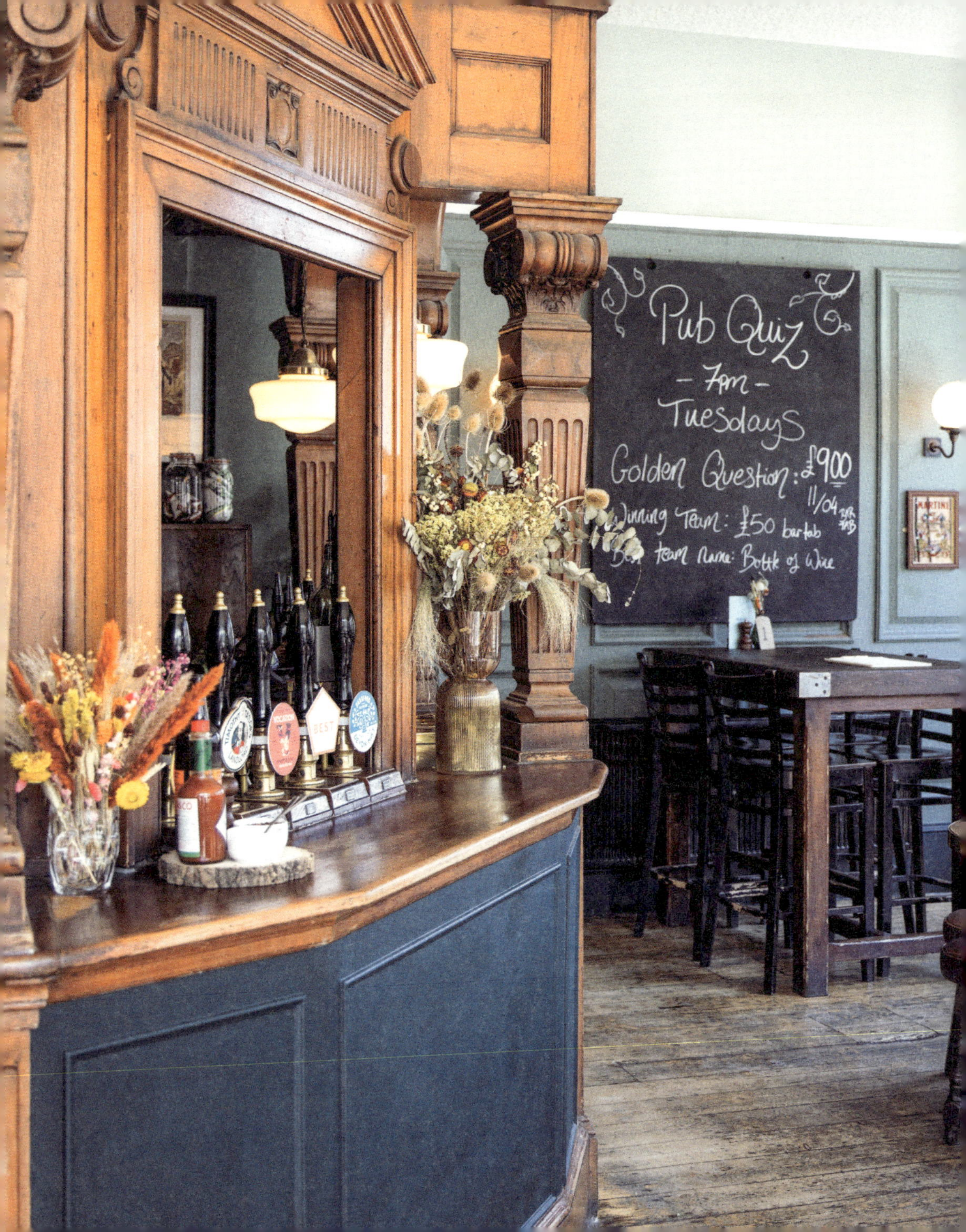

Pub Quiz
- 7pm -
Tuesdays
Golden Question: £900
11/04
Winning Team: £50 bartab
Best team name: Bottle of Wine
MARTINI

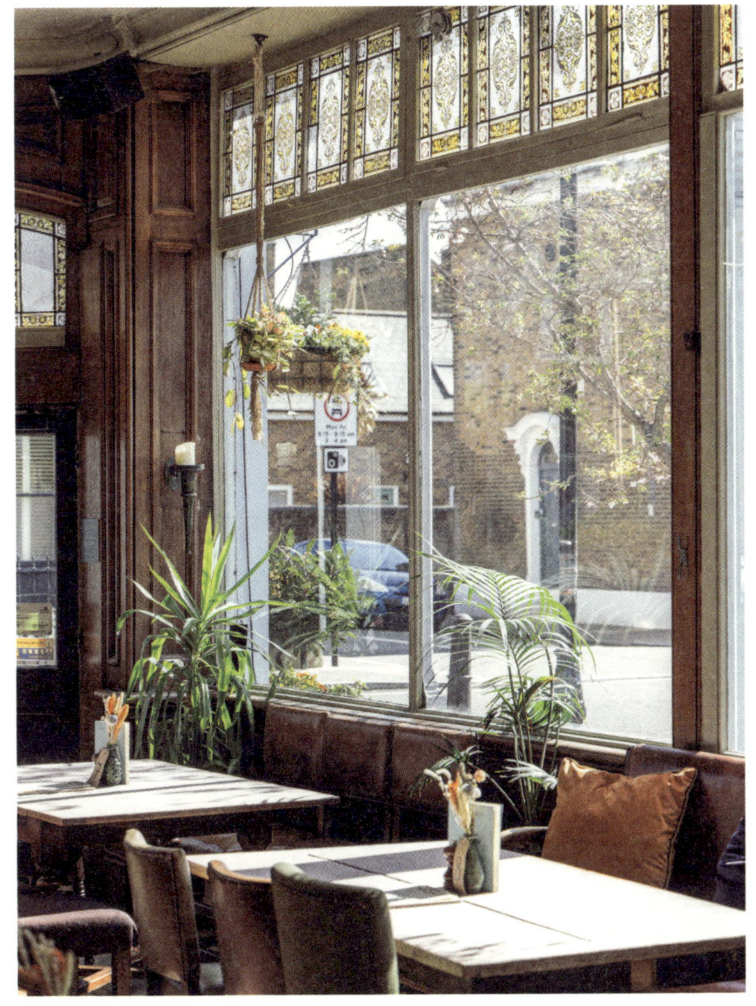

The George

The George was originally a hotel built around 1864 to accommodate those working at the nearby Millwall Dock. The present building came into being in 1932 and it has been a treasured hostelry ever since.

Most pubs on the Isle of Dogs have understandably strong links to the sea, and The George is no exception. In its time it has welcomed sailors from all over the world as well as East Enders, contractors building Canary Wharf and office workers having a quick pint before catching the train.

Not only have the type of drinkers evolved since its construction as a hostelry for board and lodgings, but so has the landscape around it. Many near neighbours have vanished, such as The Islander – a pub that once served as HQ for Millwall F.C. before they moved off the Island in 1910.

The George serves cold lager to old faces from the local estates, while Ma Baker's Bar – once used for off-sales for those who preferred to take their drinks away, rather than sit in the pub – provides a cosy nook for date nights and the rear saloon bar accommodates foodies with familiar pub classics. Catering to a diverse mix of patrons, the different bars offer something for everyone and when the weather is fair, the terrace is ideal for sun-loving punters who want to catch some rays.

Old black-and-white photographs adorn the walls (and ceilings) with scenes from the pub's nautical past, conveying the weight of the Isle of Dog's history and its impact on London. It is uplifting to see a pub bustling and contributing to Island life close to a century after it was built.

114 Glengall Grove, E14 3ND

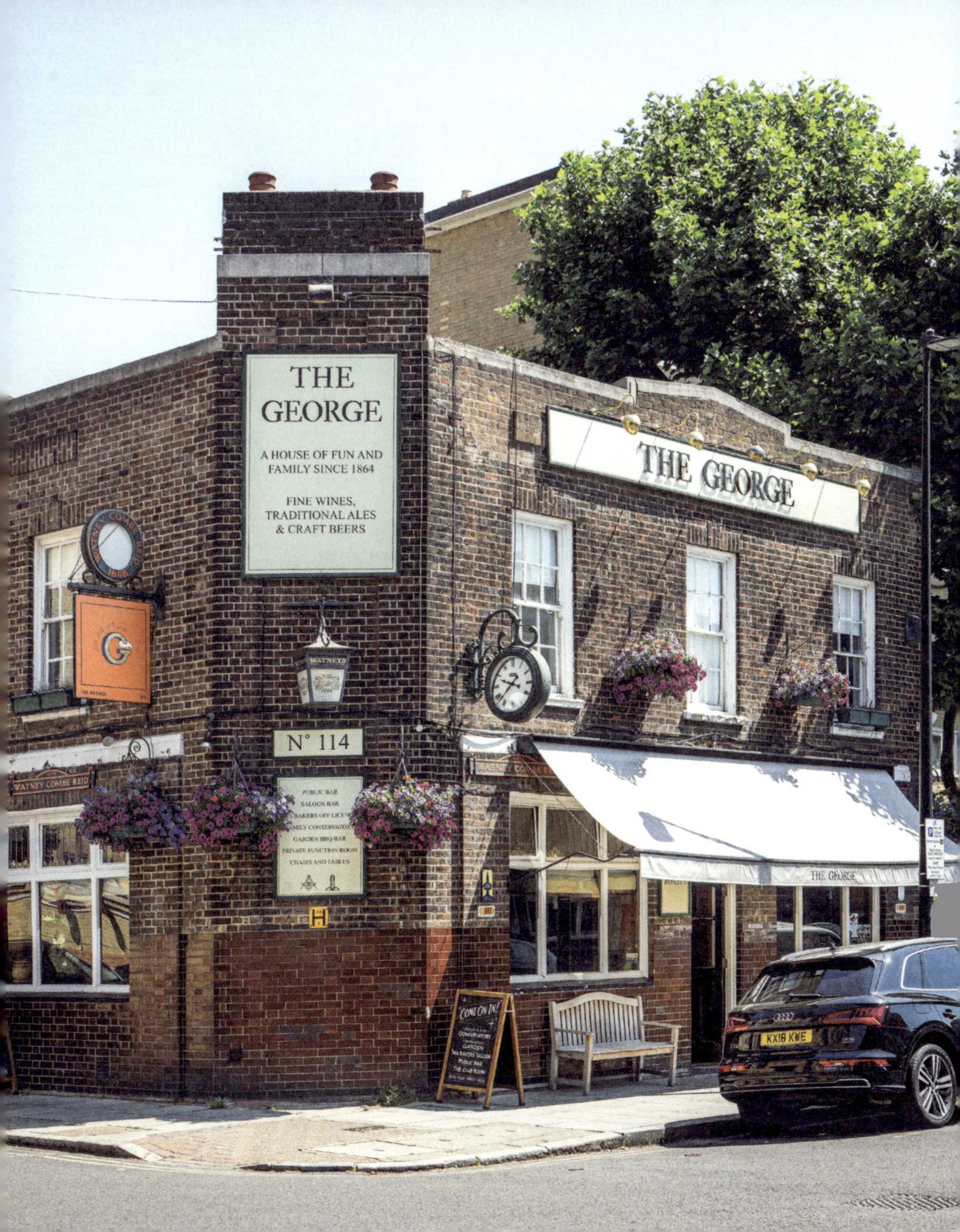

THE
GEORGE
A HOUSE OF FUN AND
FAMILY SINCE 1864
FINE WINES,
TRADITIONAL ALES
& CRAFT BEERS
N° 114
THE GEORGE
PUBLIC BAR
SALOON BAR
BAKERS OFF LICENCE
FAMILY CONSERVATORY
GARDEN BBQ BAR
PRIVATE FUNCTION ROOM
CHAIRS AND TABLES
COME ON IN!
KX18 KWE

The Star of the East

In 2015, this grand Grade II-listed boozer closed and was left to decay. It felt inevitable that the building would be carved up into flats. Prior to its demise, it was rarely busy and served only a smattering of old regulars. Anyone familiar with pubs on the brink of closure will be able to picture the scene: the electricity turned off to save a few quid, and more money being made on the pool table than the bar.

In 2019, however, after a jaw-dropping refurbishment, it opened once more. It's hard to do justice the amount of money, love and care that has been poured into the pub. Consultation with English Heritage has seen the retention of many original features and the new gilding and wood burners have made The Star well worth lingering in. The transformation of the upstairs restaurant makes dining there a treat for anyone and the revamped courtyard, once just a place for smokers to congregate, is now the jewel in its crown.

The new custodians are Ben Tucker and Hannah Lyall. Both are born-and-raised east Londoners with a great deal of experience working in pubs. Prior to The Star, they ran the Princess of Prussia and the White Swan in Aldgate. Hannah's father, Marc, is the partner of Ann Butler, The Pride of Spitalfields' landlady (p.138), so there's no doubt they know how to extend a first-class pub welcome. The renewed Star exerts an elegance that must be seen to be believed. This long stretch of the Commercial Road was crying out for a proper pub – it's now got it.

805A Commercial Road, E14 7HG

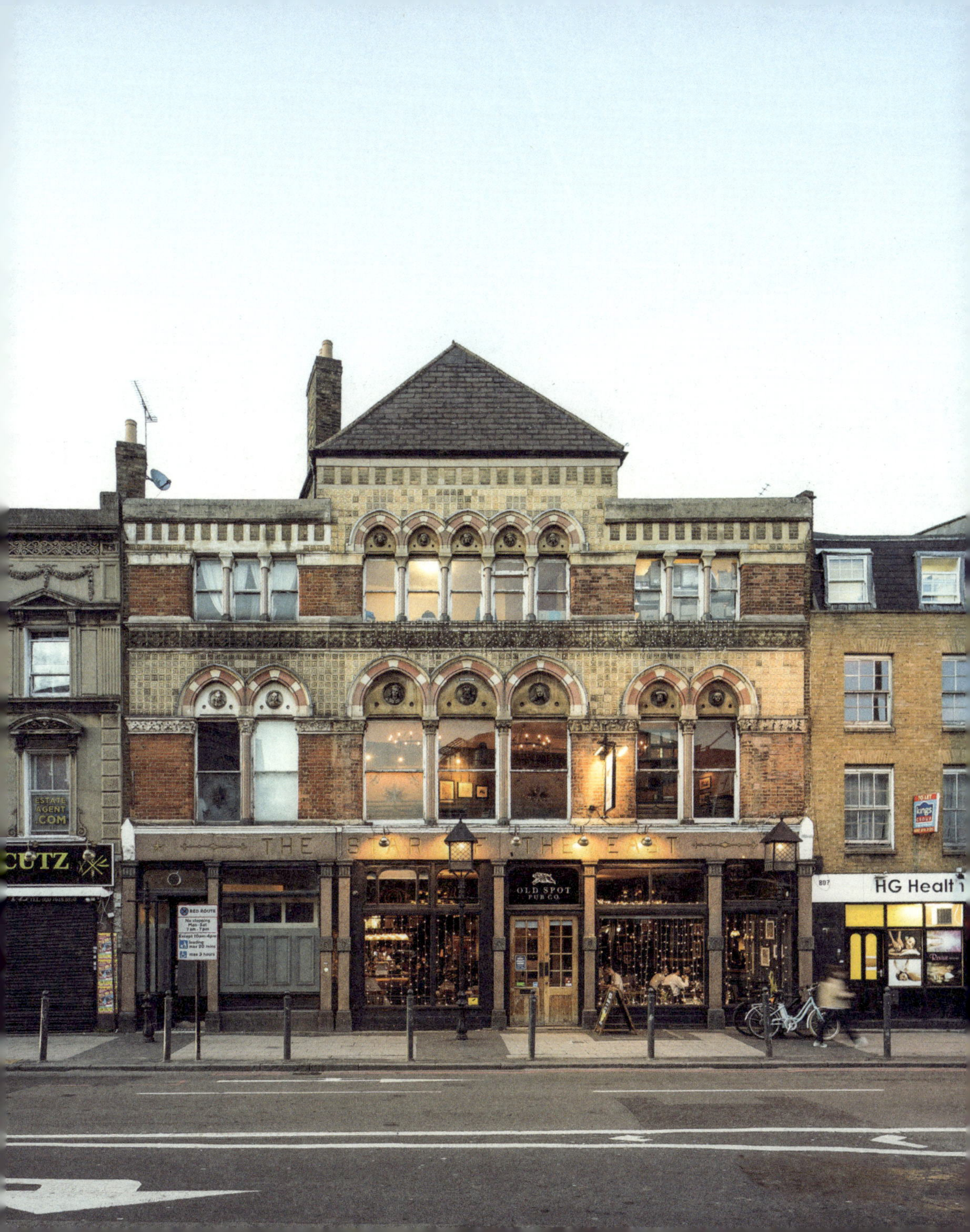

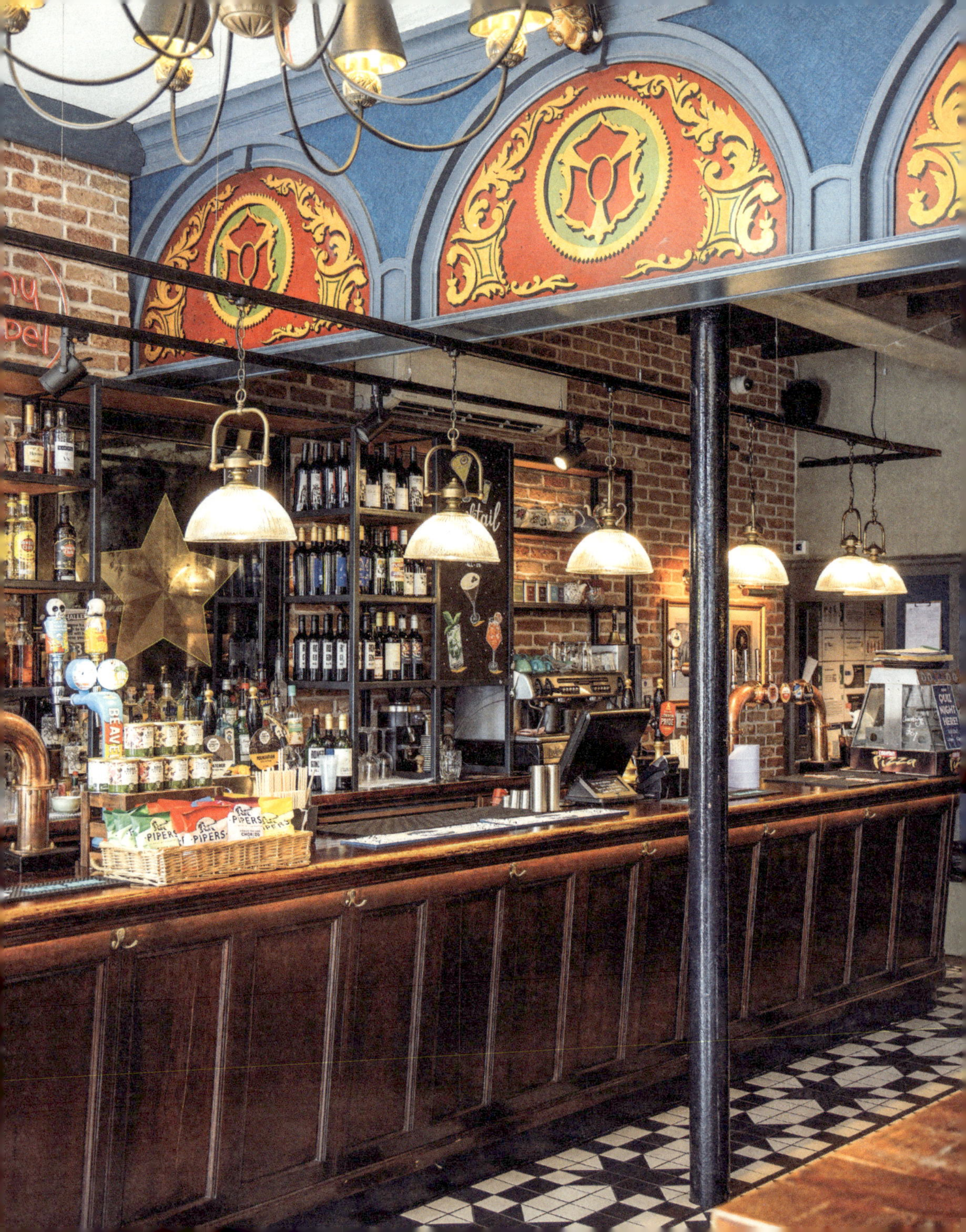

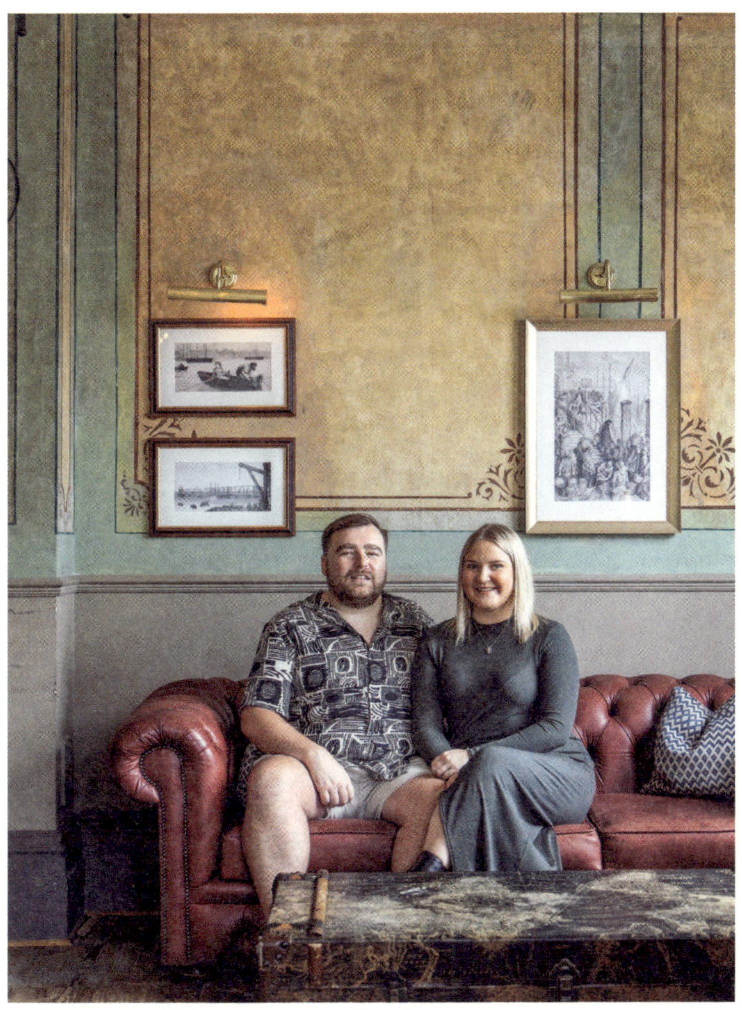

Ben Tucker and Hannah Lyall are the custodians of The Star.
Both are east Londoners with a great deal of pub experience,
so they know how to run a proper hostelry.

The Shakespeare

Lisa and Jason Kinsella have been at the helm of The Shakespeare since 2015, although Jason was a long-standing local before he became the Guv'nor, and the much-loved barmaid Mandy Handley has been working at the pub since 1973. Such long tenures (and the fact that ex-Guv'nors Brian Prentice and Micky Turner, whose combined proprietorship stretches back 50 years, still drink here) are a real testament to the pub and the loyalty of its patrons.

The Shakespeare is an unusually small hostelry; a one-room pub built in the 1870s and tiled in Truman's signature green. While the exterior delights passers-by, the interior has been stripped back and replaced with a copper-topped bar and exuberant floral displays. However, it is not the decor that local punters flock here to enjoy. Although no original features remain inside, it is the sort of establishment where everyone knows each other – outsiders will be treated with curiosity, but friendships are quickly forged and you will likely get a tip for a nag or a recommendation for a tradesman to go with your pint.

Famous not just for its warm welcome and affordable pints, The Shakespeare also prides itself on hosting local acts, such as firm favourites Jodie Stone and Brian and Debbie Spence, several times a month to entertain those thirsty for a singalong to go with their drinks.

The Shakespeare is very much a slice of old East End life and drinking here is just as much a history lesson as a good time. The Cockney legacy of good pubs and good beer lives on here in spades.

460 Bethnal Green Road, E2 0EA

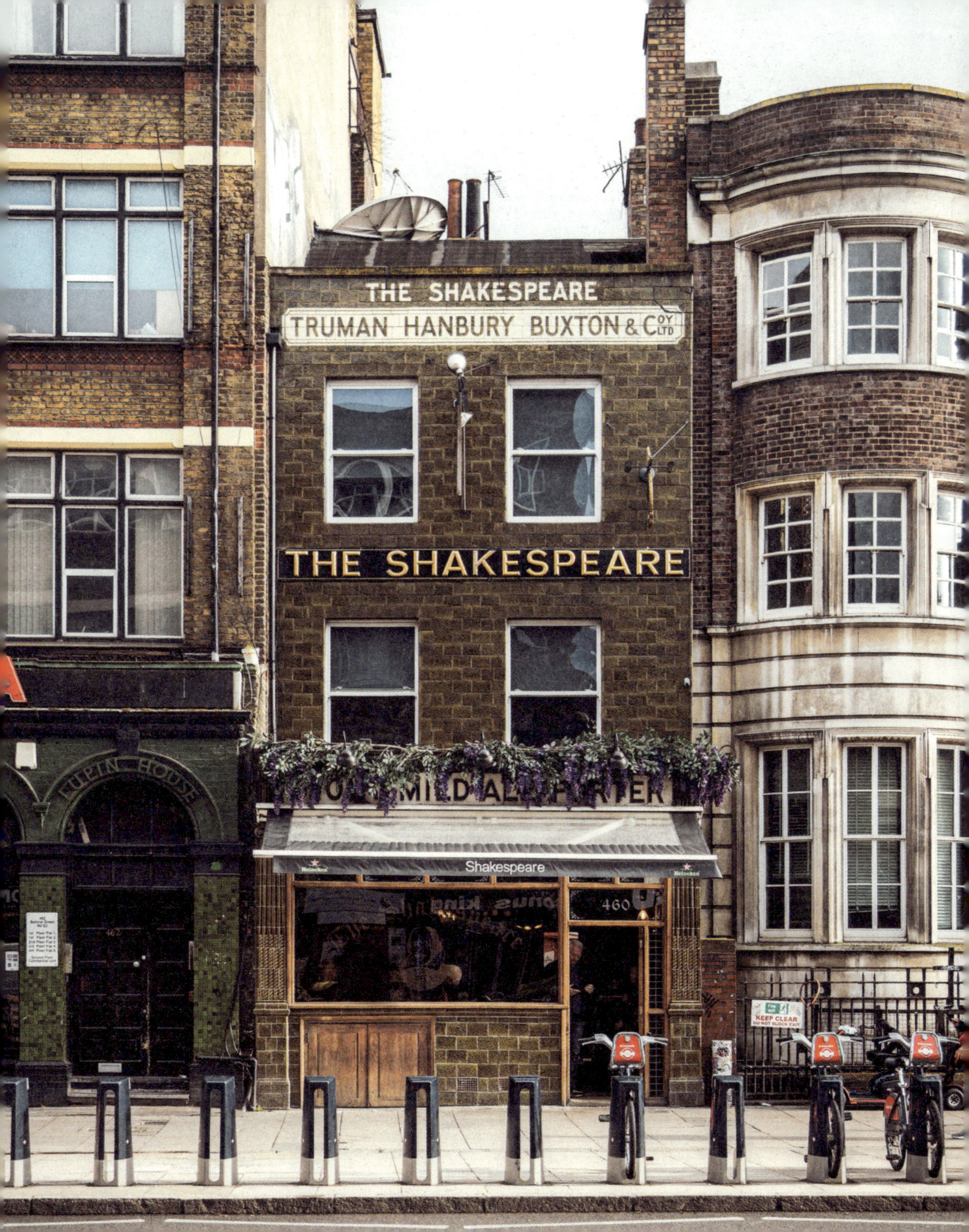
THE SHAKESPEARE
TRUMAN HANBURY BUXTON & Coy LTD
THE SHAKESPEARE
MILD ALE PORTER
Shakespeare
460
PUPIN HOUSE
KEEP CLEAR
DO NOT BLOCK EXIT

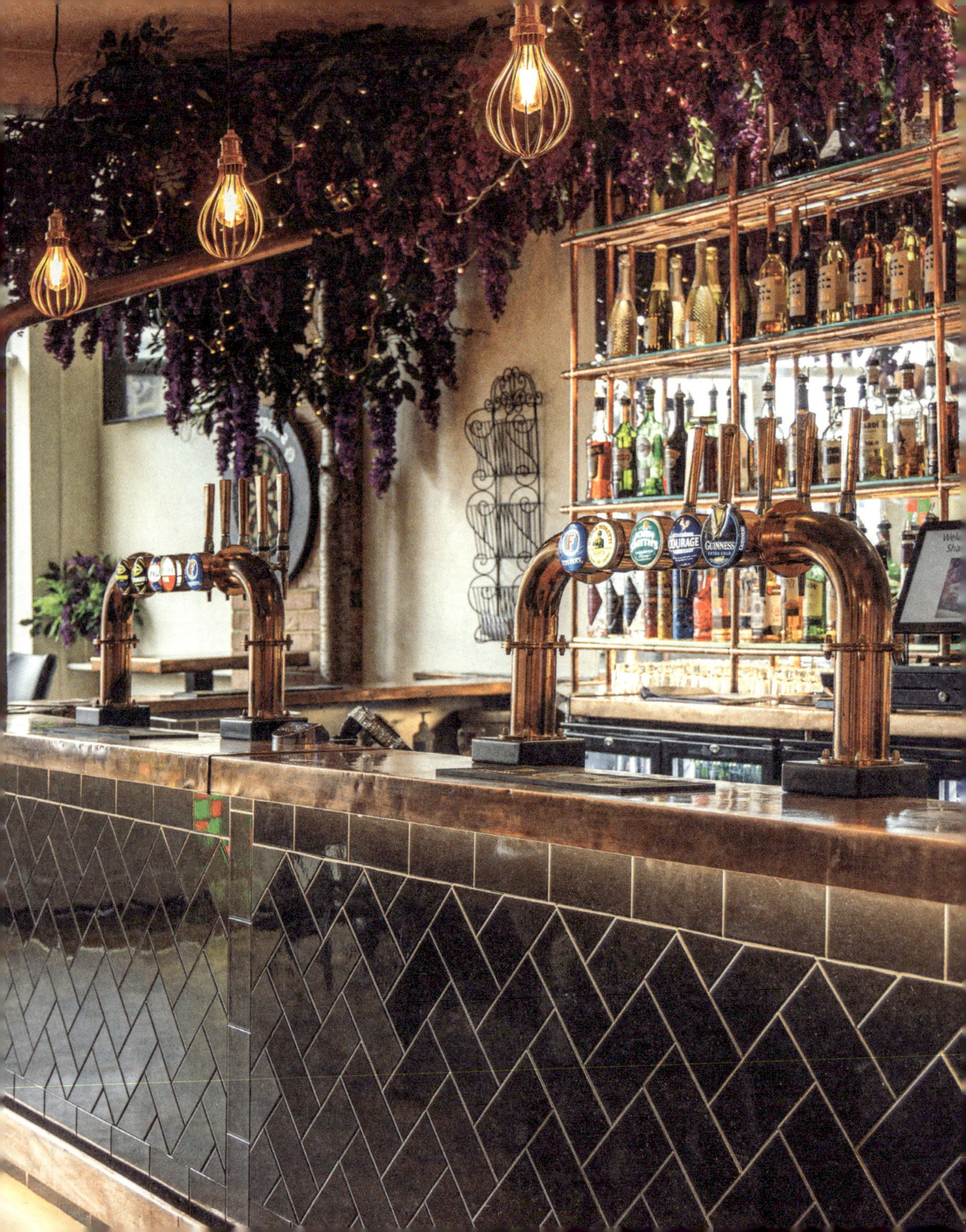

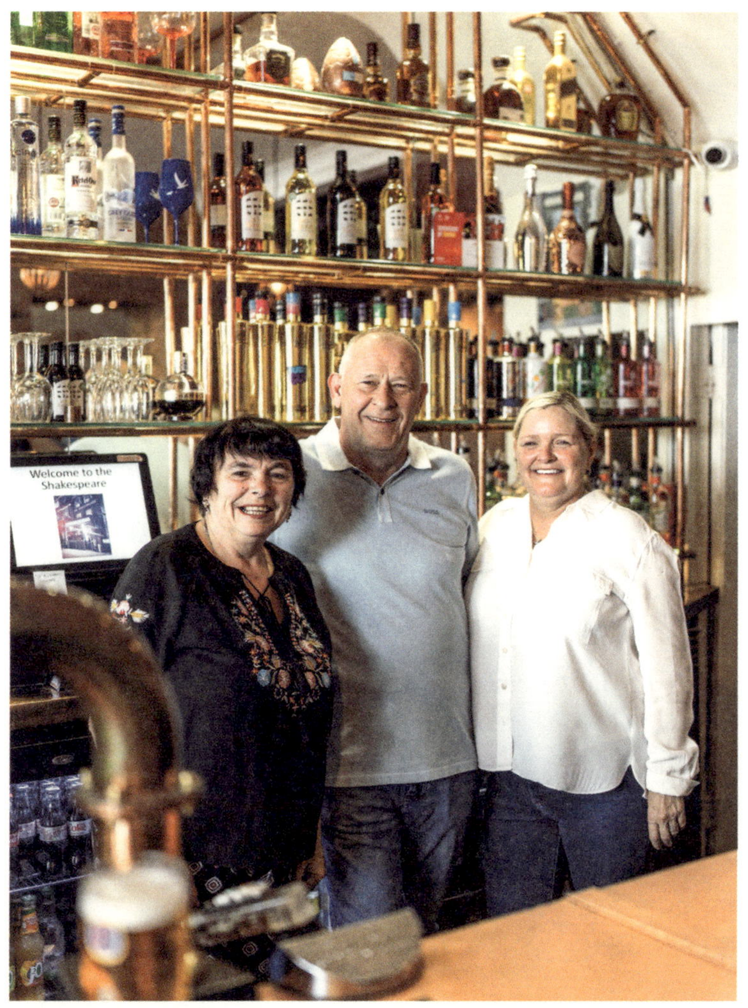

Lisa and Jason Kinsella (far right and centre) have run The Shakespeare since 2015, while Mandy Handley (left) has been working at the pub since 1973.

The Young Prince

BASTION OF COCKNEY PUB CULTURE

Wedged within a long parade of shops on the East End's Roman Road sits this curious hostelry which, to many, holds a perpetual air of mystery. Peeking into the pub through the tiny curtain-fronted windows on the street affords an inviting view into days gone by, and those intrepid enough to enter will receive a warm welcome from stalwart victualler Barry Holloway, who has been at the helm of the Young Prince since 1983.

Formerly a Charrington's pub, it was first founded as a beer house (licensed only to sell ale) in 1889 before being converted into a fully licenced tavern just a few years later. The Young Prince in question was Queen Victoria's grandson Prince George, a naval officer and popular royal who unexpectedly became first in line to the throne upon the premature death of his eldest brother, and was eventually crowned King George V. It is one of several public houses across the country named in his honour.

Today, the pub contains many nods to publican Barry's long career. Trinkets, personal photographs and curious mementoes adorn the walls to create an intimate and cosy tavern. There are sporting trophies and old etchings, as well as an electronic dartboard and 1980s video games sitting beside a glowing fish tank. Everything on display has been collected over the course of his stewardship of the pub, and it is a genuine

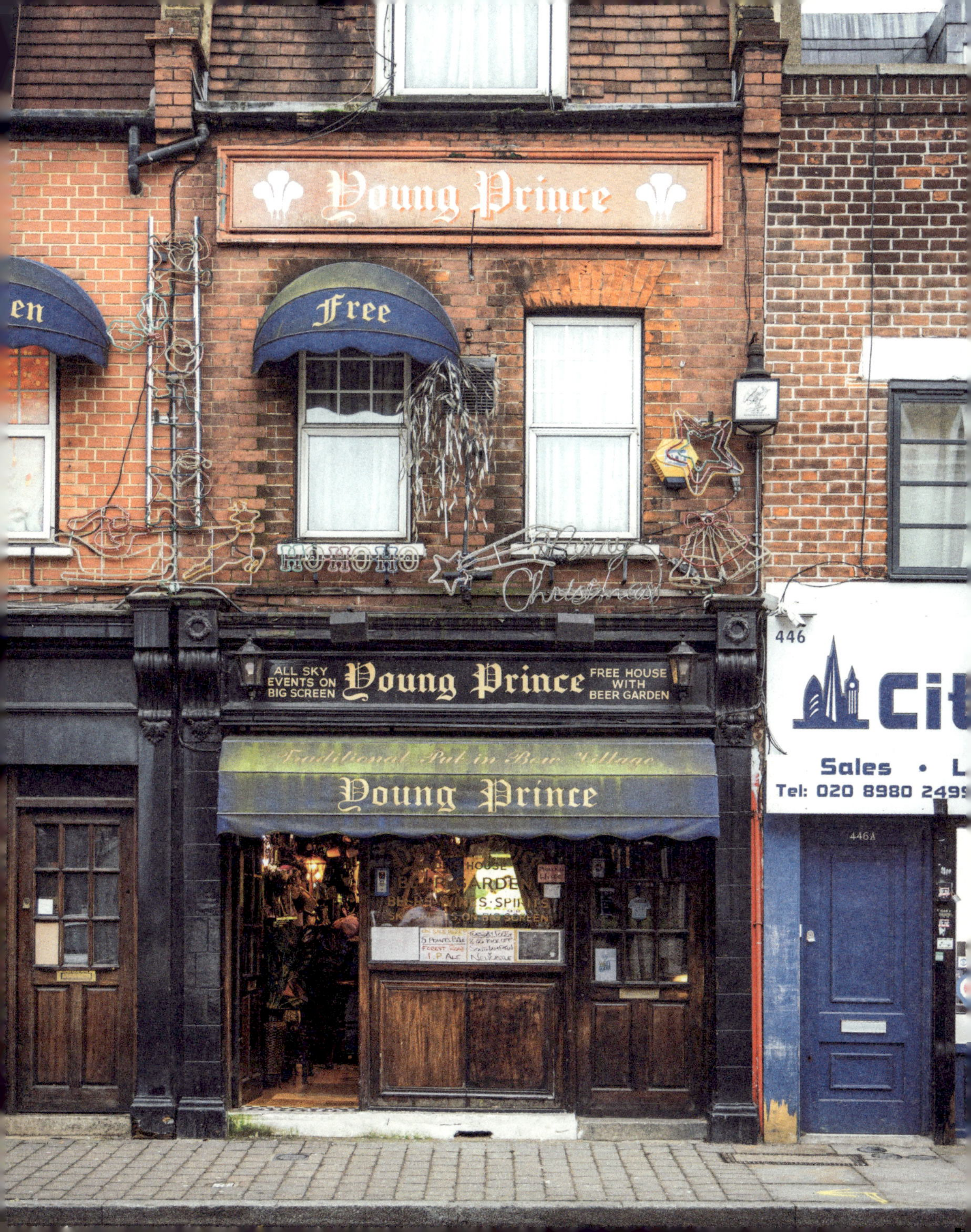

Young Prince
Free
ALL SKY EVENTS ON BIG SCREEN
Young Prince
FREE HOUSE WITH BEER GARDEN
Traditional Pub in Bow Village
Young Prince
HO HO HO
446
Cit
Sales · L
Tel: 020 8980 2499
446A

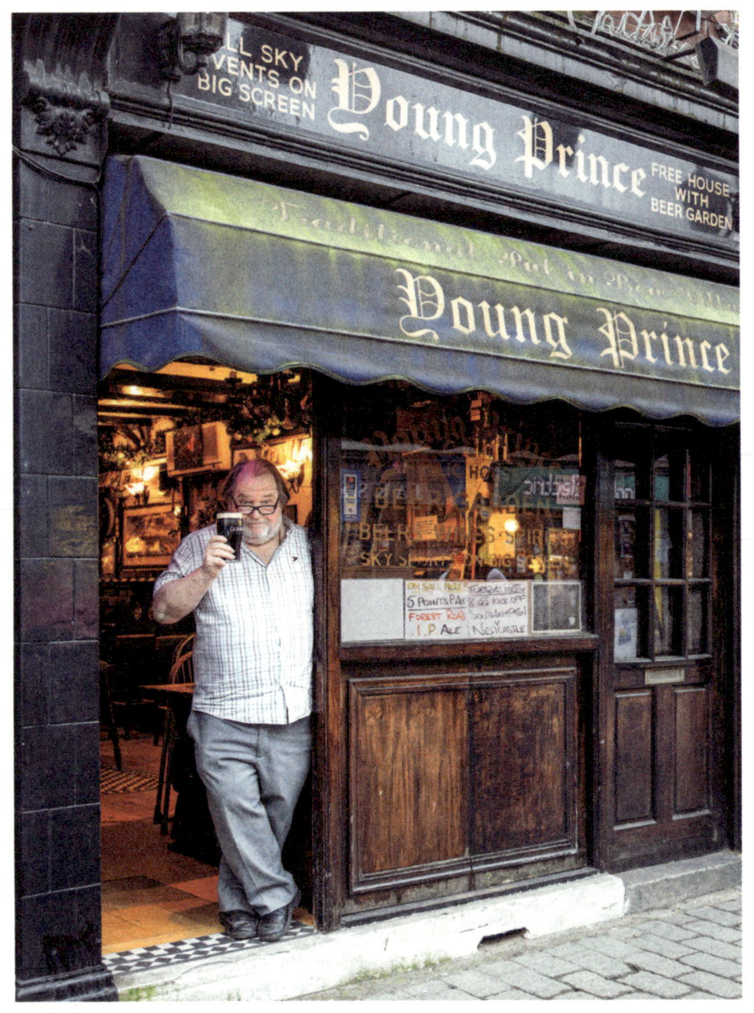
LL SKY
VENTS ON
BIG SCREEN
Young Prince
FREE HOUSE
WITH
BEER GARDEN
Young Prince
ON SALE HERE
5 POINTS P.ALE
FOREST ROAD
I. P. ALE
NEWCASTLE

treasure trove enjoyed by customers old and new. Whenever there's a royal event or a football tournament, the pub's interior is beautifully festooned with bunting, flags and other colourful adornments.

Traditional wood panelling installed by Barry himself and brass fittings run throughout this home-away-from-home. Bar stools remain very much in situ at the Young Prince, although they've been tactically removed from many establishments during the pandemic in order to introduce table service and have yet to be returned to their rightful places – eroding the simple pleasure of sitting at the bar and having a drink while chatting to other locals, or just listening to raconteur Barry's glorious pub tales. It's rare nowadays to find a Guv'nor with over 40 years' service, especially one who still lives above the pub. His personal relationship to the building and his customers understandably runs very deep.

The Young Prince is now one of only two surviving public houses on the 'Roman', which, at one time, had over 20. Its presence offers a comforting reminder of a way of life and type of drinker that has almost disappeared from the East End in the last 25 years.

It is truly a place worth celebrating, a cherished local pub filled with knick-knacks where it is still possible to pull up a stool and exchange pleasantries with the long-standing custodian as patrons share stories at the bar.

448 Roman Road, E3 5LU

Barry Holloway has been Guv'nor of the Young Prince since 1983. The pub is decorated with sporting memorabilia and local artefacts he's collected over the years.

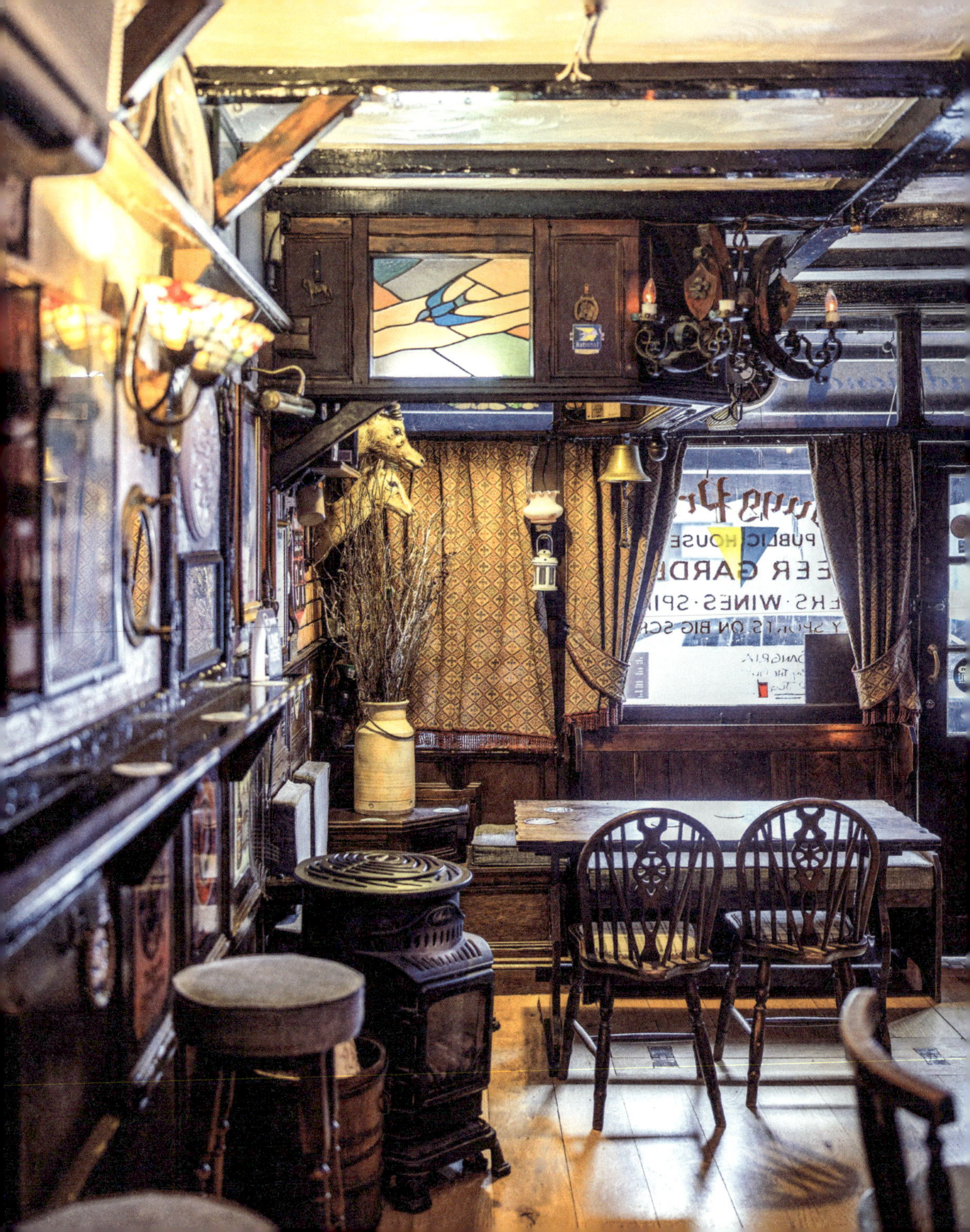

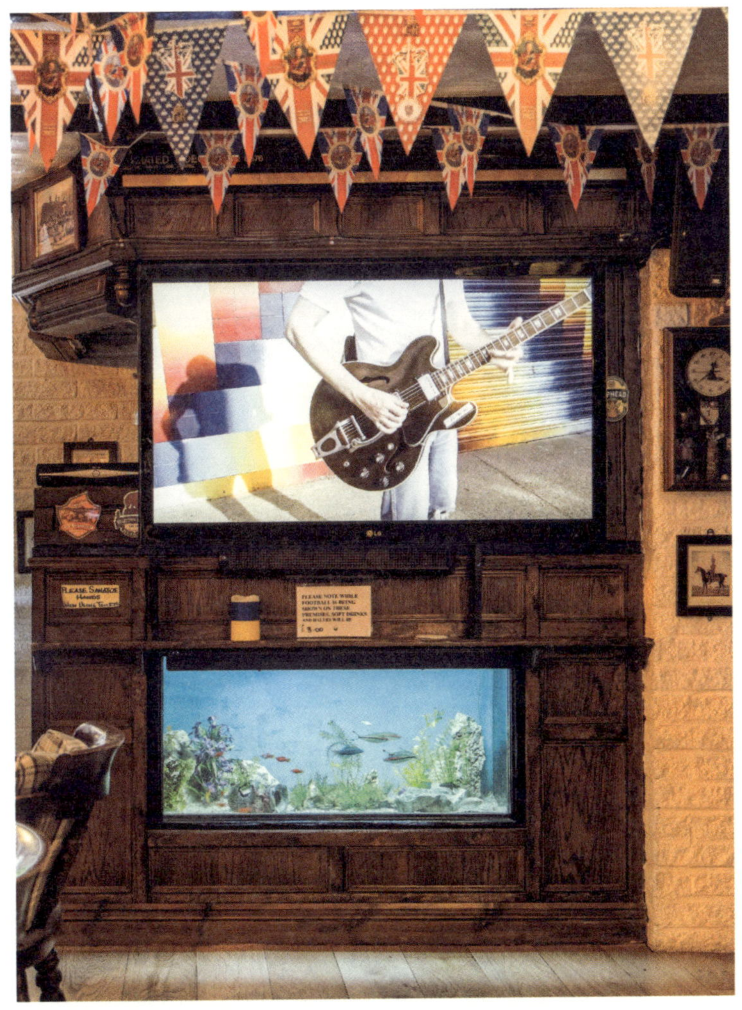

The Golden Heart

EAST END ROYALTY AT THE HELM OF AN ICONIC PUB

In the streets that surround Truman's old brewery on Brick Lane, once the largest of its kind in the world, there are few pubs left that still bear the Truman name. One of the last remaining is the Grade II-listed Golden Heart in Spitalfields. It is a well-known venue, but perhaps more for its memorable land-lady than its location, architecture or the quality of its beer – all of which are reasons for visiting in themselves.

Sandra Esquilant has been in charge since 1977, running the pub with her husband Dennis until he sadly passed away 15 years ago. In its early days, before Truman's closed, the pub served almost as a taproom to those who worked in their brewery – in fact, before he became a landlord, Dennis himself worked there. The daughter of a docker and a florist, Sandra comes from a time and part of the city where people didn't hold back from speaking their mind. She has a fearsome reputation and is without question one of a kind; known for keeping rude and unruly drinkers in line, Sandra has forthright views on how her pub should be run and the decorum with which her customers should behave while within her establishment. Most visitors to the pub en-countering the Queen of Spitalfields seem to leave with a 'Sandra story' – her love of life and people is evident to all who meet her.

Despite hardships resulting from the economic downturn of the 1980s and the relocation of Old Spitalfields Market in 1991,

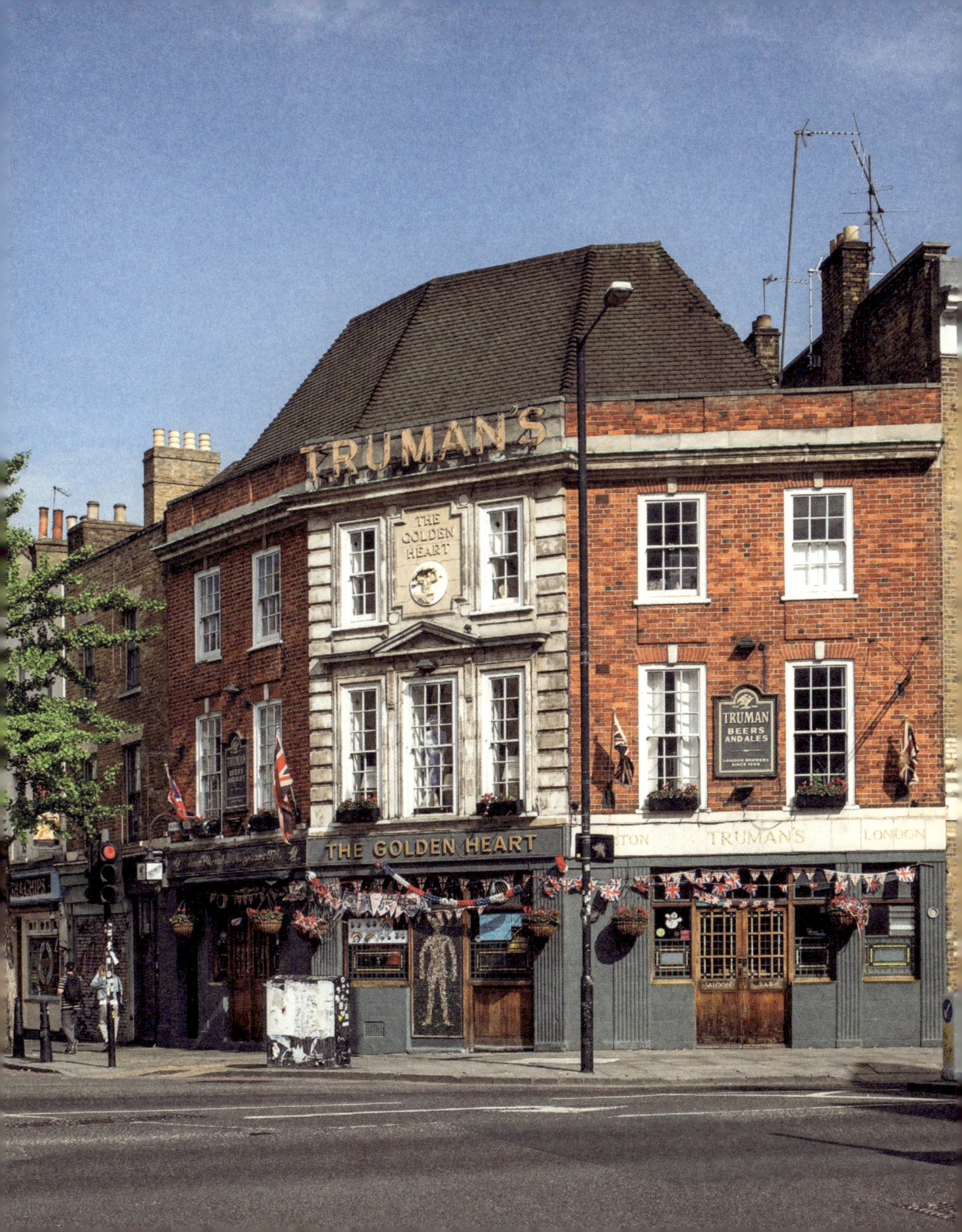

TRUMAN'S
THE GOLDEN HEART
TRUMAN BEERS AND ALES LONDON BREWERS SINCE 1666
THE GOLDEN HEART
TON TRUMAN'S LONDON
TRUMAN BEERS AND ALES LONDON BREWERS SINCE 1666
SALOON BAR

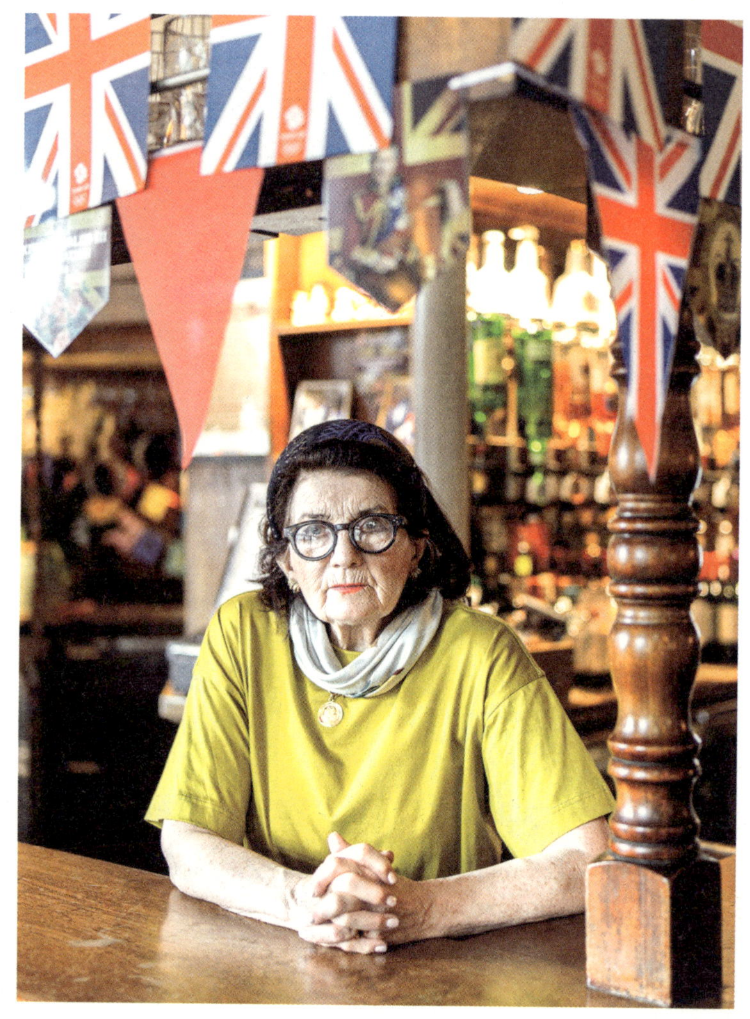

Sandra and Dennis managed to create and uphold a much-loved hostelry, which was a favourite with Young British Artists such as Sarah Lucas and Gillian Wearing, who gravitated to the pub and its warm confines. Emblazoned on one side of the pub is a neon artwork by Tracey Emin celebrating Dennis and Sandra's 40th wedding anniversary, while another from the artist declares 'I love you' from a small corner window.

As high-street brands and chain restaurants move in, the area where the City of London meets the East End is becoming increasingly sanitised. In this context, a fully wet-led pub is an anomaly, but The Golden Heart is a true independent refusing to change.

The interior feels very true to its original 1936 decor: simplistic but homely, hospitable whatever the weather. An island bar that serves both a saloon and public bar provides the ideal setting from which to survey the curious mix of market traders, city workers, tourists and artists who frequent the pub, all adding to the lively atmosphere from which it derives its continued success. According to Sandra, she wants the pub to be a party – and it's that feeling of being part of something that keeps drawing in thirsty revellers and ensures The Golden Heart sits in perpetuity as an East End icon.

110 Commercial Street, E1 6LZ

Sandra Esquilant is the longest serving landlady in the East End, loved by locals and celebrated artists alike.

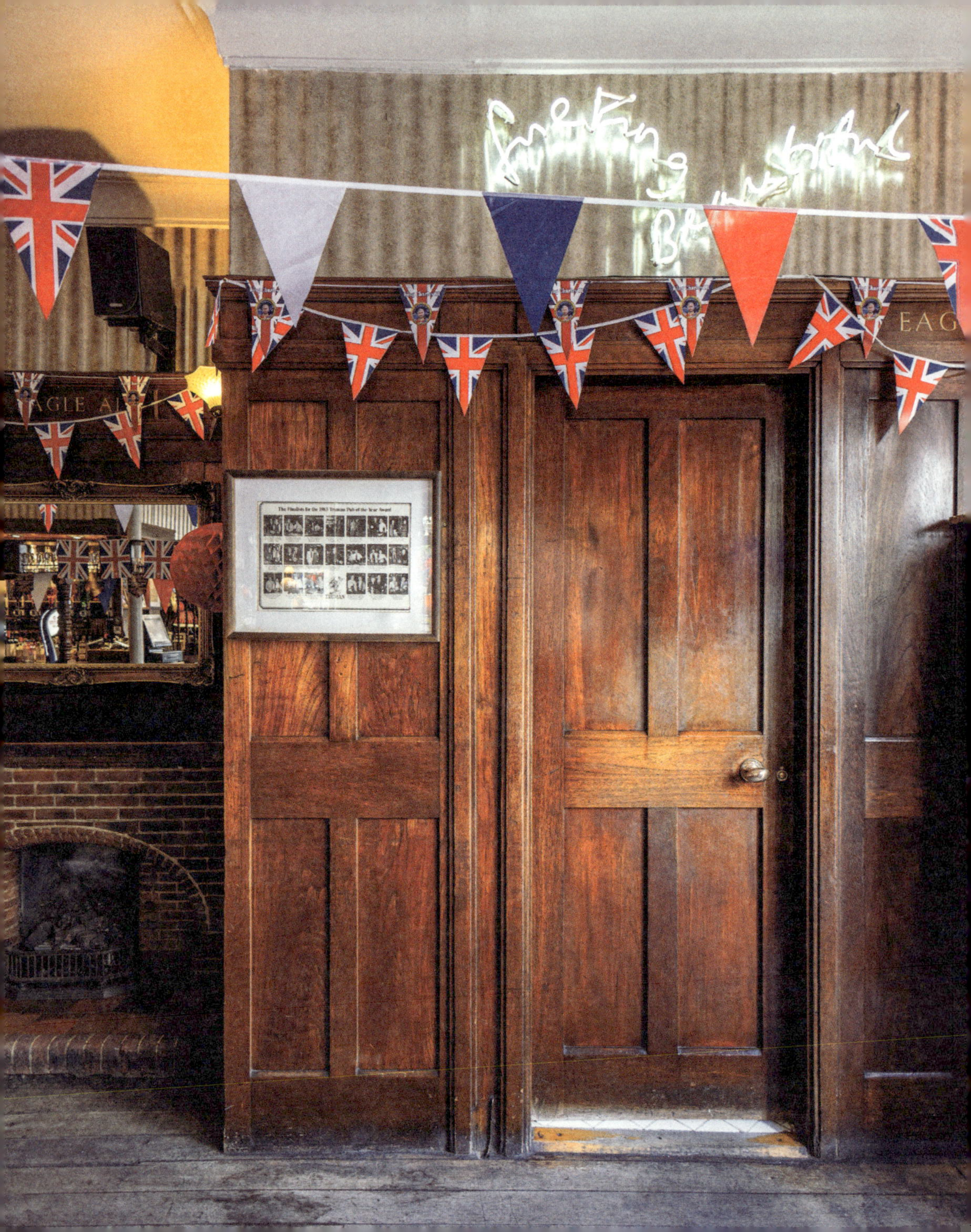

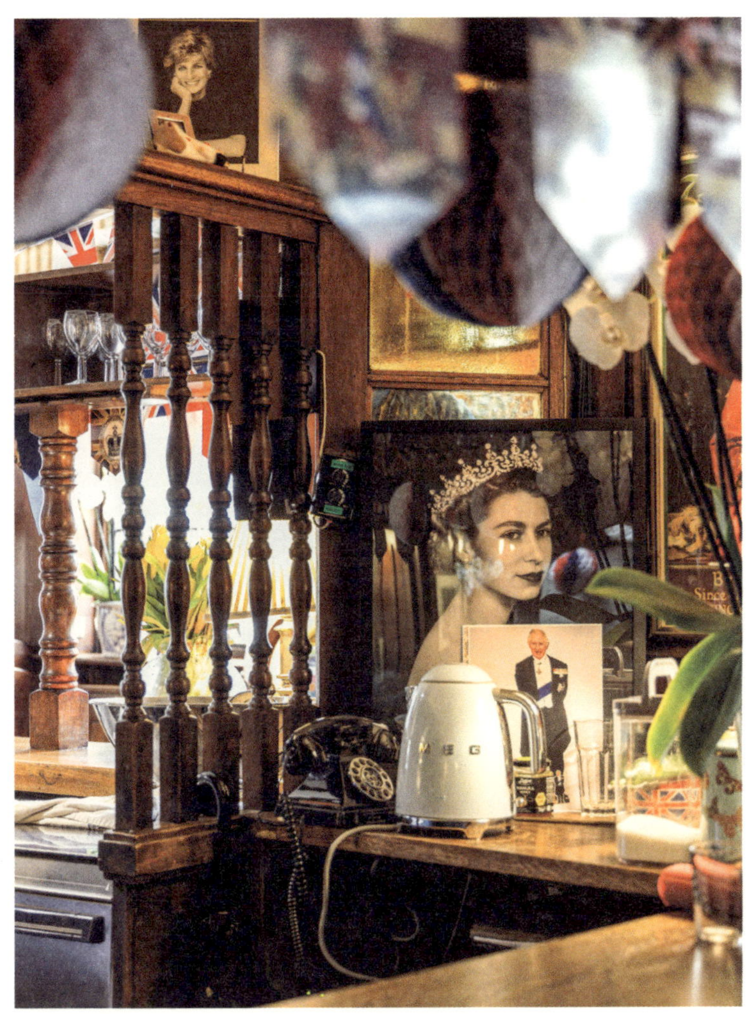

East End Pubs
First edition, second printing

This edition printed 2024
First published in 2023 by Hoxton Mini Press, London.
Copyright © Hoxton Mini Press 2023. All rights reserved.

Text © Alistair Von Lion, photography © Tim George*

*Except photography: p.2 ©PA Images / Alamy Stock Photo; p.15 ©Evening Standard / Stringer;
p.78 ©Heritage Image Partnership Ltd / Alamy Stock Photo; p.168 ©Print Collector / Contributor.

Design and production by Sarah-Louise Deazley
Additional design by Richard Mason
Editing by Octavia Stocker
Proofreading by Lizzy Silverton at First Pages and Florence Ward
Editorial support by Megan Baffoe

Alistair and Tim would like to thank the Guv'nors of the East End for kindly giving
up their time and allowing them into their lives and businesses. In addition, Tim would
like to thank Gareth Gardner for his invaluable technical advice. Lastly, both authors
offer up their deepest thanks to their wives, Isobel and Natalie, for allowing them
to spend the best part of eight months 'down the pub'.

The rights of Alistair Von Lion and Tim George to be identified as the creators of this
Work have been asserted under the Copyright, Designs and Patents Act 1988.

No part of this publication may be reproduced, stored in a retrieval system,
or transmitted in any form or by any means, electronic, mechanical, photocopying,
recording or otherwise, without the prior written permission of the copyright owner.

A CIP catalogue record for this book is available from the British Library.

ISBN: 978-1-914314-43-8

Printed and bound by OZGraf, Poland

Hoxton Mini Press is an environmentally conscious publisher, committed
to offsetting our carbon footprint. This book is 100 per cent carbon
compensated, with offset purchased from Stand For Trees.

For every book you buy from our website, we plant a tree:

www.hoxtonminipress.com

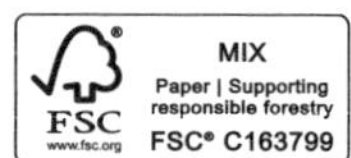